Carol Lynn Pearson Writes Play for Sundance
Carol Lynn Pearson, Noted
next at PTC
PRESIDENT AND UTAHN
RELIGION
Mormon speaker a compassionate promoter of respect, acceptance
New single parenting book is touching, hilarious, informing
Carol Lynn Pearson's New Book of Poetry Stirs Deep Emotions
Carol Lynn Pearson to highlight women's forum
Author Carol Lynn Pearson to address SUSC convocation
Dealing with AIDS
Mormon poet comes to terms with disease
There will be some people who will be terribly shocked that I wish to address this subject, but most will want to understand
Mormon parents of gay children form support group to understand

Carol Lynn Pearson

The Diaries of

CAROL LYNN PEARSON

Mormon Author, Feminist, and Activist

VOLUME 1: 1956–1990

Signature Books | 2025 | Salt Lake City

To our women ancestors who did not have a pen
or a voice, but gave their hearts and their hands
to creating the good things we have today.

Join our mailing list at signaturebooks.com for details on events and related titles we think you'll enjoy.

Design by Jason Francis
Frontispiece photo by Michael Schoenfeld

FIRST EDITION | 2025

LIBRARY OF CONGRESS CONTROL NUMBER: 2025939810

Paperback ISBN: 978-1-56085-524-8
Ebook ISBN: 978-1-56085-505-7

CONTENTS

PUBLISHER'S FOREWORD

I owe much of who I am to Carol Lynn Pearson.

I remember, growing up in the 1970s, singing along with her *My Turn on Earth* musical and laughing at her humor with my mother and grandmother as we read *The Model Mormon Mother's Notebook* together. But the real impact came in 1987.

I had just read her latest book, the nationally acclaimed *Goodbye, I Love You*. This memoir provoked in me profound compassion for the gay community in what was a worldwide AIDS crisis. The power of Pearson's writing prompted me to record in my diary, on January 14, 1987:

> I decided today that I want to be a writer. I want to start out in journalism, maybe magazine journalism, and then move on to books, etc. I don't know if I can do it, but it's a dream I have, a dream that's just beginning to wake up inside of me. It's been there for a long time, but I just haven't acknowledged it. I know that I'm afraid to try. Why? I don't know.
>
> But I've been reading a book by an author I admire and respect, Carol Lynn Pearson, and I suddenly realized—she started out just like me! She had to realize her dream just like me, and she was probably afraid, also. But she did it, and so can I.

In the years and decades that followed, I did indeed go on to major in journalism, work at three different magazines, author my first book, and edit and publish numerous other books. That nineteen-year-old girl who recorded these dreams in her 1987 diary would have been astonished to know that she—some forty years later—would be privileged to work with Carol Lynn Pearson to publish *her* diaries. And discover that Pearson, too, at about the same age, recorded her dreams of making a difference through her writing.

I am well aware that I'm just one of countless people whom Carol Lynn has inspired throughout her long life. Whether you are one of them or about to become one, I hope you'll cherish walking with her through the pages of her remarkable journey as much as I have.

Barbara Jones Brown
Director, Signature Books Publishing
May 6, 2025

PREFACE

My first diary, a gift for my seventeenth birthday.

In September of 1956 I was given a small book: red, with an alligator cover, a little brass lock, and nearly an inch of blank pages. *A diary! Intriguing! Inviting! A secret place to store my words, my thoughts!* Writing in my diary quickly became an addiction, the only addiction I have ever had. I wish I could remember who gave me that gift for my seventeenth birthday. I would thank them for changing my life. On one of the many thousands of my diary pages are these words: "I find that the more of my life I can put down on paper, the more of my life I can understand."

I did not begin writing these diaries for you. I did not write them for the woman who speaks to you now. And I certainly didn't write them for history. I began them selfishly for that immature, insecure, dramatic teenage girl who needed a loyal pen and page. I am grateful to her. And I think she is grateful to me for being her guardian, her forgiver, her appreciator, her faithful friend.

A decade or two after beginning this adventure, I realized that a diary, perhaps anyone's diary, is valuable to the future. If we discovered today the makeshift diary of a milkmaid in Slovakia in 1649, it would be a real find.

Gradually it dawned on me that the day-to-day record of a Mormon girl in Utah in the 1950s, 60s, and well beyond might be of some interest to history. Even if she had a dull life. But especially if her life was rich with thoughts to think and things to do. I knew that after I died some historian would be poking around in these pages. Only a couple of years ago did I suddenly have the thought, *perhaps that person ought to be me.* So here I am.

I was born a smart girl child into a very solid patriarchy. Approximately half the population of the planet is born female and into a patriarchal system—meaning "the rule of the fathers," or "a society controlled by men in which they use their power to their own advantage." For many, the system is just there like the trees and the wind are just there, not to be questioned. This girl child did question, long before she had words to frame the questions. And then when the words came they would not be stopped. Therein lies the development of this drama—the bewilderment, the grief, the anger, the action.

I was born on September 27, 1939, the very month that Hitler invaded Poland and Great Britain declared war on Germany. Hitler's patriarchy was so perverse that he trained his citizens to say in their prayers, "Adolf Hitler, you are our great Fuhrer. Thy name makes the enemy tremble. Thy Third Reich comes, thy will alone is law upon earth." All across the globe patriarchies were on the march. Thankfully that September, I chose—or was assigned to—or just happened into—a much kinder, gentler version of patriarchy—the Church of Jesus Christ of Latter-day Saints.

This is not a "hate the men" book. It is a "love everyone" book that insists we move into new territory. Frequently I rise up in what I call my "spiritual helicopter" to survey the land. Over on that side is "what was"—our history, where patriarchy brought us innumerable injustices, even unspeakable horrors.

And over here on the other side is "what can be"—our future, whatever we are intelligent enough and brave enough to create here in this small space between past and future, the space we call "now." It is here that my writing and your reading are happening—where our mutual desire for something better than the past erupts into a new vision, a new invitation, to join hands—all of us together—and happily walk the rocky road of patriarchy toward a new land. This is a historical necessity—as urgent and as inevitable as was the evolutionary move out of the Middle Ages into the Enlightenment. The new land we are both discovering and creating comes with a new name. It will be known as *partnership*.

I believe I volunteered to participate. Two days after I was born, my mother wrote home to the other children and said of my birth: "The Baby did not cry—but opened her eyes and looked all around."

Carol Lynn Pearson
Walnut Creek, California
May 6, 2025

AUTHOR'S NOTES

The excerpts from my diary that appear here, chosen to develop my intended themes, are only a fraction of the entire work. Every diary entry is authentic. Some words or sentences have been deleted for the sake of brevity. A word or two or a sentence have occasionally been added for the sake of clarity. Comments I've recently added in preparing this manuscript for publication appear in italic blocks before or after my diary entries. The exception is the first three pages, which briefly summarize my life before the first entry on October 3, 1956.

My diary occasionally uses terminology that reflects proper usage at the time of its writing but may not be today. Recently, for example, the leaders of the church to which I belong have requested that it be referred to by its full name, "The Church of Jesus Christ of Latter-day Saints." During the decades in which nearly all of my diary was written, the term "Mormon" was widely used and accepted. It is the term primarily used in this book.

1

THE BEGINNING

Starting first grade in 1944.

I loved being a Mormon girl. My roots in Mormondom were deep and I treasured the stories of my valiant pioneer ancestors on both sides—George Warren Sirrine, who sailed from New York to San Francisco on the ship Brooklyn and later was a founder of Mesa, Arizona—Thomas Morris, who marched cross-country in the Mormon Battalion during the Mexican-American War—my own grandmother, Sarah Oakey Sirrine, who at age eight walked across the plains beside a covered wagon and later was active in the women's suffrage movement in Idaho. I was proud of them and their devotion to the Lord's restored church.

My own parents, Emeline Sirrine Wright and Lelland Rider Wright, had both served missions for the Church of Jesus Christ of Latter-day Saints. They married later in life, and at thirty-nine my mother gave birth to twins, Donald and David, soon after to Warren, followed by me, and then by our sister Marie. The Church was in our blood, in our home, in our conversation, in our expectations. It was our world. I was a perfect little Mormon girl, and I loved it.

When did I begin noticing this thing that I later came to understand as "patriarchy"? In the wider world I observed that nearly all the voices on the radio were male, and that all the people in charge were male, like President Roosevelt and President Truman. In my smaller world I noted that all the people on the stand at church were men (except for maybe the chorister)—that God our Heavenly Father was male, as were Jesus and the Holy Ghost—that all the prophets were men, and all the angels. There was one hymn we sang sometimes in church that said about our heavenly source: "Truth is reason; truth eternal tells me I've a Mother there." But She didn't seem to be important and She never showed up for Her children. Most of the Bible stories—and all but maybe two of the stories in the hundreds of pages of the Book of Mormon—were about men. All the leaders of the Church were male, like President Heber J. Grant. The boys were ordained to the priesthood and got to pass the sacrament on Sunday. Everything important seemed to be done by a him, not a her. This was very puzzling to me, because I was good, I was smart, always one of the smartest kids in the class, but I was a her and somehow everyone knew that a her wasn't quite as important as a him. Our mother and father never seemed to treat their three boys and two girls differently, except for work assignments that made sense. It was just something in the air. Everywhere. Boys are better. It didn't smell right.

Salt Lake City was our home for my first eight years. Church was a warm, fun part of our lives. In Primary, when I was six or seven, I made my first appearance on stage in a little musical operetta. I was cast as Raggedy Andy, and when I asked our director why I wasn't cast as Raggedy Ann, she said that they had lots of girls who could play Ann, but no boys who were capable of playing Andy. I took that as a compliment. I still remember the costume my mother made, cream-colored flannel with red, yellow, and green stripes, the feel of it on my skin, and the scary delight of being on stage and singing:

Me: "I'm Raggedy Andy."
Her: "And I'm little Ann."
Both: "We're sewed together, you see.
If some little girl chooses one of us
She'll have to take both you and me."

There was a separation, of course, and great grieving, and then a happy reunion.

When I was eight, because my father got a job with the government teaching veterans how to farm, we moved out to the Uintah Basin on the Ute Indian Reservation to the tiny town of Gusher. Two of our five years there saw our family of seven in a two-bedroom farmhouse with no electricity or running water.

With siblings on the family horse, Tim, in Gusher, Utah, 1949.
Front to back: Marie, Carol Lynn, Warren, David, Donald.

One winter the temperature reached 40 below. I was the only kid in my classes who had no American Indian ancestry. In fourth grade I had my first writing success—winning four dollars in a school district essay contest on "Why We Should Eat a Better Breakfast."

Our mother taught school and saved every paycheck to get us out of Gusher. When I was thirteen we moved to Provo and I entered Brigham Young High School, essentially a training school for blossoming teachers at Brigham Young University. Two years later our mother died of breast cancer. When an event as harsh as that happens, the world is reconfigured in many ways. Marie and I took over fixing the meals and ironing the clothes. And—because death is so huge—I began to think more deeply.

The following year when I was a senior, the diary entered my life, a gift for my birthday, and suddenly my thinking had a home. Crushes. Silly escapades. Big hopes. Hurts were noted as "gargantuan"; good things were "neat"; disgusting things met with "Gag a rag bag!" Life's little heartbreaks brought devastation throughout the land. But there were riches even then, thoughts that were destined to become hugely important in building the themes of my life. As early as the third diary entry in that first little book, a profound sentence introduces the very serious subject of this book:

That's me on the far right, among the winners of the high school "I Speak for Democracy" speech contest, 1956.

October 3, 1956

All day long I was distraught about the idea of polygamy in heaven.

I did not elaborate. But I know what prompted this entry. I told it in my 2015 book, The Ghost of Eternal Polygamy: Haunting the Hearts and Heaven of Mormon Women and Men. *Our much-loved seminary teacher told us, as he introduced himself on the first day, that his first wife had died and he was now married to his second. Both of them were "sealed" to him by priesthood authority in the temple. His words are still imprinted on my mind: "I bear you my testimony that when I arrive in heaven I will claim both of these women as my wives. The doctrine that we call plural marriage, or polygamy, restored by the Prophet Joseph Smith in these latter days, is an essential part of the gospel. I promise you young women that as you grow in unselfishness, as you become more pure, you will realize the beauty of this principle and yearn to live it. If we are righteous we will be called to live this highest form of marriage in the eternities."*

Thus opened the first chasm between me and God, between me and my church. This is what God has in store for me? The God who created me, who loves me? If I'm sufficiently righteous I'll be one of many wives forever? I was seventeen, very aware that I was developing into a woman, dreaming about love. And now—this!

I put it away in a far closet. But I knew it was there by its particular bad smell.

Meeting President Dwight D. Eisenhower in the Rose Garden in 1957, as I represented Utah by winning the Alexander Hamilton Bicentennial oratorical contest. This photo appeared in *The New York Times.*

I had plenty of good things to pour myself into. I was not one of the popular kids, I was one of the smart kids and I found my people in the arena of speech and drama and journalism, sort of an adolescent intelligentsia. I was elected editor-in-chief of our newspaper "The Y'ld Cat" and president of the Thespian Club.

I won first place in the school's poetry contest; won the speech competition, "I Speak for Democracy"; and won the Alexander Hamilton oratorical contest that gave me a scholarship and sent me as Utah's representative to Philadelphia for a mock constitutional session in Independence Hall and a visit with President Eisenhower in the Rose Garden, during which I was lucky enough to be standing beside him for a photo that appeared in newspapers, including the New York Times.

I was on a winning streak. But it was never far from my consciousness that in the kingdom of God I came in second. Autumn of 1957 found me at BYU, enjoying life on campus. The Woman Question faithfully followed me there, like a rock in a shoe.

October 6, 1957

In Sunday School they discussed what a wife had to do to make a happy home. It indeed painted a dark picture. I don't intend to go through life acting the part of a stupid, inefficient, fragile idiot to make men think they're

Playing Lady Bracknell in Oscar Wilde's
The Importance of Being Earnest at BYU, 1957.

superior—they're not! I doubt if I shall ever find the type of man I want—one who'll want me—as an equal, not an inferior ego-builder.

And the Ghost of Eternal Polygamy was never far away.

December 16, 1957

My English teacher called me in for consultation on my polygamy theme. He gave me an A on it, but wanted to straighten me out. We had an enjoyable discussion—but that's all.

I did not include the background on this. Dr. Bruce B. Clark, a prominent professor, assigned his freshman English class to write a theme on "A Fate Worse than Death." I wrote on polygamy because death does not solve the problem—the horror of polygamy is guaranteed to go on forever.

"But, Miss Wright, if a man marries a woman and she dies . . ."

"But, Dr. Clark, if a woman marries a man and he dies . . ."

"Well, that's just the way it is."

I threw myself into college life. My days were filled to overflowing with good

Playing Joan of Arc in *The Lark* at BYU.

things to do and good people to do them with. I knew I would be majoring in theatre. My first quarter there I performed in The Importance of Being Earnest, *by Oscar Wilde. I loved being on the stage. I loved thinking, dreaming. After rehearsals and studying I was often up until 12 or even 2. Pondering. Imagining.*

October 22, 1958

I wish I could do something great.

Over the course of my five years at Brigham Young University, I was in many plays and received the Best Actress Award twice—once for Joan of Arc in The Lark *and once for Sarah in* J.B.*, a contemporary poetic version of the story of the biblical Job. Both of those powerful women seeped into my cells and live there today. A drama professor once introduced me as "The First Lady of BYU Theatre." The president of the university, Ernest Wilkinson, knew who I was. I traveled for six weeks with the Drama Department to the Far East for the United Service Organizations (USO) and Defense Department, performing Madam Arcati in Noel Coward's* Blithe Spirit.

I was asked to write scripts for assemblies, writing and directing one honoring our prophet, President David O. McKay. I was the winner in the poetry division

Helping with costumes at the famous Hill Cumorah Pageant near Palmyra, New York, in the summer of 1958, where I was also a performer.

of BYU's Wye Magazine *for a compilation of original work. I was the back end of a bull in a halftime routine for a BYU v. University of Utah football game with my dear friend, Tom Macaulay, who was the front. I received my B.A. in 1960 and my M.A. in 1961, graduating with high honors.*

I had a few boyfriends in my early college days, but often preferred to stay home and read. Or write.

June 2, 1959

I'll just sit here and ferment in my own virtue.

May 3, 1960

If being a *woman* means giving up one fraction of what I am as a *person* I can never do it.

The Woman Question became more central.

July 12, 1960

I've read every scripture regarding woman that exists in all four of the standard works. Each one only upsets me more; I don't mean casually bothers me—I mean upsets me at the core.

Were those spirits who were designated "women" so designated because as original intelligences they were somehow lesser to those designated "men"? And—is the ultimate highest order of family structure one of polygamy? I must find the answer to these two questions very soon, and if the answer to either or both is "yes," I am very much afraid of what will happen.

July 26, 1960

Suddenly it has occurred to me that in 50 years when someone reads this they will not have any idea at all of the appearance of the main character. I will therefore attempt to give a slight description of myself. I am 5' 6" and weigh 117 pounds. I have always felt conspicuously underweight, but perhaps that is not so. My unglamorous measurements are 34-24-34. My hair (brown, already sprinkled generously with pure white) is now comparatively long, and I wear it at present in a bouffant page boy. At my best I look "pleasant" or "interesting"—never approaching the beautiful. Some people have admired my profile but I have always disliked it. Among all my physical features, however, I do possess something that saves me. My eyes. They are wideset, of a very deep blue with extremely long and dark lashes. And that is a sufficient description of the author.

August 5, 1960

I like to think that I have the ability to someday write really good things.

Throughout the college years I wrote lots of short poems, or verse, much of it lighthearted, some satirical, even flippant (I was much influenced by American poet Dorothy Parker) some embarrassingly emotional, much of it really bad, some pretty good.

January 17, 1961

I wish that I could pray in poetry.

January 21, 1961

"The greatest artist is the one who develops the soul in greatness." I just ran across this statement in an old talk of my mother's as I was preparing a short talk for church tomorrow. I think it would be just the thing for repetition before I get out of bed each morning.

February 15, 1961

After seeing *Anne Frank* the play, I am truly so ashamed of myself for the weaknesses that I allow to creep into my soul. If only I could raise my thoughts, fears, pains, and hopes above my own person! If only I could concentrate my energies toward humanity in general, with the basic assumption that human existence is fundamentally good and beautiful—and that the exertion of my energies, however slight, will add a little to that goodness and beauty.

June 13, 1961

It's just afternoon, and I have been reading Brigham Young's Discourses on the pre-existence and plan of salvation. There is no peace within me. Why must my goal be to ever press onward to eternal increase? This strikes me as being told that I must stand in a line for 24 hours a day in order to help pass bean-bags down the row. I am repelled.

July 3, 1961

I am reading *Women of Mormondom*, a book published in 1877 by Mormon feminist historian Edward W. Tullidge. On page 177 he writes, "Presently woman herself shall sing of her divine origin. A high priestess of the faith shall interpret the themes of herself and of her Father-and-Mother God!"

I suddenly found myself crying, and then on my knees in prayer. The most glorious dream that I have ever dared to let play upon my consciousness is that of, in some way, discovering and singing the divine existence of woman. I have no way of knowing whether or not God has given me the capacity even to approach this dream, or whether or not I am personally worthy to make an attempt. All I know is that my soul cries out—almost audibly—with an overpowering desire both to experience and to proclaim the rightful fulfillment of woman's creation. Whether or not I bear the potential of being a "high priestess," able to sing the themes of womanhood and my Father-and-Mother God to ears other than my own—at least I shall sing them to myself.

August 1, 1961

Tonight I am in complete spiritual chaos. I finished reading *Women of Mormondom*. This is the age of woman, he says: a great dawning of the feminine triumph that man cannot stop. Zion, the women of Mormondom, will rise to meet Messiah, the Bridegroom, and accomplish a regeneration of the human family.

And the throning, the crowning of woman in her Royal Court, is to be accomplished through a great cry of gladness for the divine Patriarchal Order (polygamy) that is a necessity for exaltation.

As I read this, I sobbed so that I had to shut myself in my bedroom so I would not be heard. Is this the answer that I have searched for, studied for, prayed for, since I first discovered that I was a woman?

I am told that this is a principle to be enjoyed only by the "pure in heart" and unselfish. Must I believe that my own soul is forever damned to wretchedness because I am unable to rise to this plane of higher existence and more perfect love? Unless I deny completely the divinity of the Church, this is the only thing I can believe.

I feel that the reader may be shaking their head. Why is she taking all this nonsense so seriously? I was a very serious young woman. To me, my life and my church and our God were very serious business, and they were entirely intertwined. My grief was serious too.

August 2, 1961

I know neither what is woman nor why I am a woman. But this I do know: The sun still shines from the heavens to warm the body; the earth still is green and the crickets still sing; there still is blood that pushes life through my veins; it is still good to walk, to eat, to laugh. At present I must say, as I did onstage as the wife of Job: "I am—and that is all my answer." But there is a larger answer, and one day I shall know it.

August 7, 1961

I talked to Dr. Lael Woodbury, professor in BYU's Theatre and Media Arts Department, for a short while today. It's almost refreshing to hear a man stop beating around the bush and admit that woman is an inferior creation.

I recall our conversation, though I did not write it in the diary.

Me: Dr. Woodbury, do you think God values maleness more than femaleness?

Him (after a moment's thought): Well, I guess I would have to say yes—because God, being God, could be anything God wanted to be. And God chose to be male.

August 13, 1961

I just finished re-reading the 132nd section of the Doctrine and Covenants, that terrible "revelation" to Joseph Smith about the necessity of polygamy, along with the commentary. No just God—no God of love and sympathy—would ever have inspired that. I am not able to pray. How can I bring myself to kneel in love and supplication before a God who recognizes me only as a tool and a possession for the use of His MAN? "If any man have a wife and he teaches unto her the law of my priesthood, as pertaining to these things, then shall she believe and administer unto him, or she shall be destroyed, saith the Lord your God."

August 14, 1961

The sun arose this morning, and so did I. The day carried a certain peacefulness, and so did I. Somehow there is something innate within me, a heart whose intuition is infinitely wiser than my own intelligence.

And I just kept on thinking.

October 27, 1961

I think that I would rather be a poet than a prophet—I mean a *real* poet. A prophet has to be told that his words are divine. A poet knows it intuitively.

In the interest of name-dropping, a fun little story here. I spent the Christmas break of 1961 in New York with my boyfriend Fred Dixon, with whom I had co-starred in The Matchmaker, *and who was now working there. We attended church and I met Lola Redford, who invited us to come over that evening (Christmas Eve) and spend it with her and her husband Robert Redford, who was then performing on Broadway in* Sunday in New York. *Writing about this took up many pages in my diary.*

November 27, 1961

A visiting professor in the speech department, Grace Stewart, said in class today: "Don't you think it interesting to watch Carol Lynn think? So often we see people just let words roll out; but you can just see Carol Lynn thinking every minute."

January 12, 1962

Studying Joan for "The Lark." So excited I get to perform her on the stage. I hope that sometime in the great beyond I meet Miss Joan of Arc and have a nice friendly visit with her. I wonder just how much of her legend is true. Did she really act under literal command from heaven? Why not? The idea appeals to me—especially because she was of the race of Woman—whose primary function historically is to go unnoticed. And while I'm on the subject, let me say that I've had no more crises about Woman's Worth since the last I recorded. I move about in a carefully nurtured sort of pride that discards all doubts and questions as absurd. For the present this must satisfy me. In fact, I almost feel as if I have a secret—a secret that for some reason is still hidden from present theological understanding. And until it is known, I shall live by intuition and trust.

A poem I wrote today, a sonnet:

Joan of Arc

Her fingers were not meant for chafing wrists
Where skin is raw from rusty shackles' bite.
Nor were her lungs intended for the mists
Of filthy dungeons, fouled with tallow light.
Those fingers loved the touch of horse and leaves,
Of white sword flashing with her soldier stride;
Those lungs were meant to swell with scent of sheaves
Fresh harvested in her French countryside.

And though the judgment strained with wisdom's wit
To bow her with the rod of holy birch,
Her soul was not intended to be lit
A sacrificial candle to the church—
And on the sacred stand her body stole
The flame and died a martyr to her soul.

I loved that image—"her soul was not intended to be lit a sacrificial candle to the church." Joan was my soul-sister, each finding our places in Catholicism and Mormonism.

I see that I have not reported on my love life at BYU. No college girl is immune. I had two significant crushes and one very important relationship. We loved each other truly, but fate intervened and ours was a star-crossed love. I wrote many poems about that:

There's something strangely false in our
Assured, complete goodbye,
For love's the blood in the flesh of the soul
And the soul will never die.

So—friendly, fondly, as I may
In God's approving view—
I'll call across eternity
For messages of you.

After I received my MA degree from BYU, I accepted a position teaching English at Snow College in Ephraim, Utah. It was a successful year, but I knew I didn't want to remain a teacher. That summer my friend Fred Adams called and asked me to come to Cedar City and participate in the second annual Utah Shakespeare Festival, playing Rosalind, the female lead in As You Like It. *I not only liked it, I loved it!*

June 13, 1963

I have decided that it is not a good custom to pray just before going to bed. Often I am so entirely fatigued and brain-weary that I don't get much accomplished. Tonight I took a walk and sat me down on a pile of rock: it was the best half-hour of prayer I've had in a long time.

The next year was my vagabond year. I had saved $5,000 from my school teacher's salary and this little Utah girl was hungry to see more, know more. A group from the Shakespeare Festival traveled to the major places in Europe. Then, when they flew home, I stayed on for ten more months. Sharing here only a few short paragraphs about those months, as the stated themes of this work did not really emerge until later.

Greece: I arrived in Athens on my twenty-fourth birthday and, trusting little Mormon girl that I was, I failed to keep an eye on my suitcase, which was stolen during the overnight journey, leaving me with only my jacket, my purse, my passport, my traveler's checks, and my virtue. But, smart little Mormon girl that I was, I quickly found the US Air Base and asked for the Mormons. Just as you would hope to hear in a good inspirational story in testimony meeting, I found them and they took me in and gave me a little brown suitcase and food and clothes and helped find me a place to stay.

I ate Athens with a big spoon, specializing in the ancient ruins. I would take a library book that held the plays Medea *or* Antigone, *position myself center stage on the restored, outdoor Theatre of Dionysus, and read the entire play aloud—quietly when tourists showed up. Ah, and my fabulous time on the island of Mykonos in the Aegean Sea. I would buy enough bread, cheese, and fruit for a full day and wander, stopping at a special "rock throne" that I deemed mine, where I sat and meditated on how the ocean meets the sky. And occasionally The Woman Question showed up, wanting to sit with me and talk with me.*

November 4, 1963

From Deep in the Mind of a Woman

The philosophic enigma that puzzles my soul
Is this more than any other:
Why was the world made by a father and son
Instead of a father and mother?

Russia: From Greece I flew to Russia to join a Soviet sponsored theatre tour. It was in Moscow that I learned of the assassination of President Kennedy. The

Russians I spoke to were very kind and told me they had admired Mr. Kennedy. At the Moscow Art Theatre School where Stanislavsky had taught, the head professor stopped his class to acknowledge me and the tragedy my country was going through. I later wrote an article about that and sold it to Playbill, *the NY theatre magazine. I was a good missionary whenever possible. I had smuggled a Book of Mormon and some church tracts into Russia and gave them to the minister at the Baptist church in Moscow.*

Kenya: I spent three months with my dear friend Selene Oates and her husband Ernest and their new baby. Ernest worked for the State Department. Beautiful white beaches, dense forests, elephants, crocodiles, giraffes, leopards, water buffalo. Independence Uhuru celebration. Time to think. And to write.

December 10, 1963

I must record a few things I've written since being here in Kenya, actually prior to arriving—before I lose the scraps of paper.

Day-Old Child

My day-old child lay in my arms.
With my lips against his ear
I whispered strongly, "How I wish,
I wish that you could hear;

"I've a hundred wonderful things to say,"
(A tiny cough and a nod),
"Hurry, hurry, hurry and grow
So I can tell you about God."

My day-old baby's mouth was still
And my words only tickled his ear.
But a kind of a light passed through his eyes,
And I saw this thought appear:

"How I wish I had a voice and words;
I've a hundred things to say.
Before I forget I'd tell you of God—
I left Him yesterday."

In the Israel Museum in Jerusalem, one very interesting piece of conversation I absorbed from my two friends (the director of the museum and an elderly scholar from Copenhagen) was regarding the 1600–1700 B.C. change from worship of the female to worship of the male. This, said the director, is why the Bible is so against Woman—simply out of jealousy. To get the people to worship the male God Jehovah, this was necessary. Very interesting.

Performing scenes from Greek tragedies on the stage in the ruins at Epidaurus. Occasionally a tourist stopped by and applauded, and one of them took this picture!

"Very interesting," she says, like a detective who has stumbled upon a clue that may become important. "Very interesting indeed." My first real glimpse into the ancient, hidden history of our Divine Mother.

Israel: Three and a half months with other young people on Kibbutz Ein HaShofet (a communal farm with a population of about 500), half the day in "ulpan" (a school for the intensive study of Hebrew) and half the day doing manual labor picking oranges, weeding the vegetable garden, mending blankets, setting tables in our big dining hall—whatever work needed to be done. One day I ironed twenty-two shirts. I developed a reputation as a very good worker. And before I left Israel I could carry on a decent conversation in rudimentary Hebrew. Later my friend and renowned BYU professor of history and religion Hugh Nibley liked to walk across campus with me to practice his Hebrew. (Our family and the Nibley family had lived in the same Provo neighborhood for years and, as early teenagers, my sister Marie and I were babysitters to the Nibley family, back when the going pay was twenty-five cents per hour—and that included doing the dishes and folding the laundry).

July 14, 1964

From the air most countries look pretty much alike. The land of America is just part of the soil of the earth. And the people of America are just part of the people of the earth. I was born to a part of America that has a unique destiny; there is no fulfillment for me apart from it. And it is there that I am going.

I was still a totally devoted and good little Mormon girl. I had continued to obey all the rules. A boy I had a crush on at the kibbutz and who really liked me but never made a "pass," explained, "Carol Lynn, you radiate a kind of purity." I had decided something at the beginning of my trip. My church's "Word of Wisdom," a health code that readily showed who was "in" and who was "out," forbade all use of alcohol. But I decided that—just for a minute—I would be a bad girl. I had one ceremonial sip of wine in France, one sip of vodka in Russia, one sip of beer in Germany. Of each one of them I thought, "This might have tasted good before they let it go bad."

2

FROM WRIGHT TO PEARSON

How I miss my maiden name, Carol Lynn Wright. Back in Provo, I accepted a job writing screenplays for BYU's Motion Picture Studio. The writing department consisted of two people—Scott Whitaker, former Disney animator, and me. We were a great team and became fast friends. I was thrilled to be able to use my abilities on behalf of the Church.

And I could be on stage again! The drama department had scheduled By the Skin of Their Teeth, *a comedy by Thornton Wilder. Even though I was no longer a student I was allowed to try out, and I got the role of Mrs. Antrobus, one of the two main characters.*

February 19, 1965

Oh, one other person in the play I must mention: Gerald Pearson. He's a 22-year-old returned missionary and we've struck up a marvelous little friendship. He has beautiful blond hair and is completely open and unfeigning. I like him. And he likes me. He thinks I'm terribly witty and a fantastic actress and that I have beautiful bright expressive eyes that shine from deep, deep down. If I didn't know better I might develop a crush on him.

Gerald lived only a few blocks from me and when the play was finished he would often come over just to talk. Once he brought a notebook with him and started taking notes. "You always say so many wonderful things that I need to write them down!" I laughed.

March 17, 1965

Gerald is one of the sweetest, most unspoiled, refreshing honestly spiritual people I've met. And I'm very fond of him.

Of course the plot thickened. The more time Gerald and I spent together the more we liked each other. Loved each other. I truly did fall in love with Gerald Pearson.

And I continued to love my work at the Motion Picture Studio. Some were educational films. Many were films for the Church, which always needed approval from the General Authorities (top church leaders, colloquially referred to as "the Brethren." We were the creative team and the Brethren were the establishment, something that led to significant frustrations and sometimes disillusionments. But there was also significant appreciation.

April 7, 1965

Read my script about changes made in the temple ceremony to apostle Richard L. Evans in Salt Lake. He said it was "beautifully written and beautifully read."

In addition to writing scripts for the Studio, I helped there wherever more hands were needed. I traveled to Arizona to help with And Should We Die, *a film about the extraordinary sacrifices of Mormons in Mexico. Here on the wall of my office today is a framed photo of me as an extra, a soldier to Pancho Villa, sitting by a campfire with bloody bandages on my head and coffee grounds on my cheeks for a beard.*

April 10, 1965

Whenever I see Gerald a warm light bulb goes on inside of me and I don't want him ever to go away. I dreamed about him last night and the night before.

April 13, 1965

I received a check for $1.25 from the *Improvement Era* as payment for one five-line poem— "Written with Toes in the Sand."

Because church magazines paid twenty-five cents per line, I had developed a habit of writing poems with very short lines, increasing their length and obviously their value.

April 14, 1965

Gerald Pearson is just about the most remarkable person I have ever met. Such a clear and total dedication, such an absolute and friendly commitment to things spiritual I have never seen. I shouldn't be surprised to find that he was translated on his way home from here.

Yes, I would be surprised. Gerald will stay on earth: he has a huge work to do—and he's going to do it. I have complete confidence in him. He still trails clouds of immaturity—but beneath them there is pure angel and strength.

Before he left he asked if we could have prayer together, and we did, he offering it—praying that our association would be binding, that we might help one another and accomplish that which the Lord wants us to accomplish.

Dear God—bless Gerald.

April 18, 1965

My week was occupied with seeing the dentist. He filled two cavities and then proceeded to extract a wisdom tooth—the last one I had, leaving me now entirely without prudence.

April 23, 1965

As I opened the door tonight, the light fell on newspaper headlines: "100,000 to Viet Nam?" No, no, please no!

May 23, 1965

I want to be somebody—not necessarily to be famous, but to do what I want to do so well that it makes a mark that is visible.

June 12, 1965

Truly Gerald is a thing of beauty and a joy forever. Last night he came over and we talked until late again. "My wife has got to love God more than me" he said. He told me about his home life in Murray. His father had problems. His mother built their house almost single-handedly. They lived in the garage for a while, he in the attic where he could see snow sifting in through the shingles. Gerald worked full-time from the age of 13 in a grocery store after school, four to midnight.

June 14, 1965

Perhaps my painting of Gerald in this book has been a bit one-sided. He is not a pious, sober young man—not at all. He is exuberantly joyful and silly and giddy and fun, fun, fun. And marvelous.

June 20, 1965

Ah, me—what a state I am in! How is it that in so short a time a mature intelligent young woman can be reduced to a sighing, quivering wreck?! I cannot open a book and keep my eyes and my mind together on the page.

Am I a fool? Ah, no, no, no. To love is the only wisdom.

Gerald and I continued our fine friendship through the summer.

December 5, 1965

Tonight Gerald and I sat here with our arms around each other.

Him: I've been so confused about you. And I still don't know what to say—except that I love you very much.

Me: I love you too, Gerald.

Him: But now I don't know what to do with it.

Me: Don't worry about it.

Him: I don't worry about it—I love it. And I'll just go on loving it—loving you.

And he kissed me. A real, true kiss.

By Christmas time we were engaged. Even though Gerald was two and a half years younger than me and less accomplished, I felt it was the absolutely right thing to do. We were a good match. I was in love. I was thrilled.

February 20, 1966

Last Sunday Gerald and I had a long talk about a certain thing I'm not going to mention. He had been fasting for two days. This could have been a shattering experience, but it wasn't. I was utterly wrapped in the assurance: "It's all right. It's fine. Don't give it a second's worry."

I did not want the pages of my diary to hold any further information than that. The full story is told in my memoir, Goodbye, I Love You *(Random House, 1986). Gerald told me that in his past there had been homosexual feelings and some homosexual experiences. But, he assured me, that is not who he really was. He had repented and he loved me and he knew that would not be a problem for us. I knew almost nothing about the subject of homosexuality. I knew our church taught that it was a great sin, that it was just giving in to Satan, that a man needed to repent and find a good woman who loved him and all would be well. I was a good woman. I loved him. And I knew that the leaders of our church were inspired by God. Truly, all would be well.*

March 2, 1966

Gerald and I are no longer engaged. I know he's felt wrong about us since the Sunday he confessed to me the problem in his past. I believe that the thought of perfection is vital to Gerald and knowing that he had shown me his imperfections made him extremely uneasy.

He came over tonight and we talked. After I gave back the ring I asked if we could have prayer together—saying that if he'd like, I would offer it. I prayed with all my heart that God would be with us and lead us to the things He wanted us to have.

Then he left.

And only a few days later . . .

March 7, 1966

Yesterday I had an experience that shook me to the core. Marge and I went to the "fireside" up on campus. Rodney Turner of BYU's religion department spoke. He chose as his subject "Woman." By the time he was five minutes into his talk I was so near to sobs that I had to get up and leave. I stood by an exit and listened to the rest.

His thesis was that women have got to submit themselves to their husbands entirely or find themselves in hell where Emma Smith is.

He reminded us that *man* was God's supreme creation, and that because he was not fulfilled, God created woman to glorify man.

Man contracts with God—but woman contracts with her husband.

Woman's circumference is *within* the circumference of the man, but man's circumference is *not* within that of woman.

Woman is a branch of the tree, of which man is the trunk.

I was thrown off onto the sea of despair I so often sailed before when this "Woman Question" was foremost in my mind.

So I came home and called Gerald and told him I needed his help. I wanted him to help me understand wherein I failed.

He feels that he's not secure enough in his own manhood to help me in my search to be a woman. And that I'm not secure enough in my womanhood to help him be a man. "It would be the blind leading the blind."

Reading how I was affected by the words of Brother Turner, I shake my head, as I hope you do. But I was as true a believer as you could find, taking in the words of the Brethren—and their appointed teachers at BYU—as gospel truth. After all, they were consistent with those dreadful words in Section 132 of the canonized LDS scripture, the Doctrine and Covenants, that were really the beginning of all the pain.

March 15, 1966

There is much I have learned from this, I suppose. I will keep trusting people. But I will not let someone else be my direct line to God. I have a testimony of myself. I hereby pledge to keep my testimony of myself in the face of all. It is something between God and myself—and none else.

I threw myself into life without a man. I enjoyed my work in the Motion Picture Studio and was highly regarded there. We had been commissioned to write a series of films dramatizing the Book of Mormon and I was very much involved. I wrote the story of Alma, which my superiors very much liked, and was instructed to take it to the highly-regarded professor Hugh Nibley for his response.

April 12, 1966

I visited today with Dr. Nibley in his office.

Him: Who wrote this?

Me: I did.

Him: It is very, very good. Dialogue, characters and all. Obviously a committee did not write it. This is much better than what we usually produce around here. It's the best thing I've seen done on the Book of Mormon.

As a side note, the Book of Mormon series was never filmed. The General Authorities ultimately decided it would not do to put any words in the mouths of the characters that are not found in the book itself.

April 17, 1966

I am trying a little experiment. It's called diary by typewriter. Writing in long hand is such a tedious effort. This may be a good thing for me.

At a poetry reading event, my old high school drama teacher, Max Golightly, read a poem he had written, "Discovering Woman," which led into a discussion of why woman was created second. "It's usual," he said, "for us to make a rough draft of something we're creating, and then from that form the more perfect, more refined creation." He's always felt that way about woman, that she is a more refined man. Interesting—not doctrinal, but interesting.

April 19, 1966

I went to interview Dr. Reed Bradford, much-loved sociology professor, about a film I'm working on, and in the course of the discussion he brought up the talk given by Rodney Turner. He takes strong opposition.

"Many girls," he said, "liked the talk greatly. And do you know why? Because they're immature. It's easier to accept a subordinate role and just be led along. But this is not the way it was intended. When one person dominates another, he deprives that person of growth and fulfillment. Very few people in the Church understand what a woman is supposed to be."

As for me and my house—we're not at present in a great state of wondering what a woman is supposed to be. A woman is supposed to be a person—a good, kind, giving, loving, trusting, confident person. The end.

My writing career was blossoming. I had sold poems to Woman's Day *and other magazines, as well as articles about my time in Russia to several magazines. A children's play,* Pegora the Witch, *was produced at BYU and a few other colleges and was accepted for publication by Anchorage Press. A play,* Think Your Way to a Million, *was performed at Snow College in Ephraim, Utah.*

June 24, 1966

News. Surprisingly not surprising news. Gerald has asked to re-enter my life. "Could you marry a blind man?" he said. He knows he behaved badly. But pride and fear and confusion stopped him from coming to me. But he knew he would. Nothing has been right since March, he said. It's been very difficult for him to keep the Spirit of the Lord.

"You know, I used to think that you wouldn't be much without your poems—but what I've discovered is that your poems aren't much without you. I've admitted to myself that I do love you, and that it's the kind of love that endures. I've discovered that I just cannot live my life without you."

What did we decide to do? To try again—this time for keeps.

On September 9 in the Salt Lake Temple, Gerald and I were married by Elder Marion D. Hanks, one of the General Authorities. He had become a favorite of ours, and he graciously agreed to perform our ceremony. This began a friendship that developed over many years.

September 12, 1966

I sit at our table up here in the mountains on our honeymoon while my

Gerald's and my wedding day, September 9, 1966.

husband does the dishes. I have a husband. Isn't that amazing? I am a wife. The thing that's really amazing is how non-amazing it is. How extremely natural it is. I was told the marriage state would be kind of difficult to adjust to—physically—that psychological holdovers of long-lived modesty would cause inhibitions. This was not the way with me at all. Sharing a bed with Gerald—having his body close to me, and in me, is utterly natural. I accept it, and love it.

September 25, 1966

The Judgment

I have been judged.
Already, mortal,
I have stood at heaven's bar
While my soul was read aloud
And (oh, listen) not proud
But too full for silence
I sing the decree.

God smiled at me—
And all of heaven did too—
Smiled as He gave
My sentence of salvation—
Gave me you.

September 29, 1966

Oh, dear—Gerald is bad for my diary. I no longer feel the urgency to confide in something. I have some*one.*

3

SURPRISING CELEBRITY

I suppose that everyone who writes poetry dreams of someday having a book published. I did. But I would never have made it happen. Gerald made it happen.

October 20, 1966

Gerald asked a group of Mormon visual artists to come to our house and serve as an audience for a hearing of my poems and suggest those that they think should go into our book. I read about forty that I think are good candidates. They honestly were greatly moved and most enthusiastic, saying they would all go out and sell the book once it's out.

October 26, 1966

I think I should be honest in my writing. A week ago Sunday I had a big upset because at the dinner table Gerald asked me (half-jokingly) if I would mind if maybe he had Christie Lund Coles, our much older poet-friend whose husband had dropped out of the Church, as one of his wives in the next world. I ended up crying—for the first time in my married career. Gerald tried to comfort me, saying that was in the plan so every righteous woman could have a righteous husband. I hardly knew what to say.

January 11, 1967

It's fun to be married. Last night Gerald and I just stayed awake in bed giggling and having fun. We do have good times. And even the once in a while that we have a small tension it doesn't last long. It's very peaceful to be married.

August 1, 1967

Yesterday Gerald and I went up to Salt Lake to see if Bookcraft Publishers would be interested in my collection of LDS poetry. We talked to Marvin Wallin, who was very nice but who stated unequivocally that a book of poetry would not sell. I think we're still going to go ahead and put the book out, financing it ourselves. Gerald is very determined that we do it. He has established a company, "Trilogy Arts."

September 6, 1967

The book is at the printers now. We're using five illustrations by our friend Trevor Southey. Gosh, it's scary to do all this. It seems so presumptuous to print in a book, in black and white for all to see, your very own thoughts that you have framed in the privacy of your own mind and must now expose to the perhaps unsympathetic eye of the casual book-thumber. It's scary, but all things of value have a little scare attached to them. And I believe in the poems. Who was it—Emerson?—who said that genius is to believe that what is true for yourself is true for every other man.

In the late '60s and early '70s, Trevor Southey and I were part of what became known as the "Mormon Art and Belief Movement," which also included artists Dale Thompson Fletcher, Dennis Smith, and others.

October 10, 1967

My book is out! I have published a book of poetry—Latter-day Saint poetry! This I have dreamed of for years. *Beginnings.* On the cover is Trevor's "Embryo of a God." Everybody seems to love it. The books are now tucked away in my Daddy's garage, almost all two thousand of them. This is truly an adventure in faith.

Here is the title poem:

Beginnings

Today you came running
With a small specked egg
Warm in your hand.
You could barely understand
I know
As I told you of Beginnings—
Of egg and bird.
Told, too,
That years ago
You began
Smaller than sight.
And then
As egg yearns for sky
And seed stretches to tree
You became like me.

Oh
But there's so much more.
You and I, child,
Have just begun.

Reading from my first book, *Beginnings*.

Think:
Worlds from now
What might we be—
We who are seed
Of Deity.

October 15, 1967

These are really quite amazing days. My book seems to be a most unusual success. The lady at the BYU bookstore wanted at first to take only five because "poetry just doesn't sell." But we left her twenty on consignment. She put it up on a display table for new books and in two hours she was calling for more books. And it didn't stop. In the first week now she sold two hundred copies. Donna Gregory wrote a review of the book for the *Universe,* headlining it, "Authoress Compiles Bestseller."

And today a review of it came out in the *Provo Daily Herald*, by Theron Luke. He started by saying, "If you believe in God, Carol Lynn Pearson's poetry might bring Him closer. If you don't, her poetry may make you wonder why you don't."

When Gerald and Mario Aranda, our good friend and best man at our wedding, picked the books up in Salt Lake, the manager of the bindery said that he went back to check on things while it was being bound and the whole operation was stopped. Everyone was sitting there reading the poems.

I'm kind of like a celebrity.

October 17, 1967

I must comment on a phone call I just received from Bruce B. Clark. He thinks my book is "exquisite." He said he's delighted with it, that the poems are simply lovely. This thrills me of course, as he is a very knowledgeable and discerning man, now BYU's Dean of Humanities and past chairman of the English Department, not to mention my freshman English teacher. He said he's already had an argument about the book with someone who claimed it wasn't poetry, but short little essays. But he defends it as poetry, though not highly imagistic and complicated—just as Emily Dickenson's poems are poetry. And he wanted permission to choose several of them for inclusion in *Out of the Best Books,* which he compiles for the Relief Society lessons. This makes me feel better than any comment I've received since we got the book.

October 25, 1967

Last Tuesday we got a letter from Marion D. Hanks. We had left a copy of the book in his office in Salt Lake. He wrote:

> Dear Folks: I had my first chance yesterday to really move into the book a bit and I loved it! This is great material and will be appreciated far and wide. I am grateful to know you and grateful for the special gift you have honored enough to develop and use. God bless you always. I am off to the Orient for a time and hope to see you sometime when I get back.

We have now sold to the BYU bookstore 440 copies of *Beginnings* in a matter of two weeks. And BYU's a capella choir is going to sell the books as a fund raiser. They decided today to take 1,000.

Decades later I still am surprised at the immediate and remarkable success of this little book. I have no way to account for it except that what I offered was sort of the right thing at the right time to the right people. Just recently the Association for Mormon Letters posted a list of "100 Works of Significant Mormon Literature." Beginnings *by Carol Lynn Pearson was on the list. I know that, among other things, this book opened the door to many other people creating their own contributions.*

Something else: there's a possibility that I may be pregnant. My period is a week and a half overdue. This is my first month off the pills in a year. I hope I am. And Gerald is terribly excited about it.

November 28, 1967

It's true. I'm going to be a mother. Right now there is a little being inside of me growing and becoming a person. I feel happy and calm, just like I did about getting married.

I gave Dr. Webster a copy of my book. He immediately called in his nurse and his secretary and showed them.

"Why, look—this girl wrote all these poems."

They both responded, "Oh, you're the one!" and "I've been trying to get a copy of that!"

So it's official that I'm with child. Gerald has been more than delighted at the prospect. In fact, if my visit today had revealed that I wasn't pregnant, I wouldn't have dared come home until I was!

My celebrity continued to expand—even to the thirty or so General Authorities of the Church at that time. Gerald and I had sent them each a signed copy of Beginnings *at Christmastime.*

January 2, 1968

While in Salt Lake we dropped into the Church Office Building. We ran into General Authority S. Dilworth Young, and I was introduced as having just written a book of poetry. Brother Young promptly said, "Oh—are you the one? Let me shake your hand again! I've never seen a collection of poetry that I've enjoyed more." As he left he said, "I bow to a real poet." And he did.

August 8, 1968

This is shameful—my first diary entry since February. I am a mother. We are parents of a beautiful little girl whom we named Emily. I am nursing her—have from the first, and I have plenty of milk. I love to nurse.

First Child

I savor this mutual feast:
You at my breast
Desperately drinking life—

And me
Watching, touching,
Sipping eagerly
On your sweet evidence
Of immortality.

January 5, 1969

Some time ago Elder A. Theodore Tuttle called me (he had called previously to tell me how he enjoyed our book) and asked if I would come to the Lion House (a mansion in which Brigham Young housed a large number of his plural families) to give a program from the book to a monthly luncheon of the Wives of the General Authorities. Of course I was extremely excited about it. His wife and Mrs. Boyd K. Packer were in charge. I met Sister Packer the preceding week as she and her husband addressed a meeting on BYU Women's Week, where I had been asked to give 20 minutes of my poems. When I finished, Brother Packer asked me if I would also read "The Forgiving," which he said was his favorite.

One awfully funny thing happened at the Lion House event. I was standing with two girls who were to give musical selections. Richard L. Evans's wife surmised that we were the program and asked, "What are your names and what are you doing?"

Nervously, I replied, "I'm Carol Lynn Poetry and I'm reading—." I blushed. We laughed.

The luncheon was lovely. I sat at a table between Sister Marion D. Hanks and Sister Eldred Smith, wife of the Church patriarch. Also at my table were Sisters Oscar Kirkham, Spencer W. Kimball, and N. Eldon Tanner. Sister Hanks was very gracious, telling me that her husband had told her how wonderful my poems were.

Sister Packer introduced me, and when I got up, Jessie Evans Smith spoke up, saying, "I hope you read my favorite one—the one about the new baby!" I assured her that I would. When I came to "Day-Old Child," she mouthed the words with me. As I finished, she said out loud, "Isn't that beautiful? Isn't that beautiful?" She then asked for the two poems on page sixteen.

Reading this, I have to wonder why it was Brother Tuttle and not Sister Tuttle who called to invite me to present the program. And, of course, I grimace at reading that I named them in my diary only by the names of their husbands. I expect that's how they were introduced to me. All except for Jessie Evans Smith, the wife of Joseph Fielding Smith who had established an identity of her own as a renowned opera singer.

January 29, 1969

Among those present at the dinner party we attended last night was J.D. Williams, well-known liberal professor of politics at the University of Utah. I read from the book later in the evening and everyone seemed quite captivated. Especially Brother Williams. He said several times how touched he was and that he was a better person for that evening. He asked if the U of U bookstore had the book and we said that no, they had refused to take it. He said to leave a package of books with him and that they would be on their shelves the next morning. He called the next day and said yes, the book was now in the bookstore. Brother Williams is now using the poems in all the talks he gives—used five of them at the missionary farewell of his nephew. Back at a Stake Conference, he based a whole talk on the book, devoting quite some time to the book itself and its author. Really quite astonishing.

March 13, 1969

About a week ago Jay Todd, managing editor of the Church Publication the *Improvement Era*, called to ask if I would write something for the May issue on what it means to be a woman. The whole issue is devoted to that, especially the Centennial of the Young Women's Mutual In Action (MIA). And they're having various notable women—Belle Spafford (Relief Society General President) and Florence Jacobsen (Young Women President)—write articles on women. Then they decided they needed a personal expression and asked me to send something in poetry or prose. Here's what I finally came up with:

The Woman

God fashioned me for feeding
And set me in a hungry land.

I give—
To satisfy the unconscious appetite
Of the unborn
And the child's first thirsting need.

I give—

To be sweet sustenance
To aching man,
And then quiet comfort
To a weary, wanting world.

There is much hunger here.

Oh, Father—fill me
That I may nourish
Generously.

I continued my work at the Motion Picture Studio and often found it so frustrating to work with the small bureaucracies within the Church. I love the following story.

March 23, 1969

I had to go to Salt Lake to read a filmstrip to the MIA missionary committee, a leadership thing for the branches [smaller congregations], which I have been working on with [educator and soon-to-be author,] Steve Covey. Covey told me what he wanted, I did it, and he was delighted.

So I arrive at this meeting and the committee tells me they want quite a different thing, that there isn't enough meat on the bones of the script, not enough specific how-to on all the problems faced.

Then Brother Covey arrived; he had had another meeting to attend. I told him that we had to start all over again. He asked what they objected to in the filmstrip we had created. They gave him some of their objections and he listened. And then I saw Steve Covey in action. It was truly amazing. He was firm, forthright, kind, and absolutely masterful in presenting his case. The people out in the branches, he said, get instruction "up to here." What we wanted to do in this filmstrip was to give a little motivation. He asked if they had heard the script read. No, they had just read it individually earlier that day. Well, he said, would they take the time to have me read it aloud in order really to see how it would sound? Yes. So I did.

When I finished one man said, "Well, I think that's great!" And everybody else began to say, "Hmm, that sure sounds a lot better when you read it." So the upshot is that we're moving forward with it. As I say, it was an amazing evening. Steve Covey is a master.

April 6, 1969

Last week our new order of books arrived—ten thousand plus—all stacked in one room of our little four-room apartment. We have now sold 20,000 without any promotion at all.

I was definitely on the Mormon map. Speaking invitations came in regularly and I accepted all that I could—for Young Women Conferences, Relief Society dinners, stake events, firesides. I was honored in high places. And usually I took little Emily with me. She was the light of my life.

Elder A. Theodore Tuttle quoted "The Lesson" in his talk at the Sunday School session of the Church's biannual general conference. He said, "And now I'd like to quote a poem by Carol Lynn Pearson. She's a very talented young lady who has the gift of saying things very succinctly and beautifully."

Wow. I'm pooped. And it's my turn to get up with Emily in the morning. Her day begins about six, so Gerald and I take turns sleeping in. Good night.

Clearly, Gerald and I deserved a vacation. We arranged for business to be taken care of, packed our bags, picked up our Emily, and headed off to Scotland. I was told that the island of Tiree was the sun spot of the Hebrides. I think there were three days in which it was warm enough that we did not have to wear our jackets. We joked that if the sun came out we had to run outside and follow its path until it disappeared.

Our six weeks on Tiree were happy and productive ones. Gerald and I each took half a day to be with Emily and half a day to do our personal work. Gerald worked on his own projects and spent intense time studying the scriptures, making new discoveries about light and love. He was a philosopher and loved to talk about the infinite.

I had brought a typewriter and planned to write my musical play, The Order is Love. *The story is set in Orderville, Southern Utah, where early Mormons were attempting to live the United Order, a communal living arrangement. Early on I realized I needed some information, so I sent an emergency letter to Church Historian Leonard Arrington, saying, "Help! I'm in the middle of writing a musical on Orderville and I need to know more about how and why the Order dissolved. Help! Help!" Happily, I had previously created a friendly relationship with Leonard. Having read something of mine in one of the church magazines that mentioned my ancestors, he telephoned me to ask some questions. That was the beginning of a lovely friendship. Just in time I received a letter from him with the information that I needed to keep my momentum going. How I did love writing that play!*

July 20, 1969

10:30 Tiree time. Over an hour ago men landed on the moon. The "Eagle" landed within 35 seconds of the time scheduled two weeks ago. On Mrs. McKenzie's wireless (radio to us guys) I listened to the voices of the crew as they landed and described the rocks and the colors. What a day!

And the Israelis and Egyptians are bombing again.

And Gerald is wonderful.

And Emily is likewise wonderful.

And yesterday I finished the first draft of my musical. Wrote it in two weeks.

Leaving Tiree, we spent some time in London, absorbing as much as we could and seeing a lot of plays.

September 4, 1969

Last night we went to *Boys in the Band*, a play about homosexuals. It was intriguing, particularly because both of us have come to know quite a bit about the problem. Some of the elements in the story I appreciated. Like when Alan decided to go back to his wife. I just cheered.

4

SMOOTH SAILING INTO ROUGH WATERS: THE EQUAL RIGHTS AMENDMENT

October 1, 1969

We left London with no tears. I write now from my very own study in our new house.

In London we had finalized the purchase of the family home of my dear friend Dave Jacobs—a fine house on Ninth East in Provo, Utah, right off of Center Street. I was thrilled.

In summary: Gerald published a book by artist Dennis Smith, titled Star Counter, *followed by a second poetry book of mine,* The Search. *I continued to be a guest speaker on many occasions. Renowned LDS composer Lex de Azevedo wrote the music to* The Order is Love, *which was scheduled to be premiered the following year as part of the Festival of Mormon Arts at BYU. Our son John was born and was thriving and seemed to want to nurse nonstop. Gerald referred to me as "Johnny's leftovers." Gerald wrote a book about the drug scene in the Church,* There is a Way Back, *showing how a lot of kids have turned things around by using the principles of the gospel. He also continued to perform a church calling at the prison. We participated in "The Group," helping kids who have made it back from drug addiction or were trying to.*

September 27, 1970

My birthday. Time is a trick, and one cannot master it. One can just hold each moment close, hold Gerald and Emily and Johnny very, very close, for time takes. I sound sad. I'm not. I'm very happy. But real happiness brings melancholy as a twin. Awareness—that's it—awareness of being so full. The happy are vulnerable—so vulnerable.

October 10, 1970

For the last two weeks my brother Warren has been here. He and I and Johnny drove out to our childhood home in Gusher. It was a little painful for me. The greyish wooden house—still the same, except for other people living in it. A family of nine. The parents weren't at home, but several girls were there. The oldest was thirteen, a little older than I was when we were there. She was shy and wore her Primary bandelo. They had moved there about a year and a half ago, after many, many moves. Their father was trying to make a go of farming. The place has electricity now and running water. We used coal oil lamps and went to the outhouse even in winter. The well was gone; only the tree nearby was still there. But we found the pump in a junkheap not far away. I reached down and pumped the handle. It worked. It squeaked. And my heart filled up with sadness in remembrance of my mother. How hard it was for her there—teaching school and then having to cope with life like that—and with five children that were sometimes not very helpful. As we left I said a little prayer for the girls that their parents could someday get them to a place where a few of life's opportunities might find them.

March 27, 1971

My musical play, *The Order is Love,* went very well indeed! The response has been overwhelming. Tickets to the four performances in BYU's de Jong Concert Hall that holds over 1200 soon sold out and so they scheduled a Saturday matinee. That too was sold out and for the last three performances there were people standing and sitting in the exit ways.

The audiences were really moved. Moved and warmed. And excited. That was the great part. I've never had such enthusiastic approval heaped upon me.

August 25, 1971

And now we two are five. I am the mother of three. Dear little Aaron is down in his cradle sleeping peacefully while I take a moment to note his arrival.

December 3, 1971

I am deciding that the most one is entitled to in this world is to simply get through it with a little courage left in your heart and your ability to love intact.

I'm reminding myself of this because of late I feel concern for the position of Trilogy Arts, our publishing company. We are way over extended and have debts that we ought not to have.

Trilogy Arts's pie is being split into more and more pieces without the pie itself becoming any larger. Gerald and I have not been taking out any money for about five months now. I tell Gerald we need to be more cautious. Just because we are striving to build the kingdom does not give us an open door to financial success.

Gerald had published a second book of poetry by me, which did well but not as well as Beginnings *had. And he was captivated by LDS musicians, going out on a very big limb to record their albums, which never recouped the large investment. I continued to support the family with my screenplays for BYU Motion*

Pictures. One of my best was Cipher in the Snow, *a short film that went on to win international awards and is now something of a cult classic.*

And then—suddenly and without warning—just as 1971 was drawing to a close—Enter: the Equal Rights Amendment! When I first heard of the ERA and learned it was something about women's rights, I was on the alert. What did it mean? "Equality of rights under the law shall not be denied or abridged by the United States or by any state on account of sex." I did not see any reason to be frightened by it.

January 6, 1972

Toward the first part of December I called KBYU and suggested they have a panel discussion on the Equal Rights Amendment, because there's so much confusion about it. They set up the program. On the pro side: Virginia Cutler, former head of the College of Family Living, State Senator Robert O. Bowen, and Carol Lynn Pearson. On the con side: BYU Professors Rodney Turner and Carlton Marlowe. For the first time in my life I came face to face with and shook hands with Rodney Turner. First Virginia spoke, declaring her endorsement of the amendment. Then Senator Bowen spoke, from a plane of democratic philosophy. I then spoke, mostly giving a perspective for the woman's movement in Utah by rehearsing some of my significant finds in the early *Woman's Exponent*. Just that day I had received in the mail from Leonard Arrington a copy of the *Utah Woman Suffrage Songbook*. I selected one of the songs, words written by Louise Lula Green Richards, to be sung to the tune "Hope of Israel." I slipped a copy of it to Virginia just before we went on, and I had her join me in singing it on the broadcast:

Woman, Arise

Freedom's daughter, rouse from slumber;
See the curtains are withdrawn
Which for long thy mind have clouded;
Lo! Thy day begins to dawn.

Woman, rise, thy penance o'er;
Sit thou in the dust no more;
Seize the scepter, hold the van,
Equal with thy brother, man.

I was told the camera flipped to Rodney Turner while we were singing, and he had his head down, scowling. Dr. Turner came across as a very belligerent man. He kept saying, "This amendment will strip women of the rights they hold most dear—to be protected, to raise a family, to be provided for, etc." Some of the arguments need to be seriously considered, I will admit, but things like forcing integration of public rest rooms is incredible nonsense. In fact I called up my friend Liane's father, Provo City Judge Maurice Harding, that day and asked him if that was a possible logical extension of the amendment. He laughed and said it was ridiculous. "We don't throw out common sense and propriety just because we amend the constitution to extend rights."

P.S. The typing is not up to par on this today because my fingers are freezing: my room over the garage is icy, and my heater only gets to my feet. Pity I can't type with my feet.

January 14, 1972

Last week Utah Governor Rampton in his State of the State address called for ratification of the ERA. He was deluged with letters condemning this from various places—particularly Sevier County, where there is a strong John Birch Society and where the people are ultra-conservative. A group has organized there called HOT DOG (Humanitarians Opposed to Degrading Our Girls). They are convinced that the amendment is an evil plot.

The Governor's Committee on the Status of Women asked Mildred Bushman and me to go down there and speak on the radio to present the other side on this issue. I agreed if a very informed man would also go.

A couple of days later I got a long-distance phone call from someone in Richfield. He pled with me not to come—the people down there love me and my books, and my reputation will be utterly destroyed if I go. He tried to make me see that all this is a Satanic plot to destroy the family. He said they had tried to contact me earlier to ask me to be one of their leaders in HOT-DOG. (Great heavens! Would I join any organization named "HOTDOG" unless I were a meat retailer?) I will admit I was a little bit shook. I guess I am too used to people loving Carol Lynn Pearson.

Friday night Gerald and I took my friend Stella Harris Oaks with us to a public meeting held by a group against the amendment. Stella, who acknowledges herself to be a feminist, is the mother of Dallin Oaks, current president of BYU. Carlton Marlow discussed the amendment. Some of the changes he indicated would result—like ultimately forcing the woman to bring in as much money as the man (in a private home situation)—such incredible logic!

I made a brief comment to the effect that there must be some very good reasons why Congress passed it so overwhelmingly—why President Nixon has said that for the last 21 years he has not altered his belief that equal rights for women warrants a constitutional guarantee—why the three presidents preceding him were all in favor of it—why Governor Rampton is very much for it. Are these men "evil and conspiring"? And I challenged them to look at a more thorough picture of the whole issue. Surprisingly, I received a great round of applause.

A little later in the meeting, Stella Oaks got up and spoke briefly, saying she was very much in support of the amendment, that she knew we make progress by legislation, and that this amendment is a definite piece of progress. (Today in the *Herald* was a report on that meeting, and Sister Oaks was quoted in it; she didn't bargain for this.)

I made a phone call to Wendell Ashton, with whom I had worked on motion picture business and who was very appreciative of me. He was serving as head of External Communications for the Church. I asked his advice on how to handle certain things in public. He didn't know much about the amendment but suggested that I call General Relief Society President Belle Spafford and he gave me her number.

Sister Spafford answered the telephone. I identified myself; she knows me from several contacts concerning a film I wrote for the Relief Society and also skits I've done for their R.S. Conferences. She said right off, "Well, I have always encouraged women that when they feel strongly about something they have the right and the responsibility to speak out on it." She said she has watched the ERA for twenty years and has always been opposed to it. "Equal rights means equal responsibilities, and I don't think women want that. Women are essentially different from men—biologically, emotionally, spiritually. There is a natural division of labor that we shouldn't overlook."

I went on to tell her that the amendment thing was really a sideline of my major efforts, which were to study Mormon women historically and currently and endeavor to raise their self-image.

"Why, there's nothing wrong with *my* self-image," she said. "I think the Church has given me everything I could possibly ask for."

I indicated that I thought a lot of women had the misunderstanding that they did count less than men. She couldn't understand that at all.

We concluded our talk on good terms. I assured her of my loyalty to the Church, to the Relief Society, and to her personally, and she appeared to appreciate that.

I ultimately did go down to Richfield and spoke on the radio along with Carlton Marlowe and Mildred Bushman. I generally kept my comments to women's history and women's rights and didn't push the ERA.

The experience wasn't so bloody as I thought it might be. No one met me at the station to shake their fist and say how disappointed in me they were. One of the officers of HOTDOG called to tell me she was glad I had stayed out of it and she would defend me to all the ladies down there.

January 16, 1972

Yesterday Stella Oaks called here, spoke to Gerald while I was out and then he and I went over to talk with her. She has been in some turmoil over the amendment business. From her own point of view, she is for it; but her position is vulnerable, just like mine is. She had called her son Dallin to talk with him about it (she was kind of taken aback to see her name in the paper and the quote from that meeting). He in essence told her to be very cautious about it. He has been an attorney, and did seem to feel that right now there are so many people who would use this to a wrong advantage. She has decided that she is going to say no more about the ERA.

So what do I think of it all now? Jesus said: "In me there is neither black nor white, bond nor free, male nor female." I would wish that the law could say the same thing.

Something happened yesterday afternoon that I found very exciting, and quite amazing right in the middle of all this. BYU called and invited me to be the Devotional speaker in the Marriott Center for Women's Week, February 6th. This is not a small deal. I am very excited indeed.

Just now I was speaking to Dorothy Rea on the phone (*Deseret News* reporter, columnist and photographer). A lot of people are worried, she feels, that the ERA has an implication for the priesthood in the Church. (I guess I mean *against* the Church.) She spoke quite frankly, saying among other things: "I'm glad you're as young as you are, Carol Lynn. I'm just too old to fight Mormondom anymore. I know that the Lord does not discriminate against women, but some of these self-made Church men certainly do. The priesthood is the only 'power' some men will ever have, and they grind it right into the ground."

I continued to inquire of a number of women and men what their thoughts were on the position of the genders. Many said that—even though it puzzles them—they felt that somehow men are the superior beings.

May 12, 1972

I have thought, for many years, that one day I must write something on the theological implications of womanhood—one day when I am quite wise. But in the meantime, there's a whole bunch of pain going on, there's a whole bunch of women whose spiritual self-concept is suffering, and probably a whole bunch of men who need to take a look at the subject too.

I am not yet entirely wise. But these many years of thinking and searching and asking have sparked some bit of light that I believe in. And, however small my candle, anything that lessens darkness is good. I ought to get busy.

May 31, 1972

My Aunt Mamie's final comment on the different valuing of men and women: "All I can say is that if a baby's going to be born, it's just better off if it's born a boy."

Last night we went over to the Arandas to eat pizza, and we started talking about the woman issue. Mario told us about a girl who works in his office at the department of Seminary and Institute Curriculum Development, a very sharp, bright girl. She got engaged to a boy she was deeply in love with, but clouds arose on the horizon. The night they got engaged he read to her Rodney Turner's address on Women and the Priesthood (yes, the very one that had sent me out sobbing).

Him: When we marry, I will be completely in charge. Everything I say goes. If I say it is raining outside and it is not, you say, "Yes, dear, it is raining."

Her: But—but I can't do that. If it's not true, I can't say that.

Him: That's the way it has to be. It's the only way it can work.

They married. Recently the office was planning an office party. This conversation ensued.

Mario: Are you coming to the party tonight?

Her (a little troubled): No.

Mario: Why not?

Her: Well, we were going to. But my husband made arrangements for us to go to a barbeque at some friends.

Mario: Did you remind him that you had already made plans for the office party?

Her: Yes. He just smiled and said, "The matter is closed."

June 29, 1972

I met a really remarkable lady, ex-wife of a BYU professor. She is much more scarred by the whole problem of Mormon womanhood than I will ever be. Mine is all theoretical—hers is practical. From the moment she walked out of the temple with her husband, she existed only to serve him. Anything he didn't want to do was "squaw work" and she had to do it. She had actually talked to a man who told her that the primary reason he joined the Church was that it gave him the authority to put down his wife.

I was on campus one day last week and I ran into two ladies I know who work there. I asked both of them, "Does BYU discriminate against women on the staff?" They seemed surprised that I would even ask. "Of course," said both. My friend Blaine Porter, chair of the Department of Human Development and Family Relations, told me a few weeks ago that in a meeting with President Oaks, he heard the president say that the woman thing was going to be stickier than the black thing, as far as being accused of discrimination goes.

I accepted an invitation to go to Southern California as a presenter at BYU's Education Week. The family accompanied me and had a fun time playing on the beach. As preface to the next diary excerpt I need to mention the influential book, Fascinating Womanhood *by Helen Andelin, published in 1963. Just now*

I reviewed my copy of the book to see my underlinings. I'm all for the encouragement to make your man feel important, but here's what I found: "Make your man feel superior as the leader—be inefficient when consulted on major decisions—flounder and flutter—do not train for a career—do not appear as an equal partner." Tell him, "You know best, dear."

August 12, 1972

My class on "One Look at Womanhood" was quite popular. Most responded enthusiastically. A woman came up after the class and asked me how I felt about *Fascinating Womanhood.* I told her kindly that I had strong reservations about it. She told me she knew it was inspired and pure gospel. She tried to proselyte me to the philosophy, saying that only a few intellectuals find fault with it, that the honest in heart accept it with open arms. She asked me to give the book another reading—and this time prayerfully. I did not promise.

Later in the day. Pending some miracle, the worst is here in terms of the life of Trilogy Arts. We are insolvent. Everything we have tried to recoup our losses has failed. And right now I find myself in the very uncomfortable position of having gone along with the whole thing *in spite of very strong feelings* I had to the contrary at many points along the way, points at which my stomach hardened and said, "This is wrong."

I abdicated my responsibility to guard carefully what was in part my stewardship. I abdicated it to the damnable doctrine of a femininity that says a woman's place is to quietly influence or keep hands off as she chooses. I did violence to the promptings of the Spirit and the assessment of my own good judgment.

Reading this now many decades later makes me very sad. Gerald and I were not practicing what we preached, the philosophy of partnership in marriage. I loved him. I wanted him to be successful. He was the man. He held the priesthood. I wanted to support him. I didn't want to be the only "star" in our family. I constantly gave in to his stronger personality and never said, "No, we absolutely will not do that." I never said, "You know best, dear," but I always found a way to support Gerald's vision and not my own. I, Carol Lynn Pearson, eminent supporter of women's rights, had unwittingly become a "Fascinating Woman."

But people can grow and learn and begin anew. We still love each other and we have learned a lot.

August 26, 1972

And what an interesting adventure in learning I have had last week. I've spent a number of hours in the special collections room at the BYU library reading the very earliest issues of the *Woman's Exponent,* the forerunner of the *Relief Society Magazine.* Wow! They are way ahead of the women's movement of today. These ladies are really something—Eliza R. Snow, Susa Young Gates, and others. Eliza has some essays in the *Exponent* that are very outspoken about developing a larger sphere for women. I intend to put together excerpts for an article which I hope the *Ensign* will use, or maybe the *New Era*. If they dare.

Yesterday I spoke for an hour with Leonard Arrington on the subject. I knew we were kindred spirits. He said, "I'm so happy to hear you say all these things, and see you doing these things. And you're a good Latter-day Saint for doing it." He said that since he came to the Church Historian's office, they are giving much greater emphasis to the role women have played in Church history. I am ever so grateful for him.

September 23, 1972

I just finished the first draft of a screenplay for the Studio on the subject of women. When I got back from L.A. I submitted two proposals for films on the theme that a woman doesn't have to make the untenable choice of either/or as far as family and life-work of her own goes. An educational film, the one I've been working on. And a Church film, using an example from Church history (Susa Young Gates) and the general climate of the early Mormon women. I think the Church one will go through too; Wendell Ashton responded very favorably to the proposal, saying it was a "capital idea."

What a wonderful thing I have to report! The article I wrote from my research into the first year of the *Woman's Exponent* and sent to the Church's *Ensign* magazine—Jay Todd, editor, bought it the day he received it, and it will appear in January or February. I have received a check for $100.00. I'm just delighted they're going to use it. I was afraid it might be considered rather too controversial a subject to get into. Ran into Leonard Arrington on campus yesterday and told him. He was very pleased.

October 23, 1972

Thursday night I had a long talk with Amy Valentine on the telephone. She's on the Relief Society General Board and is a very intelligent, lovely lady. Also she is very active politically. I called especially to get her idea on how the Equal Rights Amendment would fare in Utah. Here are a few of her comments as I remember them:

"In Utah politics women don't have a chance; they're never permitted to act in positions of real influence. Or on BYU's Alumni fund-raising committee either. The other day I got really brave and told them they ought to let more women have a chance at some of the top positions—that if the truth were known it was probably their wives that did most of the work anyway.

"Back at the Republican convention I made special pains to go to the women's section and was *so* impressed at the women there, and their plans for day-care centers. But the Utah delegation just threw cold water all over me.

Now, the truth is that lots of women *are* working, and their children are not being well cared for.

"If I was not a member of the Relief Society General Board I would be out in the forefront of the women's movement."

I asked, "What is Sister Spafford's position about it all?"

"Her position is that she supports the Brethren, *all* the way. But I can say without hesitation that sometimes she gets pretty hot under the collar. I felt so bad when funds were taken out of our hands recently; all the Relief Society presidents have to go to the bishop whenever they need anything. I felt it was a real step down."

This is a reference to what is known as the Priesthood Correlation Program, a church-wide reassignment of leadership power, completed in 1972, intended to "provide consistency and uniformity of doctrine, policy, and programs." It also brought an increased level of patriarchy, centralized authority, and bureaucracy. Historians today suggest that it was in some measure a response to the cultural revolution of the day. Women, who had in some ways been able to act independently or sometimes as partners in church leadership, were put firmly in their place under the men. Prominent Mormon sociologist Armand Mauss wrote that "Correlation" resulted in "a reduction in the power and autonomy of women."

The following diary excerpt is out of chronological order, but it belongs in this section to give context to the damaging results of what is known as "Correlation." Visiting England on a book tour for Goodbye, I Love You, *I wrote:*

March 10, 1987

I had received a letter inviting me to dinner from Wendell Ashton, mission president in London. He used to be editor of the *Deseret News* and then head of Church Public Communications. His wife, Belva, is a good woman whom I had talked to on several occasions about our mutual concerns regarding women in the Church.

On February 7, 1977, I had asked her, "What do you see as the future for women in the Church?" She said, "Well, I'll tell you, Carol Lynn. I think we've hit the bottom, and the only way now is up." Belva called me back and invited me to stay with them for my second week in their flat. I gratefully accepted.

I must write down some of the things Belva and I talked about. I won't write down everything, as certain things should remain private. But my commitment to history showing the fuller picture is very important to me, and so I'm going to write down some things.

Belva was on the General Board of the Relief Society for a long time, and saw the whole thing deteriorate as Correlation came in and put the R.S. down further and further on the charts. It was happening at the end of Belle Spafford's reign. She remembered Belle saying to the Board when she saw the damage: "They closed us down. They've closed down the Relief Society." And when Barbara Smith took over she had not much power. The budget was taken out of the hands of the R.S., they could not call their own counselors, could not have control over their own lessons, lost the R.S. magazine, etc.

Seeing how crippled they were as leaders, Belva and Alice Smith offered to write a letter to the Brethren, telling them how they viewed all that had happened and asking for some concessions. Barbara agreed and sent the letter over to their advisors (some of the Twelve Apostles, some Seventies).

Barbara was called in (by one of the Seventies whose name she would not give me) and he "tore her apart." He told her never, never to do anything like that again. Barbara went back to her office and locked the door and sobbed and sobbed. She didn't go home. Her husband called that evening and she didn't answer the phone. Finally he went to her office and found her just devastated. Belva was very sad and bitter about all this.

Going back now to the time period prior to the above important interjection:

October 23, 1972

Friday night Gerald began to quiz me about what would be the end result of all these things I'm into about women.

"Why should women have a larger sphere?"

Well, for this reason and that.

"But beyond that, what?"

Then, when we had gotten to the ultimates, he said, "People have to see that the end result is to make women—and men too—better children of God. That's all that will count in the long run."

That's true. And I believe that the things I'm working on are truly toward that end.

November 4, 1972

Last Thursday evening I attended the Utah State Historical Society's meeting here on campus. Brother Arrington spoke. I had the previous week written to him asking about several things, and in the letter I asked him to read Rodney Turner's new book, *Woman and the Priesthood.* When I asked him about it after his talk, he raised his eyebrows and shook his head and emitted a long "Ohhhwwww. He sure is off on that one."

At that same time I sprang on him my current idea for a book I'm in the process of working on—a very well documented compilation of instances in which LDS women in early history exercised the gifts of the Spirit, likely to be titled *Daughters of Light.* I think this is the *best* way to go about raising the vision of women regarding their own spiritual horizons, and the vision of men too that women have power.

When I told Brother Arrington about it, asking if I might come up and see what I could find in his office, he got really excited, began to wax enthusiastic. "Oh, I will help you," he said. "I will help you! Say, this is the perfect answer to a book like Brother Turner's—call it '*Woman—WITHOUT the Priesthood!*'"

November 18, 1972

Time is so precious these days that I hesitate to write much in my diary. And yet I've never believed more strongly that it is important that I do so. My motivation years ago was a therapeutic one, a romantic one perhaps. Now I feel the imperative of history. Few modern Mormons have kept a journal for as long as I have, I think. Add that to my being a household word to many and I cannot escape the feeling that in many, many years there might be a number of people interested in these pages.

I was honored as "Utah's Outstanding Young Woman of 1972"—as chosen by the Outstanding Young Women of America Association, made up of many women's organizations. All the publicity came out last week and everybody has been quite impressed.

Dorothy Rae of the *Deseret News* came over to interview me about it. In our conversation she told me a very interesting thing that I hadn't heard before. I guess around the time that the *Relief Society Magazine* was discontinued and economic independence was taken away from the Relief Society—the Brethren asked for the deed to the Relief Society building that the sisters had worked and worked so hard to get for so many years. She said Sister Spafford was obviously very, very hurt. And that the feeling of those sisters that she has talked to was that it was sort of a put-down—that in the face of all the move for independence that women are getting into, the Brethren were making a gesture that said, make no mistake, you sisters are not independent, and you will function *under* the priesthood.

Amy Valentine concurred in this, and I've been told BYU President Ernest L. Wilkinson's wife, Alice Wilkinson, made some statements expressing the same thing. So. If it was a step up—why not present it as such, and in such a way that everyone felt good about it? If it was a step down—why should it happen at all? Just today Gerald told me he remembers, when the change in the position of the R.S. was explained in Ward Council, that good Bishop Jameson made a little wry fun about finally being able to bring the sisters back where they belonged. And he got a little rise out of Fern Gardner, our Relief Society president. From the general to the local level there were feelings about it—feelings that the women were being "put in their place."

We had an interesting meeting here at my home to talk about leadership and women. When I brought up Rodney Turner's book, Stella Oaks commented, "Brother Turner is in my ward. I was asked to give a speech about

Martin Harris in church, and I prepared for it extensively (Harris was her relative). Afterward Brother Turner put an arm around me and said, 'Sister Oaks, that was as good a speech as could have been given by any man in the Church.' Then later when she met him in BYU's Sky Room restaurant where he was with a group of men, he said to them, 'This woman gave a speech the other day that was as good as any man could have given.'"

December 9, 1972

It was a good thing that I went to Salt Lake on Monday, for as I checked on my article the *Ensign* had accepted, I found they had taken out two significant parts—the lady lawyers being admitted to the bar and Eliza R. Snow petitioning the sisters in Ogden to join a program to make them medical doctors. I asked Jay about it, and he said he and Doyle Greene (director of all publications for the Church) had done it because of some trouble they had had a month earlier on the problem of an article that appeared to encourage women to work. Elder Boyd K. Packer's philosophy reigns supreme among the Brethren, he said, that women are to stay in the home.

In Salt Lake I ran into Dean Wheelwright as he was delivering to all the General Authorities a copy of his new book, *Mormon Arts*. He showed it to me; it's really quite beautiful. My musical, *The Order Is Love* is given a big spread, and he also quotes one of my poems. As we were talking, the door opened and out poured *all* the General Authorities. Wow, what a sight.

I spoke to a few of them. Brother Packer, who remembered hearing me read my poems at a program he spoke on, told me he quotes from me. S. Dilworth Young told me again how very much he enjoyed my play *Move On* last Saturday. Brother Hanks overheard Brother Young, and put a hand on my shoulder, saying, "Well, you're great—may you live forever."

I have been writing for two hours. There's too much to do in this world.

I spoke to Briant Jacobs, professor in the English Department of BYU, who volunteered that there is a great deal that ought to be done for the position of women nationally and in the Church as well. Picking up the cue, I began to probe him on his observations of the situation in the Church. He said that anyone who would deny there is a problem had "already sold his soul to the devil."

He told of hearing a young girl at the Church College of Hawaii bear her testimony, and in it say that she knew the proper role of women was to be doormats to help men get into heaven. He was appalled and asked her afterward where she got that image. It was given to her, she said, at an education week by Rodney Turner. Brother Jacobs also said that as he observes the women teachers on campus, too few of them are really vibrant (Virginia Cutler and Leona Holbrook are exceptions, he said). And he said that I am one of the few women he knows who has achieved an identity in spite of being a woman, a phrase he did not like to use but had to. "There are so many women I know and love," he said, "and I just do not want them to feel in any way secondary."

January 24, 1973

Such a lot to catch up on. Yesterday I ran into Bishop Robert L. Simpson of the Presiding Bishopric (now of Social Services) in the cafeteria. I took the occasion to ask him if he was aware of a stated Church policy on women participating in blessings or administrations, telling him briefly about my project of writing about the spiritual gifts of women. He suggested that the best one to inquire of would be Boyd K. Packer.

So today I dropped into Brother Packer's office and was successful in seeing him for about fifteen minutes. I told him about my project and he nodded his head approvingly. I then asked about current policy concerning a woman's prerogative in the area of administering to the sick. He said he wasn't aware of a stated policy, but he was quite certain that only when priesthood was "completely unavailable" should a woman undertake such a thing, and then not doing it in any way *through* the priesthood.

Policies change, he added, with the needs of the times. Satan uses certain tactics, and so the Lord's work has to respond to those tactics. In our day, he said, Satan is making us confuse the roles of the sexes—making men want to look like women and women look like men. Even some Church programs have made mistakes like that; the boys have a camping program, so the girls need a camping program. The boys have a big leadership conference, so the girls have to have one too.

I tried to explain to him that that's a natural result of everybody assuming that what men do is naturally more important than what women do; and that we need to change our values. I didn't dare go much into my belief that some of women's striving to be "men" isn't that at all—it's just striving to be a full "human being," of which unfortunately men have been sometimes the only models. I wouldn't have dared to lay on him some ways in which I receive with joy the blurring of some of the hard and fast sex roles.

His main advice about my research was to avoid whatever would appear to be an invitation to women to participate in "ordinances," or to feel that there were things going on back then that we're denied the privilege of doing today.

Also yesterday Brother Arrington and I went to see Jeff Holland, recently appointed to the new Melchizedek Priesthood MIA superintendency; he's giving a talk on "Woman and the Church" tomorrow in the Institute at the University of Utah. I like him; he's young and aware and honest. He and young general authorities James Faust and Marion D. Hanks and Tom Perry are on a committee to plan the future of the Young Men's MIA, and Brother Holland asked me if I might be willing to come and talk to them about some of my ideas concerning women. Of course I said I would be delighted.

Regarding the ERA, I must back up a bit. After the Richfield episode, I thought I had put it all away. Then, a week ago today Algie Ballif called and told me that Utah's House of Representatives had scheduled a public hearing, and particularly wanted Virginia Cutler and me to come and testify. Wow—there I was again. What should I do? Should I just decline? Or should I make a statement and risk disappointing some people whom I do not wish to disappoint?

Let me tell you, I suffered. I called my bishop that night—Richard Cracroft (who served as chair of the English department) and talked to him for an hour. He encouraged me to go and to make a statement; said he was proud of me. He said he has some emotional reservations about things like women in the military, but that in general he hoped the amendment would pass, and that his wife Janice felt the same way. He also has been reading some things about the early sisters in the Church, and feels we have taken a few steps backward in some ways. I appreciated his talking to me. Gerald was at the prison late that night with his church calling, so I had to do a lot of contemplating on my own.

I decided that night, after a lot of prayer, that I really ought to make a statement.

That day, Friday, was really quite a day. It was storming, and as it turned out, I didn't get to the capitol until about a half an hour before the hearing was over. As we came in a girl said to me, "Are you Carol Lynn Pearson?"

"Yes," I answered.

"They called your name twice to speak." The place was packed and people were loudly applauding as one speaker spoke for the amendment and then one against. I went up to the front and told the secretary they had called my name before and that if they had time I would like to make a statement. In a few moments, the moderator said, "There is just time for two more speakers, one representing each side. Speaking for the amendment, we will now hear from Carol Lynn Pearson."

I got up, went to the microphone, and said, to the best of my remembrance, something like this:

"Dear ladies and gentlemen of the legislature: when I elect a public official, I do so because I believe he or she knows more about some things than I do. (Applause.) Therefore I would not presume to tell you anything about law or economics. I think the best we can do for our lawmakers is to give them our philosophy of life and ask them to find the best possible means of legal implementation.

I would like, therefore, to give you my philosophy of men and women. I yearn for the day when men and women can take one another's hand, regarding each other as full human beings. First of all on the level of the home—equally devoted to creating the kinds of human beings the world needs. And then on every other level of human endeavor—in church, community, profession. Oh, we are not speaking of women's rights! I believe, with Tennyson, 'The woman's cause is man's—they rise or fall together.' How I wish that men and women could join hands—and together, rise."

There was a good deal of applause.

Yesterday Nixon announced agreement for a cease-fire in Vietnam. And in Utah—this afternoon the House of Representatives voted on the Equal Rights Amendment. It was roundly defeated.

5

BLACKLISTED

February 7, 1973

It was a good day. I spoke in the Marriott Center at BYU as the featured speaker for Woman's Week. They had asked me to speak on love, reading from my poems and having three musical numbers from *The Order is Love*. Gerald introduced me and did a wonderful job—was tender and admiring and also personal. The audience roared with laughter as he told of my writing him a letter from the Provo Sanitation Department when he forgot to take out the garbage for the third week running.

Injecting a little levity here. In the first year of our marriage Gerald and I both tried to take on our roles according to our abilities. We agreed that he as the man really ought to take the full garbage cans out to the curb. But he forgot. Frequently. So in my inimitable and witty way, I managed to write a letter to Gerald from the Sanitation Department. Believe it or not, Gerald greeted me one evening with, "Blossom—you won't believe what I got in the mail today.

"Dear Mr. Pearson,

We, here at the Sanitation Department, miss you. For the third week now you have not contributed anything to our company. Are you dissatisfied with our service?..."

Of course I burst into laughter.

"You! You did this! Ohhhh ..."

Lovingly, he pummeled me. Actually Gerald loved it when I pulled a fast one on him. And yes, he had for some time called me "Blossom" because I continued to bloom so beautifully.

I felt good about my talk. President Oaks asked me for the middle part of it, in which I talked about men and women, and invited the men to come home. He said he had never heard it put so well, and wanted to use some things I said. There was a large crowd there in the Marriott Center, about 5000, unusually large for the assemblies this year. Klea Worsley, my friend on the MIA General Board, said that last week only about 2500 came for President Oaks's talk. I was really pleased that so many came.

For a few weeks now I must cease this diary and everything else and get my book written—*Daughters of Light,* stories of the early Mormon women exercising spiritual gifts—healing, receiving revelations, visions prophesying, etc. The research could go on and on, and will, throughout my lifetime. I think it's going to be a terrific book.

February 8, 1973

Last night when Gerald and I came home from the movie *Funny Girl,* I had a message to be in Marion D. Hanks's office this morning at 9:30. I think I mentioned that Jeff Holland, who is recently appointed to the newly organized Melchizedek Priesthood MIA Committee, told me that he was meeting daily with Brother Hanks and James Faust and Tom Perry on getting the whole thing organized. All the adult single people in the Church are in their charge, and their responsibility is to make them feel like they belong to the Church, really belong, and not as unwanted step-children. Brother Holland was interested in my thoughts about women and asked if I would be willing to meet with them sometime and give them some ideas. I said I would love to. So this morning I did.

I was with them an hour and a half. They were very cordial, very warm, very responsive. They mostly just sat back and let me talk. I told them this was the fulfillment of one of my best Walter Mitty daydreams—to have a captive audience of some of the influential Brethren and be able to talk about the subject of Mormon Womanhood. The essence of what I said is found over and over in these diary pages:

My belief that the woman's movement in general is one of the most exciting of modern developments—some of the problems that face the Mormon woman as she comes to absorb our utterly masculine theology—stories of the women I've met who can only conclude that women count less than men—my own struggle with the two seemingly mutually exclusive propositions: 1-the gospel is true, and 2-women count as much as men count—my belief that revelation and religious progression is an ongoing thing and that one day full light will be cast on this subject, but that in the meantime there's a bunch of human suffering going on—some of the problems in Mormon marriages that stem from this—a woman saying to her husband, "Well, dear, what would you do if you'd been born a woman?"—and his answer, "I guess I'd just make the best of a bad deal."—our enormous need to encourage women to become *somebody* as well as somebody's wife and somebody's mother. Etc.

I asked them as we were concluding if the things I had said surprised them. Brother Hanks and Brother Holland said no, they didn't. Brother Faust said he was really pained to realize that all this existed. And Brother Perry was surprised—are there men who treat their wives so unrighteously? Brother Holland responded that there were many men in the Church who treat their wives like chattel. I added that there were also many who treat their wives as pets, love them dearly, worship them even, but do not regard them as human beings to be encouraged to grow.

Oh, yes—I also mentioned to them this Institute home study lesson I was asked to respond to: "The Elect Lady"—emphasizing submission and glorying in your husband, painting the woman's movement as "the bad guy." I told them that in the portrait that lesson painted for the Mormon woman, there was no place for me, that between the lines they were saying, "Sister Pearson, if only you had stayed in the background and inspired your husband to write fine things—if only you had done his typing while he wrote *The Order is Love.* Brother Hanks showed some feeling at this.

As I write this, I so miss the time when membership (at least some) had access to visit with the top authorities in the Church. I clearly recall the graciousness, warmth, and honest interest these men showed, and that—on this occasion—it was they who had requested my presence. I know, I know—the number of members continued to grow, and the Brethren could not spread themselves as thin as they might like. I hear lovely stories of some of the General Authorities extending themselves to the members in moving ways. But my feeling is that there also came to be an organizational separation created by hierarchy.

March 5, 1973

I did it. The book is finished. *Daughters of Light.* Most of it's at the press. I'm more anxious to get it and give it than I ever was about *Beginnings.* I really do think it's needed. I hope it does not offend unnecessarily any of the Brethren or threaten unduly any of the sisters, but I feel strongly that both need to seriously look at the spiritual powers available to women even without their being ordained to the priesthood. I found some wonderful, wonderful stories. Gerald gave me the title. Brother Arrington talked me into introducing each chapter with a verse, so I have a running poetic tie that brings it all together.

The one thing I've not written that must be given full accounting for is the adventures of my *Ensign* article. February's issue didn't come, and didn't come, and didn't come, and I got a very strange feeling that not all was well. Then on Wednesday the 14th, Leonard Arrington returned a call I had placed to him. His first words were, "I have bad news for you. Your article has been pulled from the *Ensign.*"

I felt like someone was standing on my stomach. He had heard it unofficially and knew no more than that. As we went on talking I started to cry—cast again into that blackest of pits that says, "Mormon woman, get down, down, down, down. Let the Brethren do your thinking. Give up." Brother Arrington volunteered to call Jay Todd and then to call me back. He did. Jay gave him a noncommittal answer.

Last week I went to Salt Lake to do some things and dropped in to see Jay Todd. I asked him for the whole story and he gave it to me. Two days before the presses were to run, Wendell Ashton, the Church's Director of Public Affairs, called and said, "Jay are you running an article about the ERA?"

"You think I'm crazy?" said Jay.

"Well, are you running an article by Sister Pearson?"

"Yes, I have a very excellent article."

Brother Ashton then went on to tell him that he understood I was becoming known as a spokesman for the ERA, and that to avoid a bunch of letters and inquiries being sent to the Brethren, he might want to investigate it. Brother Ashton said that he had nothing but the deepest love and respect for Sister Pearson. So. Jay said he took the article to two apostles who saw nothing wrong in the article itself, but agreed that it was very bad timing. So Jay pulled it.

So there you have it. The first major defeat of Carol Lynn Pearson in her work for a better image of the Mormon woman. But the battle is one of years—a whole lifetime—and I still have a great deal of energy, and determination. As I learned from Joan of Arc whom I played on the BYU stage, "What I have done, I will not denounce—what I am I will not deny."

I will likely be denouncing and denying things as I discover things that are better; but the essential direction that I'm in, I think, I shall not be denying. I feel comfortable in my prayers as I talk about it. And I think we're going to be all right.

March 17, 1973

Have I written here about "The Elect Lady"?—that correspondence lesson for the Institutes of Religion. William O. Nelson of Church Correlation, whom I met in Washington last year, gave me a copy to read and asked that I give my reaction to it. Just over a week ago I wrote a five-page letter, pointing out how I was seriously disappointed in it. My dear friend Mario works in a neighboring office and I had him deliver it. He and his department had received copies of it for their own use; he calls it "the yellow peril."

Mario knows the secretary in the Institute office quite well; Barbie is her name. She told him that the day she had to type that lesson she went home and wept. Next day she tried to tell some things to Brother Nelson's boss, but they didn't take her at all seriously. Barbie's report the next day was that they were going ahead with sending it out as is, that they considered my reaction very emotional and didn't take it too seriously. He said he observed Barbie talking to Brother Nelson and saying, "If that lesson has caused that much pain before it goes out, what will it do to all the girls it's going to?"

April 4, 1973

One week has passed since last I wrote—one of the most difficult weeks of my life. Last week Gerald and I drove into Salt Lake City, where we both had things to take care of. Just before five o'clock I walked into the office of *The New Era* to give Brian the article about Connie and her family.

I had written a lovely article about a young woman who had confided in me that there was no warmth in her family, or even good communication. They never had "family home evening." I helped her form a plan to create a fun and meaningful home evening herself, and with great excitement she told me it went beautifully. I thought it was a fine story, so I wrote it into an article to give to The New Era. *This is the article I came to give to Brian.*

Brian Kelly, editor of *The New Era,* happened to be sitting there by the door, and when I handed him the article he got a very strange look on his face and said quietly, "I can't use it. I've been instructed that I can't use anything of yours for the next while."

I couldn't move. His assistant, Lowell Durham Jr., said, "Brian, you're kidding."

But it was clear that Brian was not kidding. He and Jay had both been instructed by Doyle Green, director and editor of Church magazines, that until further notice they were to use nothing of mine. Pain like I have seldom known covered my body. I put my face into my hands and began to cry. Brian tried very hard to comfort me, but there's not much to be said in a situation like that. I told him that I wanted to speak with whoever above him is responsible for decisions like that. He told me he was sure Doyle Green would be willing to see me.

I succeeded in getting myself out to the car and in telling Gerald what had happened. Gerald is so great—so very sympathetic. I had to give two talks that night—one at the University of Utah Institute on Mormon Art, then one to the Taylorsville Stake's Laurel Standards Night. It was a challenge, and I had to do it with eyes that looked a little strange. But I felt like I gave two of the best talks I have ever given.

The next morning Jay Todd called to tell me Brother Green said he would be happy to talk with me.

Monday I got up at 6 and drove to Salt Lake in Mario's car pool. I went firstly to Leonard Arrington's office to get a little friendly encouragement. I did get it, but I also got some additional bad news. Brother Arrington had heard of some letter I had written in response to a book or something. It dawned on me in full color. William O. Nelson had given my letter to the Brethren—my letter written in response to the "Elect Lady" Institute lesson. Brother Arrington didn't want to tell me which General Authority it had been sent to, but later he let it slip, and still later Brian Kelly confirmed it. Nelson gave my letter to Boyd K. Packer.

Brother Arrington was as kind as he could possibly be. He is very much a realist about the imperfections that exist in the Church. He said he has been in my position before. In fact, he said he is enough of a realist that he makes two copies of his journal—one that stays in his office, and another that goes home with him. He said that no matter what happens to him, he wants his true story to be preserved.[1]

I told him that I also write down all of these details in my diary, and we were in agreement that truth has got to be preserved, whatever the cost. I know now for a fact that my diary will one day be important as a Church document. Having seen the importance of the early journals, and recognizing the amount of influence I have already obtained, I could not possibly deny that. And so with full knowledge that the things I write here belong to history, I am going to tell the story in complete accuracy.

Until ten o'clock I paced in the ladies' room and in the halls, praying and trying to gather composure.

Brother Green was very cordial. His first statements were to tell me how he had enjoyed my poetry. He then stated his position. "Now, Sister Pearson, the Church Magazines are in business for one reason, and that is to promote the policies and the practices of the Church. You are a very influential person, very popular, and widely-read. Anything in the future of yours that our magazines would use would serve to further promote you. And with your involvement now in 'woman's lib'—we simply cannot do that."

He went on to mention a letter he had received, which I had written, and which had been given to one of the Brethren, who, with underlinings and comments written on the margins and at the end of the letter, had sent it down the ranks through Brother Fyans, who is Brother Green's supervisor. The General Authority to whom my letter had been given—he didn't use Brother Packer's name, but this is evident—had found some things in the letter that disturbed him a great deal. At this point I asked Brother Green if the things in that letter also appeared radical to him. He nodded his head.

I then told him about my involvement in the women's movement and my philosophy about women in the Church. I explained my awareness of and struggles with the theological problems that a woman must face.

When I was through, Brother Green appeared to have accepted what I said. He took out the copy of my letter that he had received, and said that he hoped he wouldn't be breaking confidence if he let me look at it. We then went over

1. Excerpts of Arrington's diary–which include many references to Gerald and Carol Lynn Pearson, including this meeting—are in fact preserved and published in Gary James Bergera, ed., *Confessions of a Mormon Historian: The Diaries of Leonard J. Arrington, 1971–97* (Signature Books, 2018).

together the parts underlined in red and annotated in the margins. At the very end of my letter was written three sentences. To the best of my memory:

"Carol Lynn was in the forefront of lobbying for the Equal Rights Amendment. She is in the forefront of the move to recall the legislators who voted against it. She is a frequent public speaker, and preaches this philosophy." I assured Brother Green that those statements were a gross misrepresentation. I did no lobbying, only made one general statement to the legislature; I'd never heard of a movement to recall the legislators who voted against the ERA; and I have never mentioned the ERA in any of my talks. I felt that he believed me.

Brother Green suggested that I write him a letter outlining all the things I had told him, which he would send on up the ranks. This I will do.

Leaving his office I went immediately to the office of Marion D. Hanks. His secretary told me he was busy writing, and with conference coming up, she didn't want to disturb him. But I believed that knowing how urgent this was Brother Hanks would want to be disturbed. So she went in, and then called me in to him. He was, of course, wonderful—utterly gracious and warm. I said to him, "Well, Brother Hanks, you know that when you start talking about women in this Church, you are in for trouble. And right now I am in big trouble."

He leaned back and smiled as if at a joke. "With whom?" he asked, very disdainfully. "Name it."

So I named it. It took quite a while for me to convince him that it was indeed a fact that unless I succeeded in righting my image I would not be permitted to contribute to the Church magazines. "There is nothing wrong with your image," he contended.

As I told the story, he wanted to know the identity of the General Authority to whom the letter had gone. By that time I felt so violated myself by Church protocol, and so very much in need of a friend, that I told him it was Brother Packer. He shook his head and said with feeling, "The worst kind of provincialism. That man's head is as impenetrable as an armadillo."

I asked Brother Hanks to tell me frankly what kinds of things came across from me as he and the other three men listened to me for an hour-and-a-half those several weeks ago.

"Oh," he said as he leaned back, "honesty—beauty—truth—tenderness—none of us felt anything negative from it—we all found it an elevating experience."

That was, of course, most comforting. And the truth is that I spoke more frankly to them than I spoke in the letter regarding the "Elect Lady" Institute lesson.

I told Brother Hanks what I intended to do, and asked that if there were an occasion in which he might say a good word for me that he would do it.

"There's a lot that I can do," he said, "and I certainly intend to." As I left, he assured me that nothing was going to happen to stop me from making the contribution to the Church that I am supposed to make.

Of course that visit was very comforting to me.

The rest of the day is somewhat a blur. Gerald had prepared supper for me and the children; he was fasting for a few days. Later in the evening, Gerald and I lay on our waterbed while I told him all the events of the day. As I finished I could tell that he was crying. He pulled me over to him and said only, "I love you, Carol Lynn."

This has been, of course, a shattering experience. But my general faith in the Church is not shattered. I guess what's happening inside of me is called growing up. It's very clear to me why the millennium is not here yet. For when you couple my own inadequacies—regarding women and everything else—with the uncompassionate judgment shown to me from high levels in the Church—you do not have a people prepared for the Lord. Brian Kelly and Leonard Arrington were my only friends among those who knew I was in trouble. Except for them, nobody would have come to me. I would have been cut off without a hearing. That hurts deeply.

April 5, 1973

Now, three days later, I cannot think of it or write of it without tears coming to my eyes. I will very soon write my letter to Brother Green. And I have asked some people to write letters in my behalf. Bishop Cracroft and Jerry Taylor, my Relief Society President, and my friend Blaine Porter, Dean of the College of Family Living. And I gave a letter—through Stella Oaks, who has been with me through a lot of this—to her son, BYU President Dallin Oaks, asking him to state that on the occasion of my talk to the student body I spoke of men and of women in a way that he found appropriate and useful.

I am finishing this now on Saturday, between sessions of conference. It has occurred to me that I'm meeting this blow with some better inner resources than I met a similar one precisely seven years ago. Rodney Turner in the fieldhouse made me run out in the middle of his talk in tears. At that time it was a judgment on me; the only answer was that I was out of line with the whole eternal plan.

But now I am content—with Gerald beside me and my own spiritual confidence strengthened—that the general direction in which I am going and thinking is right.

Just a few minutes ago President Dallin Oaks called me. His mother had given him my letter, and he said he wanted to call and tell me to be of good cheer—that this sort of thing happens to people when they start playing in the big league. It's happened to him, he said, and to his mother, and the test is in how you weather it and how you come out of it.

He said he went through the whole "prayer in the schools" issue, when even to talk about not allowing prayer in school (which he did) was to attack God; but he said that things have changed considerably now. And he feels the same kind of thing will happen regarding women's rights. The prayer issue took seven years to work out, he said, but he thinks this one will take not as long. He said he would be pleased to write a letter stating his reaction to my "splendid talk at BYU," and also would find an occasion to put in a good word for me with whomever it was that needed it.

It is now after the afternoon session of conference and after supper also. I've been enjoying conference a lot. This afternoon Brother Packer spoke. It was really an excellent address, geared to children. I went out in the backyard and got Emily and Johnny and their friend Mimi to come in and listen to him. I felt only a good spirit in hearing him talk, for which I was very grateful.

April 18, 1973

I think I have done all I presently can about righting my life in the Church. I prepared a seven-page statement that I took to Brother Green's office. I am hopeful that my statement will find its way back up to Brother Packer.

April 25, 1973

I am reading the *Woman's Exponents* that Aunt Mamie and I brought down from Idaho months ago, wrapped in an old white curtain and with the names of my grandmother Sarah Oakey Sirrine and my great-grandmother Mary Oakey written on them. There are several years' worth. Right now I'm in 1880. What an adventure. Brilliant essays on the sphere of woman. Emmeline B. Wells, after whom my mother was named, has already won my devoted admiration. They were so much in advance of us. What happened?

April 28, 1973

A very strange synchronicity occurred today. I spoke at a Stake Laurel Conference along with Glen Roylance, who was a member of the stake presidency. Afterwards he asked me if I knew who he was. "I don't think I do," I said.

"I work with Bill Nelson. I wrote the 'Elect Lady' Institute lesson."

Oh, boy. What are the chances? For almost two hours we sat there and talked. He had loved my poems, and when he read the letter from me responding to the "Elect Lady," he was astonished.

Brother Roylance has spent years forming his own ideas about women and men; he knows they are true, and he will not give them up. In the 1960s, he said, many things came to the surface—the Civil Rights movement, the God is Dead thing, Women's Liberation. All of these are of the devil and, if allowed to flourish, will destroy our homes. He knows of some places where I have spoken to Relief Societies that I have sown seeds of discontent—that some women have felt, maybe I ought to be doing more. Discontent, he warned, is of the devil.

I told him that I thought "The greatest thing that has come from the whole woman's movement is that we have been given more of the world to drink in; we have been given the opportunity to fill ourselves up on the best that the world has to offer. And consequently we can come to our husbands and our children as fuller people, having more to give."

"There is where we disagree," he said. As we finished our conversation he very humbly asked me just to consider the possibility that I am wrong. He feels that I have a great gift and he does not want to see it "taken away" from me.

He asked if I would pray with him. How would one refuse? We knelt down together and he asked me to pray first. I did, praying as I have in private hundreds upon hundreds of times that on the subject of women we may receive all the light that is possible for us to receive, praying that I would not be misled or mislead others, and that the Church authorities and membership at large would be given good understanding on this subject and the wisdom to act on it.

He then prayed, a good honest prayer that I could only appreciate.

So. Another chapter in the great drama. Deeper and deeper we go. There is no turning back. There is reappraisal, there is gaining of new insights, there is holding onto what proves to be true despite the pressures of high and low. But there is no turning back.

May 7, 1973

Something good. Brother Green just telephoned me from Salt Lake to say that he had passed my statement and the letter from my bishop back up the line to Brother Fyans, and to the Brethren above him. Everyone involved accepted it very well and "feel very good about the situation." He has been instructed that his office should view me just as any other contributor to the magazines, though he did say that material dealing with women would have to be looked at very carefully.

6

CELEBRATED BY THE BRETHREN

May 9, 1973

Daughters of Light is in the bookstores. We published it through our Trilogy Arts company. From pre-publication orders we have already sold 1500 copies of the 5000 that we had printed. I do so hope it does for other women what it did for me. And for men too. Gerald and I stayed up until 1 a.m. filling orders.

I know, of course, that you my reader are primarily interested in the aspect of this tale that focuses on The Woman Question, but I expect you are also curious about my personal life backstage. Our family life was a happy one. Gerald was a warm husband and a fun and devoted father. Our children's friends loved being in our home. I, like so many "working women," had to juggle a lot, had to plot a way to hopefully be successful at family life and at career.

One of my tactics was that whenever I was invited to speak away from home base, I always required a plane ticket for me and one for a child and that they made sure my child had a fun time. All my children have good memories of these travels—to Florida, to Canada, to Washington, to dozens of other places. I was in high demand. In the middle of all the "women's doings," my personal life went on.

May 30, 1973

Walking over to the Church Office Building from KSL, I saw an old man lying on a bench in the sun. He was whiskered and as I leaned over him I smelled whiskey. I looked around to see if there was anybody to help such a poor derelict—a policeman or anybody. Nobody else was paying any attention. I took out a dollar bill and spoke to the man.

"Sir?" I said. He didn't stir. I tucked the dollar bill in his shirt pocket and walked on. That poor, lonely, wasted old man used to be somebody's beautiful little boy, full of light like my two beautiful little boys. The story of all that went into putting out that light must be a tragic one. I hurt to think about it.

Speaking of beautiful little boys. Tonight I put them to bed the way I like to. I sent Emily and Johnny to the neighbors while I bathed Aaron alone and played with him and nursed him (he's mostly just a social drinker now) and rocked him and heard his prayers and rubbed his back and sang to him and very leisurely told him goodnight.

Then with Emily still in the tub I took Johnny out and had a nice little private time with him, rocking and singing and being silly the way he likes to, then heard his prayers and made him a bed on the floor because he decided that would be more fun than the bunk bed.

Then I got Emily out and gave her a little chocolate milk and gradually got her to bed, heard her prayers, and lay with her for ten or fifteen minutes, talking about things. On Monday we all walked over to the cemetery to take some flowers to my mother's grave. We firstly had a little family night discussion about death and burial and resurrection, and I showed pictures of my mother. Emily has known for a long time about my mother's death. She took the whole thing very seriously and didn't want to leave the grave; spoke very tenderly of her grandma.

About this time there began to be serious thinking about "Mormon Art" in the area. Gerald and I met a number of times with Dennis Smith, Trevor Southey, Dale Fletcher, Gary and Diana Stewart, Brian Kelly, and others. This movement grew, with the stated theme that the arts were a wonderful way to preach the gospel to the world. Certainly this was the vision Gerald had in 1967 when he insisted on publishing my little book of poems, Beginnings.

June 29, 1973

Gerald and I just got back from a surprise birthday party for BYU instructor and therapist Richard Wooten. We stayed and visited with them for a while. I told Richard that I'm into studying a lot of things about women, with an intention to write. I asked him from his professional point of view, having counseled as a therapist with hundreds of women, if he sees a pattern of problems that relate to their Mormon background. He said he definitely did: tremendous depression tied into compulsive perfectionistic visions of what they ought to be—the "starched apron" perfect Relief Society lady baking cookies and bread every day, spotless house, and wonderfully happy with it all.

He said that when women come to him for counseling, many times his first step is to have them stop going to Relief Society; he said they come home quivering. Everybody else is doing the perfect womanhood thing; why aren't I? He told me it's much easier for Mormon women to be self-condemning than Mormon men.

I saw Brother Arrington for a few minutes. He told me something I want to record. He attended one of the sessions of the new Aaronic Priesthood MIA, and heard Ruth Funk, the Young Women's President, speak. She told of receiving her call last year and how it transpired. President Lee came to their home. After pleasantries, he addressed himself to Brother Funk, explaining the new MIA program. He then, still looking at Brother Funk, said, "We wish now formally to call Sister Funk to serve as president." Brother Funk looked over at his wife, then back at President Lee, and said, 'We accept.'"

My days of innocence are over. I am not yet prepared to say that the Prophet or the Church are not 100% in tune; but I cannot avoid saying that I am not in tune with every word and every gesture that emanates from 47 E. South Temple (church headquarters) in Salt Lake City, Utah. It takes a lot to admit that. May my reader be kind.

July 11, 1973

I dropped into the office of Jeffrey Holland. I hadn't seen him since that good experience with him, Brothers Hanks, Faust and Perry. He was very glad to see me and we had a nice, warm conversation. He knew nothing of my adventures since our meeting, so I very briefly indicated what had happened. He was really surprised, but assured me that was not the prevailing and continuing picture for women.

He told me he really feels there is a wonderful era dawning for women in the Church and that I'm doing some significant things in that direction. He said he's more content than he's ever been that the Church is indeed being guided by revelation. But, as he told me when he walked me to the elevator after the other meeting, "The mills of the Gods grind slowly." He said he hoped that I would be a "sweet agitator" to kindly make people aware of the problems. It may not be a comfortable position, he said, but it's a necessary one, and the Church has always needed people to do that. It was good to talk with him. I appreciate his confidence.

July 15, 1973

I am stunned. I can't think when I've been more startled and amazed. This evening after sacrament meeting the bishopric came over to call me to be ward Relief Society President. Nowhere, in any of my ambitions, have I ever coveted the office of Relief Society President. When Bishop Cracroft first told me, I was certain he was joking (he does have a goodly sense of humor), and when he convinced me he was serious I was absolutely speechless. Then I looked at him and said, "Do you feel this decision was inspired?

"Yes, I do," he said.

I accepted.

Later in the evening Gerald gave me a blessing and I took the occasion to read through my patriarchal blessing. A certain section hit me with entirely new power. The blessing was given by Joseph Harold Eldredge in Roosevelt when I was twelve years old. After speaking of marriage and children, he said, "Remember that through obedience and through proper observance of the principles of life, you may in due time hold, in conjunction with your husband, the priesthood of God, for in the Lord the man is naught without the woman and they are equal in responsibility and in privilege as they live in harmony together."

And so my life was even more full and my balancing act even more challenging.

Invitations to speak did not wane and I accepted as many as I could. Always I brought books along and sold them afterwards. Back then there was no policy against that and for us was a major way to help pay the bills. I have a clear memory of taking Emily up to Washington state, where 650 girls attended a three-day Laurel Conference, many from Idaho and Canada. Emily stayed with a family that had a girl near her age, and they would bring her to me on the campus at five and we would eat together, then spend the evening together in whatever activity the Laurels had. One of the events of that conference is still clear in my mind.

August 22, 1973

Being free that afternoon I attended the workshop of a woman on the subject, "The Fascinating Girl." She was a very sweet, unsubstantial little lady whose first words were, "I hope you don't mind if I lean on the desk—I'm a leaner." A very symbolic statement. Also symbolic was a word on her chart, showing us how to be the perfect woman, "Angela Human." One of the qualities we're to cultivate is our "Feminity." Yes. On the chart. F-e-m-i-n-i-t-y.

August 25, 1973

Among the letters that I opened when I got home was a very interesting one from Theodore M. Burton, Assistant to the Council of the Twelve. He and Brother Packer and another young general authority, Loren Dunn, are in charge of an entertainment program for the traditional gathering of the Brethren and their wives the Tuesday evening following conference. They are planning it after the early meetings of the Polysophical Society (pioneer cultural event of the 1850s) and would like me to write an original poem and read it on the program.

And the morning that I opened the letter I received a long-distance telephone call. A female voice said, "One moment please. Boyd K. Packer is calling."

I felt faint and nearly began to shake. He came on the line, very pleasantly asking how I was, then asked if I had received a letter from Brother Burton. I replied that I had, that I was thrilled with the invitation, and that I would do my best. He gave me a little background on the Polysophical Society, then went on to suggest a theme of unity and cooperation. The Church membership has never been so united, so cooperative; and that he feels in part it stems from the General Authorities being more united than they have ever been.

I mentioned that in Brother Burton's letter he suggested a theme for the poem could be the early women of the Church and their influence of refinement. Brother Packer thought a moment, and said, "No, let's not make it just about women." Well. I don't know quite what I'll come up with, but what an amazing opportunity, to speak to *all* of the General Authorities.

September 16, 1973

Today Frances Boyden dropped in for a moment during rehearsal of *The Order is Love,* which is being produced by the Promised Valley Playhouse. On her way out she said, "Oh, I think it's so wonderful—you have those beautiful children and your husband, and you continue to do all the other things you do." I responded, only half-jokingly, "But I'm not supposed to be doing it, you know."

She went on to say that she has lived through a number of "regimes" in the Church, and that things come and go. I asked, "You mean the current stand is tighter on women than you've seen it before?"

"Heavens yes! I've never seen it so tight." Frances is a long-time member of the General Board—MIA, Drama. Some months ago she told me that her daughter said the best thing that happened in the whole ERA involvement in January was my speech at the Capitol.

September 23, 1973

Must mention our dinner with Hugh Nibley and his wife Phyllis the other day. I have further developed a relationship with Brother Nibley through my work writing screenplays for BYU's Motion Picture Studio. The other day on an impulse I walked to the telephone, dialed their number and invited them to come to dinner on Friday night. Phyllis accepted. When I called back to confirm it I asked her if her husband had whipped her soundly for accepting the invitation. She laughed and said, "No. I told him he has to eat supper every night anyway."

So they came. Gerald fixed his wonderful chicken spaghetti, and a tasty time was had by all. Among the things I asked Brother Nibley was to verify that story of his prayer at BYU graduation exercises. I gave it the way I had heard it, then he gave it the way he had really said it: "Our Father in Heaven, we are gathered here in the black robes of a false priesthood—." No one said anything to him about it. The Brethren must have built up a terrific tolerance for him. And they must recognize his value to give him such rein.

We also probed him a bit about sexuality of spirit. He feels that according to the things he's read of the documents on the teachings of Christ and the apostles—and what he believes—that one condition that must occur before the establishment of the millennium is that we will cease to think of ourselves primarily as male or female. I asked him if he realized how heretical that would sound to the Brethren today. He said that yes, he realized that. Again I told him how pressing was the necessity that he turn some of his scholarly genius in the direction of the status of women, for there is human pain going on.

We had a pleasant visit. I think they enjoyed it. When we first sat down to dinner I said, "Now, Brother Nibley, we know that you would ordinarily spend this time in study. But then all work and no play makes Hugh a dull boy." He agreed and said that he had certainly become dull lately.

October 11, 1973

Last night was the major event—the dinner with and performance for the General Authorities of the Church and their wives. An unforgettable occasion. On the program with me were Delos Jewkes, an actor who was the voice of God in *The Ten Commandments*. And Alexander Schreiner, famed organist of the Tabernacle Choir, who sang and played a variety of tunes that were used for our hymn "O My Father." I was last on the program and I gave two poems, surreptitiously chosen to address my dangerous gender issues, first regarding women:

On Nest Building

Mud is not bad for nest building.
Mud and sticks
And a fallen feather or two will do
And require no reaching.
I could rest there with my tiny ones
Sound for the season, at least.

But
If I may fly awhile—
If I may cut through a sunset going out
And a rainbow coming back
Color upon color sealed in my eyes—
If I may have the unboundaried skies
For my study
Clouds, cities, rivers for my rooms—
If I may search the centuries
For melody and meaning—
If I may try for the sun—

I shall come back
Bearing such beauties
Gleaned from God's and the world's very best.
I shall come filled.

And then—
Oh, the nest that I can build!

And then, specifically for men, in this case "The Brethren":

HE WHO WOULD BE CHIEF AMONG YOU

And he rose from supper
poured water in a basin
and washed the disciples' feet.

Those hands
hardened by the heat of a desert sun
comfortable with cutting trees
and turning them to tables
in Joseph's shop—

Those hands
that with a wave could stop
the troubled sea
could touch a leper clean,
or triumphantly turn death away
from the loved daughter on Jairus' couch—

Those hands
that could gesture the heavens open—
poured water in a basin
and washed the disciples' feet.

the lesson lies unlearned
but to a few
who trust the paradox
and hear the call:

"He who would be chief among you,
let him be the servant of all."

I was very well received. When I started, Brother Hanks straightened up to get a good view. And when I finished, he lifted his hands above his head and clapped as loud as he could. When the program was over, he said it was wonderful and kissed me on both cheeks. A couple of minutes later he came over and slyly said, "Why, I just learned that you wrote those specially for tonight! Brother Packer told me that, and he was very proud of it."

Indeed, Brother Packer did seem pleased. And his wife also. Sister Funk raved about "On Nest Building." She wants a copy to take to England with her. "Our sisters *need* that. So many of them marry later. And what you have said there is so important."

Gerald and I shook hands with most of the General Authorities, receiving nice comments from them. President Lee said he had wanted to shake my hand and that he so enjoyed the poems.

Indeed a memorable occasion.

7

DOOR MAT OR RED DRESS?

October 24, 1973

I'm off for the first private adventure I've had in years. I'm speaking to-night in Grand Junction, Colorado, for all the Relief Societies there, then in Kansas speaking at a Laurel Conference, then on Monday I'm going to Boston for a week—expressly to meet the Mormon women there who are doing such interesting things. It's Claudia Bushman that I've been corresponding with. I'll miss my little family. But I will enjoy missing them. To be responsible only for my own body is something I will delight in for a while.

A few weeks ago what should appear in my ward bulletin but that dreadful little "doormat" verse that Rodney Turner uses—

> Women are doormats and have been—
> The years those mats applaud—
> They keep their men from going in
> With muddy feet to God.
> — by Mary Carolyn Davies

I nearly fell on the floor. Now, there is nothing I can do about it when Brother Turner uses it in a talk, but there is something I can do about it when it appears in my ward bulletin when I'm Relief Society President. So I wrote a little sequel and sent it in for the next bulletin, asking them to print that verse again with my response directly under it:

> And I think I can hear the Lord's answer
> When those feet He will sadly see.
> "What you have done to her, my son,
> You have also done to me."
> —by Carol Lynn Pearson

November 1, 1973

I am staying with Claudia and Richard Bushman, and writing on Claudia's typewriter as I look onto their front yard here in Belmont, Massachusetts. I talked to Gerald and my little ones last night on the phone—they were just ready to get into their Halloween costumes and I felt dreadfully homesick for them. Gerald has made it clear that I am to have no guilt about being gone, but to enjoy myself thoroughly.

November 12, 1973

Of course I did not keep up with my diary while I was gone, so here I am having to do it. I met many great women back East. Stephanie Goodson was elected editor of the *Woman's Exponent II* that they have decided to publish. She and I talked a lot about it and I gave her my best words of caution and balance. Stephanie is planning a "Dear Abby" type column, hoping Laurel Ulrich will write it.

Thursday night they all met for a pot-luck dinner and conversation. They are an impressive bunch. They told me they had solved the housework problem some time ago by deciding it simply wasn't as important as they had previously thought.

The most important thing I put to them was this. I explained that within myself I have come to feel very good about my own value as a woman, my own capacities, relative to manhood, womanhood, personhood. But that I have come to this in spite of, not because of, our religion's doctrines concerning the sexes. And my question to them was if anyone had come to these feelings by *dealing with* our doctrines. I had no takers. Claudia's attitude is just to put all of that away and not worry about it—to concentrate on the here and now, doing with your life what you want to do.

In one of our last conversations, Richard Bushman said that he was getting tired of the "woman question." I agreed with him heartily. I myself am sick to death of it. I wish to solve it in some reasonable way and move on. Sitting around talking about it is like studying your bicycle for days and days and never getting on it and going anywhere. I want to go somewhere. Except that some study and work in the area will always be pertinent, for there are such a lot of women who don't even know they have bicycles.

Gary and Diana Stewart came and took me to Amherst for a couple of days. Diana and I went through the Emily Dickinson house, really a treat. In her bedroom was a shawl on the bed, which Emily used to wear out walking in the garden. I coaxed the guide to let me put it on (just because I was a poet too) and in fact to let this fellow who had a camera snap a picture of me in it by Emily's portrait. What fun. We drove to the nearby cemetery and saw her grave. On it was simply, "Called Back."

December 10, 1973

Just a minute to try to catch up a bit. If this diary were not so deeply ingrained in my conscience, I would never in this world get around to it; it calls for too many sacrifices. But here I am, a diary on my back.

Never truly wore the mantle of Emily Dickinson, but for a moment I wore her shawl.

Must comment on a very interesting and satisfying meeting I had with Ruth Funk and her counselors in the General Presidency of the Young Women's Aaronic Priesthood MIA. Sister Funk invited me to a meeting they were having with a number of women to get ideas for directions they should take with the young women of the Church. Sister Funk had me recite my poem "On Nest Building," saying again how thrilled she was with it.

Among comments in the beginning discussion, a woman voiced the need to give our girls direction against all the things that are going on in the world. Sister Funk then said that we must utilize any good thing that the world is doing. I raised my hand and said how glad I was to hear her say that—that what I feared greatly was that we would force our girls into an untenable choice, by painting it all in black and white, us against the world. My comments seemed to be taken very well.

The following Tuesday we did our "Polysophical Society" program for the Young Women's General Board party (the same one we had done for the General Authorities and their wives). I was sick with the flu, but I went. I threw up right before we went on, but I braved it out and my performance went well.

As I studied the paragraph above, I thought—Surely I must have made an error: "The Young Women's Aaronic Priesthood MIA"? Could not be. But with a few moments of internet research I learned that was correct: "The Young Women's Mutual Improvement Association, so named in 1934, merged with the Young Men's Mutual Improvement Association to form the Aaronic Priesthood

MIA Young Women in 1972, then split to form Young Women and Young Men organizations in 1974." Aaronic? Ironic?

Last night Harold B. Lee, President of the Church died, very unexpectedly. It occurs to me now that I do not mention many events of the world in these pages—the fact that we're going through shortages and energy crises and Watergate and Nixon's resignation and Agnew's resignation and war in the Middle East and all manner of challenges.

I just finished typing a poem that I really like, "Millie's Mother's Red Dress." Written from the true account that my friend Millie Bushman gave me, and she insists that I keep her name on it. I find myself inclined toward writing poetry again after a few years of neglect. The poems are longer, more dramatic, and many are tinged with my thinkings and studyings about women. Here is that poem:

Millie's Mother's Red Dress

It hung there in the closet
while she was dying, Mother's red dress
like a gash in the row
of dark, old clothes
she had worn away her life in.

They had called me home
and I knew when I saw her
she wasn't going to last.

When I saw the dress, I said,
"Why, Mother—how beautiful!
I've never seen it on you."

"I've never worn it," she slowly said.
"Sit down, Millie—I'd like to undo
a lesson or two before I go, if I can."

I sat by her bed
and she sighed a bigger breath
than I thought she could hold.
"Now that I'll soon be gone
I can see some things.
Oh, I taught you good—but I taught you wrong."

"What do you mean, Mother?"

"Well—I always thought
that a good woman never takes her turn

that she's just for doing for somebody else.
Do here, do there, always keep
everybody else's wants tended and make sure
yours are at the bottom of the heap.
Maybe someday you'll get to them
but of course you never do.
My life was like that—doing for your dad
doing for the boys, for your sisters, for you."

"You did—everything a mother could."

"Oh, Millie, Millie, it was no good—
for you—for him. Don't you see?
I did you the worst of wrongs.
I asked nothing—for me!

"Your father in the other room
all stirred up and staring at the walls—
when the doctor told him, he took it bad—
came to my bed and all but shook
the life right out of me. 'You can't die,
do you hear? What'll become of me?
What'll become of me?'
It'll be hard, all right, when I go.
He can't even find the frying pan, you know.

"And you children.
I was a free ride for everybody, everywhere.
I was the first one up and the last one down
seven days out of the week.
I always took the toast that got burned
and the very smallest piece of pie.
I look at how some of your brothers treat their wives now
and it makes me sick, 'cause it was me
that taught it to them. And they learned.
They learned that a woman doesn't
even exist except to give.
Why, every single penny that I could save
went for your clothes or your books
even when it wasn't necessary.
Can't even remember once when I took
myself downtown to buy something beautiful—
for me.

"Except last year when I got that red dress.
I found I had twenty dollars
that wasn't especially spoke for.
I was on my way to pay it extra on the washer.
But somehow—I came home with this big box.
Your father really gave it to me then.
'Where you going to wear a thing like that to—
some opera or something?'
And he was right, I guess.
I've never, except in the store,
put on that dress.

"Oh, Millie—I always thought if you take
nothing for yourself in this world
you'd have it all in the next somehow.
I don't believe that anymore.
I think the Lord wants us to have something—
Here—and now.

"And I'm telling you, Millie, if some miracle
Could get me off this bed, you could look
For a different mother, 'cause I would be one.
Oh, I passed up my turn so long
I would hardly know how to take it.
But I'd learn, Millie.
I would learn!"

It hung there in the closet
While she was dying, Mother's red dress
Like a gash in the row
Of dark, old clothes
She had worn away her life in.

Her last words to me were these:
"Do me the honor, Millie,
Of not following in my footsteps.
Promise me that."

I promised.
She caught her breath.
Then Mother took her turn
in death.

This narrative poem has proven to be one of my most popular pieces. Often

I used it in a talk to a hall full of women and I would glance up to see many listeners in tears.

March 2, 1974

Stephanie, our baby sitter, told me a funny thing that Johnny said to her a week or so ago. "Stephanie, do you know what my mommy and daddy do in their bedroom late at night when they think we're asleep?" "No," she said, "what do they do?" "They eat cheese."

Johnny and I are home again from our trip to Arizona. My two talks went very well. I did my "Flight and Nest" basic speech, and it was very well received both places. We had about 450-500 each night. In Tucson we stayed at the home of the Institute Director, Paul Dahl. He's a good man and was very enthusiastic about my talk.

He told an interesting thing: last year on the series, they had Belle Spafford, General Relief Society President, speak, and he invited one of the Institute officers, who was a girl, to conduct; also they had girls give the prayers and introduce Sister Spafford. Afterward about five of the young men came up, dreadfully upset that a woman had conducted the meeting. One said, "If you'd taken the name of the Lord in vain, it wouldn't have been any greater sin." Brother Dahl laughed and tried to reason with them, but they were still convinced the priesthood had been terribly abused. Two of those who were in on it are this year's officers, and Brother Dahl noted that they had now decided to have the secretary, a young woman, conduct and introduce me. "I understand about women better now," one of them told Brother Dahl.

May 6, 1974

Must mention a fireside group I had here on Sunday evening. Martin Nalder, a psychiatrist who has been doing some speaking on Mormon women. He told me an interesting little item as we were chatting afterwards. His mother is a frequent sacrament meeting speaker in California. Just last month as she spoke in a ward—upon her conclusion the bishop arose and said, "As it is not appropriate for a woman to conclude a sacrament meeting service, we will call on Brother So and So to come up and bear his testimony." She was absolutely livid when she came home, he said.

June 7, 1974

Have I written about how *The Order is Love* went in Salt Lake? It was a tremendous success and was packed practically every night. The final Friday the First Presidency and their wives were in attendance. I spoke to them all, and afterwards President Kimball and wife both told me how much they enjoyed it. He said, "I especially appreciated the way you handled the ending. I was afraid there would be a feeling of failure, but you surprised me. It was very elevating." That truly pleased me. And it was quite a heady experience to know that I had the entire First Presidency captive for two hours.

Gerald talks more and more of our moving away. He doesn't want to leave the Church, but he wants to leave the kind of atmosphere that exists here. I don't know if we will go away. But we are certainly moving along to somewhere.

August 26, 1974

I read the two film-strips last Wednesday to Loren Dunn and Daniel Ludlow, BYU professor of religion who was also on the Correlation Committee. We were discussing the "priesthoodization" (my term) of all the programs—priesthood genealogy, priesthood MIA, priesthood missionary work. I had an impulse to say something, and I said it. "Brother Dunn, may I make a personal plea—that all of the emphasis on the priesthood be done in such a way that the sisters do not feel they are being moved further and further to the back of the bus."

Brother Dunn didn't say a word; he didn't acknowledge that I had spoken. After the meeting I approached him and explained why I had said that, telling of the woman back East who had spoken in stake conference, saying, "We want to thank the priesthood for the support they have been giving us in such and such a way." The visiting General Authority then got up and said (this was Brother Packer, but I didn't mention a name), "I want to make one thing clear. The priesthood does not support the Relief Society; the Relief Society supports the priesthood."

Brother Dunn did not comment much. He was pleasant to me as I left. As I came in he had given me a royal welcome, said I was the most famous person in his household, they were always quoting me.

I need to add a few "backstage" items to this account. Gerald was now wearing a beard and a mustache. He was one of the first Utahns to discover the "New Age." He was hungry for a new look at spirituality, and he readily dove into the concepts of the "human potential movement"—meditation and the studies of consciousness, biofeedback, the chakras, reincarnation. I found much of it fascinating—and to this day utilize the valuable tool of meditation. Both of us were enthralled by the discoveries about matter and energy in the field of quantum physics. Especially to Gerald this new, larger way of looking at life and of God and things spiritual was deeply meaningful and truly encompassing. And yes, he was looking with new and more critical eyes at his Mormonism. And yes, this was troublesome to me.

8

"I HAVE KNOWN THE STEADY PULSATION OF PAIN"

September 27, 1974

Today is my birthday. I am thirty-five years old. Carol Lynn Wright Pearson, as she has lived for these many years, is dead. I feel like I should be looking down at my body.

I have written that I believe in history, that "history requires the facts, the dark spots as well as the bright." I have been brought low. I have faced the unanswerable knowing that there will be no answers. I have known the steady pulsation of pain.

And yet I have felt the sun on me still. I have felt the dearness of my children. I have felt the trueness of friends. I have felt the goodness of service. It was comforting to bring in Sister Loper's wash from the line and to retch while I emptied and cleaned her bedside toilet.

In these days of anguish I have come to some resolves. Somehow I am going to get in better touch with myself and with God. I am going to make times of quiet and of seeking and knowing. I have resigned from my seat on the Bicentennial Commission. I have resigned from my recent appointment to the committee to plan Utah's participation in the National Endowment for the Humanities. I had considered canceling all my speaking engagements, but I decided to honor those already made and to refuse new ones. In less than a week I have turned down six or seven.

There must be peace somewhere. There must be light. I must find it.

I did not give to my diary pages the reason for the anguish. I did not place it on paper for a long time. The shame and the pain were too great. But in 1986 in my book Goodbye, I Love You, *I told everything. A day or two prior to the entry above I had learned that Gerald had broken his marriage vows, that the gay experiences in his past were not really past. I feel that now I owe the reader who perhaps has come to care about me a fuller glimpse into that terrible time.*

Gerald had been traveling and did not arrive home for a few days. I called him on the phone and asked him outright. He did not lie. He begged me not to do anything until he got home. We wept. We hung up.

I am going to print here some excerpts from Goodbye, I Love You. *These would have been the entries in my diary then if I had had the strength. Also, these words show more of my own personal experience of The Woman Question.*

* * * * *

The next morning Lynn Ann, our live-in friend and helper looked at me as if I had blood on my face.

"Carol Lynn! What's wrong?"

"I'm just tired. I didn't sleep much." I had not slept at all. I had walked and rocked and lain down and gotten up and gone in to look at the children and picked Aaron up to hold because he was the smallest.

I had to move. I had to get ready to give a talk. Two hundred women at BYU would be waiting to hear me. But it was all a lie. I was not the person they had invited to speak. I was a fraud. *They* thought I was an example of good Mormon womanhood. They were proud of me. They didn't know anything. They didn't know that my eternal marriage was in ruins. They didn't know that my children's father was a homosexual. What if they knew that? They wouldn't ask me to speak then. Still I would give my talk. I would speak on the wonderful world of women, tell them what a thrilling thing it is to be a woman. I didn't have a master's degree in drama for nothing.

On the way home I stopped in to visit my father whom I hadn't seen for a couple of days. He was going to die soon, we knew that, and now the thought brought relief. Maybe he would never have to know. He had charged Gerald on our wedding day to take good care of me. Oh, Daddy, die soon, I thought. And then you'll never have to know. If I did not have three children, I would lie down too. I would lie down and not eat or drink, and soon I would not be here.

How could this be happening to me? I had been doing everything right. I was keeping all my covenants. Something like this was not supposed to happen, something so shameful, so sinful you could not even speak of it or write it in your diary. I thought it was over, done with, washed clean. I had been promised!

Was it me? Had I not been enough of a woman? I stared at my hands and turned them over. They were small, a woman's hands. Was there something wrong with having a woman's hands, a woman's face, skin, breasts? Where could I go to find healing for the wound to the woman in me? Only to God.

But—didn't God prefer men too? God *was* male. God associated with males, did business with males, spoke to males, called males to his work. God did not transact important business with people with small woman's hands and a woman's face.

And God's Church preferred men. That was evident. But they had promised me that in this one thing I was safe. The man would want me, need me *because I was a woman.* It could not be true that everywhere I turned they would rather I be male—not God and the Church and my husband too. I did not want to be a man. I liked being a woman. There must be some mistake, something I couldn't see, something no one had told me. *I will not accept this answer,* I cried inside. *I will beat my small woman's hands against heaven until I get a better answer!*

Suddenly I remembered a statement Gerald had read to me a few weeks before. I was nearly asleep and he had shaken me and said, "Now listen to this, Blossom. Are you listening?"

"Mmmm hmmm."

"This is from Alan Watts. 'The thing is to see in *all* faces the masks of God.' That's *it,* Blossom. That's what it's all about. If we can look at each other and see *everyone,* no matter who they are, as a manifestation of God, we've solved the puzzle!"

Waiting for the sound of Gerald pulling into the driveway was excruciating. I had confided in no one, only gone over it and over it with myself.

Can you become
Acclimated to pain?
Can the shiver cease,
And some condition
Almost comfortable set in?

The polar bear has been
So long a resident of frost
That the ice he walks barefoot
Is not reported to the brain.

Can you become
Acclimated to pain?

He walked into the kitchen. It was just … Gerald. He had done it hundreds of times before. It was just Gerald walking into the kitchen. I looked at him and listened to my voice say, "Hi, Gerald."

"Hi, Blossom."

The thing is to see in all faces the masks of God.

And then we were in each other's arms, sobbing, pressing against each other and against the monumental mystery that lay between us and around us, that I knew would be there for the rest of our lives.

9

WE JUST KEEP BREATHING

November 10, 1974

There is some blessed mechanism in this life that will permit pain to go only so far. Somewhere in the darkness the momentum of living, the grace of things that yet are good takes over and the world goes on. I want to make the right decisions. I want to be able to look back in ten years, in twenty-five, in forty, or in eternity, and feel that I did the best that was possible for everyone involved. That is what I pray for.

I found the strength to just keep breathing, to go through the motions. Gerald and I continued to talk—he to try to convince me that homosexuality is an intrinsic phenomenon and not a revolting choice—me to tell him that is impossible, God cannot work that way, President Kimball himself called it "repugnant … embarrassing… perversion… a crime against nature… deep, dark sin." Through my anger and my grief I remembered the many times Gerald had gone up into the mountains to fast and pray. Surely he had tried to overcome this. But clearly not hard enough.

Neither one of us could conceive of ending our marriage, breaking up our beautiful family. We just had to hang on. Somehow we could find a way. Somehow, I thought, Gerald could make the sacrifice.

I found the energy to carry on my obligations as mother, Relief Society President, writer. Slowly I accepted a few new speaking engagements. I accepted a very prestigious but overwhelming invitation from the Utah Bicentennial Commission to write the lyrics for a choral piece, music by the noted Crawford Gates, to be performed by the Tabernacle Choir and the Utah Symphony, the first joint performance of those two organizations, celebrating patriotism, liberty, and democracy.

And I continued to participate in the large sisterhood of Mormon women searching for a place in our patriarchal church.

Have I mentioned *Exponent II*? It's the woman's paper put out by Claudia Bushman and the other Boston women, and I believe it will be a very good thing. Two issues now have appeared. The first carried my poem, "The

Steward," and the second "Millie's Mother's Red Dress." Both have had a lot of impact.

December 12, 1974

Jan Tyler and I had talked for some time on organizing a group of women interested in Mormon women's issues, inspired likely by the Boston women. Jan is a true activist for women's rights, recently left Weber State University as Dean of Women there. Our group met for the first time on December 3 and had really an amazing experience. There were about thirteen women there. I had sort of wished that the group might be able to solve once and for all the riddle of the Heavenly Mother and like enigmas. But it took a rather more personal turn, and what most everybody wanted was to *experience sisterhood* rather than do projects or conduct studies. I found that this appealed to me enormously.

We met at Jan's last Tuesday. Everyone was there except M., who came with me the first time and decided she couldn't continue. She had feelings, which she has had for years, and which she has to suppress in order to survive. Her husband has a very traditional picture of what women are supposed to be, canners, quilters, docile, home-bound. She was afraid that if she came to our group, brought up all the feelings she has locked away, that it would be risking too much, risking perhaps even her marriage.

She called me the other night, however, and said that she had had a great talk with her husband, they had stayed up late after she'd gotten home, past midnight. She had described to him all the women that were present that night, their positions in life, their intellectual and spiritual qualifications, and he was very impressed. The next morning he said to her, "You don't have to do any canning, and quilting, anything you don't want to do. All you have to do is be your own person."

February 7, 1975

How I would love to rejoice in my womanhood *because of* and not *in spite of* my religious beliefs.

More than the surprise to discover that I was pregnant was the surprise to see how thrilled I was about it. Gerald and I had included intimacy as part of healing our life together again, but barriers to pregnancy had been put in place. Several of them. But the child who came, Katy, was determined. Upon being informed of the pregnancy, Gerald told me that not long before in a deep meditation he had sensed a female spirit who let him know she was on her way. He told her absolutely no. But Gerald was thrilled that she won.

January 29, 1975

The legislature is in session now and two years have passed since the defeat of the ERA. So it's up again. I decided as part of my withdrawal not to engage in this one. Polls of the legislators showed it had a fair chance of passage. But then about a month ago Barbara Smith, new Relief Society General President, gave a speech at the U of U Institute of Religion attacking the ERA, using Phyllis Schlafly phrasing. Then an editorial against the ERA came out in the *Church News* and then one in the *Deseret News.* This was, of course, a staggering blow to the prospects. Many legislators admitted they felt they had to reverse their position. Byron Fisher, for example, is a bishop and has supported the ERA all the way, but says now he has to think of his position as a bishop first.

March 1, 1975

A very interesting morning. I met with a group of women invited into the office of Barbara Smith, General President of the Relief Society. Sister Smith had been assigned to pursue research that would help to "represent the Church well to the world in terms of women."

That such a group has been officially called to meet and talk about women's issues in the world and in the Church, is to my knowledge an unprecedented step. I will do whatever I can.

I rode up with Barbara Hales, teacher of home economics education at BYU. Also present in the meeting were a small group of well-known feminist-leaning Utah women: Moana Ballif, Alice Smith from Logan, Jean White from Logan, and Anne Decker and Mary Lou Hansen from Salt Lake.

Sister Smith agreed that women in general in the Church should be regarded more as co-partners, as companions with the priesthood. I asked her if she really thought that was feasible, saying I had sent from the Motion Picture Studio plenty of things through Correlation and knew about hierarchies. I also mentioned the woman in stake conference who thanked the priesthood for the support they had given the Relief Society, being reprimanded by the visiting General Authority (Elder Packer, whom I did not identify), who reminded them all that the priesthood does not support the Relief Society, the Relief Society supports the priesthood.

We talked about Sister Smith's plan to let the women of Relief Society take more initiative in welfare and other work—about the bind the working women are in, getting discouraging signals constantly about their evil doing—and the pressures on women to feel guilty about taking time for their own self-improvement and interests.

We were asked if we would be willing to be an ongoing committee to meet periodically. We agreed. Sister Smith said we should meet at least every third month. I said I felt we could do nothing if we didn't meet once a month. Others agreed.

In typing this just now I focused on something I had not considered before.

The Brethren had commissioned Barbara Smith to "pursue research that would help to represent the Church well to the world in terms of women." Not to do research that would help the Church better address the needs of women. Clearly a PR effort.

April 16, 1975

Last night was very interesting. I was invited to be the guest speaker at the Cannon-Hinckley Club at the Lion House in Salt Lake. This is about the most elite of groups in the state. All of the First Presidency and wives belong, plus a number of the other General Authorities and other VIPs. They had only one membership opening this year and filled it with David Gardner and wife. He is president of the University of Utah. Among those present (with their wives) were Leonard Arrington, Neal Maxwell, Wendell Ashton, Spencer Kinnard, Franklin D. Richards and a bunch of the Hinckleys. I had ridden up from Provo with William F. Edwards (a vice president at BYU) and Harvey Fletcher (scientist, invented the first hearing aid) and their wives. I was seated next to the club president, David Evans. On my other side was Lowell Bennion. He and I had a most interesting conversation.

I interrupt this program to make certain the reader knows who I'm speaking of. Lowell Bennion was one of the truly great men ever produced by Mormondom. He was a practical philosopher, sociologist, and humanitarian, once described as "A combination of an Old Testament prophet, who wants to give you his vision of what should be, and a New Testament good Samaritan, who doesn't stand back and talk, but steps in to do the good work himself." In 1989 he received the Caring Award, given in Washington, D.C. to ten Americans who had most exemplified practical human service. I recall being thrilled to be seated by him at this event.

I had heard that he had gotten into a little difficulty because of his views on the "black" question, and I asked him if it was fair dinner conversation to inquire about it. He was very happy to talk about it and told me generally the following story. I asked if he had written it down anywhere and he told me he hadn't. I hope he does, but in the meantime my memory will have to serve.

Brother Bennion was head of the LDS Institute at the U of U for something like 26 years. He had never been satisfied about the question regarding blacks and the priesthood, hadn't made any public thing about it, but admitted in private that he didn't understand it and didn't feel good about it. At one point he wrote a letter to President McKay expressing his dilemma and asking for some help. After three months President McKay wrote back a long and compassionate letter, stating that the only scriptural thing he knew of was the verse in the Pearl of Great Price about Ham. President McKay left the question open, giving the impression that he felt the policy would be changed at some time.

About twenty years ago Brother Bennion was teaching Sunday School in a ward in a little Utah town and a young man came up afterwards in tears, saying that he had been asked to pass the sacrament but that he couldn't do it. "Are you a member of the Church?"

"Yes."

"Have you been ordained to the priesthood?"

"No. My grandmother on my mother's side was from the South and was a Negro."

Five years or so later, Brother Bennion got a phone call from that same young man. He said that the next week that there was to be a family wedding in the temple, and his sister and mother wanted so much to attend it. But they had not been given permission. Was there anything he could do?

The next afternoon Brother Bennion was in President McKay's office, being asked kindly what President McKay could do for him. Brother Bennion told him of this family, that they were trying hard to do the right thing, and that it seemed to him the gospel was here to bless the lives of people and not to be a destructive force. President McKay asked what Brother Bennion suggested be done in this case. The response was that if we err on the side of mercy that the Lord would be more forgiving of us in what mistakes we might make. President McKay told him just to leave things in his hands.

At five o'clock that afternoon he received a telephone call from President McKay asking how he might get in touch with the family they had discussed. He gave him the phone number. At seven Brother Bennion telephoned the young man and asked if he had heard from President McKay. The young man said that yes, they had, and their stake president and bishop had as well, and were told that the daughter and the mother had been given permission to go to the temple.

Concerning my program for all these illustrious people—it was a roaring success. I have never been better appreciated or admired. Wendell Ashton (head of External Communications for the Church) came up afterwards and asked when I am next going to New York. He wants to set up some interviews for me with top newspaper journalists. "It would do the Church a whole lot of good; and it wouldn't be bad for your book sales either." He was really very excited about the idea.

June 9, 1975

My new book is progressing wonderfully. Once I get the research for each chapter organized, it seems to write itself. *The Flight and the Nest* is a perspective on women's issues from Mormon women during the age of emancipation. I wrote six chapters in ten days.

August 1, 1975

Lex de Azevedo and I are working on a new musical, for children—*My*

Turn on Earth. It's a story featuring children coming to earth to learn what this life is all about. Life is a treasure hunt—and the treasure is love. The lyrics have been coming quite well. Every day for a week or more I've turned one out, and they're really rather good. Lex is very excited about it.

A very sad thing happened this week. Emily's first grade teacher, Janet Bills, died of a rather sudden brain condition. It was hard to tell Emily about it and to cry with her. So many things seem so unfair. And how do you explain them—to yourself, or to your seven-year-old child who is so simple and loving. I'm glad I'm writing this little play. "The world turns 'round like a merry-go-round, and it lets some off and it takes some on."

Wendell Ashton and his New York man, Charles Graves, are making plans to get me on a national television show. Ironic. Just over two years ago the Church Department of Internal Communications put a ban on my name as far as the magazines went—and now the Department of External Communications wants to help me appear coast to coast.

September 13, 1975

She is here. Katharine Sirrine Pearson is now with us instead of inside of me. And I am so happy. These monumental events come and go so quickly and the world just moves right on. (I'm glad I finally got a new typewriter ribbon so this report can have the proper emphasis.)

I am finding it a lovely experience to hold and to nurse my little baby. I have plenty of milk for her and we're getting along great. This is a sweet, sweet time.

October 8, 1975

For the first time in my life I have started to read through these voluminous diaries that I have been keeping since 1956. Last week, former BYU President Ernest Wilkinson called me on the telephone and asked if I would contribute 5-8 pages in the third volume of his history of BYU, sort of showing one year in the life of a student during that time. He was sure nobody these days kept a diary, and was really astonished when I told him that I had for almost twenty years.

Aaron is now sitting on my lap helping me type, newly arrived from preschool, where he goes for two and a half hours in the morning while Johnny is in kindergarten. I asked if he has any messages for my diary and he said, "Yes, tell it that you love Aaron." It's true. I love Aaron. I certainly do.

November 3, 1975

I just got through speaking to Brian Kkkkk kkkk (someone is playing with my typewriter!!) I had given him a batch of poems for the *New Era*, and he's buying them all (six or eight) and sending me forty-five dollars for the batch (the most he's ever paid for poetry). One of the poems, however, is still hung-up

Writing with Katy on my lap.

pending approval by their supervisors. Somehow Brian now goes through a new General Authority, Elder Robert D. Hales. Brian said that Brother Hales is a great fan of mine, loves the poem, loves all my things, loves me. In fact he said he loves me so much he thinks he's breaking a commandment.

The poem in question is "The Cast." And I think I can see why some people are afraid of it. It suggests that perhaps spear carriers are as important as stars on the stage of life, and they're afraid it might upset some bishops and stake presidents. I don't mind making a few people uncomfortable. Brother Hales is determined to get it through. "We're going to win this one, Baby," he told Brian. And when one of the supervisors (Marvin Ashton, Brian thought) wondered if there was a little women's lib in the poem, Hales said, "Get out of this room—just get out of this room." (I'm sure in a perfectly inoffensive way, but it is nice to hear of a new G.A. that has a mind of his own and speaks it.) Brian wants me to meet Brother Hales, and we're going to try for it this afternoon when I go up to see Wendell Ashton.

Which brings me to another large subject. Brother Ashton's Office of External Communications has been arranging to send me to New York for some major interviews—on my books and also as a Mormon woman who does things. Last week Charles Graves, the Church's man in New York, called me and said, "Did you know you made *The New York Times*?"

"Oh, no," I said. "Was it another assassination attempt on the president?"

"No, it was the women's conference at the U." I remembered then that the *Times* had sent a reporter there to cover it and that she had been to the session I had addressed on our heritage from the early Utah women. The article, he said, was very damaging to the Church. But my part of it was all right; she quoted my poem "On Nest Building," which I used at the beginning of my talk.

We decided it would be a good thing for me to visit with Wendell and let him know the kinds of things I would be saying, so no one would be embarrassed or surprised. Brother Graves sounded like quite an enlightened man to me and we talked for at least half an hour. "The Church has just got to start facing some realities," he said. "We have to educate some of the General Authorities. Many of them have not gotten past the last century on some things."

He said that he would not expect me to reiterate only the same things we hear about women from the Brethren, that I should feel free to say what I want. He and Brother Ashton decided that I had a firm testimony and that they would not worry about what I said. This scares me a little. I do have a testimony, I feel, about many things concerning the Church; but I do not have a testimony that things in the Church as they relate to women are as they should be. I said to Brother Graves, "I could not come back East and pretend that I feel all is well in Zion on this issue."

"Of course not," he said. "I would not expect you to." He has evidently been fighting the battles on the issues about women for months and months and is trying to convince the Brethren that they have to start taking all this seriously. The article quoted President Kimball as saying feminists were "Pied Pipers of sin."

Little Katy's got the grippe. Goodbye again.

Having the blessing of Google, I just pulled up that New York Times *article: "Paradox in the Women's Movement: Feminists Who are Mormon." Yep, the reporter quoted President Kimball as saying that awful thing. And she wrote, "Perhaps more typical of the modern Utah woman was Carol Lynn Pearson, a young poet who came to the conference each day with her children and husband. Introducing her talk on important pioneer women, she recited a poem entitled 'On Nest Building' that lyrically epitomized the dualities her Mormon sisters are trying to resolve." She then quoted the entirety of that poem.*

November 4, 1975

My meeting with Wendell Ashton was somewhat as I had expected. He does not realize the real dilemma that Mormon women are in when asked the questions the world is asking. I told him that I could not give out the pat little answers that usually are forthcoming when people of the Church are interviewed—as when Belle Spafford was asked how it felt to be a second-class citizen in the Mormon Church. She responded that there's no way in the world anyone could accuse the Church of that.

He had read the preface and the last page of *The Flight and the Nest* and thought they were wonderful. He considers me the Church's Robert Frost. He said he's been telling the Brethren for a long time that they need to give more attention to what the women are saying. He said that apostle Bruce R. McConkie took the *New York Times* article into their temple meeting last week and read from it. As we parted he said he was confident that I would say the right things and that he wasn't worried about me.

Directly afterwards I went to Brian Kelly's *New Era* office. One thing Brian told me was that President Kimball had released Boyd Packer from the advisership to the magazines. He called that a faith-promoting story.

Then we went down to visit Robert Hales. Brother Hales is an Easterner, rather unlike your Utah breed of Mormon. He told me he loved me as much as the law allowed, and that he was determined to get my poem "The Cast" in *The New Era* and not let *Exponent II* have it. In fact, I learned that the poem raised questions that made them set up a whole new department under Correlation—interpretation of doctrine. He said that after reading *Millie's Mother's Red Dress* he's never been the same man. And he said, "I want to get some of your poems into the Melchizedek Priesthood manuals. The Brethren need to be reading those things more than the sisters do." A highly encouraging encounter.

November 28, 1975

I am writing this with little Katy on my bosom; otherwise I could not grab the time to get caught up a little. I must review my trip to New York—I just got home last night. But first a couple of earlier things.

Five or six weekends ago I took the children up to Aunt Cree's and Uncle Karl's in Midway to stay overnight. They're such terrific people. And I do want the children to have some happy rural-family-out-on-the-farm memories. Climbing up to the treehouse, riding the Shetland pony, walking through the field up to the hot springs that comes right out of the ground, seeing the milking (by machine) done in the evening. I asked Aunt Cree and Uncle Karl to tell the children some stories of interesting things that had happened to them in their lives, and they did.

And now—New York. Last Friday late afternoon Charles Graves called and asked if I could get on a plane Sunday; he had the interviews set up for

Monday. I had planned to take Katy, but changed my mind. I borrowed a breast pump and took off in solitude.

I stayed at the Roosevelt Hotel, 45th and Madison, right across the street from Charles's office. He and his wife came over and we talked for about an hour and a half.

The Brethren have become aware that they need to be on the offensive more than on the defensive about the woman question, so Eldon Tanner–counselor in the First Presidency–is going to read a statement about the middle of December clarifying the Church's position regarding women. It is being written by apostle Gordon B. Hinckley. I told Charles I felt that Brother Hinckley was a very traditional thinker, but Charles said that in the last year or so a number of the Brethren have been learning things. Brother Hinckley in particular has traveled widely and been asked questions by people that have made him think. Also Mormon women in other countries have said to him, "Now, we're not like your women in America; we don't have a tradition here of being tied to the kitchen sink."

I suggested that President Tanner's statement be read by a group of women who would appraise it honestly. He agreed, saying it should not be the leaders of the official Women's Organizations: Relief Society, Young Women's, Primary. "I'm afraid they lie," he said, "and I know why they do it—they don't want to be removed from their positions."

Evidently there has been some talk of the idea of a body of twelve women that would meet and give input to the Quorum of the Twelve. And there has also been the suggestion that a woman address one of the general sessions in the area conferences. Brother Packer questioned if that would set a precedent, making it necessary to do the same in conference in Utah. A decision has been put off.

About three years ago, I think, when reporters began covering priesthood meeting, an interesting thing occurred. A woman reporter went in (either *Time Magazine* or *The New York Times*) and the Brethren were in a fit of frenzy as to what to do with her. Eventually they sat her in a private room where she could listen to the proceedings.

And just in the last two weeks the Brethren decided that they would have a special press section at priesthood meeting and that any reporter would be welcome there, women included. This was evidently discussed in the weekly temple meeting of the Twelve. Whoever told Charles reported it this way: "Brother Packer went up to the ceiling and circled the room three times before he landed. Then he said, 'That is heresy! Women are not permitted in this meeting!'"

There is a long-established policy that unless there is unanimity among the Twelve they do not act. President Kimball then said, "For the time being we will go back to the old tradition."

Charles recalled a statement made by B.H. Roberts in 1925 to the effect that the Church seemed moving to where the mechanics and bureaucracy would get in the way of application of spiritual principles of the gospel. One difficulty, he said, is that President Kimball has been so elevated that he's afraid to say, "Which way is the bathroom?" because somebody will say, "Write that down—that's important!"

Charles said he is very infrequently asked about The Negro Problem in the Church. It's much more The Woman Question. And he thinks it's going to get bigger. I think so too.

Reading that statement now in the 2020s, and remembering too what I wrote earlier about BYU President Dallin Oaks saying the same thing, I am surprised. History played out in very different ways from this expectation. Beginning in the 1960s, in tandem with the Civil Rights Movement, there grew increasing social pressure for church leaders to examine their policy of exclusion of Black men from the priesthood and of all Black people from the temple. There was picketing. There were demonstrations. Stanford University and then other universities announced that they would no longer play BYU athletic teams due to these policies. Members of the Church put pressure where they could and prayed for the change. And in 1978 came the announcement: the ban against full participation of Blacks in the Church was lifted.

There has been no corresponding outside pressure to change any doctrines or policies regarding women. Various protests inside the LDS population have occurred, but society at large has not expressed significant interest in the doctrines and policies that belittle Mormon women.

The interviews I had in New York went very well. I spoke to Sue O'Brien of NBC radio news, Tammy Tanaka of the Religion News Service, Jean Lessing of UPI and others. They seemed quite interested in what the early Mormon women were doing, and how I organize my day to have a little writing time.

Charles and I walked to the World King of All Toy Stores—FAO-Schwarz. I bought one thing for each child and a little jumping frog to put in Gerald's stocking. I would have loved to spend more, but I have no money. We're at one of our lowest ebbs. My work is barely keeping us afloat—selling books at speaking events (only a few because I'm generally retired from going out)—royalties from *The Order is Love* and a filmstrip for BYU.

In NY I finished reading Mary Daly's *The Church and the Second Sex.* A devastating book. Her voice in the post-Christian/new feminist introduction is too radical for me, but the book itself is generally as true for Mormons as it is for Catholics. And what is to be done about it? What?

December 27, 1975

My women's group met last Monday eve. Elouise Bell, dear friend and esteemed professor of English at BYU, reported on a few things she has observed through her position on the General Board of the Young Women. She said that many of the Brethren are becoming aware that a problem exists, not because of outside pressure, but because of the condition of many Mormon women. There is evidently a high rate of drug use among Mormon women—not heavy stuff, but alcohol and amphetamines, etc.

I had an interesting discussion with our new home teachers about the subject. Last month (Gerald happened to be gone) I gave them the assignment as my home teachers to solve the Woman Problem for me.

When they came to see me on Tuesday night they both had done some reading and thinking about it, but agreed they couldn't solve the problem. They both agreed that it's a puzzling situation and that there are many inequities. I especially enjoyed Brother Lindsay's reaction. He's never really thought about it, but once being made to think about some things is very open and teachable. "I was happier before I knew all this," he said. All I did was to take him for a very brief trip through an inversion of Mormon sex-roles and a little commentary on the usual sacrament meeting. Bit by bit.

January 2, 1976

It will be noticed that I have not written much about the Pain that has been with me for over a year. I don't know that I shall ever write much about it. It is sharp sometimes, and sometimes dull. But never absent. I think now that I would have to give a qualified "yes" to the question I posed in that poem—"Can you become acclimated to pain?" Life continues to go on. And there are always good things in the day.

The last year has brought better communicating between Gerald and me. It has also seen Gerald become more disaffected from the Church. When I have the heart for it I shall write more on this.

Gerald's distress was very real regarding the Church's explanation of and policies about homosexuality. Also, he had become devoted to reading church history and found what he felt were very troubling things. At the same time he was exhilarated to discover what he felt was a widened view of spirituality in arenas apart from the Church.

January 24, 1976

At present the real estate people are holding an open house here.

There were two prongs to the distress of the past year. First, the ongoing challenge to the relationship. Second, the ongoing financial trouble. Our business debt was such that we had to sell our house to pay our obligations.

Two months later I would write:

March 30, 1976

Our present financial situation is a disaster. The things Gerald was banking on haven't come through and my first of the year money is all gone. I have about six dollars in my purse, less than twenty in the bank and none of this month's bills paid. Money from the sale of the house probably won't come until the middle of June. Between now and then things are a large question.

My father had passed away in our home from pulmonary embolism. I had continued to scramble to bring in enough money for our basic needs. My new book The Flight and the Nest *had done very well, selling nearly 5,000 copies in three months.* Daughters of Light *continued to be popular. I continued to do free-lance work for BYU's Motion Picture Studio.*

And, of course, my work for women went on.

A week ago in Relief Society Sister Lynn Lindsay came up and threw her arms around me and said, "I am so grateful for what you are doing for my husband!" I did mention, did I not, my conversations with our new home teachers? The night before Christmas Eve Brother Bill Lindsay left our house and spent a long time apologizing to his wife Lynn for all the years of treating her as he had. (He hadn't abused her, but he was just not *aware*, and becoming so was a shock to him.)

Lynn came over and we visited for about an hour. I asked if her husband's behavior was really different and she said it definitely was. Often she would feel hurt and not understand why, but it gradually dawned on her that Bill was treating her like a child, not like an adult human being. I am thrilled to have helped enlighten them both. (It certainly proves that home teaching is an inspired program!)

March 1, 1976

One other thing. Christie called last week to tell me a number of people have been inquiring of her about a rumor they've heard that Gerald and I are getting a divorce. This makes me so angry I feel like hitting somebody. What the hell business is it of anybody to sit around and discuss me and my marriage? And to pass around a story that has no basis in fact. Along with the flu, that's all I needed!

I smile a sardonic smile as I type the above paragraph. Being a public figure is a two-edged sword. "Look at me! I'm a poet! I'm a writer! Tell your friends about me!" And then, "Oh, don't look at me now! Things have gotten complicated! Don't gossip about me with your friends! How dare you talk about me!"

All of that is a major part of why we moved from Utah to California. If indeed there might be a divorce in our future, which I was so hoping would not be the case, I did not want it to play out in Utah. Imagine the talk, the questions, the disappointments, even condemnations. "See?—that's what happens when you get into that women's lib stuff."

I was the one who said, "As long as we're going to have to move—I think maybe I'd like to really move. I mean leave Utah. Go somewhere totally new. Like California."

April 19, 1976

Yesterday Dave, my friend from the Motion Picture Studio, came by. In telling me all they've gone through in getting approvals for *The First Vision* movie, he told me that recently they showed the first cut to some of the Brethren. In the film is a nice shot of the family around the table—it pans from Joseph Smith Senior around the others to Joseph and his mother at the end of the table. She reaches over and gives Joseph a warm squeeze on his arm. Thomas Monson's reaction to this: "Why did you feature the mother? We've got to feature the father. This is a priesthood-oriented Church. We've got to feature the priesthood, not the mother."

It really amazed Dave. But it didn't surprise me at all. Hurt, yes—but not surprised. Few women in our church get through their life without having their value challenged. Many, if not most, are not much aware of it. But once you are aware—as I have been for twenty years at least—it hurts a lot. Life in general is so fine. But the *Church* end of things is so painful.

Moving on to better things. Katy is asleep; what an angel. She makes me happy one hundred times a day. The boys are both warm and wonderful. Emily is still a challenging, interesting, delightful person.

April 24, 1976

I made a deal with Bookcraft for this third book of poetry, *The Growing Season*. Marve Wallin—who had turned down *Beginnings* in 1967—was, of course, very anxious to get the book. I didn't have the manuscript with me when we spoke. He took it sight unseen, giving me a thousand dollar advance on the spot, with another thousand coming in a month, and a seventeen percent royalty from the first copy on. I know the book will go very well and will ease our financial burdens considerably. I think I'm ready for bed. Now to go and move three small bodies. The children love to fall asleep in our water bed. Sometimes I'm hard-hearted and make them get in their own beds before falling asleep, but usually I'm a sucker and let them have their way. Then, if Gerald is not here, I have to wake and shake and hoist and drag and carry. And they're all getting so big.

The following event served unwittingly as the public grand finale to my presence in Utah, where I was born of goodly parents and brave pioneers, where I was gifted with remarkable opportunities, deeply appreciated, and personally challenged. And for which I will always be grateful.

What could be more thrilling? My words, Crawford Gates's music, the Mormon Tabernacle Choir, and the Utah Symphony Orchestra!

June 1, 1976

I have a thrilling thing to report. The concert at the Salt Lake Tabernacle last Saturday. Crawford Gates conducted our piece, "A New Morning," between Jerold Ottley conducting "Song of Democracy" and Maurice Abravanel conducting "The Chichester Psalms" and "Battle Hymn of the Republic." I had not heard any of the music for our piece and so it was a total surprise. There were some marvelously impressive things in it, some dramatic things. So thrilling to hear my words sung by the Tabernacle Choir. At the conclusion of the piece the audience (a packed hall) gave a standing ovation.

I had not been invited to take any bows, and during intermission somebody (Crawford likely) realized the oversight. So they sent out scouts to find me. Cliff White, my friend on the Commission, located me, and several different people—Presiding Bishop Victor Brown, Keith Engar, head of the U. of U.'s theatre department—got me set to come on after the "Battle Hymn." Maurice Abravanel gave a little thank-you speech for those making this occasion possible, and then said, "We want to thank again—and have them come out here—Jerold Ottley, Crawford Gates, composer and conductor—and the lyricist, Carol Lynn Pearson." As we came out, the audience applauded wildly. We came out twice, in fact, and it truly was a thrilling and memorable moment.

10

NEW HORIZONS, SAME CHALLENGES, AND THOSE UPPITY MORMON WOMEN AT BYU

September 3, 1976

Such a dreadful lapse since my last entry. Here we are in a new home in Walnut Creek, California, a city in the East Bay, close to Oakland and to San Francisco. Gerald had fallen in love with Walnut Creek as he spent time here with the Kruiswycks, a family that he stayed with on his mission in Australia.

My women gave me as a going away present a t-shirt that says "I Look Just Like Carol Lynn Pearson." Several times people have stopped me and said just that.

I do want a new environment in which to work out a new life. I'm sort of weary of being a public figure. I want to simply *be*. So far I am delighted in this new place just to be a person.

September 8, 1976

The first Sunday the children and I went to Sacrament Meeting and two people recognized me and came up and spoke to me. I soon learned that The Woman Question was also a member of the Church in good standing in California. A counselor in the bishopric called and asked Gerald for permission to talk to me about working in the Primary. Gerald was furious. He wasn't rude, but told him that our family does not operate that way, that if he wanted me to work in the Primary he is to talk to me and not come to him for permission. I accepted the Primary job—I'll be teaching the four-year-olds, seven of them.

I'm writing another children's musical, *Don't Count Your Chickens Until They Cry Wolf.* And Lex de Azevedo is moving along with *My Turn on Earth.* He plans to produce it in L.A. before Christmas.

Last Thursday was our tenth wedding anniversary. We went out to dinner and came home and had a pleasant, warm evening together. Somehow I had expected that this move would be somewhat of an emotional strain between Gerald and me, but it hasn't been. Things have been good between us.

September 27, 1976

So I am thirty-seven years old today. In three years I will turn forty, which is way beyond my comprehension.

With Gerald, the cook, in our first home in California.

Ever since Beginnings *was published, I had been receiving letters from Mormon women, wanting to thank me for my work, and often relaying their own personal griefs, their own distress with the patriarchy.*

Saturday I received a letter from a young woman in North Carolina. It's short and I will record it here:

Dear Sister Pearson.

I have hopes that this letter will reach you and that you might be able to help me with something that has brought me great grief and has been a stumbling block to my testimony of the gospel.

Sister Pearson, it is with tears and confusion that I have just finished reading Section 132 of the Doctrine and Covenants. My understanding is that if my husband rules faithfully over one (me) he will be made ruler over many. I have spent many nights in tears since my temple marriage a little over a year ago. It saddens my heart to think of Emma Smith and her awful grief as she finally agreed to allow her husband to have other women sealed to him for eternity. I cannot understand polygamy—nor our giving importance to such a doctrine.

Carol Lynn, I have had what I felt was a very strong faith in the gospel and yet as I feel so much love for my husband this has become "a fire in my mind" and has shaken so much of what I used to believe. I've been told to take it on faith but find it impossible to faithfully work towards a celestial glory that I dread with all my heart.

I'm hoping now to be able to lean on your testimony and faith. What will our place be in the hereafter? Do you understand what your place will be with Gerald as he loves and has children with many others?

I thank the Lord for your talents and the joys they've brought to me. I turn to you now humbly seeking your help.

Thank you.

Sandee S.

How ironic. One who is drowning calls to a life guard who cannot swim. Her letter sounds like some of my diary entries of years ago. I don't write about it anymore. I don't think about it as much as I used to, and so I don't cry about it as much as I did. But I have no better answers now than then. I don't have a testimony of polygamy. I don't have a testimony of the eternal place of woman as explained in Mormon doctrine.

As I read this now, many decades later, I feel grief. But more importantly I feel anger. I'm sure I sent a reply to Sandee, offering what encouragement I could. If I could write to her today, the words would be these:

Very dear Sister Sandee,

Thank you for honoring me with your feelings and your questions. Of course I understand them fully. I too read Section 132 as a young woman and I dropped to the floor and wept. You ask to "lean on my testimony and faith." Listen closely.

I have a firm testimony that polygamy is not and never was of God—that Joseph Smith instituted the practice in error to serve his own personal needs. Over the decades I have spoken to or received letters or emails from hundreds of women like you, whose hearts have been broken, whose spirits have been violated, whose marriages have been damaged or destroyed because of this pernicious teaching. Shame on everyone who assisted in upholding this doctrine throughout the history of our church. And shame on those today who have the power to abolish it and refuse to do so.

You asked also to lean on my faith. I have full faith that our Creator—our Divine Father and Mother—have wept with you to see your pain, to watch the damage that has been done to your marriage and the confusion pressed on the husband who I'm sure loves you with his whole heart.

Sandee—let us, you and I, have a testimony of our own selves, our own hearts and minds and spirits. From them we learn there is no truth in the terrible doctrine of eternal polygamy. Let your love for your husband be overflowing, given with no hesitation. Let the "fire in your mind" become sweet warmth. Trust.

Sending love and blessings from your sister,
Carol Lynn

October 3, 1976

Last week's sacrament meeting was very interesting indeed. John Hilton spoke, a very enthusiastic speaker, and chose of all things to speak on our Mother in Heaven as portrayed in "The Pearl," in the apocryphal Acts of Thomas. Why should a talk like this be such an amazing exception to the usual fare? The Woman Question will not be answered for me *at all* until we speak of and think of the Mother God as much as we do of the Father God. And when will this be? Not in my lifetime. Not in *anyone's* lifetime as a Mormon. Nonetheless I eat up the delicious crumbs. A starving one does not wait for the banquet.

Comic Relief:

Last night we had a wonderful exchange in the car as we were going out for ice cream cones after supper. A store we went to was closed and Johnny suggested we could break into it.

Me: That's a fine idea, Johnny. Then those two policemen we saw back there could come and arrest us and put us in jail.

John: Oh, no! Then we'd have to eat bread and water!

Emily (Pause): Well, that's what they had at the last supper.

Gerald and I went into hysterics.

We really do have good times, it's true. Often I am overcome with gratitude for all I have that is good. My children are phenomenal. People stop us in public places and tell us we're a beautiful family. Gerald and I have some depths and some warmths that have not always been here. My writing moves along. I feel good about being in California. If only I could solve the Church-Woman problem—and erase the Great Pain—I would have contentment in my time.

November 7, 1976

Last Friday was Emily's baptism. It was not an easy time. I had asked Gerald if he wanted to attend, and he said no, it would be a very unpleasant experience for him. It was hard on both of us. Hard on me because I was alone, and harder for Gerald than even he had expected.

When we came back, Gerald was out in the garage, where he has set up his office, and he didn't come in for a long time. Emily went out to find him, and in a few minutes I went out to get some ice cream from the freezer. Gerald was holding her on the big cushions. When she came back in she said, "Daddy was crying. He cried on my cheek. I asked him why and he said we'd talk about it when I was older."

I haven't gone much in this diary into Gerald's changing position in regard to the Church. He believes without question in God the Creator and in the mission of Jesus Christ. Gerald some years ago had a personal experience with Christ, which I do not feel to deny. Gerald is a man of much light and honesty and sincerely in pursuit of truth. His study over these years has brought him to an awareness of spiritual gifts evidenced by many people outside our church, and of philosophies that feel to him more in harmony with the feelings that he has for and from the Savior. The patriarchal system of the Church, the eternity of sex roles, the denial of priesthood to blacks, the exclusive spiritual powers assumed by the Mormon priesthood, the incredibly authoritarian organization—these and other things pain Gerald deeply. If Emily's baptism was unto Christ and not to the Mormon Church, he would feel differently about it.

November 22, 1976

I have started keeping a dream notebook. I got some paper to fit in my mother's BYU leather notebook, and I am using that. I'm writing down all my dreams, even those that embarrass me. I intend to learn something about my inner workings through many methods.

December 27, 1976

I was a speaker in Sacrament Meeting two weeks ago, gave a fine talk on the painful aspects of growth, used a number of my poems. Everybody seemed very impressed and many were moved.

January 23, 1977

Yesterday Gerald and I had a marvelous day. For three hours we shopped in the stores of San Francisco, buying *clothes* for *me!* Is that not amazing? Gerald, of course, thinks I need to indulge myself much more than I do. The truth is that the Deseret Industries and more recently the Goodwill have supplied most of my needs for years and years.

January 27, 1977

I fasted again today. I intend to fast every Sunday for the foreseeable future. For light on my relationship with Gerald and on my relationship with the Church.

I had accepted an invitation to speak at the Women's Conference at BYU. My heart was still with those good women struggling to make some progress there, and I missed them.

February 7, 1977

The conference was most interesting. They had 1600 women, students and mothers. Last year, the first conference, was rather a minor event, but this year they did great promotion and pulled off a real success. The school administration had pretty much ignored them, not thinking it was going to be a big deal. But suddenly, the week before it began, all these registrations came pouring in, and the administration started getting upset that there was something happening over which they did not have control. So they started looking into it.

Bruce Olson, public relations man for the Church, called and told the Women's Office that they had to change their theme—"The LDS Woman: an Ever Widening Circle." It sounded too much like being pregnant, he said. The women in charge told him they would not change the theme. Also they refused to have the publicity turned over to the administration. In the meantime, Robert K. Thomas, academic vice president of the university, looked over the roster of speakers and panel participants and exclaimed, "Why, there's not one woman here who has come out against the Equal Rights Amendment!"

To my view, the conference was a landmark occasion—perhaps the first time on any large scale that a group of Mormon women met and made a serious attempt at addressing some extremely pertinent issues. Emma Lou Thayne—that magnificent woman and poet—gave a good, warm, personal glimpse into her own marriage and gave some of her own philosophy, like a couple operating from their own strengths and not just relying on roles. Sally Hess Barlow gave an open account of some of her struggles, admitting to putting off children so she could finish her PhD.

Then Shirley Paxman got up and really started the fireworks. I took good notes.

"When I was a young woman, we didn't have to ask the questions the young women are asking today; we just went about our business and did what we wanted to do and followed a career if we wanted, and nobody thought anything about it. But today there are pressures we never even dreamed of. And when I got married and my mother gave me a talk about the birds and the bees, it was understood that we would practice family planning. But it seems the girls now feel that if they don't have a baby a year they're committing a sin. And so their husbands are going to school and coming home to a frustrated wife and screaming children—and all the financial burdens—and the relationship can hardly survive. Girls, you don't have to have a baby every year!

"And another thing that's really changed is our idea about the priesthood. When I was growing up no man ever said, 'I hold the priesthood authority and this is the way decisions are going to be.' But I hear my own sons saying that now, and I take them aside and say, 'You'd better shape up or you're going to have a terrible time.' We have to listen to counsel and then think for ourselves and have joy in the decisions we make."

The meeting was turned over to the audience for questions or comments, and the first to get the microphone was an intense little woman who said, "I want to bear my testimony. There are some things being said here that I can't agree with. I'm the mother of eleven children, and when I had our fifth child in the fifth year of our marriage, I wrote to one of the Brethren, and I said, 'Am I doing right?' He wrote me back, quoting Brigham Young and saying, 'Sister, you go right on doing just what you're doing.' And so I did."

Other similar comments were made. A woman said, "I just taught a Primary class, and I told the boys—and it was right there in the lesson—that when they get married, they will ask their wife's opinion, but they will go ahead and make the decisions themselves." This brought a few reactions.

Emma Lou Thayne stepped in at the end to pull the thing together and brought a good feeling back to the majority, I believe. She stressed that we should rejoice in our diversity and allow one another to be different, and establish our own spiritual pipelines.

I walked out with Belva Ashton, wife of Wendell, head of the Church's Public Relations. "What a fine session that was," she said. "That Shirley Paxman—I would call her a progressive woman in the Church today. She was saying the kinds of things that I would like to be able to say if I could."

We sat together at lunch and I quizzed her on some things. I asked if she felt women of her generation had more freedom in the Church, as Shirley had said. "Yes," she nodded her head emphatically.

"What do you see as the future for women in the Church?" I asked.

"Well, I'll tell you, Carol Lynn. I think we've hit the bottom, and the only way now is up."

I'll quickly report my conversation with Leonard Arrington, Church Historian. I called him on the phone, knowing that I wouldn't be able to get in to visit him. He was glad to hear from me. I told him that I was working on something about Mother in Heaven. I asked him what he thought of the situation—Her utter absence, etc.

He said, "Oh, I think She's coming back."

"What do you mean?"

"Things like the ordaining of the Episcopal women, and signs that I see of things happening among the women of our own church—She's coming back."

"But why," I asked, "is it happening in spite of and not because of the only true authority in the only true Church?"

He chuckled and said, "It seems to me that's the way most important things come."

"So what does that say about the only true Church?"

"We'll have to take an hour and visit about that sometime," he said.

And just a bit now on my visit with Hugh Nibley. Wednesday morning I called him and told him I had to see him. He agreed. I know he doesn't see everybody that comes to his door.

I put my dilemma to him. I told him I was reading things that established that historically prior to the patriarchy there was a definite time of goddess worship.

"Of course. The matriarchy. It definitely existed. There's always been this tension, this battle, one is supreme, and then the other."

"But we are told that the patriarchal order has always been and always will be. Why do we have the patriarchy now?"

(Now this next just about blew me away.)

"It was necessary to have a patriarchal interlude after the time of the matriarchy. Sort of to balance things out."

"And what role do you see the LDS Church playing in righting what is now obviously a great imbalance?'

"None. Absolutely none."

"What do you mean?"

"We're in a position where we must wait for divine intervention. And it's not only in this area—it's in many areas. But I'd better not get into all that."

He also gave me a lot of bibliographical material to look into on the Mother God. I stressed to him that I believe humanity suffers enormously from the lack of the Mother in our notion of deity. He agreed with me completely.

Those are the highlights of my trip. My sessions went well. Huge crowds. And my San Francisco coat and hat were a smash success. Cindy Bateman told me her mother, my cousin Helen, said: "Have you seen Carol Lynn? She looks like a fashion model!"

This morning Gerald and I had a good visit about "us." I say good because we are dealing honestly and without anger or pessimism. Actually our worst times have not had much anger, just hurt. I fasted again on Sunday.

11

MORMON WOMEN AT WAR

March 2, 1977

Split my day again between Work and Love. Katy played happily while I did things. When Aaron comes home from kindergarten I have to hug him and hug him and kiss him and kiss him; he is such a bright little light. Helped Johnny check his homework and encouraged his good little brain; read him a story he had brought from the library. Got Emily to practice and recorded some of her pieces on the tape recorder. Said our scripture before family prayer. This week is, "Trust in the Lord with all thine heart and lean not to thine own understanding." Johnny and I and Emily put on the play of *Aesop's the Sun and the Wind and the Traveler*, which Johnny has been wanting to do for days. Actually that was both the Love and the Work.

March 4, 1977

Saturday evening Gerald took me to see the American Ballet Theatre performing in Berkeley. Really lovely. I had an interesting experience looking around at the dancers and at the audience in general. This new consciousness that I'm going through makes me look at people differently. And I love it. When I have looked at the world as a Mormon, first and last, I have seen every Gentile as a non-Mormon, first and last.

In a crowd like this of thousands of people who were obviously not Mormon, I would sense this depressing division between us. They would be "people who don't have the truth—that I and the few others like me have the obligation of giving the truth to." But I didn't look at them that way last night. Just being able to look at people of the world in general and feel that we're all in this thing together, all of us struggling and searching and enjoying and becoming and making mistakes and helping each other where we can—just to feel that we're *not that much different*—is a most exhilarating feeling. Of course the Brethren would be horrified at that—we have to be a peculiar people—we have to be missionary-minded—we have to convert the world—the basic division of humanity is Saints and Gentiles. But I find these new feelings so beautiful.

Emily, John, Carol Lynn, Katy, Gerald, and Aaron, 1977.

March 8, 1977

Yesterday I began a new book: *The First Sex,* by Elizabeth Gould Davis. It promises to be quite as radical as Merlin Stone's *When God Was a Woman.*

April 15, 1977

Our evening last night with Mary Bradford, terrific woman, now editor of *Dialogue: a Journal of Mormon Thought.* After Gerald's excellent chicken spaghetti, our conversation touched on many things. She had spent a week in Utah, mostly Provo, and found it to be a depressing experience. "It's like a continual cell-block meeting," she said, "lots of secrecy and heartbreak." She said it looks like there will not be another woman's conference at the Y unless it's a bridal fair. Some women complained to the General Authorities about the conference and a lot of problems ensued. Emma Lou Thayne is on the firing line evidently and trying to salvage things. But the clock cannot be turned back.

I often found a way to derive humor from heartbreak. My little series of booklets—funny jottings that began with The Busy Bishop's Notebook*—had recently added* The Ready Relief Society Sister's Notebook *and had entries like this:*

"Interview Sister G. to find out why she's still depressed. Visit their trailer and talk to each of her 12 children to see if they know.

If not, call her husband in Alaska for his opinion."

May 2, 1977

Must write down something one of the Hilton girls said at our brainstorming session. Not funny; tragic. She was out with this boy named Charlie, and he wanted to hold her hand. She didn't want to. Charlie said, "I hold the priesthood and therefore I make the decisions. It's up to me to decide whether or not I want to hold your hand, and you have nothing to say about it." I quizzed her about his exact wording and she swore that it was accurate. And that he was not joking.

May 23, 1977

Friday night I did my big program for the Stake Relief Society. Afterwards several men came up, obviously both disturbed and moved by "The Steward," my long narrative poem about the man who cultivates his orchard and stunts the growth of his wife. One man in complete seriousness asked me how I am able to write critical things like that and still be accepted in the Church. I told him he could suggest to the stake president, who was standing at his elbow, that I am a dangerous woman. President Hilton replied that he thought the whole thing was just beautiful.

June 30, 1977

Just now I called my friend Jan Tyler. Last weekend was Utah's International Women's Year Conference. Every state held one. Jan was head of the coordinating committee, appointed by the Governor's Committee on the Status of Women. Held in the Salt Palace. Wanting a broad representation of the state's citizenry, they invited all the organizations they knew of to send women to participate, including the LDS Relief Society. About 2,000 women were expected. Just days before the conference Apostle Ezra Taft Benson and Relief Society General President Barbara Smith (who was, of course pressed by the Brethren) contacted all of the wards in Utah and assigned them to send all the women they could to the conference and to reject every proposal. 13,870 women showed up, the vast majority Mormon women. Buses arrived from everywhere in the state, often with a man at the helm with a bullhorn, directing the streams of women and giving instructions. There was disorder in the plenary and in all the sessions, often with women shouting down the presenters. Jan was devastated, spent a lot of time in tears.

The New York Times *ran an article headlined, "Mormon Turnout Overwhelms Women's Conference in Utah," and reported one feminist saying, "It was like a war, only they had atomic weapons and we had words. The Mormon women outnumbered us ten to one. They ran the whole thing. I've never been so rudely treated in my life." Don LeFevre, a spokesman for the Mormon Church, acknowledged that the Relief Society had encouraged its membership to take part in the convention "and vote for correct principles. We don't make any excuses for our women's participation. We're proud of them. Other women's groups could probably take a note from their book."*

The Church's anti-ERA engine continued to storm across the country, and many believe this may have been the decisive factor in the ultimate defeat of the Equal Rights Amendment.

July 15, 1977

Finished a poem about Mother in Heaven; don't know what will come of it.

A Motherless House

I live in a Motherless house
a broken home.

How it happened I cannot learn.

When I had words enough to ask
"Where is my Mother?"
no one seemed to know
and no one thought it strange
that no one else knew either.

I live in a Motherless house.

They are good to me here
but I find that no kindly
patriarchal care eases the pain.

I yearn for the day
Someone will look at me and say
"You certainly do look like your Mother."

I walk the rooms, search the closets
look for something that might have
belonged to Her:
a letter, a dress, a chair.

Would She not have left a note?

I close my eyes and work to
bring back Her touch, Her face.

Surely there must have been
a Motherly embrace
I can call back for comfort.

I live in a Motherless house
Motherless and without a trace.

Who could have done this?

Who would tear an unweaned infant
From its Mother's arms and clear the place
Of every souvenir?

I live in a Motherless house.

I lie awake and listen always for the word
That never comes, but might.

I bury my face
In something soft as a breast.

I am a child
Crying for my Mother in the night.

Actually quite a bit came of that poem, now in my book Finding Mother God. *My friend Maxine Hanks, Mormon scholar who was excommunicated in 1993 for her feminism and later rejoined the Church, told me that hearing me read that at a BYU event in 1981 was a life-changing moment for her, the first powerful thing she'd heard that spoke the truth on this subject.*

July 17, 1977

I wrote a little song last night—"Heavenly Mother's Lullaby." Tonight I put my four children on my waterbed and sang it to them. Emily said it was very nice:

I close all the curtains,
I turn out the light,
I tuck the night around you.
Your toys are away now,
The day's in its drawer.
My arms once more have found you.

Chorus:
Sleep, sleep, sleep will bring you home.
Once a day from faraway I gently bring you home.
I gently bring you home.

We'll stop and remember why you went away,
Why you won't stay forever.
We'll smile at your good times, we may dry some tears.
We'll plan the years together.

Chorus.

You will not recall it, you'll wake with the dawn.
Your life goes on in daylight.
But there may be something, the drift of a dream,
A thought that seems to stay bright.

Chorus.

August 15, 1977

While in Utah I went to Sundance twice to see my *I Believe in Make Believe*, based on Grimm's fairy tales. This is the second family musical Sundance summer theatre has produced written by me and musician friend J.A.C. Redford. The first was *Don't Count Your Chickens Until They Cry Wolf*, based on Aesop's fables. Such fun!

Finally got in touch with Aileen Clyde, one of the women on the committee that I too was on before we moved out of Utah, organized by General Relief Society President Barbara Smith. Aileen is such a great woman. We visited for nearly an hour, mostly on the International Women's Year events. The IWY is sponsored by the United Nations to call attention to the status of women throughout the world.

There was to be a conference in each of the states, then a national conference, then an international conference to be held in Mexico. Utah's IWY Conference was a total disaster, she said, and polarized the women of the state as never before. She felt that the Church was used shamelessly by the extreme conservatives in the state. The week before the IWY conference was a meeting of Barbara Smith's committee. They went over all the resolutions to be brought up at the IWY and had some challenging discussion on some of them. The last resolution was about the ERA and Barbara asked Aileen to comment on that. The General Authorities of the Church and Barbara Smith had all made public statements against it.

Aileen took a deep breath and dived in. "I have felt all along on this committee that I was not being entirely open. In my heart I am for the ERA and I do not see all of the terrible things coming that the opponents predict if it is passed. Sister Smith, would you be willing to tell us the real reason why the Church is against it? There *must* be *some* reason."

Barbara Smith's response was: "I believe the Brethren feel it would weaken the position of the priesthood." So she will admit this at last, if only to herself and a few trusted others. This has been absolutely obvious to me all along: the fear of attack upon male authority.

After the IWY played out, Barbara Smith and her committee had a lengthy meeting up the canyon. Barbara has become very fond of the committee and trusts them a lot. She said that for two years now she has been hearing things from them that were so painful she didn't want to hear them, but she's very grateful now for what she's learned. She said, in essence, that she has, during her time in office as General President of the Relief Society, been representing the Brethren to the women of the Church. And now she must find a way to represent the women of the Church to the Brethren.

This fear of weakening patriarchal authority felt so unlike the feeling I had only four years prior with Elders Holland, Hanks, Faust, and Perry when they requested that I meet with them and tell them how they could better serve the young women of the Church. These men were open, truly searching, facing hard truths, appreciative of what I said, wanting things to be better.

October 4, 1977

President N. Eldon Tanner, Counselor in the First Presidency, quoted from my song "Look for the Little Light," in General Conference, mentioning *My Turn on Earth* and my name. "Look for that bright little, right little light inside—helping you to see your way ..." That may help to dispel some of the rumors about my excommunication. Lex received the story twice, and other of my friends have as well. It's probably been as widespread as the rumor about my divorce, both of which are untrue. Mormons do love to pass on gossip.

Gerald was reading to us from "The Essene Gospel of Peace," in which Jesus is speaking of our Heavenly Mother. Aaron, *six year-old* Aaron, volunteered that we ought to pray to our Mother as well as our Father. In my private prayers I generally address both, but I've been reluctant to do it with others, even my children.

October 9, 1977

Last night after the movie we had a conversation that sparked something about the Church and about us, and Gerald exploded—like I have never seen him do before. It led into the first conversation we've had in months about the Problem. He feels on trial. I feel in jeopardy. Gerald is working his head off at the restaurant. He called me twice from work today. I'm a little on edge.

Gerald had been working at Scott's Seafood and had risen rapidly in the company. Eventually he became a Junior Partner. He had, some months ago, taken an apartment in San Francisco, which was better for his work and also, we both knew, was a step toward the inevitable.

October 21, 1977

Today I bought a car! It's a yellow Volvo station wagon, 1973, in very good condition. I am grateful, grateful, grateful. I deserve a car. Never have we owned two cars. Often I have been stranded. What a happy thing, to own a car.

October 25, 1977

Later in the day the children and I wrote letters and drew pictures for Marilza, our girl in Brazil to whom we send $15 a month through "World Vision." And then we went to visit a rest home. I had called one on Oak Park Ave. and asked if they had anyone there who needed a visitor to talk to, read to them, play a game with or anything.

"No," she said. "I can't think of anyone like that." Fifty patients? And not one needs a visitor? So I called another rest home. The girl said yes, they would love to have us come. So we all went and spent a couple of hours. They were delighted to have us. "Are these children all yours? Aren't you lucky? Four such beautiful children." The boys played checkers and dominoes with an old man. I read a woman's prayer book to her. I read a few poems to Lillian. We will go back again. I would like to develop the children's habit of helpfulness.

For years, after or before church on the first Sunday of the month, the children and I went to visit Lillian and Geneva, who were in separate rooms. The women couldn't believe we were actually coming back. How they loved us. The children didn't complain; they knew that we were doing something important. And an added incentive was that after the visit we would stop at Baskin-Robbins for an ice cream cone. I know, breaking the Sabbath. But it was a good tradeoff.

The year 1977 ended with some comfort in my heart about The Woman Question, knowing I was in such a strong sisterhood of good, smart, questioning women. There was sadness, too, disappointment that there had to be such division between good members of the Church over this. And regarding my own journey I found myself on somewhat stronger ground.

October 20, 1977

This morning I wrote a poem—on the theme that I and all Mormons must be pioneers. I like it. I am seeing my position in kind of a new light these days. I feel some poems coming that might help to bridge a gap and soothe a pain.

PIONEERS

My people were Mormon pioneers.
Is the blood still good?
They stood in awe as truth
Flew by like a dove
And dropped a feather in the West.
Where truth flies you follow
If you are a pioneer.

I have searched the skies
And now and then

Another feather has fallen.
I have packed the handcart again
Packed it with the precious things
And thrown away the rest.

I will sing by the fires at night
Out there on uncharted ground
Where I am my own captain of tens
Where I blow the bugle
Bring myself to morning prayer
Map out the miles
And never know when or where
Or if at all
I will finally say,
"This is the place."

I face the plains
On a good day for walking.
The sun rises
And the mist clears.
I will be all right:
My people were Mormon pioneers.

12

ENDINGS

January 3, 1978

These years are like little ticks of a clock—another is here before the last is gone and you can neither grasp them nor grasp what they are all about.

What has my 1977 brought to me? Or I brought to it? I believe I'm in a better place inside than I have ever been before. I feel a strength that is so welcome and will be so very much needed. It was a good year with the kids. A good year financially—something over forty thousand grossed on my own. I suppose 1977 is a year in which I experienced some distancing emotionally from the Church.

My dear Trevor Southey came on Friday night and stayed over; he's here checking out some galleries. Because of some comments he was making I said, "But Trevor, what does that mean about the only true Church?" His reply: "Carol Lynn, I have ceased to believe there is such a thing. I think the only true thing is human kindness." In his youth, Trevor was a very enthusiastic convert and the Church was a great blessing to him.

January 5, 1978

Gerald and I continue to discuss the Problem. He understands that it will probably become necessary for us to separate. Gerald is (my words, not his) seeking after his Pearl of Great Price, for which he will sell all that he has. Including me. Today I feel some anger. Last night I felt the pain. But there is still quite a lot of the strength. How I pray it will continue.

January 13, 1978

These are tumultuous days. I am optimistic; I am in despair. I am alive inside; I am entirely dead. I think I can do it; I know that I can't. I know what is right; I wonder if I know anything.

Wrote a poem this morning, "Trial Number Five." Of all the trials I have been horrified of, it has been this one. Did I draw it to myself for that very reason? Must I learn that I can face it, go on in spite of it, discover something important? I am not being shaken by the shoulders; I am being tossed from wall to wall.

TRIAL NUMBER FIVE

Carefully they laid out on the table
Trials one, two, three,
Four, five and six.

"Choose one," they said.

"Oh, any," she cried, with a horror
Born of the best of Halloweens,
"Any but number five.
It would kill me.
I promise you I would not survive."

They thanked her graciously,
Escorted her out,
Then gift-wrapped, addressed,
And labeled "Special delivery"
Trial number five—

Sent with love from
Those whose assignment it is
To make sure you know
That you can go
Through trials one, two,
Three, four, ninety-nine,
Or five—
And, incredibly,
Come out alive.

January 30, 1978

Jan Tyler called and told me that Reba Keele, BYU professor, is having a terrible time. Her superiors at the Y informed her that while they were not firing her, she could look forward to no advancement at all as a consequence of her voting in favor of the ERA at the IWY national convention at Houston to which she was a delegate.

February 5, 1978

What am I doing? I am thinking very seriously about buying a house! My home teacher, a real estate agent, took me out to see houses because I told him that when I get rich I intend to buy. We drove directly up to this house—Cornwall Court. Five bedrooms upstairs, a nice living area, lovely brick fireplace, attractive kitchen, a little balcony off the master bedroom—and just a three-minute walk from lovely green hills. The asking price is $129,000. I love it! What if?

February 15, 1978

I did it! I bought the house. In my name and with my own money, thanks to my excellent share of royalties from Lex's Western States tour with our musical *My Turn on Earth*. It's very unusual for me to make a quick decision like this, but it has all gone like clockwork.

My great-grandfather, George Warren Sirrine, had a strong reputation throughout the West as a healer. I've heard stories all my life of people calling for his gift. Especially if people were injured and bleeding—or even valuable horses—a message would be sent to George Warren, describing who, what, and where, and remarkably the bleeding would stop or the injury move toward healing. I'd heard these stories, but never from someone who had experienced it.

March 13, 1978

While visiting my brother Warren in Salt Lake, I heard him tell of meeting a Sirrine relative there who had a story about his own healing. I grabbed a tape recorder and we went over to meet him and his wife. When he was ten he was cutting a watermelon, which burst and let the knife go into his wrist. It cut two veins and he was bleeding profusely. George Warren was nearby and came and touched the hand and said, "It'll be all right now," and the bleeding stopped altogether. And I recorded Aunt Mamie telling a few stories that were similar. Wonderfully interesting.

Visited by telephone with Leonard Arrington on Thursday. He has a new book coming out soon with Knopf, a one-volume history of the Church for non-members, *The Mormon Experience: A History of the Latter-day Saints.* He said it's even more objective than Donna Hill's book through Doubleday about Joseph Smith. I asked if he expects it to make any waves. He said he's sure there will be some. He told me a sad observation he is making about some of the women in the Church, that they are just withdrawing to a position of silence and not speaking out as they had before. He does not like this.

I mustered the courage to ask Leonard some pointed questions. We have talked rather frankly before. He had volunteered when we were talking about his book that when Joseph Smith first reported his First Vision it was quite of a different nature than what we've made of it. It was a personal visitation, assuring Joseph that he was forgiven for whatever he was concerned about. I asked, "Does it ever occur to you that maybe—just maybe—all the visionaries, Joseph Smith and the multitudinous others who have had glimpses into the other side, were simply allowed to peek in and then given their free will as to how they interpreted and what they did with it? Maybe some wrote a book from it—some organized a church out of it."

He said sure, that occurs to him. "We're not as utterly unique as we like to believe," he said. "Something like an ant going along carrying a little dust speck, which he believes is the whole world. It's a great church, and I'm glad we've got it."

Had a pleasant trip home. Saw Cleon Skousen on the plane and went out of my way to speak to him. He was very pleasant, said how he and his family had been enjoying my humor notebooks.

I did not report here on hearing Daniel Ludlow speak on the Dead Sea Scrolls at the "Know Your Religion" series in Oakland. I asked: "In all the Dead Sea material, is there any mention, as there is in the Nag Hammadi stuff, of a Mother in Heaven? And what do you make of the evidence in the Nag Hammadi material?"

No, he said, there is nothing in the Dead Sea Scrolls. "And the appearance of the doctrine in the Nag Hammadi material shows how truth asserts itself here and there." He went on to say that in the 1960s for the Correlation Committee a thing was done called "The Blue Book." To a question regarding the Mother in Heaven doctrine, they were told it could be regarded as doctrine that we have a Mother in Heaven—but we cannot say that we all have a common Mother in Heaven.

April 6, 1978

A while ago Aaron was begging me for something at the grocery store, a toy of some kind: "Please, Mom, it's for my own good!"

April 16, 1978

Johnny had brought up the subject of his forthcoming baptism and Gerald had been left "in despair." A month from today Johnny will turn eight. I am torn, very torn. Jesus taught baptism—and yet … Johnny had asked Gerald, "Is it true that when I am baptized all my sins will be washed away?" Gerald had to laugh and cry at that. For Johnny, beautiful, beautiful Johnny to think of his sins being washed away. I don't know. I don't know.

I told Gerald that in spite of the things he disagrees with in the Church, I was convinced it had been an excellent force in his life. He finally said, with great pain and tears, "What makes it hurt so much is that I do love the Church. I really do love it. And it detests me."

Shall I finally explain? Shall I finally say it? (The perceptive reader already knows.) I am so weary of being evasive, so tired of protecting myself and Gerald in the eyes of history. I do believe in honesty, though it hurts. Gerald is a homosexual. That is not entirely accurate, for it implies not being able to respond to a woman. Gerald and I have had a sexual relationship that, from what little I read in the national magazines, would make many married couples envious. And yet there is this powerful force that draws him emotionally and physically to men.

April 19, 1978

Before church I took the children over to visit Lillian and Geneva. They are so thrilled when we come, and the kids are so loving and huggy. Emily told me she always remembers Lillian and Geneva in her prayers and reminded me to do so tonight as I said family prayer.

May 7, 1978

I had a good experience speaking at the "Interfaith Celebration" held in Petaluma, Marin County. I was invited some months ago, and broke my retirement to accept. There were nearly 400 people there, from different faiths. They were making special commemoration of Passover, so I began by saying—in my very broken Hebrew—the first two verses of Genesis, then sang a Hebrew song that I learned on the kibbutz. They all loved it. Then I spoke on "We Are One." Used a number of my poems and they went over really well.

May 23, 1978

What would Jesus do? "As I have loved you, love one another." He would not throw Gerald out in anger and pain. He would be unconditionally loving in the pure sense of the word. He would respect Gerald's free agency and help him along the path he truly, truly wants. These are the things I've been working on.

So what is the answer? For nearly four years that question has been in front of me daily. There must be an answer that can bring peace to both Gerald and to me. The answer may be painful, but could it be more painful than the question?

Last night as we went to bed, we talked. We hadn't for some weeks. About us, I mean. I hadn't cried for a long time. I cried, confessed again how the pain is so great I don't know if I can bear it. Gerald was, and is always, kind, and warm, and tried so hard to be helpful. I have accepted the fact that this is not something of Gerald's choice. He would have done anything in his power to avoid bringing me such pain. He has considered, and rejected, suicide. But this Thing is as much a part of him as his legs or his arms. He cannot get away from it—his need to love and be loved by a man. It has always been that way, from his earliest recollections. He truly doesn't see why his having a sexual relationship with a man should interfere in our being able to make our relationship everything we want it to be. Oh, we are so different.

June 9, 1978

Today the Church announced that President Kimball received a revelation granting the priesthood to black men. How do I feel about this? Pleased, but also a little cynical. The Church is absolutely pragmatic. Perhaps God has indeed answered all those prayers that have been sent up regarding this matter, saying perhaps something like, "Look, my dear ones, why are you asking me to change my mind on this? My mind was never against it. It's all your doing. Do what you can to right it." Of course, I could be wrong.

June 23, 1978

This morning I went visiting teaching. I didn't bring up the subject of the new policy, but both my ladies did. Dear Zula thought the new revelation was just wonderful. But she told of calling her sister on the phone to tell her. The sister said, "Oh, no, I don't believe that. Why, their skins have to turn white before they can get the priesthood." My next stop was at Sister C.'s. She thought the new position was great. But her husband's mother had said only, "Well, the whole world's going to hell."

Something Jan told me on the phone: An older group of Mormon feminists (Algie Ballif and others) have been meeting weekly and really getting into some heavy stuff. Jan attended a recent meeting. They were of the feeling that the new stance toward black men may result in an even tighter stance against women, just from some psychological reason, I suppose.

Friday I got a pamphlet from BYU that made me so angry I sat down and wrote a letter to BYU President Dallin Oaks.

> Dear President Oaks:
>
> Just this minute I opened up my invitation to participate in BYU's Development Fund, and I heaved a great sigh. "Oh, no," I thought, "I had believed that the Y was picking up on President Oaks's challenge to include women more fully in the life of the university."
>
> What do we see in this fine patriarchal pamphlet? Photos of six men using their skills to benefit the world. The only female representation is the tiny, incapacitated girl in the bottom picture receiving help. The message is very clear.
>
> I know this is not your personal fault. But I am asking you to send this on to your development office with this message from me: when you can represent to me that BYU is a place that truly desires to develop woman as well as man, then I will be thrilled to send in my contribution. Until then I'll hang on to the envelope.
>
> My very best personal regards to you, President Oaks.
>
> Sincerely,
> Carol Lynn Pearson

July 25, 1978

I have withdrawn further from Gerald than has ever happened before. The energy that would be required to participate in the relationship is just superhuman. Gerald is a true polygamist (see, the threat has followed me even here). This is not fair to either of us. He and I both deserve more than that. Through the peep-holes of my protection, I still see him: that amazingly beautiful, wonderful, desirable person that I love so much. He deserves much more than I can give him. He deserves everything. In the moments when I am really true to myself, I hope he gets it.

I fasted again—as I have how many other times—for some good miracle to be worked in the lives of those I love. For Gerald. And for me.

August 18, 1978

Wednesday night Jan called me from Salt Lake. Sitting in her apartment with her was the woman who got into the papers the other day by standing up to Orrin Hatch in the Senate hearings, Sonia Johnson. They wanted my help in phrasing a news release they were to make the following day. They were also inviting Mormon women and friends to join in a daily prayer or meditation for the national passage of the ERA.

I added the sentence: "We believe the time has come for all the children of our Heavenly Parents to regard one another with equal respect and reverence." Hatch and Garn plan to filibuster to keep out the vote for extension of passage of the ERA. If they do, the Mormon women for ERA in the area, dressed in white, will begin a fast on the Capitol grounds, and not leave until the filibuster ends. Simultaneously Mormon women in Utah will be fasting on the steps of the State capitol. Almost never do dramatic things like this really come off. I must say I would like to see it. Amazing.

August 28, 1978

I came home last night to find a message from the local blood bank here that they desperately needed some of my A-negative blood for a man having open heart surgery on Monday. So I went in the next morning and gave blood. It was a curiously thrilling experience to be really needed in some way by some other human being whom I will never know.

September 25, 1978

Gerald's anniversary gift, a poem to me, signed:
To my dearest Blossom,
In answer to your question
"How do you suppose it is that
We chose to live this life together?"

With dearest love,
Gerald
September 9, 1978

The Unmasking

It wouldn't matter what costume
We wore to this party,

Or to any other for that matter.
We would still betray the disguise.
Tracing our soul's unfailing ties
We would wander through any crowd
Seeking and seeking until finally
Hand in hand, arm in arm
We would dance together again.
We would embrace and dance again
In spite of continual masquerades,
Dancing but never knowing that
Old lovers from times and times before
Are dancing within the dance,
Are touching hands within the hands,
Are together again and always,
Unrecognized, undetected, unremembered,
Again and again and still again,
Regardless of forgetfulness,
Regardless of unknowing,
Regardless of every new mask—
Every new disguise,
Are together always and again,
Are always together again and again
Loved, loved, loved.

October 15, 1978

Just a minute ago I got a phone call from Marilyn Arnold, assistant to the President at BYU. She wanted to apologize to me for the letter that I had received from a Sharon M. at the Development Office. President Oaks had sent my letter and a copy of the brochure to a number of people, with a pointed memo from himself upholding my position. The head of Development wrote back to him a very defensive memo. It was clear to both Marilyn and the President that a sore spot had been jabbed and that it was a very, very deep thing.

Regarding the letter she was calling about. A week or so ago I received a letter from Sharon M., identifying herself as the woman who had written the brochure and really coming down on me hard for criticizing it. She suggested that instead of a nit-picky letter to President Oaks, I might use my literary skill in writing something to inspire women to break out of their stereotypes. I especially liked that part; why didn't I think of it before?

I decided to send the letter on to Oaks's office as they need to know what goes out on BYU stationery. Today's call from Marilyn Arnold was in response to that.

At the end of our conversation I said, "I hear the ultra-conservative Phyllis Schlafly is coming. How'd you manage that?"

"Oh, please," she said. "I think I'll leave town. I talked myself green against having her come, but to no avail. It's one of the things I will have to live with. It's for political awareness week, and we've asked her not to talk about women." Marilyn is a very bright, warm, good person. I was pleased to have her call me.

Last evening I went to the buffet opening of Scott's Seafood Grill and Bar at the Embarcadero. Gerald has been in charge of the kitchen and now owns 7% of the place. About twelve thousand was spent last night on free liquor and canapes. I saved them money by drinking coke. The place looks lovely.

At eleven Gerald called here; said he just wanted to tell me how much he appreciated me, that of all the hundreds of guests there that night I was the one he was most glad to see. I was happy he called, happy that some of the painful edge seems gone from my feelings. I do believe the worst is over.

October 30, 1978

I bought a present for Gerald—a charming little sand castle—real sand arranged to be permanent. And I wrote a poem to go with it.

For Gerald, a Chaser of Rainbows,
A Builder of Castles in the Sand

He builds his castles
In the sand
Despite the tide.
No, because of the tide
For he must see walls break
And if the tide did not do it,
He would.

I think him mad, of course.
Why build except to live within?
But then,
There are some, like him,
Who cannot breathe
With anything between them
And the sky.

And so he goes to the ocean
Every possible day,
Where the tide takes care
Of the threat of things that stay
And he builds his castles.

I saw one.
It was beautiful.
Beautiful—
And gone.

November 2, 1978

Two nights ago I had a lovely dream. In it I have arranged to make a telephone call to my mother who is now dead, and also to my Heavenly Mother. It all feels very natural to me.

I felt that Gerald and I had done everything we could to find a way to remain married. I had read everything I could about healing from homosexuality, contacted organizations that seemed promising. Nothing. I had contacted Wardell Pomeroy, a psychotherapist and one of the co-authors of the Kinsey Report, who happened to live now in San Francisco. He told me he wasn't seeing clients any more, but as we were Mormons and he had a special interest in the problems associated with that religion, he would see us. We had a session together and then each of us in private. I asked Dr. Pomeroy if he knew of any methods that were successful in changing one's sexual orientation. He assured me "there is no change for the homosexual." He told me that Gerald would be placed as a "4" on the Kinsey scale of 1-6—that it was possible for him to have a sexual relationship with a woman, but that his primary needs would always be toward another man. We began to make plans toward the inevitable.

November 10, 1978

Elouise Bell called me last night with more depressing news. Louise Degn, who was the woman that interviewed me for KSL (the Church-owned station), had spent something like a year preparing a documentary on depression among Mormon women. It was advertised in the papers and everything. Elouise turned it on to watch and found the announcement that the show had been cancelled. She was furious. Depressed and furious.

I called Louise on the phone to give her a word of good cheer. She said that someone in the station who was a friend of Barbara Smith had invited the Relief Society Presidency to see the film. Barbara was going to let it go with someone prepared to rebuttal if necessary. But one of her board members started calling General Authorities, and soon the whole thing was put under wraps. Of course depressing. Mormon women have enormous cause for depression. Cancelled. Just like the film. We are not only negated. We are cancelled.

November 28, 1978

I must look outward for a moment from my own personal difficulties to record the incredible events that are happening in the world. All last week has been the astonishing horror of the mass suicide-murder tragedy of the

People's Temple group in Guyana. Over 900 people dead. What can happen when a group of people turn over their conscience and their own reason and responsibility to an "authority" outside of themselves.

In family night last night, I stressed as hard as I could to my children that on matters of conscience you do not give up your own feeling to *anyone* else in the world. You do what you know to be right regardless of the instructions of anyone to the contrary. Finally you must trust the light that is inside of you. Always.

Worse and worse. Yesterday morning the Mayor of San Francisco, George Moscone, and a supervisor, Harvey Milk, were shot and killed in City Hall by a former supervisor, Dan White. I called Gerald this morning to give him my sympathies and tell him I had been thinking about him through it all. Harvey Milk was the leading homosexual public figure. His success meant a great deal to the gay community. Last night on TV was a scene of thousands and thousands of gay marchers with candles and a men's choir. Gerald had been with the choir. He told me that just last week he had eaten lunch with Mr. Milk.

Some time earlier Gerald had requested that the children call him "Gerald" instead of "Dad," supposedly because he wanted them to see him as more than just his "role." The kids were reluctant, and I did not approve the move, but gradually it came to be.

December 4, 1978

Gerald came out Saturday about noon. We had a full weekend of fun things planned to serve as a context into which to give the children the new information. We put Katy down for a nap, sat in the family room by the fire, ate chocolate chip cookies and talked. I took the initiative.

"You children will be glad to know that Gerald's work schedule is easing off somewhat, and he will be able to come out and spend more time with us. He's missed being able to be with you and we've missed having him too. Gerald will keep his apartment in the city. But we're still a family. We will always be a family. But there is one change coming up that you children need to know about. Gerald and I have decided that as we go through the rest of this life that we can help each other best and be happier as best friends instead of as married people, as husband and wife. Does that sound okay to you?"

Everybody nodded. We continued talking. Finally when the word "divorce" came up it sort of sunk in. Emily was the only one who really grasped what it meant. She was sitting on Gerald's lap in my wooden rocking chair. She looked stunned, confused, amazed. She cried a little.

I went on to assure them that Gerald and I didn't have bad feelings toward each other. We instructed them not to talk about this to anybody yet—to say nothing at all at school or church or anywhere. Johnny said, "Not even at show and tell?"

Gradually the children will understand the real story. Right now they will just have to have faith in us. Of course it's confusing to them. They have never seen us fighting or even arguing. They have never heard either one of us speaking unkindly of the other.

After we finished our discussion and the children left the room, Gerald and I were hugging. Aaron ran back in and said, "Let me join you."

We are blessed.

Blessed—but not without pain. Soon there was an event so poignant that I can never forget it.

December 15, 1978

Gerald had invited me to come and see the Winter Concert of the choir he had joined, the San Francisco Gay Men's Chorus. I was reluctant to go, but I knew it meant a lot to Gerald, so I went. I took BART, Bay Area Rapid Transit, and then a streetcar. I went up toward the front of the theater and sat down by a woman. I thought to myself, her presence here must be a whole story, just like mine is. After a few minutes I turned to her and said, "Do you have someone singing tonight?"

"My son," she said. "And you?"

"My husband," I said.

She gave a short laugh and we didn't speak further.

The Gay Freedom Marching Band played first. And then came the choir. From the back of the hall, marching down all the aisles, came the choir. Perhaps seventy or eighty fine-looking young men in white shirts, dark pants, and a red carnation pinned at their left. They were all smiling and singing "If My Friends Could See Me Now."

The instant I heard those voices I began to cry. And as I watched the men take their places on the stage I felt as if I must burst with the incredible poignancy of it all. I spotted Gerald, right in the center, smiling and with all his good light shining. Gerald in white. Gerald with white all around him. Gerald with light shining on him and from him. I had seen him in white many times before—in the temple in white—in the delivery room in white—and now in white in the San Francisco Gay Men's Choir. The pain and the heartbreak and the complete irrationality of the whole thing washed over me and I was as helpless as a cork in the ocean.

13

THE EXCOMMUNICATION OF SONIA JOHNSON: BURNED AT THE STAKE CENTER

January 8, 1979

Had a really good evening with the children tonight. Good work with each on the piano. Good private time with each. Good family night, reading more of our book *Return From Tomorrow*, a book about a man's death, glimpse of heaven, and coming back to his body. Emily is especially excited about the information these travelers bring, that we are mostly on earth to learn about love. We learned and sang the first verse of "Lead, Kindly Light." I've always loved that song. I told them that someday in the future when their world looks very dark they would remember that song and remember our singing it together by the fire, and it would bring them great comfort.

January 12, 1979

Afternoon. I must record a dream I had when I took a nap a short while ago.

DREAM: MY MOTHER IN A BOX ON THE SHELF. I have come to our old house in Provo because I have learned that my mother is still alive and I want to see her. My brothers are there. They tell me that our mother has been in a coma for a long time, and indicate a little room like a closet. I go in and look around and cannot see her. I then see a box up on a shelf. I climb up and look in it. There is my mother, sort of shriveled up, but her face is still life-size and recognizable. As I look at her she opens her eyes. She is very glad to see me and says, "Well, it's about time you got here."

Suddenly I was able to interpret it very clearly. I am telling myself to get back to my project on The Mother. It has, for about two years now, been the thing that I yearned to work on, but put off. Symbols:

Our old house—History.

The Mother: The female in our Source.

In a box: Literally all my research, all my files are assembled in one cardboard box.

On a shelf: I have shelved this project.

She is still alive: The project is still viable.

I have taken too long to come to Her: The Mother says, "No more putting it off. Get to it."

I find this dream terribly interesting—even moving. Okay. The time has come.

I've not mentioned much about this project. It's been on my mind consistently. I want to do a substantial but not terribly scholarly work that is poetic, popular and moving—turning our hearts to our Mother. I don't know just how, but it will come.

January 26, 1979

Talked to Gerald on the phone last night. He's been very ill with a cold and of course continued exhaustion from work. The night before he had been to a rehearsal of the choir. As he left the place and was walking toward his apartment two "punks" drove by, spat, and got him right in the face. Harassment of the gay community in this and other forms, many of them incredibly ugly, are commonplace. It is, of course, an outrage.

February 1, 1979

Sat down with a notebook to see what might come.

The Days We Shared

They were generating days,
The days we shared,
Bright
As when two fires combine.

I leave
Wearing some of your light,
As you leave
Wearing some of mine.

Having good days with the children. Had Johnny's cub scouts this afternoon (have I mentioned I'm den mother?) I'm teaching them "Don't Be Anything Less Than Everything You Can Be" from the musical "Snoopy" for the blue and gold dinner on Tuesday. Also took Emily to ballet. Did piano with each of them. "Mork and Mindy" on TV. Prayer. Lullabies. A little bedtime talk with each one. I'm much more a participant in all that's going on here than I was with Gerald around. Somehow his high level of energy overwhelmed me so that I capitulated on many levels and stayed in the shadows, even in some ways with the children. As Napoleon Hill said: "In every adversity there is the seed of a greater benefit."

February 12, 1979

First day of BYU's Women's Conference. At lunch with Elouise Bell, Jan Tyler and Emma Lou Thayne, I learned that Emma Lou was dreadfully upset by the panel she had just participated in. It was on education for education's sake. And one of the panel members, who announced herself as the mother of 11 children, took it upon herself to make her contribution a testimony to the fact that motherhood was the only needful thing in a woman's life. She said she had fasted and prayed and knew that she was telling the women what the Lord wanted them to hear, and now they had heard and were responsible for following it. It served to make the other women look like they were way out of line. "Spiritual blackmail" is what Elouise called it.

Dropped in to see some of my old friends on campus. Talked for an hour to Blaine Porter, still head of Human Development and Family Relations. He and I have always felt, in spite of rather infrequent visits, quite close to each other. We talked for a bit about the Church; he is as frustrated as I on many counts, but has not taken the time or grasped the courage (according to his own admission) to think many things through. Gave him my poem "Pioneers" and he loved it, wanted a copy. I decided to tell him about me and Gerald; in fact I told him the whole story. I wanted to talk about homosexuality in the Church; I knew that in his position, as Dean of the College of Family Living, he would be more knowledgeable than most. He was very much in agreement with me that the official Church position was damaging and archaic. He was very interested in the fact that Gerald and I are working things out with such good feelings between us. He is doing a book on divorce, and wants to talk with me further on how it can be handled better than it is. So often, he said, both parties do so much to destroy each other.

While there I placed a call to Gerald's parents in Murray. He had been there to talk with them and told them everything. We were both very apprehensive about it. But it had gone really well. He cried as he told me that it was "wonderful," that he's missed so many years with them through fear. "I'm so angry at Spencer W. Kimball I could punch him in the nose. He has no right to make me and everybody like me feel dirty. I should have talked with my parents years ago."

At the conference I learned that Loneta M., League of Women's Voters member and active ERA supporter, had gone to her bishop for her temple recommend, been given it, and then the next week the stake president wrote her a letter telling her that he had changed his mind and that her recommend had been rescinded.

That evening at Jan Tyler's house she and I entertained Grace and Leonard Arrington for supper. Pleasant visit. Such good people. He seemed fairly guarded, though, in talking about some of the difficulties I think he may have been through. He was thrilled on the pronouncement about our black members. I asked if there wasn't a direct tie in it to the opening of the Brazilian temple. "Of course," he said.

February 28, 1979

The next morning Emma Lou Thayne and I arrived early at the chapel so we could visit. Her perceptions of the Church are not far from my own. She never really grew up with a concept of "the one and only true," and has never entertained that idea. She uses the Church as she wants to, takes the good, and doesn't let the rest concern her. I took the occasion to let her know what is going on in my life at present. She is aware of the incredible situation of Mormon homosexuals, knows some, and has wished she could get the ear of someone at the top to let them know what great damage is being done by the Church to these people.

March 6, 1979

The KSL TV documentary on depression among Mormon women that Louise Degn produced finally was shown, I understand, and received widespread acclaim, lots of women writing in saying what a relief it was not to feel so alone. As for me? I do not believe in work, work, work, worry, worry, worry about not quite making it to the celestial kingdom. I believe in happiness. I believe in peace of mind. I have no place for fear and trembling.

March 18, 1979

Have I mentioned Trevor Southey is here? I want to write down the whole story, so I asked his permission. I guess I see myself now as a documentor of the situation of the Mormon homosexual.

Gerald told me some time ago that Trevor is gay. And Trevor and I have talked about it in the last year. Right now he and his wife are at the same point that Gerald and I were a year ago. Trevor has long since rejected the "only true Church" concept; but here he is in the incredible challenge of being a homosexual in an "only true" framework that has absolutely no place for one.

The Church is pressuring into marriage people that should never be married and is doing a heinous thing in this. And in making all those who have tried to change and tried and tried and tried again feel they are miserable failures, sinners. Trevor is now submitting to a humiliating experience—going to counseling from a BYU professor, Alan Bergin, who is supposed to be an expert on change.

Trevor is here to do a portrait of the children. Last year I arranged with him to do it. It's very exciting to see it shaping up. And the children love it. Emily is in ballet attire and position; Little Katy floating in front of her. The two boys are together as if "just called from wrestling," according to Trevor.

In 2020 Dr. Bergin publicly apologized for the harm in which he was complicit. Using the LDS pulpit and the influence of LDS General Authorities, Bergin had taught that self-discipline and a mixed orientation marriage would successfully overcome the problem of homosexuality. "I was among the traditionalists who believed that homosexuality was a disorder and that it could be treated and changed to some degree," he wrote. "I regret being part of a professional, religious, and public culture that marginalized, pathologized, and excluded LGBT+ persons. As a father of two gay sons and grandfather of a gay grandson, I've been given a personal education that has been painful and enlightening." See Tyler Lefevor, "Expert's apology teaches us to listen to LGBT persons," Salt Lake Tribune, *July 24, 2020.*

March 20, 1979

Tonight I read to the kids another chapter in *A Wrinkle in Time*, fascinating story, very spiritual. I let Johnny and Emily stay up for a few minutes after Aaron and Katy were in bed. I told them, "Do you know what would make me happier than anything in the whole world?"

"What?" they asked.

"If my four children, in whatever they do with their lives, would help to bring more light to the world and not contribute anything to darkness—that would make me happier than anything else."

"Hu-uh," said Johnny. "I know what would make you happier than that. If everybody, *including* your four children, would bring light instead of darkness." I told him he was right, of course.

Had an interesting conversation with Trevor last night. In 1968 one of his gay friends, who had one semester left to finish his Master's, was called in and suspended, and told he had to repent and write a weekly letter to apostle Spencer W. Kimball in order to be allowed to finish. So he wrote weekly letters, telling of his repentance, his change, his success in overcoming. All of this was completely fabricated. President Kimball used this correspondence in his book that came out the following year, *The Miracle of Forgiveness*, illustrating the fact that gay people can successfully change. I had Trevor telephone his friend last night to check out the story again, because I knew I wanted to write it down. The above facts were verified, and it's probably a story that happened over and over.

March 22, 1979

My dear friend L. called from Salt Lake. He said people from "Sixty Minutes" are very, very interested in covering the subject of gay Latter-day Saints. There is evidently a lot of underhanded, inhumane stuff going on. He said that last week there was another suicide of a young man, directly attributable to some advice one of the General Authorities had given him. This is the second suicide L. knows of that this leader has been a factor in.

"This has to stop," I said.

"You're damn right," he replied. I told him that I knew that there would finally be some sense made of why I had spent the last twelve years in my marriage situation. I may someday be part of whatever must happen on this subject in Mormondom. And I am not unwilling to do that. I know that I am here to be part of the light that I wrote of in my last entry, and I find it quite exciting.

I said to L. on the phone, "We are pioneers, my dear, and right now we're up to our ears in Winter Quarters." He agreed.

April 8, 1979

I took the children out on my balcony and read the last two chapters of *A Wrinkle in Time.* Such a fine book. My voice kept breaking during that wonderful part when Meg pulls her brother back from IT with love. Love is the most important thing in the world. I took up some fruit and biscuits and the kids ate while I read. I had decided to fast today.

Just now I came back from upstairs going from room to room singing lullabies. Katy has to have her three with the light on; then Aaron needs his two with the light off. I went in to Emily and sat on her bed with my guitar and she said, "I don't need a lullaby." So I proceeded to sing her a song about "Everybody needs lullabies and don't ever say to me again that you don't need a lullaby." Dear Emily has pre-adolescent distress these days.

April 18, 1979

Frequently the children and I sing together in the car. And I am liable to break into song at any point. I have been given to understand that I am not to do this when we have another child in the car because it embarrasses my children dreadfully. The other kids giggle at it. Recently this happened:

Johnny: Don't pick up anybody today.

Me: Why not?

Johnny: 'Cause you'll sing and embarrass us.

Me: Well, nobody's in the car now but us. Do you mind if I sing?

Johnny: Okay, but make sure all the windows are closed.

May 6, 1979

Yesterday Emily and I got our ears pierced. Quite a wild and outrageous thing for me to do. She had been begging for some time. She was amazed that I would do it myself. "This whole year's gone crazy," she said. "First, you and Gerald are getting a divorce, and now you're getting your ears pierced."

May 3, 1979

A depressing thing to report. At the Relief Society Luncheon (to which I took three Jell-O salads) I was talking to my friend C., exchanging jokes. She said, "Here's a good one. Do you know what they did with Harvey Milk's ashes? Put them in a *fruit* jar and labeled it powdered *Milk.*" She laughed.

I said, "That's a bad joke."

She replied, "Oh, I can't bring myself to cry over spilled *Milk.*" More laughter. And she went on, "I watched the Donahue show yesterday where he interviewed Masters and Johnson and all those homosexuals. And now I've really got a thing against gays."

"Don't you know any gays?" I asked.

"No. No, I don't." I could have told her that she knows a lot of them, just doesn't know that they're gay. It really did appall me. Right there in Relief Society, whose motto is "Charity Never Faileth."

I had an impulse to shock her, which I did not. Or shame her, which I did not. Or leave the chapel, which I did not. So I just sat there and watched the program put on by our little children from the nursery, about twenty of them all dolled up in circus costumes, and—if statistics are correct—two of which will likely grow up as homosexual, grow up in a community that has neither understanding nor compassion to offer them. Beautiful, beautiful children, whose lives will be turned into anguish by other beautiful children who know not what they do. It continues over and over again through the centuries, crucifixions large and small. And we know not what we do.

Now and then I see the Facebook posts of my friend in the paragraph above. She has been through a great deal in these four decades. I can tell that she is now a wise and compassionate woman. And she loves the work I have done for our gay people.

May 13, 1979

Thursday night was the concert, the San Francisco Gay Men's Chorus, plus other gay musical groups. I sat by Trevor. The chorus sang Gerald's lyrics, set to the music of Jean Sibelius:

From the Silence

Surely, surely from the silence
Breaks the song that we never sang,
Come the words that we never spoke,
The love that we've always hidden.
Once all men feared so to say it,
The love that dare not speak its name.
At last, long last from the silence
Lovers come bringing gifts of song.
Voices sing of manly love.
No more will we hush the singing,
Never more will we hide our love.
No more will our joy be silenced.
Manly love has its melody.
Lovers too have a song to sing.

June 1, 1979

Last night I had some interesting visitors. Sonia Johnson, who is here for the National Organization of Women (NOW) Convention, came with my MIA teacher in the Provo Ninth Ward, Vonda Porter. Sonia is one of the ring-leaders in the "Mormons for ERA" organization, and she called last week, wanting to spend a little time with me. I was, of course, glad to meet her. She is a bright and intense woman, very excited about the work she's doing. She has received, of course, a lot of difficulty from her activities; even her parents have been harassed. I tried to convince Sonia to keep a diary of all her adventures; I think it's terribly important for history to have a good record of all this.

Speaking of records, I spent yesterday going over the edited manuscript of Elouise's and my "Diary" book.

A couple of years prior my dear friend Elouise Bell, author and BYU English professor, had persuaded me to let her utilize my early diaries for a book she wanted to write, showing people how fun and also important diary keeping can be. Bookcraft published it. Our title was Will I Ever Forget This Day? *And of course the answer is yes, you very well may, unless you write it down. Which today I heartily agree with, as I am going through these thousands of pages, sometimes laughing or tearing and saying, "Wow, I'd completely forgotten about that!"*

June 1, 1979

Yesterday I spent an hour with my cub scouts and another den of cub scouts making kites. I am not built for this.

June 8, 1979

On Thursday Theron and Zelda Luke came by from Provo. Spent a couple of hours visiting. I like them very much, and Theron always has some good stories to tell me. We were talking about the press, about the *Provo Herald* and then about the *Daily Universe* at BYU. (He used to be city editor of the *Herald*.) He said, "Oh, here's something interesting. Not long ago the *Universe* ran a series of three articles on homosexuality on BYU campus. I have it from a faculty advisor to the *Universe* that President Dallin Oaks was called in before the Brethren and chewed out for letting those articles be published—more than he'd ever been chewed out for anything that had happened since he took over the presidency of the university."

Isn't that remarkable? Such mild articles. So clearly on the Mormon side: repentance, change, etc. But evidently just the admission in print that there was such a problem at BYU was infuriating to the Brethren.

Friday evening Sonia Johnson called me from back East. Jan had recommended that she read Mary Daly's *Beyond God the Father*. Sonia had just finished it and was totally blown away. "It rings of so much truth to me. And much of it is so beautiful. And I say, 'Yes, yes, that's got to be the way it is.'"

Sonia went on to say that she's entered a new phase of being dealt with. "Until recently my bishop and all the ward members went out of their way to love me and tell me how much they appreciate me. They thought they could love me into repenting and giving up my trouble-making. But now they see that all their love isn't making any difference in my behavior, they don't know what to do with me. Just since I got back the bishop has had all he could do to be civil to me."

Oh, my. Things are at work.

July 9, 1979

Today Jim Conkling (broadcasting executive, head of Capitol Records, Nixon's pick as Director of "Voice of America," an international broadcasting network funded by the U.S.A.), called me from L.A. He has not been able to get the big-name screenwriters that he had hoped for his Joseph Smith film project. So he has talked the backers into a new approach; he wants five competent writers, some in the Church, some out, to each come up with a complete script by the middle of October. Guaranteed guild minimum: $16,000 for script whether they use it or not; if scripts are combined, $50,000 to be divided among writers according to how much of their stuff is used.

I am torn. My feelings about our founding Prophet Joseph Smith are quite ambivalent. Polygamy and other things. And the time it would require. I was clearing my life to get into my "Mother God" project. I told him I must sleep on it.

Walked up in the hills for an hour this evening. So incredibly beautiful up there. A full moon was coming up as I was coming down.

I accepted Jim's offer to write a screenplay on the life of Joseph Smith. The Church itself was the sole sponsor and financier of this project. Soon I traveled to Salt Lake City to do some interviews with historians.

August 23, 1979

I write from Jan's in Salt Lake. An interesting episode I must get down here. Jan had mentioned Deseret Book's latest offering regarding women: *Woman's Divine Destiny*. A few days after being here I picked it up. It is horrendous. On an impulse I called George Bickerstaff at Bookcraft to congratulate him on not publishing that book. He said he had rejected it some eighteen months ago.

Then on another impulse I called Eleanor Knowles at Deseret Book and asked her why in the world Deseret Book put out that book. She said she had not been enthusiastic about it but that the board felt it had some good things and that its point of view seemed to be what the Church is stressing these days. I asked who the Brethren were who oversee Deseret Book. She told me Marvin Ashton and Marion D. Hanks. How could this be? Both of them are enlightened men.

I went to the phone and called Brother Hanks's office. The secretary was very nice, but assured me there was no way he could see me that day or the next morning. I thanked her, hung up and burst into frustrated tears. It has been more than a year since I cried over anything, but I sat there on Jan's bed and sobbed in frustration at being so helpless in the face of something that I care so deeply about.

I called back and explained to the secretary that Brother Hanks and I had talked about some very important issues and that I had information he needed and wanted to have, and that I wanted him to know I was trying to get in touch with him. She called back and said if I could be there right at two that I could see him for a short while. I hurriedly got ready and walked down to the Church Office Building. He greeted me warmly and as we sat down he said he had heard that I had been going through a difficult experience. I told him yes, that was true, and assured him that Gerald, I, and the children are all right. Our conversation went something like this:

Me: I will talk very fast as I know we just have a short time. You will remember, perhaps, that I am a self-appointed defender and protector of Mormon women.

Him (smiling): I had heard something about that.

Me: I received a real blow when I saw Deseret Book's latest offering to Mormon women. And when I learned that you were one of the supervisors there I said to myself, I have to make sure Brother Hanks knows what a mistake this is. Did you read the manuscript of *Woman's Divine Destiny* before it was published?

Him: No, I don't read any of their manuscripts.

Me: I understand. But somebody has to. Somebody must pay attention.

I read him a few of the salient pieces. Like Lorenzo Snow saying something like: "It is harder for wives to learn than it is for husbands, for women have not the degree of light and knowledge that men have." And the part about women having access to the Lord's vast library, but men having the key to the special collections room because they hold the priesthood.

He raised his eyebrows, took note of the page, said he agreed that was a bad way to put it. I also read the analogy of the shoe and the foot—that the man is the foot and the woman the shoe that helps him climb his mountains. He said that was as bad as Rodney Turner's doormat.

Him: I know that President Kimball has a very high regard for his wife.

Me: Yes. But how do you suppose he would react, and all the other Brethren in this building, if when they got to the other side they were told, "Now Brethren, you've all been so faithful and done everything so well that your reward is that in the next world you get to be women."

At this Brother Hanks threw back his head and laughed long and loud. I believe he got my point.

Me: I have a fantasy of gathering together all the men in this building and providing for them what I call "A Walk in the Pink Moccasins" so they can understand what many women in our church experience every day. It's a brief address to the "Boys of Comparable Age" given by "One of the Presiding Sisters." (That term, "of comparable age" is currently used in this way to identify the young people in the Church organization: "deacons and girls of comparable age, priests and girls of comparable age," etc.) Would you like to hear my Walk in the Pink Moccasins?"

Him: "Yes, go ahead."

The following is a little fuller than what I presented that day to Elder Hanks.

"My dear young Brethren, I want first of all to let you know how much our Heavenly Mother loves you. She loves you just as much as She loves her daughters, and I hope you can believe that. What a glorious time it was when our Eternal Mother planned out our existence. The Mother and the Daughter created this world together, and then placed upon it Eve, their crowning creation, the first woman.

But of course our Mother could see that Eve was not complete, that she needed a helpmeet, someone who could love and assist her, and so that's where you come into this glorious plan, my dear young Brethren. Our Mother gave to Eve a worthy companion, Adam, to cherish and to rule over. What a glorious time that was, and how you, dear Brethren, must have rejoiced as you saw the part you were to play.

Study the words of the prophetesses as they have been revealed to you. Be humble and sweet and pure. Follow the Sisters. And keep yourselves clean, that one day one of the fine daughters of our Heavenly Mother might look with favor upon you and lead you to the temple, there to have you sealed to her for time and all eternity, that you might go on to become a priest unto your priestess, adding glory upon glory unto her as she adds glory to the Mother.

For this marvelous purpose you will be called to welcome other of our Mother's precious sons into your family circle to share your responsibilities of peopling worlds in that glorious principle of celestial plural marriage. What a marvelous assignment has been given you, dear Brethren. And in conclusion I want to remind you of the glorious truth revealed to us by one of our Mother's prophetesses—that although we don't know much about him, somewhere there's a Father there! Just think of it, Brethren. Somewhere there's a Father there! How glorious is the role of man!"

Brother Hanks didn't say much; smiled and nodded.

Me: The problem all starts from our having been kidnapped from our Mother, making for ourselves a broken home and being content in it and saying that's the way things ought to be.

Him: How did that happen?

Me: My research tells me that the earliest civilizations worshipped only the Mother (which is no healthier than worshipping only the Father) and then came the "patriarchal overthrow," after which we have only been allowed to see through male eyes. And now it's time for a better balance. I don't blame God for any of this. We've done it to ourselves. I have to have more respect for God than to think that He—She—They came up with a plan like this. Right now I have more confidence and faith in God—more faith in life—than I have ever had.

Him: And how do you feel about Joseph Smith?

Me: I'm very fond of Joseph Smith. (I mentioned all the research I'm doing for the film.) Brother Hanks, are you given the privilege of confidential conversation or do you have to report heresies when you hear them?

Him: I don't report anything.

Me: Well, I have no doubt that Joseph had his spiritual experiences. And that he did his very best to perceive them, to interpret them, and to convey to others what he had experienced. But I also believe that untold thousands of other people have had profound spiritual experiences and done their best to perceive, interpret, and share them.

Him: I do feel that his followers perhaps made him into something that he didn't quite intend.

Me: Of course. And we've continued the process.

Him: I do sometimes feel that we've carried our position of exclusiveness a little too far.

Me: I cannot look at this organization that we have and say this is the only institution claimed by God.

Him: Well, you only have to read history to know that that isn't true. But perhaps in the seeds of what Joseph Smith gave us we still can find the answers.

Me: I must tell you that if I ever want to get really depressed, I just start thinking that maybe everything the Church has ever told me is absolutely true, that that's really the way things are. As a woman, that is really depressing.

We ended our conversation pleasantly. He said he would like to hear more about my heresies sometime. One other thing: early on in the conversation he said he had been talking to Neal Maxwell, who resides in the next office, and had said to him, "Neal, when are we going to take some time out to just think about the things we're doing instead of putting all our time into doing them?"

I also visited with Leonard and Grace Arrington. Told them about the Conkling project. Leonard knew it was in the planning stages for some time. He was very happy to know I was working on it, got up and came over and gave me a kiss.

Here are a few of the interesting points that I gathered from those I asked to interview for the Joseph Smith film. Ron Esplin feels that it's possible Brigham Young's account that Emma poisoned Joseph in the fall of 1843 is accurate. I'd never heard of that.

All of them feel that probably Eliza and Emma did have some kind of a physical confrontation (like the pushing down the stairs story). Esplin is the only one who gives a totally divine origin of polygamy. The others allow for a considerable amount of human intervention. Marvin Hill, for instance (co-author with Dallin Oaks of the book *Carthage Conspiracy: The Trial of the Accused Assassins of Joseph Smith)* feels that in 1831 there is a period of time when Joseph is writing of a great anguish that he is going through. It can't be accounted for in anything that is going on at that time. Hill feels that he had fallen in love with Fanny Alger and didn't know what to do. Joseph then writes that he had found his peace. It was during this time that accounts have it that he married Fanny Alger. Also during this time Joseph is retranslating the Bible and, being in the dilemma that he was, found in the marital style of the patriarchs an answer to his problem. So—according to Brother Hill—he put it through his mechanism for getting revelation and came out feeling a divine sanction.

Leonard and I didn't get too much into polygamy, but Eugene England—prominent sage and scholar at BYU—told me in Leonard's new book, *The Mormon Experience,* he had written polygamy from very much of a naturalistic development, but then changed it somewhat feeling he couldn't get away with it.

Speaking of polygamy, isn't it interesting. I am one of the few women you will find that has in essence lived Emma's experience. How many times have I been told by a husband who truly loved me that there was a higher law than sexual exclusivity. That my desire for monogamy was immature and selfish. That if I could just rise above these feelings I had been conditioned with, I would be all right. I truly loved my husband, as Emma did hers, but could not find in my emotional capacities a way to deal with all that. Is that not interesting?

Must move along. Have so much to say but must get on with my work. But I feel so strongly about getting all this down in my diary. In fact I feel somehow that of all the writing I am doing, my diary is the most important. In future years it will be a tremendously important record of an important journey.

Saturday morning Jan and I went to a Symposium on Mormon Thought at the U of U, sponsored by Sunstone, an independent, liberal organization devoted to Mormon concerns. A talk by Carlisle Hunsaker, Institute teacher, I found quite interesting, encouraging us to examine the metaphysics of Mormonism. Afterwards Jan and I walked to another building with him.

Jan asked, "How do you feel about the ERA?" He answered that it was long overdue. I asked if he had ever really considered the metaphysics of being a Mormon woman. He said yes, somewhat, and agreed that it was pretty horrendous. As an illustration I went through my "Pink Moccasins" address for him. He laughed all the way through and loved it. I told him I was planning a book on the Mother, on our creating this broken home, etc.

To my comment that Joseph Smith likely perceived God as male because he could function only through the patriarchal consciousness, he agreed entirely and offered to send me some quotes that back it up. I told him that I go into the writing of the book about the Mother with full expectation that they might be forced to invite me to leave the Church.

"No," he said. "You can get away with it. Perhaps someone else couldn't. But you can. You have too much stature. Too many people know and love you. They would not do that to you."

August 30, 1979

I forgot to write here about the play. My *Don't Count Your Chickens Until They Cry Wolf.* I had agreed to direct it for the ward here. Mainly I wanted to involve my children in a good enterprise for the summer. It went very well—Emily's song and dance as the sun in "The Sun and the Wind"—all three as the mice in "Belling the Cat"—and their little mouse entrances later on. "A Wolf in Sheep's Clothing" was really cute with all the kids in a song and dance routine. Played three nights to good crowds. The audience really loved it. One night I brought Lillian from the rest home, a monumental job, but she really enjoyed it, has so few pleasures in life. She got stuck in the restroom and I could hardly get her out.

September 19, 1979

Katy is lovely. Several times a day she asks me, "Guess who I love?" And she will grin and point her finger at me. Some few days ago I was singing and she said, "Don't sing, Mommy."

I said, "Oh, Katy no. You must say, 'Sing, Mother, sing!'"

So ever since then when she catches me singing she says, "Sing! Sing!" She is truly wonderful. They all are.

Jan called me from Utah last night. Wanted to give me a rundown on the recent subversive activities of the Mormons for ERA group in the East. She said that recently at the Area Conference the Church held there, 75 people from an Ecumenical group of Mormons and Catholics and others, formed to challenge religions that are against women's rights, staged a protest, holding homemade signs along a mile or more of road that all the cars had to drive past leaving the conference.

A plane flew a sign, "Mother in Heaven loves Mormons for the ERA." All the major news back there covered the demonstration. The Brethren were terribly distressed by this; their PR people had spent three weeks courting the press and getting ready for good coverage. They were "beside themselves."

Some of the signs read: "Men of Quality are Not Afraid of Women of Equality," "Save Our ERA," "Catholics for ERA," "Bigots Don't Make Good Missionaries," "Lutherans say, Mormons Get off Our Equal Rights," etc. Salt Lake Channel Two was there, covered it all, talked a lot to Sonia and other people, tried to interview her bishop in the chapel—he got so frustrated that he walked into a utility closet and refused to come out.

October 1, 1979

Drove with the kids down to the Civic Arts building to see the cast list; the kids all went back for more tryouts on Saturday. They are all in the show, *A Christmas Carol.* Aaron is Tiny Tim. Johnny and Emily are in the children's caroling sequence, plus Johnny is one of the Dickens children. They are all excited to do this. And I'm excited too. It will be a lot of work, coming and going, and juggling things around. But I believe so strongly in the theatre as an unsurpassed educational institution that I will do whatever is necessary to give them this.

October 18, 1979

At Relief Society they passed around a petition sponsored by some other religious group—to be sent to President Carter urging him against any legislation that supports homosexuality. It also called for a day of prayer that these misled individuals might be "brought back into the light." A day of prayer. How about the years and years of prayer that I invested in the subject?

I've continued working on the Joseph Smith screenplay. Yesterday, in writing the Christmas celebration scene in which Porter Rockwell comes back from Missouri and Joseph is a candidate for president, I thought up one of the most marvelous lines I've ever thought up. Joseph says, dancing with Emma, "You would make a wonderful first lady, Emma." Emma replies, "Thank you, Joseph. I *did* make a wonderful first wife."

Last night the children said one of the most delicious things they've ever come up with. We had dropped Emily off at rehearsal and were driving back home.

Aaron: Oh, Mom. We don't have school on Monday. It's Veterinarian's Day.

John: Aaron! Don't you know what a veterinarian is? It's a person that doesn't eat meat.

November 8, 1979

The other day four-year-old Katy and I had this conversation:

Her: Mom, did you used to be a little girl?

Me: Yes, I did, Katy.

Her: So did I.

November 17, 1979

I sit here in the kitchen of my sister Marie in Newberry Park, just outside of Los Angeles. At this moment Marie is in the hospital following a mastectomy, little Cherene is at my left drawing, and Sonia Johnson is in a church court.

So it has come. Yesterday in the hospital I was downstairs reading and the TV news was on. Suddenly I heard the words "Mormon Church" and "Sonia Johnson" and I jumped up. I caught only that "She fears excommunication because of her pro-ERA activities." Lynn Ann telephoned to tell me that in Utah the news about Sonia is now very big.

Marie told me Thursday morning that there was cancer in her right breast and the breast had to be removed. This is the way, I believe, that the Brethren see uppity women—they must be cut off so as to preserve the health of the whole.

I had flown down here a week before and here I was again. I had come to read my Joseph Smith screenplay to a small group of people. It was held at the home of the Conklings. Jim had invited about eight people over—only one that I knew, actor Gordon Jump. I read without interruption for three hours, sang my theme song with a borrowed guitar. I was very pleased with the reaction, much more positive than negative. Gordon Jump was thrilled, said much of it was brilliant, especially loved what I did with Porter Rockwell and Emma, and bringing in Mary Todd Lincoln. Jim Conkling came over afterwards and gave me a kiss and a hug and told me I was incredible. I think they were all as impressed with my performance as with my script.

November 19, 1979

To catch up on the Sonia business, from my conversations with Jan. When Sonia got to the chapel this morning at nine, all set for the church court, she had to fight her way through 40 people from the press. All the major networks were there with their cameras. Also there were about 60 feminist supporters that suddenly showed up with signs saying "Religion and Politics Equals Oppression," and "This Is Not Iran." When she got inside, the bishop and stake president were already there. Sonia took a lawyer in with her, I believe. Christine Durham, Mormon feminist lawyer in Salt Lake, had advised Sonia to type up documentation regarding everything she would have presented at the trial had it been held December 1st as scheduled, along with documentation on what her witnesses would have presented had they been allowed.

As the proceeding started there was discussion over why the tape recorder wasn't there—Sonia had been told the proceeding would be taped, but they had changed their minds. "Why are you so distrustful of us that you require a tape?" the bishop asked. She then went into a long list of specific ways in which she feels her case had been mishandled and said, "That's why I am distrustful of you." When Sonia handed them the papers she had stayed up all night typing, evidently the Brethren began to backpedal quite rapidly.

I expect they got uneasy about doing anything prematurely or looking any worse than they already do. So they said, "Let's not call this meeting a trial; let's call it a pre-trial planning session."

So they reset the date of the trial back to the original December 1st, and began to discuss the issues that would be brought up at that time. Some of the questions were: "Are you influencing members of the Church and those outside to move away from the counsel of the Prophet?" "Are you hindering the missionary work by undermining confidence in the Prophet?" "Are you teaching false doctrine—i.e. the existence of a Mother in Heaven and the overthrow of the priesthood?" (Now this one really boggled me. The concept of a Mother in Heaven, while certainly kept in the background, cannot be labeled as false doctrine.)

Toward the end, Sonia said, they put away some of the angry feelings and got quite a good spirit between them. Sonia does not feel they want to destroy her and feels they are attempting to be quite fair. At the end of the meeting they asked Sonia to give the closing prayer. This she did. So there they all were on their knees: the patriarchy and the woman heretic. Both sincere, both wanting to do the right thing, both beloved of the Father and of the Mother, close on many counts—on others worlds and worlds apart.

I told all this to Elouise Bell when she called the next morning. The Provo group—Algie Ballif and the other great matriarchal stalwarts of the Alice Louise Reynolds Club that has lately become the "Grey Panthers"—were meeting later that day and Elouise wanted my input for them. I told her I was hoping that whatever Sonia wanted would happen, but that a part of me said, let the Church go ahead and do this foolish thing in front of the whole world. At this point the bigger the better. Surgery is indicated.

Elouise said she felt the same. "I just keep saying to myself, 'By their fruits ye shall know them,' and the fruits are getting more and more rotten." She said she has watched the Church go into an extreme of "Prophet worship." We are not taught to think for ourselves anymore, but to look to the Prophet. I told her I had watched the same pattern play out in Joseph Smith's life as had happened over the course of the Church in general—from welcoming inquiry to brooking no opposition at all from those who sought to question.

It's all quite amazing. At the same time as I am grateful not to be involved in it I wish also that I were. I don't feel this is my time, but I don't feel honest just sitting back. I told Elouise that my comments to the court were I in Sonia's shoes would be something like this: "I love the Church. I want to remain in it. But I only want to do so if I am allowed the ability to help right the wrongs that I see in it." How could you look at the body of a friend or your own body and see signs of disease and agree to not notice? Rather like my sister's cancer surgery. Love requires action.

November 27, 1979

I was putting Katy to bed after a very pleasant evening of being alone here together. She was being even more charming than usual and I grabbed her and shook her and hugged her and said, "Oh, bless my little Katy!"

"Well," she said, "that was a short prayer!"

December 3, 1979

Sonia's trial was indeed held on Saturday the 1st. I had been thinking about her a lot, sending good thoughts and praying for her that the very best thing would happen, whatever that may be.

I telephoned her on Saturday morning. A woman answered the phone and said that Sonia was unavailable. I proceeded to give her my message. Then the woman said, "Sonia just read your name on my pad and said that she wants to talk to you."

She was really glad to hear from me. I asked her how she was feeling. She said she felt good, calm, had turned all of this over to a higher power. She didn't predict what the outcome would be. I told her my major concern was that she not feel in any way that the men who were judging her had any jurisdiction over her eternal soul, for I knew that they did not. She said that no, she really did not believe that they did. I cautioned her that whatever happened she had to present herself with absolute dignity and love and not say or do anything to make anybody say, "You see how she's lost the spirit?" She said she felt she had been handling that well and would continue to.

I called Jan late that night to find out what happened. The trial was held at 8:30 that night to avoid the press as much as possible. Sonia's mother was there with her; she is very much in support of Sonia, but is horrified at the prospect of excommunication. The witnesses were allowed to give their statements, but were told they were not to use the term ERA or Equal Rights Amendment or they would not be permitted to speak. A verdict was not rendered. Sonia was told that she would receive it in the mail in a few days.

Really, this is making the Church look worse all the time. After the trial Bishop Willis read a short statement that indicated Sonia was not being tried for her belief in the ERA, which met with boos from the 300 people outside the chapel.

We've had heavy coverage of it in our local papers, articles yesterday in both the *Contra Costa Times* and *San Francisco Chronicle*. And another today in the *Times*.

December 5, 1979

I went to Relief Society this morning. After the meeting Lee K. asked if she could talk with me. We sat outside in the sun and visited a while. She has been having a very hard time with the Sonia Johnson case; it's really shaken her faith. She has a sister who is not in the Church who tells her that the Mormon Church is just like Jonestown. Lee said, "I know the *gospel* is true—but all these other things …" At the end of our conversation she said, "I do not believe that prophets don't make mistakes."

Writing now after eleven at night. It happened. Sonia was excommunicated. She received notice in the mail that she was found guilty of preaching false doctrine, speaking evil of the Lord's anointed, and damaging the missionary work. Everyone in Utah seems to have been discussing it. There was a demonstration in support of Sonia in Palo Alto. Fifty Mormon women were walking back and forth in front of the Los Angeles temple with gags over their mouths. I turned on the TV and saw sections of the news that featured Sonia. She made a brief statement:

"I'm not bitter against them—they're just insecure and small men. When you have to excommunicate your opposition, that's really being weak. Most people have to deal with their opposition and it helps them become stronger and better." Another clip showed her near tears saying she hadn't had the time in all this to cry. "I want just to get in the car and drive into the woods and cry."

14

VISITS WITH THE MOTHER

January 1, 1980

A new year. A new decade. The sun came out this morning and it was quite warm. May it be a good omen. May the year and the decade be good for all of us.

Just now Katy is at a friend's playing. The boys are out in the court. Emily is cleaning the kitchen. And I am putting aside the rest of a very messy house to get this diary caught up. Both bother me a lot, a messy house and being behind in my diary. But I am taking the quiet hour to do the quiet thing.

This morning my neighbor Joan called and told me that Sonia was on Donahue. Emily watched it with me. I have not mentioned one word of the Sonia business to the children. And I have never said one word in criticism of anything about the Church. My impulse now was to find some reason for Emily to leave the room. But then I thought, I can't protect her forever. I did not make any commentary to her as it went along. But she voiced disgust at some of the comments the callers were making. Emily has a very good mind; she is not going to stand still for ridiculous things. And I think it will happen without my having to point things out to her.

Sonia came off looking good. She is a smart woman, not without humor, and the position she has been put in of "martyr" makes her very attractive and the Church look like the bully. Sonia speaks intelligently and says good things about the Church rather than just criticizing it.

Maybe the thing that would most disturb the Brethren is this: "I didn't want to leave the Church. It has given such a lot of good to my life. You don't just walk out on a good friend when the friend is in trouble. The Church is now in a moral crisis. This is no time for people who love it to leave it."

January 6, 1980

At Fast and Testimony Meeting today a new bishop was appointed. Robert Anderson replaces Ted Christensen. I like Brother Anderson. He and his wife Joyce have had us over to dinner twice. They are both very lovely, down-to-earth, humble people. It is so easy to get drawn again into positive feelings about the Church—the sincerity, the commitment, the love expressed between members—it is all so real, and so good. Bishop Anderson radiates such purity; I know his motives are entirely Christlike. Maybe he will have to deal with me through some difficult times. I hope we can both be blessed.

I spoke to our Sunday School teacher after class today. The lessons are on the various sections of the Doctrine and Covenants. "So next week you're going to tackle Section 132 and the doctrine of eternal marriage," I observed.

"Yes," he said. "Do you have trouble with the idea of polygamy?"

"None at all," I replied. "I used to, when I believed in it, but it doesn't bother me at all now because I know it has nothing to do with eternal truth."

He blanched a little.

I have not been mentioning the trying international scene. The hostages have been detained in Iran for nearly two months now. Russia has seized control of neighboring Afghanistan. America retaliated by cutting off the wheat supply. Gold has sky-rocketed past $600 an ounce. Gasoline continues to climb in price, now over a dollar a gallon. I keep the thermostat to 65 or below these days, and we wear thermal underwear. The world is uncertain. Life is risky. But here we are.

January 17, 1980

Quite a witty girl, my Emily. Last night after a fairly unrewarding day, I decided to indulge myself. I took a hot bath by candlelight, lit incense and everything. Really enjoyed it. Phone rang in my bedroom. Emily ran in to answer it. Then took a quick peek into the bathroom.

Emily: Do you have a candle in there?

Me: Yes, I do. It's *very* romantic.

Emily (pause): Are you alone?

Later the phone rang again and Emily came through again.

Emily: Goodnight, Mom.

Me: Goodnight, Emily.

Emily (pause): Goodnight, Mister.

January 22, 1980

Went with some of my radical friends to San Francisco to be in the audience where Sonia appeared on "People Are Talking." Afterwards we had lunch and a laugh fest. Nadine Hansen, California head of Mormons for ERA, came up with a priceless one, a wicked takeoff on First Nephi 4 in The Book of Mormon: "It is better that one woman should perish than that the whole Church should dwindle and perish in equality."

January 25, 1980

Wednesday I had a good day. My Relief Society lesson went very well. I was in top form and we had a fine discussion on overcoming loneliness (while emphasizing too the great virtue of sometimes being alone). It's true that I am a very good teacher; I can put a class at ease, lead a discussion spontaneously, build on their comments, and make it a good, warm experience for all. I so enjoy doing that.

There is so much good to be done in this world. So much building. I want really badly to get this "woman thing" settled, so I can move on to the really heavy issues of life, and to the simple living of life. But that's hard to do when something so basic is left unsolved. Perhaps it's like the idea that you can't talk to a hungry people about democracy. You have to take care of the most pressing needs first. Women—many Mormon women and many others—are hungry. We have been deprived of the most basic sustenance, an honest view of our own spiritual selves. Until that hunger is met we can't fully address the large problems of humanity. Let's get it taken care of, over with, and move on.

January 26, 1980

Speaking of the book I'm working on, I had a dream last night that I'm sure is related. I have accepted by now that when I dream of my own mother, Emeline, I'm using her as a symbol for our Mother God.

DREAM: BRING MY MOTHER BACK FROM THE HOSPITAL; NURSE HER BACK TO HEALTH. My mother, whom all thought dead, has really been in the hospital all these years. I find her, arrange to bring her home with me. I rub her hands a lot as I work on healing her. In just a few days people are commenting on what a miracle it is that she is getting better and looking so well. I am really pleased.

It occurs to me now that the first few dreams I had in recent times about my mother were that she had been totally forgotten and was in the basement of the hospital. Then that really impressive dream in which she was "in the closet, on the shelf," takes it many steps further. Then this one, in which I bring her out and have considerable success in the healing, takes it even further. These dreams are so terribly interesting. And they give me further confidence in the Mother project.

February 2, 1980

Speaking of money. If nothing comes through on the Joseph Smith film I am in big trouble. I will find a way to manage, but I'll have to come up with great ideas fast. Haven't heard from Jim Conkling.

February 11, 1980

So I came in second out of five on the Joseph Smith script judging. I don't know whose got first. But I don't get depressed over things like that. I did the very best I could, and that's that.

February 15, 1980

I had sent Jim Conkling a postcard with the statement on front, "Disappointment isn't as romantic as I thought it was going to be." On Wednesday I got a call from him. He wanted to know why I was disappointed.

I said, "Well, coming in second isn't too bad but one hopes for more than that." He replied that he was taking the top two scripts, which were the only ones that were any good at all, and trying to make something of them. The other script was by his son, Chris. Jim said they needed all my humor; nobody else had any humor in theirs. And my point of view on Emma. Jim asked if I would be willing to come down to L.A. to read what they'd come up with and give my suggestions. I said I would be happy to. I don't know how much hope to place in a patchwork approach, wedding the two scripts. I'll have to wait and see.

February 21, 1980

What a mess the Joseph Smith film project is in just now. Jim had given Chris (his son) the assignment of using the best elements in his script and in mine and coming up with a great screenplay. It is not possible.

The biggest criticism my script drew from everyone was that by the end of the film Emma and William Law looked much better than Joseph looked. (Law, a highly placed figure in Nauvoo, had lost faith in Joseph and called out Joseph's polygamy publicly in a newspaper. Joseph promptly had the press destroyed.) I felt that I gave everyone a good showing, that my Joseph was very likeable and sympathetic. But it's true that there is some William Law in me, and certainly a lot of Emma. Well. The end.

February 25, 1980

Later in the evening Elouise Bell called, just wanted to talk. She said, "I went to church today, and then I asked myself why?" She's seriously looking for another job so she can leave BYU. I told her one thing that has become clear to me—how absolutely grateful I am for the closeness that's developed between us through all of these tribulations. It is a very, very rich and lovely thing. I'm almost glad there was such a thing as the Mormon Patriarchy that forced us to find each other and comfort each other, and help each other see beyond it. The personal rewards have been profound.

I'm deep into the Mother research again. Re-reading *When God Was a Woman.* And my excitement is building. It's time. I will not put it on the back burner again. I don't know the consequences, but whatever they are I will take them.

February 29, 1980

Yesterday my former visiting teacher G. came by with a friend R. to get some books. I told them what I was working on, and the instant I said the words "Heavenly Mother" their faces lit up and they leaned forward.

"Really? Oh, tell us about it." So we sat and talked for close to two hours. I asked them if they felt a loss at not having the Mother in their lives. Their reply was an overwhelming "Yes!"

G. said, "Sometimes in my prayers, I say, 'Dear Father, take this to Mother and talk it over.' Especially as a teenager it was hard, and I wished I could go to Her. Sometimes I would plead with God, 'Why can't I talk to my Mother?' But I've never really prayed to her. I've been chicken. It's a 'no-no.'"

R. said, "I have prayed to Her. Not frequently, but I've done it. I just have the feeling that there's no love as tender and as compassionate as that of a mother. I take to Her things that only a woman could understand. I don't think that even the Father could give me the kind of love and understanding that Heavenly Mother could, He's so busy doing other things. I know in my heart that She's there. And when I've seen the weaknesses in my earthly mother I knew there was some better model for me. It's hard being a woman. And when I have asked about things like this the bishop says that women just have to be long-suffering."

G. said, "I wonder what She's been doing all this time."

And then we joked, "Oh, watching the soaps. *All My Children*."

We laughed. We yearned. We hurt. We were exhilarated just to talk about it.

Elouise called me later in the day. She mentioned that on Tuesday Ezra Taft Benson had spoken at the Y. His message was the importance of the Prophet. He said that the Prophet is more important than any scripture. There is no division between things secular and things spiritual. It doesn't matter if the Prophet has any particular knowledge in the area he's speaking on; his words are still to be regarded as more binding than scripture.

Elouise said, "That made it easier for me. I can't stay here. Probably I'll be here one more year, then take a leave of absence while I get established elsewhere, and then that's it."

March 9, 1980

On Sunday the kids and I were learning "Let there be peace on earth ..." Emily suddenly said, "Hey—why do all these songs say things like 'brothers all are we?' We're not all brothers." I do not bring up with Emily any of this. She brings it up.

Exciting thing yesterday. Our cat Juliet had her kittens. I was working on my Mother research when Katy came down to tell me to "Come look!" Indeed, Juliet was starting her labor. I told Katy to watch and comfort Juliet and then went to the phone. I called the school and said to the secretary, "This is Mrs. Pearson and I need to come and get my children right away on important family business."

"Oh!" she said. "I'll have them out front in five minutes."

So I left Katy in charge and jumped in the car. When I told the kids Juliet was having her babies they were terribly excited, but when we got home we couldn't find her anywhere. Katy said she had gone upstairs. We looked everywhere in every room in the house. Finally I found her in the linen closet in the hallway. We all knelt down by her and said a prayer for the safe arrival of the kittens.

Pretty soon Juliet was having contractions and wailing. We watched, and sure enough, soon something was on its way out. It was really a remarkable experience to see that amazing thing happen. Out came the first one. Katy got quite upset because Juliet seemed to be in distress, so Aaron took her in the other room and read her a story.

When Juliet began eating the placenta, Emily freaked out. She rolled on the floor. "Oh, gross. Oh, sick!" Out came another kitty. We counted five.

The truth is that none of these five babies survived. Juliet was not old enough to be a mother. But somehow as she had been out catting around she got pregnant. And yes, I used that to point out to my children the dangers of teenage pregnancy.

Yesterday in my reading I found some lovely things. The Quakers are very inspiring people. An article from their *Inward Light* developed the "Theology of the Couple," telling how erotic love is actually the yearning of all of us to get to the state of Godhood that embodies both the masculine and the feminine principles. *All* of the things I am reading are so incredibly interesting, and it's clearer and clearer to me how we all are suffering from living in our Motherless house.

March 18, 1980

Well, whale watching. Not the highlight of my life. I paid for the trip and invited Gerald. The first ten minutes was great, plowing out into the ocean, huge waves dashing us. I had taken Dramamine in preparation and thought it was working. But then—I got sick. Sick. I grabbed a plastic bag from my purse and threw up and up and up. Then I lay down and tried to die.

It reminded me of the dreadful voyage from Odessa, Russia, to Athens, and also from Athens to Crete. How I wanted to die. But finally boats do stop, as this one did. We did get to see whales spouting and saw fins and tails. But—not worth it.

My research continues, and how I do love it. Today I read the first part of Joseph Campbell's *Occidental Mythology.* He has some very perceptive and strong things to say about the early worship of the Great Mother. I don't believe I have ever been so excited about a project as I am about this book. I am fully aware that it may complicate my life dreadfully, but I must do it.

March 23, 1980

Today I lost our goldfish, the one lovely goldfish Johnny had won at the school fair. I was about to change the water, lifted the goldfish out with a small sieve and rested it on the counter. Immediately the goldfish leapt out of the sieve and landed—right in the sink and slid into the drain. No! Gone into the pipes. No way to retrieve it. What can I tell the children?

I jumped in the car and drove down to the pet store and looked at the goldfish. All were about half the size of the fish I had lost to the sink. So I bought two.

Later:

Aaron: Hey, look there's two goldfish in the bowl!

John: Is not.

Aaron: Is so!

John looked at the goldfish. Looked at his mother.

Me: I cannot tell a lie. I did it. I dropped your goldfish and it broke right in half.

March 26, 1980

The funny Ashleigh Brilliant "Pot Shots" postcards I ordered arrived and I have been using them with great delight. I sent one to Leonard Arrington: "History is on Our Side—If We Can Just Control the Historians."

He loved it so I sent him a package of 18 to spread around. I also sent one to Marion D. Hanks that said, "The Purpose of Our Organization is to Perpetuate Our Organization," and suggesting he might post it in an elevator in the Church Office Building. When I saw that a letter from him had arrived, I thought, Oh no, maybe he's calling me to repentance. This is what he wrote:

> Dear Carol Lynn:
>
> Everybody ought to have a good belly laugh once in a while, and you have provided mine for this month. I thank you.
>
> I have never seen a more perfect rendering of the situation as it seems to exist.
>
> While I do not have the key to the faith-promoting thought boxes in the elevators, I will try to give this appropriate exposure where it will do whatever good it can do.
>
> You report that you are well and happy and that life is good. All of this impresses me strongly since I question these matters on occasion. The recent announcement of my appointment to live in China for an indefinite period causes me to consider a future wherein I may have adequate time to consider my blessings.
>
> Thanks for thinking of me. I have profited from that in my deep-down inward self. (And my skin-deep outer self.)
>
> The Lord bless.
>
> Duff

The dear man. I am really so very fond of him. I have long looked at him as one bright light among lots of darkness. And now they're sending him to China. That's the Mormon equivalent of Siberia. To keep him out of trouble, no doubt. How discouraging. He's such a great man. I wish there were something I could do to help him. Perhaps I will just send him a good joke every now and then.

I seem not to have written it in this diary, but I remember a conversation with Elaine Cannon when she was President of the Young Women's organization of the Church. She had been close to Brother Hanks years before—they had even dated—and they continued to have meaningful conversations. Together they edited the youth page in the Improvement Era *for years. She said to me, "I tell him, 'Duff—the only way you're ever going to get appointed to the Council of the Twelve is if you stop offending the Brethren!' But he won't! He just keeps telling them what he thinks."*

Today I went down to teach a half hour at Johnny's class, as I have weekly for a while. I led a discussion that got quite interesting. The teacher had asked if I had anything on mythology, so I talked about the Greek goddesses like Athena being deposed by Zeus and a similar thing happening in other cultures and what all that means for us today about God being male.

We had watched the little film I had written for BYU Motion Pictures, *Cipher in the Snow*, about a boy who just dies in a snowbank for no obvious reason—a boy who nobody seemed to know or to care about. I said I had read an article that morning about the possibility of women becoming "rare," because of sex pre-selection techniques and why people, both men and women, seem to feel that maleness is more valuable than femaleness. Read some outrageous quotes by the philosophers putting down women.

The girls got properly angry and the boys laughed. Then I had the girls read out loud with me from a sign I had inherited: "When God made man, She was only joking." The girls laughed and the boys booed.

I ended on assuring them, as I had before, that I know that being male or being female are both prizes of equal value—and that whatever God finally turns out to be will be a perfect balance of male and female.

Evening now. Just before supper I answered the door to find the Mormon missionaries. I invited them in. My heart really went out to them. Such dear, devoted, naïve boys. They had had a rather discouraging day. I told them to go out and play basketball with my boys for a few minutes and then come and have supper with us. So they did and I'm sure it was the best time they'd had for a while.

And our Easter tree is now in full décor. Our Christmas tree just would not die or even dry, so we kept it up and turned it into a fine Valentine tree and had lots of little red and white candy hearts and paper valentines hung on it. The tree is still alive and green. So now we're preparing our Easter tree. Over the last few weeks I personally blew about six dozen eggs before eight a.m., a monumental achievement. Night before last we dyed the shells and placed them over the tiny lights still on the tree. The effect is really quite dazzling. Such fun.

April 7, 1980

I met Linda Silitoe at Jan's while in Utah. She and Sonia are contracting with Doubleday to do a book on Sonia's life. A few insights I got from our conversation. Evidently it was really the Mother in Heaven doctrine that was the most frightening thing to Bishop Willis. He began calling in women in the ward to ask if Sonia had been talking to them about the Mother in Heaven. He was afraid she was getting them to pray to her, organizing a Cult of the Mother. Wouldn't he be amazed to learn that many of us consider that we have been involved for centuries in something like a Cult of the Father—that we want to move on and just unify our Spiritual Family at last?

I had a good visit with Helen Stark of Salem, Utah. She is one of the grand old dames of Mormondom who has suffered a lot and not had much support on The Woman Question. She gave me one of the first things I received on the Mother—a pamphlet called "Feminine Aspects of Divinity," from the Quakers. It was very exciting to me at that time and I'm going through it again now with my other research. I told her about the book I am preparing and she was thrilled.

She told me one of the great horror stories of all time on the subject at hand. She had read how the Quakers, and perhaps others, have written on the topic of the Holy Spirit being the feminine counterpart of God. Some few years ago she spoke with Bruce R. McConkie, a General Authority, and asked him what he thought of that as an interesting possibility. He said, "Sister Stark—if you will go home and get down on your knees and pray for forgiveness and never mention such a thing again, you may be forgiven."

Is that not incredible? But when one has the divine right of kings, or presides over the only true Church, one can make pronouncements like that. I assured Helen that those of us who are coming after are grateful for those who have come before, and that we will not let them down.

Blaine Porter, head of the College of Family Living at BYU, took me to lunch. At a nearby table was Terry Warner, philosophy professor. He was aware of my work on the Heavenly Mother and asked me if I had completed it. I told him it was still in progress and asked if he had any further observations. He said, "Well all I know is that She are!" So there you have it, again the ridiculous position that polygamy puts us in.

May 1, 1980

Must mention the "nuclear holocaust" that was supposed to happen last Monday night. A prediction by a famous man in Montana. The world, of course, is still here but in a precarious position. The American hostages are still in Iran; our attempt to airlift them was a failure and feelings are running high.

I talk about these things with the children from time to time and emphasize how we must send helpful thoughts to try to bring peace. Each night over the weekend I led them in a meditation (we've done this before). I had them relax, close their eyes, breathe deeply, receive light into their bodies, and send the light, which is love, out to the whole world, to the leaders of nations. I had them visualize the hostages returning to their families, visualize President Carter and Khomani of Iran shaking hands, visualize people all over the world shaking hands and singing and dancing. Then they went into their evening prayers.

May 9, 1980

Being responsible for the house and the yard is not something that comes naturally to me. It is so easy for my environment to master me, and when that happens (frequently) I hate it, I just hate it. Having to worry about poison for the snails that are eating the petunias we put in two weeks ago—that kind of thing is so utterly bothersome. I do not deal well with the material world and I never have and likely I never will. Sometimes I think I have no business in mortality; I should have just stayed on the spirit plane. But evidently I chose to come here. So let's get on with it.

June 9, 1980

I think Katy and I have ESP. Several times as we've been driving in the car she has suddenly made a comment on something I was thinking about just at that moment. And the other day we were both in the kitchen and in my mind I was going through "My Turn on Earth," explaining to someone that it is a spiritual explanation for children of why we came to earth and what we're to be learning. At that very second Katy spoke up. "Mom—why we came to earth?" I was really taken aback.

My dear Trevor Southey had been commissioned to do a portrait of President Kimball. Boyd K. Packer came down to Alpine a couple of months ago to view the work. While they were talking Packer quizzed Trevor about some things and Trevor confessed to him that he was something of a heretic.

On their way home, Brother Packer said (one of the riders was a friend of Trevor and later told him): "I don't trust the artistic mind. I just do not trust the artistic mind." Brother Packer later made a call to Trevor's bishop, found out more about him, and now Trevor is on the black list. Whether the portrait of President Kimball will be used is unlikely, I think.

July 1, 1980

Last night Mrs. Tate, across the court, told me that her son Chris said to her, "The Pearsons have a very special family. There's a lot of love in that home. They may not have the greatest garden in the world, but there's a lot of love there."

15

PARADIGM SHIFT

September 9, 1980

I wrote today's date on a letter and realized it is my wedding anniversary. Isn't it strange. I do not feel sentimental. I do not feel lost. I do not feel regretful. I was going to call Gerald to tell him "Happy Anniversary," but he called me first. He said, "I just wanted to tell you that I love you." He does. And I love him. And it doesn't hurt. Sort of like a miracle.

September 11, 1980

Yesterday afternoon Gerald came out as usual. We were able to talk a bit and I asked him if things were all right about Kevin being in his life. He replied that no, they're not. Kevin is behaving very immaturely and Gerald knows that "like attracts like" and that he's got to learn what he must so he won't have such bad experiences in his relationships.

And then he said something to me that I will never forget as long as I live.

"Oh, Blossom. If I could only find a man just like you I would be in seventh heaven."

I laughed right out loud, it startled me so.

But Gerald wasn't laughing. In fact, he had tears in his eyes.

I wish Gerald could find a man like me. I am not everything, but I am mature, and I am loyal. I hope someone good will come into his life. I really do.

October 5, 1980

I watched the one hour of General Conference that was broadcast here in California. I had the children sit down with me and listen to the choir. Emily said she wanted to hear the Prophet speak. I never refer to "The Prophet." We never used to call the Presidents "The Prophet." That is an innovation of the last few years. We always said, "President McKay" or whomever.

It's now the next morning. I called Jan Tyler in Utah and spoke to Cherry Dalton, who was staying with her. She asked me if I heard what they had done the day before. I said no, I had not. She and two other women had stood up in Conference when they asked for the sustaining of President Kimball. They called out, "No! Women for ERA say no!" They also flew a banner—"Mrs. God Hates Sexism. Repent and Ratify."

Jan said she was listening to the radio when the sustaining took place and was amazed at how loud the "No" came. There was a ripple through the large congregation in the tabernacle, then conference went on with hardly a pause. One of the General Authorities went to the podium and said, "There seem to be three dissenting votes. Would those women please see Gordon B. Hinckley directly after the meeting."

I look at these women making these protests and I have mixed feelings. I could not do it that way. But I cannot say that they shouldn't.

November 1, 1980

On the plane I sat by Keith Merrill (Mormon filmmaker who won an Academy Award for his documentary "The Great American Cowboy.") I'm very impressed with him; he has a great mind. We had both been thinking of movies about people preparing for the end of the world. Mormons love end of the world stuff.

Keith said there's a man in his stake who has become the local guru on the subject and has some tapes prepared by someone in Utah who has unlocked the timetable of when the end is coming. It clearly works out to the winter of 1981 that the great earthquakes begin that usher in the end. The man in Keith's stake is an extremely wealthy orthodontist and has his food supply and everything else in readiness. His wife is deeply committed as well. In fact, Keith's wife was speaking to her on the phone and the woman said, "Oh, yes, it's definitely coming this winter. And the Saints have to get prepared. The Relief Society is going to have to study new things. We're going to have to learn how to identify and tag dead bodies."

Here I nearly flew out the airplane window. What a wonderfully Mormon thing to do. We will be the ones spared. What a cute mini-class. "Sisters, today you will choose from the following: 1) Christmas tree ornaments—2) Crocheting toilet seat covers—3) Tagging dead bodies."

November 21, 1980

When I came back home, I learned that Sonia Johnson had been arrested for demonstrating outside the Mormon temple in Bellevue, Washington. Her picture was in the newspaper being led away. She and others had chained themselves to the temple gates as a symbol of the chains that Mormondom places upon women.

I called Jan this evening to get filled in. She didn't know any more. Sonia was permitted to fly back to her home. She had been trying to get arrested, I do believe. Jan said Sonia has been studying civil disobedience for months. Evidently this chaining of the women to the temple gates became a big story up in Washington. What can I say of all this? I understand her anger and her hurt. It isn't my style. But I wish her well.

November 21, 1980

I am moved to remark again that there have been hidden benefits in this hard thing of being a single parent. I have been forced to get involved with the children in a way that I never would have if Gerald had been here. He is such a good initiator, so full of energy, so really fun and full of life that I let him carry much of the burden of letting the good stuff happen. I do not do it his way. But I have grown enormously in doing it my way. And frequently it works. I am grateful. Really.

November 29, 1980

I've started reading a book I picked up at the library, *ESP in the Bible: the Psychic Roots of Religion.* Very interesting. It correlates the ancient paranormal experiences with modern psychic accounts. I've been convinced for a long time now that there is one reservoir of other-worldly experience from which comes all the remarkable things that happen to people—some of whom call it "religious," some of whom call it "psychic."

But how "godly" are those experiences? Clearly some people receive information from or invite spirits that are of a very undeveloped, even "evil" nature. The woman in Reno whose story is in today's paper, who killed five people with her car on a sidewalk and injured many more, was "directed" to do it by voices from on high, telling her to kill. Was this just her perverted mind? From where came Moses's command to kill—to kill thousands upon thousands in the name of the Lord, slaughtering villages, men, women, children? Was that from a godly source? Or, most likely, I think, from his own rationalization? Terribly interesting. Wonderfully interesting.

December 28, 1980

Yesterday while Gerald and the kids were fixing dinner, I went for a private walk in the hills, went clear up to my highest place. It was wonderful. There was fog all around. At the top it was like heaven. I could only see a few trees and felt as if I were cut off from all mortality. Thinking about the end of the year. A paradigm shift. A pulling back to see that what I believed was not wrong, just partial, and there are many, many new things to add to the picture.

January 7, 1981

Been working very hard these days. Yesterday Marve Wallin and George Bickerstaff called from Bookcraft to tell me they love the book adaptation of my musical play, *The Dance*—three couples at the church dance, each working out their own challenges. It really is charming and moving. They definitely want to publish it.

Writing down a thought before it slips away, 1981.

"Where have you been all our life?" said Marve, the man who about 15 years ago turned down *Beginnings* cold without reading it.

January 14, 1981

Have the first draft of *A Motherless House* completed. Have been doing some good rewriting. Will take it to Utah with me the first week of next month. I agreed to be on a panel at the Y's Women's Conference. Will have a number of trusted people look at it. I'm very excited about it.

This book that I have referenced by various titles, was finally titled Letters from a Motherless House. *It was a collection of ten letters from me to God the Mother, telling her the sad things that have been going on in the family without Her throughout history, and asking Her to come home. I was not able to find a publisher for it. Here are the opening lines:*

Dear Mother,

Why do I find it hard to breathe as I begin this letter? I've put it off for a long time. But I must talk to you.

Do you remember me? Never mind that question. If your eye is on the sparrow I'm sure it's on me too. I'm one of the billions that you and Father brought here for your own godly purposes, and if you looked up my file you would recall exactly which one. But it really doesn't matter. I'm just one of them, and that's all that counts. Because we all count.

Well, I'm breathing a little better now that I've begun, so I'll just plunge in and tell you the whole story. I've been going through some hard times. Some really hard times. And I think that mothers want to know when their children are suffering.

I guess the worst time was when I thought we had no Mother—that contrary to all the laws of nature, contrary to the wonderful balance that brings everything else under the sun, human beings, animals, fish, birds, flowers—our own souls, our essence sprang from the male alone—that God was the only Being who could not enter the ark male and female.

How can I tell you what it is like to be female and to believe that the divine is male?

*****

And then at the end on page 103:

I pledge to do whatever things I can, large and small, to pave the way for your homecoming. I will keep you alive in my thoughts and my words and awaken others to remembering you. We will join together to redecorate the house in warmer tones. We will compose new hymns to a God that is truly holy, a God that is whole. We will weave our yellow ribbons for your welcome.

And you, Mother? What can I ask of you? Stay close. Brood upon the world as you did in the beginning, giving us light and life. Hold us in your great arms and speak to us of peace and of love. Sing to us of the better time that is coming—a time when the family can sleep better and live better and love better because Mother and Father are both at home and it feels so good.

What more can I say? We miss you. We need you.

Mother—come home.

With love,
Carol Lynn

January 20, 1981

Wonderful day! The hostages were released from Iran after 444 days. Such a nightmare it has been. Algerian planes lifted the 52 hostages from Teheran this morning about nine a.m. our time. At the same moments Ronald Reagan was being inaugurated as the new President of the United States. The whole nation today experienced a strong and thrilling revival of the American spirit. Even the newscasters got emotionally involved. The families wept. Every once in a while I burst into tears. How I love the drama of people caring for one another. And what I feel in myself I know exists in millions of others all over the land, all over the world. And I say again with Anne Frank, I still believe, in spite of everything, that people are really good at heart.

Must report on my trip to Texas. I accepted a speaking invitation primarily so I could take Johnny on a private vacation. We were treated royally, of course. The conference went very well. They had 480 women in attendance; they had anticipated about 300. When I am before an audience a magical thing happens. I really turn on and so do they. And they love me. All of this is a mixed blessing for me. I love the feeling of having accomplished things and being recognized for it, but I hate the feeling of being—what, set apart from others.

Our first afternoon there and our last day there we went over to Juarez, Mexico. Saw the 1500 A.D. cathedral, beautiful. Talked with the Mexican woman in the ward who went with us about the miracle of Guadalupe—the Lady that appeared to the young man and left her imprint on a piece of cloth. The sister who brought us said she believed this vision just as she believed Joseph Smith's visions. Of course I agreed. She is a recent convert to the LDS Church from Catholicism. Wouldn't it be wonderful if we could accept all the lovely visionary experiences that have happened from time to time as one great and mysterious mosaic and not have to single out one or two as the only true pieces, making of the others mirages, much less significant, or even Satanic.

January 27, 1981

Last night Aaron and Johnny and I were saying our evening prayers together, silently. But I heard Johnny mumbling, ". . . and bless yourself. . . and bless your wife, and bless the Holy Ghost."

I have avoided having any really heavy discussions with the children on the subject of the Mother in Heaven. I frequently refer to Heavenly Father and Mother, but don't make a real point of it. I have long in my own prayers related to both. And in the last several months once in a while, in prayer with the children, I've addressed both. None of them have said anything about it; it must have sounded fairly natural to them. I do intend soon to have a more active discussion with them on this. I think I have hesitated from cowardice. What if I encourage them to include the Mother in their prayers and they do that in Primary or Sunday School or the home of a Mormon friend? Well, so what? I think I have been quite remiss in my duty to them.

February 7, 1981

I'm at Jan's typewriter again in Salt Lake City. As Jan met me we stopped to see Trevor Southey's painting that's had so much controversy. Did I mention this? A whole wall in the airport. Two nudes in flight, very tastefully done; criticized by the anti-smut people as lewd and possibly inciting people to rape or kill. Incredible. It is in our San Francisco papers. I wrote a letter to

The Salt Lake Tribune, also to Paul Gaines, head of airport authority. We went to the airport office and told them how much we liked the painting; they said their mail had been running about four to one in favor of it.

Next morning Jan and I drove down to Provo. I had already made appointments with Hugh Nibley and Truman Madsen to have them take a look at my manuscript. I had called Nibley's home, spoke first with his wife Phyllis. She said that Hugh was so inundated with everybody wanting him to read their books that why didn't I let her read it and if she thought it was worth his time she would pass it on to him. I said may I just speak to him for a moment and then they could work it out as they wanted.

So he came to the phone. He remembers me, of course, from our ongoing sporadic conversations on the lack of the feminine in our theology. I from time to time have told him it's a theme he needs to address, and the closest he's come to it has been some writing that touches on the matriarchy. On the phone I explained my current work to him, the Motherless House book. He right away sensed that it was important and agreed to take a look at it. In fact he volunteered to put his editors off on his own manuscript on the Book of Abraham from Thursday to Friday so he could see me on Thursday.

So on Thursday at the appointed time I walked right into his office and gave him a hug. He took the manuscript, sat right down and began reading. I told him I was going to drop one off to Truman Madsen and I would be back. So Jan and I walked over to Madsen's office, waited a while for him to be free, then went in.

He greeted us pleasantly, but then—and this seemed rather odd—he seemed not to want to look at us. And his body language was very strange. He sat perpendicular to us, protecting himself with his legs and his arms. He really would only give us furtive glances. I truly think he felt threatened by us. I told him just a bit about the project. I told him Hugh Nibley was the only other person on campus who was looking at it. He was dumbfounded.

"Nibley is reading this? Nibley doesn't read anybody's stuff. I can't get him to read a word of mine. Four hundred people are lined up to get him to read something and he won't. Why does he read yours?"

I told him that Nibley could sense that it was an important project. As we talked a little he said, "I don't like you, Carol Lynn, and I always will." He went on to say that means he really does like me, but that some of the things I write frustrated him.

We went back to Nibley's office. He had finished it (skimmed some of it). He said, "I don't see one syllable in there that anyone could object to." I asked him if my treatment of historical matters, of the matriarchy and the rise of the patriarchy were fair. He said, "Yes, very fair. It has a nice feeling to it, a healing feeling, sort of like the balm of Gilead." I asked if he would write an endorsement for me and he said he would.

I really wanted to have Sterling McMurrin read my manuscript. I had heard of him all my life as *the* Mormon intellectual who was saved from excommunication by President McKay. I just felt somehow that he would be a good one to contact. It was gutsy, of course, but that's necessary in this life.

So last night I called him. I told him who I was, and my name meant nothing to him. I just plunged right in and told him about my study and the manuscript and how important I felt it was. He responded very well and said yes, he would be happy to look at it for me. So Jan and I dropped everything and ran up to his home.

He was very generous and gracious. I offered just to leave it with him and let him look at it later. But he wouldn't let us go. He invited us into his study and sat down and opened the manuscript. After about a minute's silence, he said, "Well, it's obvious you're a very good writer."

"Thank you," I said.

He browsed through every chapter, making such exclamations as, "You have certainly got something here." "This is really something." "I can't believe how you've packed so much into this." "You are certainly not the typical Mormon writer." At one point I asked him if he had had much contact with the Church in recent years. He said, "Well, there are Mormon chapels all around here. I drive past them from time to time. That's about all the contact I've had."

And he said several times, "Don't let those male chauvinists down at the Church make changes in this. They'd ruin it for you." I told him I might be looking for a good agent. He said, "Oh, I think you'll have no trouble getting a first-rate national publisher for this." He made a few suggestions, such as to be careful not to "instruct" deity. And he felt it needed a more interest-catching title. I agreed and had been thinking about that.

He's going to read the book more carefully and send me a written response, something I can use as an endorsement if I wish. I was really, really pleased at our encounter.

February 22, 1981

On the way to church this morning I told the children I was going to give the prayer, and Emily said, "Are you going to pray to Father and Mother in Heaven?" I told her no, I wasn't. I asked her if she thought I should. She said, "Well, I think it might offend some people." I told her my purpose was not to offend people.

April 2, 1981

Must mention a visit I had with Carma P. She had written me from Salt Lake some weeks ago, a desperate, painful letter. She had heard me read my poem "A Motherless House" at the Y's women's conference. She wanted to know how to keep her sanity as a woman in the Church. I wrote her that I would call her next time I came to Utah. So I did.

She is in her early thirties, a counselor at a high school, a returned missionary. Only within the last few months has she begun to see what it really means to be female in the patriarchy. And she is in agony, has dropped out of the Church, though her family and friends don't know it yet. With her it's still a "What's wrong with me?" more than "What's wrong with the Church?"

Sometimes she truly feels that she would like to end her life. She still believes in God, but feels that there is no place for her in whatever plan He has. We spent a lot of time talking. I let her read the manuscript of "The Motherless House" and asked her what it did to her. She said, "It reminds me of all the things I've felt about how bad it is to be a woman—and gave me a brand-new thought—maybe they're not true!"

Yesterday I answered my door and there was a huge arrangement of red and white carnations—with a card that said, "To the celebration of life—Carma." I was thrilled.

April 12, 1981

Friday night my friends Vonda Porter (my old MIA teacher from Provo) and Nadine Hansen (Northern California head of Mormons for the ERA) came down to read my manuscript. They loved it, were both overjoyed. We had a wonderful time and they stayed until 2:30 a.m. I'm so grateful to the patriarchy for providing us with such a bond against it. It has served us well. In no other way, I think, would women come together and feel so close and affectionate as in our mutual pain.

They told me about three women they knew about recently who were "thrown out" of the temple here in Oakland for refusing to covenant to obey their husbands.

May 7, 1981

Speaking of money, I am down to my last few dollars. My financial life is strange. Twice a year I get my royalties and have to make it last. Recently it has not lasted, but other things have come up to make ends meet. Like the fourteen hundred I will get from the Utah Arts Council for judging the two categories of manuscripts in their annual contest. Found such an interesting manuscript in the biography category—"In My Father's House." It was written by a daughter of Rulon Allred, the polygamist leader who was murdered a few years ago in Utah by rival fundamentalists. Interesting story, very well written, by Dorothy Allred Solomon.

May 31, 1981

In a few minutes Gerald is coming and we're going to the Lafayette reservoir with a picnic. This is the last time he'll be out for a few weeks; he is leaving with the Chorus for their national tour. He's worked his head off, being in charge of scheduling, fund-raising. Hundreds of little details he's had to take care of. And he's just about broken his health; he hasn't been well at all.

This reference is to the first National Tour of the San Francisco Gay Men's Chorus. Gerald had been one of the organizers of the tour and had donated much of the money he got in severance from Scott's Seafood to the cause of the tour. His commitment to this work was absolute. The nation needed to see gay men as they truly were—beautiful and talented and with great things to offer. This tour would change hearts and minds, he was certain.

I adopted a cat yesterday. Just what I do not want. This large yellow cat has been hanging around here for months. He has a home some blocks away, Emily tells me, but he just will not leave our house. He sneaks inside for food and I throw him out. He sneaks in again and I throw him out again. This has gone on for months. Yesterday it dawned on me that he must be Juliet's husband, and father of Caesar, the kitten we gave away which looks very much like this big yellow cat. (I have written the tragedy of Juliet's first batch of kittens, all of whom died. But she did have a second batch that lived.)

So here must be the husband and father and I suppose he must be deeply in love with Juliet. He has certainly proved his affection by refusing to be dissuaded in the face of all my rejection. The reader will not believe this, but I was quite moved when all this dawned upon me. I believe that people who love each other ought to be together. I guess I can even buy extra cat food for one who is in love.

June 30, 1981

I spent the weekend with Emily at the Youth Conference, speaking on journal keeping. And here I am again having to catch up in mine, as it has suffered from undue neglect. My workshops went well, small groups but very interested. In each of the groups the most pressing question that arose was how much shall I put in of my really personal things?—the things I don't want anyone else to know. I encouraged them to—in general—be honest, to believe that the people who finally inherit the documents will be relieved to see that you too had times of darkness and even of anguish. I told them that being honest is a courageous thing to do. And I admire courage a lot more than I admire perfection. I had many enthusiastic comments about the workshops.

Gerald got back from the national tour of the Chorus and reported a triumphant time. Everywhere they had great reviews and felt they engendered a whole lot of good will.

I had a bad experience with the children on Saturday night. Johnny was just bursting with a string of sexy jokes he had heard from Davy, I suppose. And when Gerald is here they always like to show off. Anyway, in front of us all, including my friend Carma, Johnny, now eleven years old, came out with this little story that is rather sexy in a very juvenile and dumb way but finishes off with a clincher that is as X-rated as anything I've ever heard.

I was shocked, furious. Emily had been egging him on, having heard it already. I sent them both to sit in the bathrooms and think about it (my usual punishment). Gerald talked to both of them, explaining the importance of not offending people. I could not even speak to them until later, I was so flabbergasted and hurt. Finally we talked about it and made up. I cried right in front of them. I don't very often do that. I don't know exactly why I have such a strong reaction against vulgarity and filth, but I do.

At the theatre in Berkeley, Anne Cullimore Decker came up and spoke to me. I had met her before; she was with me on Barbara Smith's committee to study women's issues. I asked her what the committee was doing. She said Aileen Clyde and someone else did a yearlong study on depression among Mormon women, and finally it was shelved "due to lack of funds." Lack of courage, more likely.

I asked if she saw any good signs for women in the Church. She said no. I said, "What then does it all mean?"

She said, "I'm afraid the writing's on the wall."

July 13, 1981

Another troublesome thing. Bill McCracken wants to do a non-Mormon touring company of *My Turn on Earth*, playing to non-Mormons. He's getting the backing of a number of ministers. Evidently the only concept in it that the ministers are having a lot of difficulty with is the Mother in Heaven concept. Bill wants to rewrite those lines. That is something that could easily be deleted in the play. Except that it will *not* be! This is *my* play, and *my* lifework! I told him no.

August 5, 1981

I had bought Johnny a nice pair of tennis shoes at the thrift store for two dollars. But he had stopped wearing them. I asked where they were. "I don't know," he said.

"Did you lose them?" I asked.

"Well, what can you expect from cheap shoes? You pay two dollars for shoes, you lose them."

Forgot to mention a good telephone conversation I had with Leonard Arrington. He is always very friendly and helpful. He's in process of publishing a new book, *Saints Without Halos.* I asked if the book was going to get him in trouble. He laughed and said, "You mean I could get into more trouble than I've already been in?"

He is such a great man. The word is that he is in enormous frustration with the move of his office from Salt Lake down to BYU in Provo (exile, some called it), the closing down of lots of things he'd had available, and his personal demotion from the position of Church Historian. But he doesn't talk about it.

August 20,1981

I challenged a statement that was made in Sunday School marriage class today. That men are to love their wives and wives are to reverence their husbands. The point was that men need respect more than women do.

I said, "I don't think the feelings men and women have for one another are all that different, and that when they are it contributes to things in our society that are unhealthy. Women need respect as much as men do. The list on the blackboard up there of 'causes for depression among women' has as its number one—'Lack of Self-Esteem.' Of course. How can a woman have good self-esteem when all of society is telling her that femaleness is second prize and not first prize? And when men are taught to love but not necessarily to respect? You can love a puppy dog, but the puppy dog is not an equal creature. Women need to be respected as equal creatures."

There were a lot of nods as I spoke. And immediately after, one man recommended that all men must read Sister Pearson's two poems, "Millie's Mother's Red Dress" and "The Steward."

November 4, 1981

A woman I met told me she was in a meeting a long time ago in which Jessie Evans Smith (wife of President Joseph Fielding Smith) referred to me as being "very gifted," and being "in a position to lift and heal the women of the Church."

November 13, 1981

At church today, in the Family Relations class, which I attended to escape the Old Testament, the teacher placed before us on the blackboard that grand old diagram, the vertical "God—Man—Woman," describing how the Divine Government works. I raised my hand and said something like this:

"Lonnie, I think we've got to stop relying on that old vertical, hierarchical totem pole. That diagram has done incalculable damage to women and to men, placing as it does femaleness further away from godliness than maleness is. Let's look at the concept you're talking about, that man is the head of the home and woman is the heart. That's lovely until you really look at it. We do not value those two things equally, we do not. Brethren, how long has it been since you were taught, 'Now, Brethren, you have got to remember that the woman is the *heart* of the home. That's the way God has set it up. But you should not envy that and feel bad about it—because *you* get to be the *head.*' Our values are way, way out of balance."

Some of the men smiled and chuckled. They could see. Sort of.

Sunday morning Susan Randall telephoned me. She said, "I'm grinning and I'm crying and I'm jumping up and down. Just finished your manuscript about the Motherless House. Please—can I let my children read it?"

Last week I went with the Tates to hear famed American writer Joseph Campbell in San Francisco. One of the things I remember: "Myths are other people's religion. And religion is misunderstood mythology." Very thought provoking.

I had taken along a copy of my Motherless House manuscript in the hopes I might give it to him. I was able to speak with him afterwards, but he refused to take it, saying he did not have time to even look at the things people asked him to read. As I explained the project, however, he nodded and smiled with some enthusiasm, saying it was a wonderful work.

November 16, 1981

Susan Randall called me this morning. She wanted to tell me that last night she had her giant high school football-playing son read chapters nine and ten of my manuscript.

"He cried," she said. "Not as much as his mother had cried the night before at two in the morning. But he cried. And he said, 'She's really got something there, doesn't she?'"

"You cannot believe how much perspective the whole book gave me," she said. Throughout she kept thinking, "Did Carol Lynn have to go through all this pain alone?" I told her, no, I didn't. By the time I was writing it I had a number of people to share the pain. But before that, when I was just trying to grab onto the concept—I was alone. Very much alone. And it was dreadful.

November 21, 1981

I am so torn. So torn. How I yearn for some good resolution to my conflicts with the Church. So much emotional energy is going into my ambivalence, that I know could be used more productively. I am walking a tightrope with my breath held. I am living a double life. Not dishonestly. Very honestly. I am *truly* on both sides of the fence. There is the person in me who wants terribly to remain a Mormon and have my children be the best of Mormons. And there is the person in me who yearns to just extricate myself and build from scratch with my children some satisfactory self-and-world view.

November 24, 1981

This evening I was looking through the old Sunday School manual prepared by O.C. Tanner, *Christ's Ideals for Living*. What a wonderful, wonderful, rich book. And of course I can't help comparing it to recent manuals—they are so impoverished, so sterile, so bland, so egocentric, so totally Mormon. Tanner's book draws wonderfully from the thinking of the great minds of the centuries. It is warming and inspiring. I had a brief association with him as he was head of Utah's Bicentennial Commission.

If I remember correctly I was told he no longer is active in the Church. That would not surprise me. I can sense that a mind so at ease with expansive thinking might come up against severe conflicts in the Church. As I turned the pages I had a sense of tragedy. Are the best days of the Church past? I have seen in so many ways deterioration before my very eyes. The Church that I knew—the Church that brought me to Mutual with its posters "Be Honest with Yourself"—the Church that was courageous enough to let O.C. Tanner quote the brilliant non-Mormon minds—where is it? Is it I who have changed? Some. But the Church has changed too. It has been correlated into poverty.

November 29, 1981

Emily's friend Stacy Goff's family was robbed; someone broke into their house while they were away, stole an old coin collection and a lot of gold jewelry that her father had brought back from his travels. I had a little meeting with the children and asked them if they thought we could do anything for the Goffs, who are reasonably well off and will not suffer too much from this except emotionally.

I suggested—and they all rose to this with enthusiasm—that we all chip in a dollar or so and buy them a gift and leave it on their porch as a surprise. So we all went early to rehearsal and stopped at Cost Plus and bought for ten dollars a lovely brass planter. I wrapped it and wrote a note that said, "Please remember the world is full of people who would rather give than steal. Love from some of them."

Coming home late from the theatre we dropped by and Johnny snuck up to the porch and left it and ran. We hope it proves to be a heart-warming mystery.

December 27, 1981

On Christmas Eve afternoon we went over to visit Lillian at the rest home. She was more disoriented than I've ever seen her. The week before we had gone to see Geneva; her daughter had called and told me she was moving her into a home in San Francisco to be nearer to her. So we all went the next day and sang Christmas songs to her. The kids were wonderful. As we sang, Emily went over and took Geneva's hand, then later hugged her and cried. Bless Geneva; we will probably never see her again. She was so thrilled that we had come, and for all the times we had come before. Aaron gave her a little house he had made at school, a gingerbread house made of graham crackers and candies. She loved it.

Got a brief note from my General Authority friend Marion D. Hanks the other day. He wrote it dashing somewhere, just wanted me to know that he got my letter and that he loves me. I had decided I wanted to tell him about Gerald and me, so I did. A long letter, telling everything. I'd wanted to tell him for some time, as he was the officiator in the temple who performed our marriage ceremony.

Years later I learned that another couple whose marriage was also performed in the Salt Lake Temple in 1966 by Elder Hanks ended in divorce because of the husband's homosexuality. This man, who "came out" to Elder Hanks in July 1976, was renowned historian D. Michael Quinn.

16

PAINTING A NEW PICTURE OF GOD

January 5, 1982

New Year's morning we learned that someone had taken all the bulbs out of our string of Christmas lights that were in front of the house. Later we learned that a boy up the street, P.N. did it (a boy whom Emily hates because he tells everyone she loves him and she thinks he climbs the tree to watch her get dressed). Emily marched to his door and in front of his parents demanded that he give the lights back. Sheepishly he went and got them. His dad was very angry with him.

On Sunday evening I told the kids I had been thinking about it and had tried to find out how Jesus wanted us to feel about it all. I told them I had looked in the New Testament index under (the boy's name) and under "Christmas lights stolen" and I had found the answer. I had them turn to Matthew, chapter five, verse 44. "Love your enemies and pray for those who persecute you." We talked about returning good for evil and I asked what we could do to return good for the evil P. did.

Johnny, blessed Johnny, lit up like the Christmas tree and said, "Oh, I know! We could get him a special surprise present out of our giving fund!" That's what I had in mind, so we discussed it. Did I mention our fund? I'm going to raise the kids' payday to $4.00 per week. Out of this they will continue to put 25 cents to Marilza, our girl in Brazil through World Vision and also put 25 cents in our giving fund. We decided to buy, in keeping with the symbolism of the lights that he took, a little flashlight, and just put a note on it, "To light up your life."

Johnny spoke to do the running again, but Emily told him he didn't get to it all the time. So I guess Emily gets to run the gift to P.N., whom she hates.

Yesterday I was visited by a woman from "Battered Woman's Alternatives." I had read in the paper that they need volunteers to take in a woman and her children for a couple of nights while they arrange for her to get into the shelter or put her elsewhere. I called and arranged to meet with this woman. We had a good visit. I had talked with the children earlier in the day and they were all very agreeable to do this. We will probably have a woman in need every one or two months.

January 19, 1982

Yesterday I was invited by BYU Continuing Education to speak at two Women's Conferences, L.A. and Oakland. The man who called me (I forgot his name) said, "We feel many single mothers could benefit greatly by hearing someone who is doing such a great job as you are doing."

"And how do you know what a great job I am doing?" I inquired.

"From your stake president and your Relief Society president." So. He had been doing homework on me. The subject he suggested was "An Eternal Mother." Seeing the door open, I jumped in.

"Actually, that topic interests me a great deal," I said. "I've done a lot of thinking and research about the Eternal Mother, meaning our Mother in Heaven. I really feel that we can better appreciate our own roles as mothers if we can better view the Mother in our eternal source. Throughout history all people have yearned for some knowledge of their Mother and the hunger is very much evident today. We need it badly and it would help us enormously in our feeling about ourselves as mothers."

He was very enthusiastic about this. Hmmmm. Maybe doors are opening.

Just now I got the kids into bed. It's Wednesday night. Ten thirty. Was working with Aaron on his Captain Hook poem he has to give to the class. And Johnny's cookies. And Katy's piano. And Emily's still-somewhat-sick body. Then they all climbed in bed with me and we laughed and giggled and sang and had a good time. They really are wonderful people. We have awful times, but they don't last. We have wonderful times, and they last.

January 27, 1982

My speech in Ogden went well. I used a certain amount of material from my Motherless House book. Tried to inspire them not just to reach for the things that men have been reaching for, but to reinforce a respect for things female. Perhaps the young coeds didn't have the experience to understand what I was saying. But a few middle aged women approached me afterwards who had been deeply touched. One said. "This is the only thing that has ever been said in the Church on the subject that has made sense. You have changed my life."

My old home economics teacher from BY High, Mrs. Jacobs, was there and came up before the talk. I remember sewing a dress in her class in high school. I said to her, "Mrs. Jacobs, I don't know how to tell you this—but I do not make my own clothes. I don't even make my children's clothes—sometimes I don't even *wash* them all."

"Well, of course not," she said. "You've got lots more important things to do than that."

Gerald picked me up at the airport. His friend Ned was with him. Have I mentioned Ned? This is the real thing, we hope. He seems like a very nice person, very bright and able to appreciate the good qualities that Gerald has. Gerald told me about him some weeks ago. Ned wants to "marry" Gerald, wants to get a real commitment out of him. I asked if I could be bridesmaid. We had a pleasant time together. The San Francisco Forty-Niners had just won their football game that day to make them world champions in the Super Bowl. And the city had gone crazy.

January 31, 1982

In Sunday School I contributed one of my rare observations. The teacher, a young, enthusiastic man, was building his lesson about the temple of Solomon. After some time I rose and said, "I'm interested in your theme of the layout of the temple as a symbol of going from the outer to the inner, from lower to higher, from alienation from God to full communion with God. Would you please address for me what that means in terms of Sister Haws's observation that women were allowed in the court of the temple and not in the inner places?"

A real ripple went through the chapel, some laughs, some "Ows,"—one "The handwriting was on the wall." The teacher was a bit taken aback. "Uh—yes, I will be happy to address that. Next week. I'll have to do some research and we will take a look at that." I hope he doesn't paint himself into the corner trying to defend the indefensible.

Only at this point in my history did I muster the confidence to tell in my diary the full story of my life with Gerald and his struggle from his earliest days, three full diary pages of all the details. Just a line or two I will record here:

March 7, 1982

Gerald had been entirely straight during his mission, had confessed in fact before his mission, but after his mission had gotten involved again. At one point he had discussed it with apostle Spencer W. Kimball, in charge of such things, who counseled him to continue to fast and pray and not to touch himself much when he went to the bathroom. And, of course to find a good woman to marry.

April 1, 1982

Financially I am stretched to my limit. Waiting for expected checks. I have had only a few dollars in my purse for more than a week now—have used up everything in the refrigerator and replenished only the milk. The kids have been taking lunches instead of buying. I am weeks behind on their allowances. Can just barely make the house payment now and Kaiser's medical plan payment. The rest will have to wait. Something will come. It always has.

Gerald occasionally gives me what he can, but I have not pushed him for child support. Early on his efforts were all toward my creativity and not his own. Truly I would like Gerald to have the resources to pursue his own dream.

I am in such a quandary about something—what to do with the boys and the Church. The Sunday before last I caught them sneaking out the window so they could run up into the hills and not have to go to church. I confronted them, furious, then mellowed and tried to have a reasonable conversation about it. Johnny burst into tears. And Aaron too.

"Why do we have to be Mormons?" Johnny said, "Why can't we just be decent people? Why do we have to go to church for three hours and be bored? They get you into the priesthood and they brainwash you so you can't ever get out."

I guess my years of stressing good Christian values without using much Mormon vocabulary has caught up with me. So what do I do? I had to give my Relief Society lesson that day, so I made the boys come. But I told them the next week they would not have to go and we would talk about it all. I talked John into going to the scout meeting at the church last night, and he said it was okay until they turned it into a Sunday School lesson.

How do I handle this? The other night John and I were lying on my bed together, and he said, "Mom, do you think you've raised us pretty good?" "Yes," I said. "I'm sure I haven't done everything perfectly, but I'm generally very happy at how you're turning out." "Well, what are some of the things you're not happy about with me—so I can try to correct them?" John is so beautiful. They all are.

Anyway I have been truly puzzled about what to do. I am dismayed at many of the Church's teachings. But I am not ready to voluntarily disassociate myself from it. And I am not ready to let the boys do that either. I know so many good Mormon men. I think Mormonism is a good and gentling and refining influence on men generally, though it likely contributes to male chauvinism. And the whole scope of the Church has pervaded my life so deeply—mostly for good, somewhat in pain—and I want them to have all the good things that I had. But it is so hard to take Mormonism à la carte. It doesn't work that way.

As I was talking to Gerald on the phone on Monday I told him that I wanted to visit with him about the situation with the boys and the Church. I told him I was not emotionally prepared to let them drop out. We made plans to talk with them together. Later that evening Gerald called me back, and said something like this:

"I just wanted to tell you how much I love you and what a wonderful person you are. And I want you to know that the kids are getting far more good stuff from you than they will ever get from the Church, and I don't want you to underrate yourself in that, or think that without the Church you have nothing to give them." We made plans to talk with the children together.

April 4, 1982

Our visit with the children went well. Gerald told the children that they do need some religious base to start developing their spirituality from, and that there are things in Mormonism that could start them on that, even if they decide later on to leave it. He stressed to them my own deep involvement in the Church and the thousands of people who look to me and who I influence.

What I stressed to them then—and I'm not sure they quite got it—was the truth of the little statement, "Grow where you are planted." For some reason they were planted in Mormonism, and until such time comes that their roots and branches can no longer develop in that place, it would be good to stay there and grow.

The boys were still quite reluctant, so Gerald did not push it fully, but said to think about it for a week and we would talk again the next Saturday. I coaxed Johnny to go with the scouts (ward troop) to the Exploratorium and he seemed to have a good time. And Brother Sutton came over and explained basically what Deacons do, so that may have taken a little of the fear out of it.

A beautiful dream. I am outside with a lot of other people. There is a lovely white bird flying up in the sky. The bird comes lower and flies right into my arms. I pet it and it is very happy, doesn't want to leave. But I know it has to go back, so I toss it back in the air and know that it will come back to me. Everybody is very impressed that the bird came to me.

I had such a good feeling waking up from this dream.

Did I mention that I am judging manuscripts again for Ed Hart of the Utah Arts Council? Light verse and non-fiction books. That will help me financially. I'll get $1400 for both categories.

And Johnny has a dog. It was found at the creek and John decided it was sent to him. A black Labrador retriever. John named it Jesse. He sleeps in John's room and John loves him.

Spoke at the BYU Continuing Education Conference in Oakland, titled "The Eternal Mother." Was very well received; many hugged me and told me it was wonderful. I had been asked to be on a panel and brought in a fair amount of material from my "Motherless House" manuscript. Again I was struck with the irony of holding a conference focused on our becoming eternal mothers with me being the only one there to reference *The* Eternal Mother.

An especially odd thing. At the event was the artist who had created a beautiful painting that was featured, a painting beautifully showing a mother in a spiritual setting. The artist is a lovely, humble woman. She gave her thoughts on the painting, beginning by saying essentially, "To my Heavenly

Father, to our brother Jesus Christ, my own parents, friends and loved ones, I dedicate this painting."

Always I am stunned. Does nobody *hear?* Isn't there somebody *missing* from that list? Especially at a conference called "The Eternal Mother"? I am boggled.

May 5, 1982

And last week I was burned at the stake center. Four times. I had been asked months ago to do an eight-minute scene of Joan of Arc. It was a multi-stake cultural arts program, mostly music, orchestra, chorus, solo numbers. Themed to France. There must have been a couple of thousand people there. It turned out to be a wonderful experience. I did three small scenes—the very beginning, then when Joan submits, and then when she denies her confession.

I started working on it on my weekend in Utah. Then when I went through it all for the first time here in my house, I was so taken by the poignancy of it all that I cried throughout and found nuances of interpretation that I had never even thought of before. Which is all so very interesting. I was a much, much better Joan now at age 42 than I was twenty years ago at BYU. And it's because of the deepening of my own personal experiences. And especially the parallel that my life has taken to Joan's in my relationship to the Church. All of the anguish that is mine—*mine*—in being in a profound relationship to a church that I love and that asks me to deny a very central part of my own self—spilled over into Joan's words and actions.

And what came out was really wonderful. Each night the audience was absolutely entranced and did not make a sound. And every night but one I cried real tears.

Which, synchronistically, brings me to another story. A couple of weeks ago Marve Wallin of Bookcraft called to tell me he had a hard question to ask me. He had been informed that I had been called before a bishop's court. I told him, of course, that no such event had ever happened, gave him the phone number of my bishop, and told him this was another evidence of the giant Mormon rumor mill. I continue to be astonished at the giant appetite that Mormons have for gossip, especially unsavory gossip. My friend Duane Crowther, author of many books, has had to live with this for years and years—the story went out again and again that he had been excommunicated. And nothing had happened at all.

A few weeks ago a woman called from Chula Vista to invite me to speak down there to their singles. I told her I just couldn't leave my children as I had traveled so much lately (even though I always took one along).

She said, "Well, what if we are able to bring down you and your four children too?" I told her if they were crazy enough to do that, I would accept. So she did it. They'll be taking us around for a few days—to Mexico, to the beach, to the zoo. Should be great fun. And free.

A lovely quote from Katy (my fourth child, it is to be remembered). I was hugging and kissing her and I said, "Oh, Katy, how did I happen to get *you?* I must have won the contest and you were first prize!"

"Oh, no, Mom," Katy said, "I was *fourth* prize."

May 10, 1982

Yesterday was Mother's Day and I had a very good day. The kids brought me breakfast in bed around nine—omelet, toast, orange juice. And a bell to ring whenever I needed anything else.

After church, I did something I should have done years ago. Why didn't I? I brought all my children into my bedroom and had a long discussion with them on Mother in Heaven. I have for years brought this concept in every once in a while. They know about my still unpublished book, "A Motherless House." And they know that whenever I pray or say the blessing I address it to "Heavenly Father and Mother." Katy is the only one of the children that in teaching her to pray I have consistently used the inclusion of the Mother.

I told them how important this concept is to me, how I had felt femaleness was left out of the divine picture all my life, that it had been terribly painful, and that the human family needed to have its Mother back in its consciousness. I stressed how nature here indicates the need for male and female to be together.

I then had them close their eyes and paint in their minds whatever picture they had of God, and to describe it to me. Aaron said that his God was an old man with a long beard sitting by the fire and reading the Bible. I asked if he liked Him and he said, "No. He's boring." I told him that if God was boring then he had painted a wrong picture and that he could redesign that Being into one that he could enjoy being with. "His face has to radiate love and power. He cannot be sad or angry," I said. So Aaron put God on a bicycle, dressed him in O.P. shorts, gave him a suntan, took quite a few years off of Him and they rode up into the hills together. Aaron grinned as he described all this. He and God had quite a good time.

I asked Emily about the God that she saw. She saw a man dressed in a long robe and sandals, standing with a very stern expression on His face. I asked if she liked Him and she said, "No, I'm afraid of Him." I then had her do the same thing and repaint that God into one she could like and enjoy being with. Her God then turned into a ballet dancer. Emily said, "I like this."

I can't recall the specifics of John's, but he took a similar journey. Katy just watched and listened.

I then told them that they were to add to that picture a female that would be the perfect companion of this male God. She was to be as happy and powerful as He, radiating love just like He does. Aaron put his on a bicycle too and away they went. Emily brought in a female ballet dancer and God and Goddess danced together. They liked this a lot.

I told them to try to keep those two Beings in their minds as they prayed and went about their lives. The Beings would change in what they looked like and what they did, but they would remain male and female and they would continue to be powerful and loving and helpful.

That evening as we had family prayer, I asked Johnny if he would talk to Heavenly Father and Mother for us. He did. And I felt very gratified. I cannot relate to the single, stern Father anymore. Somebody's mind invented him and we have all just sat still and passed along this sad image from generation to generation. It is time for us to try for a better view of God.

As I went to sleep this Mother's Day I was filled with gratitude. Emily is really a wonderful, thoughtful, sensitive person. Have I mentioned she is now taller than I am? She does a lot to make me happy.

And Johnny is a delight. Frustrating at times, but a beautiful, beautiful person. Clear and buoyant and tender.

And Aaron is a darling, even though we have the least in common and he seems to be involved in whatever explosions happen in our family. He is bright and aggressive and fun and affectionate. Well, more than he used to be. He spontaneously comes out with "I love you" frequently these days to all of us, as he goes out the door to school or as he goes to bed.

And Katy is really blossoming. Her teacher called last week to tell me how she's improving in school, paying better attention and finishing her work better and smiling more. She's doing very well on the piano. And she claps for herself and asks for tickles as a reward. Katy is wonderful.

As I went to sleep last night I was truly grateful, truly, actually grateful to be their mother. And I was really overwhelmed by how wonderful they are.

June 29, 1982

I failed to mention that the ERA is on the point of expiring. It will doubtless be brought up again, but the seven years are up at the end of this month. It's been a long and painful conflict. I am not in sympathy with all of the tactics used by the proponents; some of them have been sort of ugly, such as throwing blood on the windows of the governor of Illinois when the vote was no last week. I can understand the rage. Most of the proponents, however, have been behaving in a more dignified way. Putting this in the constitution seems to me a reasonable thing to do. I feel that most of the energy that has been directed against the ERA has been very calculatedly misogynistic. And that is sad indeed.

June 30, 1982

So today is the day. The ERA failed. But I believe the issue is not dead. Certainly the change in consciousness about women that it represents is not dead. And probably the issue of a constitutional amendment is not dead. A new perception is here and it will not go away.

Have I mentioned Sonia's fast? She and eight or so other women undertook a very long fast in Illinois at the state capitol on behalf of the ERA. After 37 days they broke their fast.

Reading about that fast now on Google, I see that the Washington Post reports: "'*I think it's worth dying for,' Sonia says softly, lying on a bed in her darkened motel room. 'Certainly justice for women is as worth dying for as justice for men has ever been, and men have always died for justice for men. Because men's rights are worth that, right? Because men are worth that.*'"

Two days ago Anne Mauss and I did our visiting teaching. Somehow the idea of including Heavenly Mother in a prayer came up. "Oh, that would be entirely inappropriate," Zula said. "We are commanded to pray to the Father only." I asked why.

"Well, we know that God is a jealous God. I wouldn't want to annoy Him by praying to the Mother."

July 10, 1982

The big thing I have to report is that I attended my high school 25th year reunion last weekend. And it was wonderful. I had not planned on going; I could not afford the money or the time. But suddenly I changed my mind.

Everybody shrieked as I came in and I went around and hugged everyone. I was indeed the celebrity and was besieged with all kinds of attention. But I've learned to handle it well.

The major event was that evening at the BYU reception center. I had a wonderful, wonderful time. Probably about a third of the class came with a spouse (our class had consisted of not much more than 100). I was *so* interested to observe my own reactions. I hugged *everybody*, and I felt a real, overwhelming affection for them.

David Grow and Joan Peterson Fisher were in charge of the program and they asked me if I would say a few words. So I did. Spontaneously.

I first told a joke about changing, which is what much of the evening had been themed to. "Do you know how many psychiatrists it takes to change a light globe?—One, but the light globe has to really *want* to change."

I then said something like—

> But I was not asked to tell you jokes. I was asked to tell us why we're all here. I can tell you why I am here. I thought I could not afford it because this is an indulgence out of the past, and there are so many things in the present that are so demanding. But in a way there is no such thing as the past.
>
> I said to myself, I ought to be there because these are my people and I love them. I was a little surprised to say that to myself, and I asked, "Do you really love them?" (Laughter.) and I answered, yes. It's sort of like

family—having a group of people that go way back, that sort of came from the same womb and wish each other well.

I'm trying to decide why I was so thrilled to see each of you tonight, and I think it's because it's so great to be all grown up, without all the trappings and the insecurities of adolescence, and be able to appreciate you far more than I ever did in high school. High school was not the highlight of my life. (Here, laughter again.)

I can look at each one of you now and feel nothing but pure empathy and affection. I can look at you and say, "I know what has happened to you. Twenty-five years of life has happened to you." And I know something of the anguish that has touched each person here, because it's touched me. And I know the joy that has come to each person here, because it's come to me. I know what's inside of you now, because I know what's inside of me. And as Matthew Arnold said, "The same heart beats in every human breast."

I concluded by giving my poem "Optical Illusion":

Time is a stage magician
Pulling sleight-of-hand tricks
To make you think things go.

There
Eclipsed by the quick scarf
A lifetime of loves.

Zip—the child is man.
Zip—the friend in your arms is earth.
Zip—the green tree is gold, is white
Is smoking ash, is gone.

Zip—Time's trick goes on
All things loved—
Now you see them, now you don't.

Oh, this world has more of coming and of going
Than I can bear.
I guess it's eternity I want,
Where all things are and always will be,
Where I can hold my loves a little looser,
Where finally we realize
Time
Is the only thing that really dies.

They stopped the program after me. They had planned to give some awards (silly ones), but the fact is I had quite an impact and they did not feel to change the mood. I had many people tell me what my little talk had meant to them. Some said it was the highlight of the entire weekend. I was sharing my humanity, and it felt *so good.* To have all the crippling insecurities of adolescence behind me was so gratifying.

July 10, 1982

Horror Story from the recent local Youth Conference: An Institute teacher was telling the guys what to be prepared for in dealing with girls.

"I came home one day from a hard day's work at the Institute and found my wife standing at the sink peeling potatoes and crying. I asked her what was wrong. She couldn't tell me what was wrong. And do you know why she couldn't tell me what was wrong? Because there *was nothing wrong!* Do not try to understand women, Brethren. You cannot hope to understand those who do not understand themselves."

For a couple of hours I talked with Robert Gottleib, a prominent non-Mormon historian who is writing a book on current Mormon Church history and wanted to interview me. A chapter in his book is on the woman problem in the Church, which problem, he says, is the major one faced by the Church today and in the foreseeable future. I shared my personal experiences, and when I told of learning from editor Brian Kelly that years ago my name could no longer appear in Church publications, I was in tears just telling it, as I had been when living it.

His book that was released a year or two later was titled, American Saints: The Rise of Mormon Power.

October 3, 1982

On Thursday a young woman called me from Billings, Montana. She was in tears. She said she had to talk about the problem of women in the Church, and she apologized for crying. I told her if she knew how many hours I had spent in my life crying about that same thing, she would know she didn't have to apologize. She wanted to know how I had managed to stay in the Church.

I told her as best I could what my position was, what my hopes were. Essentially I bore her my testimony, I guess, that whatever God turns out to be is a profound balance of maleness and femaleness, a Father and Mother or Mother-Father, working in perfect harmony, nobody presiding. And that inasmuch as we are given teachings that cause women to feel in any way less, those teachings are a bunch of baloney. I went on and on, telling her I was weary of women having to cry about this—that things had to change and I was going to help them change, pushing until things happened or they asked me to leave. At the end of our conversation, she felt a lot better and was grateful for what I had said. She was afraid I was going to tell her, like everybody else had, to just have faith and not question the system. She said that on a number of occasions when a woman has spoken to the stake president or bishop about difficulty in the marriage, he has responded, "What did you do wrong? What did you do to make him angry?"

The two women who were her visiting teachers had just left and she was terribly distressed over their conversation. They were talking about this very thing, and they lovingly cautioned her not to question authority, reminding her that that's how Satan got people into his grip.

Is this even to be believed????

October 14, 1982

When my good friend in the ward, A.M., was to speak along with her husband in Sacrament Meeting, the two of them decided that he would speak first and she second, but when they relayed that information they were told no, it is not allowed. She went in and talked to the bishop, such a very good man. He told her he understood, but he had no power over this. It is made clear in the handbook that the priesthood ends the meeting (somehow stemming from the thought that if anything doctrinally incorrect is said in a prior talk he can correct it). A. told me it made her feel like she'd received a slap in the face. Of course. And we're told time and time again that we Mormon women are not second-class citizens in the Church. A year ago on Mother's Day when I gave a very good talk, I was followed by a newly returned missionary who told how grateful he was for his mother. He was embarrassed to follow me and told the congregation so. But it's protocol.

Speaking of the bishop. He received a kidney transplant yesterday. Suddenly a donor came through and he dropped everything and went in. I called the children back in from bed and we had a prayer for him. We had already had our evening prayer, but I wanted them to know you pray for particular things, not just because it's a certain time of day. They were glad to do this. I can't give Bishop Anderson all the right answers for a recommend to enter the temple, such as belief in our Church's exclusive authority to act in the name of God. But I can give him my prayers and my children's prayers.

December 6, 1982

At the Johnsons I read my new poem about the depressed woman being assigned by her husband to go out and spend a whole day doing nothing but whatever she wants to do. "Laura and the Empty Tray." Afterwards, a woman told me this story:

She had lived in Denver a couple of years ago when some of the Church members there felt it would be a helpful thing for husbands and wives to see the videotape of that KSL program on depression and Mormon women. The meeting began. The tape started playing. About ten minutes into the program the stake president got up and said that he didn't feel it was appropriate for them to be watching that and closed the meeting and sent them all home. The woman was devastated. Later he said he felt the women were just jumping onto the media stirred up by the Sonia Johnson thing and all.

December 23, 1982

Just wanted to mention that two days ago was Emily's half-a-birthday. She is 14 ½. I have lately taken to celebrating the children's half-a-birthdays. We served her breakfast in bed—half a Swedish pancake on half a plate (paper) and half a glass of orange juice. And, of course, we sang to her: "Half-a-birthday to you! Half-a-birthday to you! Half-a-birthday, dear Emily. Half-a-birthday to you!"

17

STILL NO HOUSE FOR OUR MOTHER

January 28, 1983

Elouise Bell called me this morning from Provo, saying, "Madam! Why didn't you tell me you had hit the big time?" I was about to ask her if the *Chronicle* in Dingle, Idaho had come out with a report of my visit there, but she went on, "We just received the new Houghton Mifflin anthology, *Structure and Meaning, an Introduction to Literature*—and there you are with all the greats—right across the page from Christina Rosetti. My dear!" Elouise was stunned. Briant Jacobs (who had established the American Literature Program at BYU) brought the book down to show her and he was terribly impressed. No writer they know has ever gotten into one of the big anthologies.

I had forgotten all about this. But a few years ago I was approached by letter by someone who was helping to edit a textbook and wanted to use some poems. So now this—really remarkable! I will write the publisher and see how I can get a copy.

Actually it is pretty remarkable. I open the book in front of me now and see: "Optical Illusion" (on a page opposite of John Keats and Robert Frost). "Of Places Far" (on the same page as Robert Browning). And "Millie's Mother's Red Dress" (Between Wilfred Owen and Sylvia Plath). Thrilling of course, of course.

And another interesting thing to report. Yesterday Ann Landers quoted a poem of mine as "Author Unknown. I was reading the paper and suddenly found myself reading my own words. "To an Adopted," which she called "My Own Child." That same poem was published in *Parade Magazine* a year or so ago, also "Author Unknown." I wrote to Ann Landers this morning, calling her attention to the error.

I read the most horrendous letter from Apostle Bruce R. McKonkie to Eugene England, in which England is reprimanded for differing with him in public. "It is your place to echo what I say or to be silent," he tells him. Hard for me to believe.

And, in direct opposition to that, here is a fine church story. I gave a really great lesson a couple of weeks ago in Relief Society on "Personal Responsibility."

A faith-promoting story was right there in the manual, telling the sisters not to depend so much on church programs but to follow their own spiritual impulses. Really wonderful.

After Relief Society, Donna Shea came up to me and said, "I've been wanting to tell you how darling your little Katy is. I teach her in Sunday School, and I think it's so beautiful the way she prays, saying 'Dear Heavenly Father and Mother.' I think it's wonderful."

This really thrilled me. I had wondered what the responses might be. And Anne Mauss told me that the Jr. Sunday School coordinator's husband had said to them something of a suspicious nature about me because my daughter prays to Heavenly Mother as well as Father. Anne told me she is having her daughter Jennifer pray that way. Now when somebody hears her at church, what is going to happen? They'll know I am leading astray others too.

At Aunt Mamie's funeral service I was last on the program. I said that the final loveliness of Aunt Mamie's life was the wonderful way in which the people she had produced loved and treated her. I mentioned going to the rest home here with my children to see our adopted friend Lillian, and how her daughter who lives just miles away seldom comes. And how the woman in the next bed at Christmas time would not let me go. "I want you to stay here all the time," she said again and again. I pointed out how fortunate Aunt Mamie was to have people who stayed there "all the time."

As I came into the chapel for lunch the bishop grabbed me and said, "Sister Pearson, the local press is on the phone. They would like to interview you." (I giggle to remember this.) So I talked to the girl in Montpelier, eight miles away from Dingle, who was terribly excited to talk with me. We talked about my writing career and how I was certain my Mother is thrilled that I am now known in her birthplace.

February 28, 1983

I just this minute hung up from speaking with Sterling McMurrin in Salt Lake City. I had called to see if he might have any other suggestions of a place where I could send my Motherless House manuscript, which he had been so enthusiastic about. The book has been sent to fifty different publishers. Fifty! I know the project is important. Tremendously important.

Dr. Sterling McMurrin told me again how beautifully written and important the manuscript is and that he would like to help me in whatever way he could. He is really a lovely person; I trust his tone and his sincerity.

I told him I had recently enjoyed his interview with the Seventh East Press in Provo and that I'd heard the Press had just been banned from BYU campus. He said yes, that was true, and it was because of his interview. There has been a lot of publicity around it, TV, newspaper coverage and all of them indicate his interview as the reason for the banning. He said Jeffrey Holland, BYU president, didn't want to ban the press, but Ezra Taft Benson (next in line to be president of the Church) insisted and it was done.

He told me things have never looked so bad for the Mormon intellectual as they look now. "It's the worst I've ever seen it in all my years," he said. "The historians can't even breathe around here in the last twelve months."

He said a journalist from Denver who was scheduled to speak at BYU cancelled his appearance because of the university's censoring and gave the story to the national press. And that an organization of journalists voted to censure BYU for it.

Moving right along. Something hilarious to report. My BYU friend Tom Stone (former vice president of Columbia Pictures and also former president of the French Polynesian Mission) had invited me to come to his stake and speak in Modesto. It went very well. The next day I spoke at a luncheon Tom and Diane held at the mobile home park that they own. They had invited 170 friends, about half non-Mormon. And they bought a copy of *The Growing Season* to give to each one. For the luncheon I read poetry and made comments. Tom and Diane were thrilled.

One terribly funny thing happened. Bookcraft had to hurry and get out some more *Growing Season* as they were at the end of a printing when I ordered the large amount that I did. As I was autographing some of the books, I opened one to see, instead of my poems, "*And They Shall Be One Flesh: a sensible sex guide for the married couple.*" I laughed aloud. A wonderful glitch at the binders. I hurriedly checked all the books. They were fine. Tom called me the next day to say at least one woman had received the *Sensible Sex Guide* and called to tell him. Truly, one of the funniest things that has happened to me.

I really had a fine time with Tom and Diane. The perfect Mormon family. Eight bright and charming children, a flawless house, Church magazines here and there, pictures of their children with various General Authorities of the Church, a sign in the hallway, "Where in the world are you going on your mission?" with a map.

And again I realize that for many people absolute dedication to the Church works beautifully. There is a part of me that is the Stones. And a part of me that is Sterling McMurrin. And Sonia Johnson. And William Law. All authentic parts.

Good Housekeeping wants my "Obscene Phone Caller" article. They want it for their "My Problem" feature and will pay me fifteen hundred dollars, which I certainly need.

This is the story of a dreadful incident in the neighborhood where for weeks we had frequent obscene telephone calls. By quizzing my neighbors for clues (some of whom were also receiving the calls)—with the help of my boys who "knew for certain"—by observing that when the suspect boy's family went on vacation the calls halted and then started up again when they returned, I acted. At the next call—instead of hanging up as I had before—I spoke the boy's name and said, "If I or any other woman in the neighborhood receive another of these calls, the police will be at your door within ten minutes." The calls stopped. I then made the agonizing decision to talk to the boy's mother. She was devastated but grateful. This is the story I told—all characters anonymous—to Good Housekeeping.

March 13, 1983

There's a woman in the ward whom I have just said hello to a few times, but never had a conversation with. Gladys Martineau, a woman in her seventies. At the Relief Society birthday party some of her work was on display, really gorgeous patchwork embroidery. I spoke to her and told her how beautiful it was.

Her: Well, it gives me something to do—keeps me off the streets and out of the bars.

Me (laughing): Hey, that is *my* line! I've been using it for years!

Her: I've been a professional tailor for fifty years. People used to tell me I had no business doing that, I'd be ruining my children and all.

Me: I guess you've seen some changes in the national consciousness about women in the last few years. What do you think of that?

Her: It's wonderful! Wonderful!

Me: And what about the consciousness regarding women in the Church?

Her: Worse and worse. No improvements.

Me: How do you deal with that?

Her: I just go about doing what I want to do and let the rest go to hell.

Me: But if things are not good for women in the Church, God can't want that.

Her: Of course She doesn't!

I collapsed into uncontrollable laughter. THAT'S MY LINE! And here was a seventy-year-old woman saying it to *me!* I was so delighted that I could not contain myself. I grabbed her and hugged her and gave her a kiss.

March 29, 1983

I just sent Eileen off. She is another battered woman that was brought to me for two nights of shelter. I may not have mentioned each as they came. Eileen is about the fifth, I guess, maybe the sixth. The Shelter called on Sunday evening and asked if I could take her for one night. I said yes. She came at six, with only her purse and a jacket. I washed her clothes, stained from her husband having thrown oranges at her. She is a small young woman with two children, whom she left with a neighbor.

Her husband had threatened her life, has beaten her many times before. I didn't ask her about anything the first night. I gave her some books to read, put harp music on and put her to bed. We did talk the next day. Her husband tells her that he loves her—and she feels that he does. She wrote a letter telling him the conditions of her return were that he sign up for and complete a counseling session, meeting with men who have the same problem. And she would meet with a support group to change her behavior also. I do so hope this goes well for her. I gave her a copy of *The Growing Season*.

Saturday I spent with Mary Bradford; we were together on a panel at the Berkeley LDS Institute of Religion. She called to see if I could meet her in the city for lunch. We met at Ghirardelli Square down by the wharf. She had a friend with her, Brenda Keller. All of us are radicals. And all of us love the Church. And all of us don't believe everything we have been taught there. The last time Mary was here we decided to put to rest the phrase "only true" as too absurd even to entertain.

May 8, 1983

Gerald is here. He and the kids are out back barbecuing chicken for dinner. A bit of catching up. Gerald has broken up with Ned; Ned had been too smothering for him and does not have a life of his own. I hate to see Gerald starting over and starting over and starting over, which I fear he'll be doing for the rest of his life.

Anyway, Ned called him some days later to tell Gerald that the blood test that he took indicates his immune system is impaired. Evidently he may be in the first stages of AIDS.

I have not mentioned AIDS. For months now it has been a horrendous new threat on the health scene of the nation. Primarily it attacks homosexual men and those who have had blood transfusions from a carrying party and intravenous drug abusers. It is a baffling disease that impairs the immune system so the person can fight off nothing. Hundreds have already died of it and statistics indicate those infected double every month. It has struck terror in the gay community and most men have revised their lifestyles considerably. Which I believe is all for the good. In so many ways promiscuity is tremendously damaging.

So might Gerald be infected? He's going to have another blood test next week. Could it be spread through non-sexual contact? I told Gerald to kiss none of the children while he's out here. Unless some real evidence shows up, I don't want to suggest that he not come.

This whole thing is crazy. Crazy.

May 14, 1983

Did I mention that my new poetry book is out? *A Widening View.*

It looks lovely. Trevor did a beautiful job with his illustrations. And it is selling very well. My dear Dr. Hansen (BYU Drama professor and director) and his wife Betty called last week to tell me they were thrilled with it. Had already bought five copies before mine got there.

May 16, 1983

I just hung up the phone from talking with my General Authority friend Marion D. Hanks. He called me at nine this morning to tell me how he loves my new book. I had sent him a copy a week or so ago. He said he has used a few of the poems already in speaking. He used the one about "working out our salvation in fear and competition" with the temple workers, whom he said are often at each other. (He is currently Temple President in Salt Lake City.)

I asked him why the Brethren don't let him speak at Conference these days. He laughed and said for the same reason they sent him to China. But a lot of good came of that—the refugee work, which now has spread to Africa. So they now keep him safely ensconced in the temple, but good is coming of that too.

I told Brother Hanks that in spite of my heresies, which he knows about, I continue to participate and intend to as long as everybody is comfortable with me. He remembered that blacklisting problem of a few years ago and me telling him that I had been cleared to submit things to the Church magazines on any subject except the subject of women. He asked if anybody had been getting after me about anything, and I said no, not that I was aware of.

It was great to talk to him. He is such a lovely man. And it was so nice of him to call.

June 2, 1983

There is a purge going on in the Church—sort of the latest chapter in the ongoing war between the Brethren and the intellectuals. I called Sterling McMurrin, who told me some of the story. I also called Leonard Arrington.

Two underlings decided that the people who write for *Dialogue* and *Sunstone* are destroying faith in the Church and needed to be hedged up. So they drew up a list of eight names. Those that Leonard remembered are Lester Bush and Armand Mauss, both of whom wrote on the black issue, Jeff Keller, who wrote on evolution, David Buerger, who wrote on the Adam-God doctrine, Scott Faulring, who wrote for the Seventh East Press, and Brent Metcalfe, scholar, who was fired from his position with Church Security because of troubling documents he unearthed and shared. These names were given to Mark E. Peterson, who arranged for each to be "called in" by their bishop or stake president. With one exception the leaders stood by the people on the list, reporting that they were good members.

Somebody at the top (Leonard would not tell me who) decided the best way to handle it was to give the information to the press. So the *Provo Daily*

Herald ran an article indicating that Mormon writers were being called in and told their writing must be faith-promoting or they would be in trouble. That article was picked up by other papers and other articles followed.

On my way out of Utah I called Leonard again and he told me the latest. Evidently Gordon B. Hinckley (next in line to become Church President) became so upset that he decided he had to do something. So in the weekly temple meeting of the top leaders he reprimanded Peterson and Packer and told them this was tremendously damaging to the Church and he wanted it stopped. So that may be the end of at least this phase of the purge.

And about my musical play, *The Dance*. It went very well and the audiences loved it. The total impact was very moving. Richard Anderson (religion professor) called and asked Chuck Whitman, the director, if he could purchase five nights of the play so each of the wards in his stake could see it. They're performing it again for education week in August.

July 10, 1983

A couple of days ago Gerald and I had a large run-in. We've been getting along very well for months and months. But all of a sudden, without consulting me, he invited the kids to go with him to the Gay Freedom Day Parade in San Francisco. I was horrified. I called him and told him no, they would not be coming. He asked me what I was afraid of, and this led to a few sharp words.

I was terribly upset. I went for a walk and cried and cried. I hate to have conflicts with anybody, and I have never done well in conflicts with Gerald. He has always intimidated me. But I am getting stronger now. Anyway, by the time Gerald and I spoke the following Monday when he came out here, we both were in a position to talk reasonably. Gerald admitted that he was asking too much, and agreed that he would just let it go. We ended on a very warm and respectful note.

I am so grateful for that. I cannot live with conflict in my life. On Gerald's birthday, July 3, he came out and I took everyone out to dinner (ridiculous in my present poverty, but I had promised the kids I would take them out every time I sold a new book, and this was in celebration of the Indian story I'm doing for Randall Press). We also looked at old photos, read from Emily's little diary (kept by her mother) and had a good time. Gerald later called to say it was about the best birthday he'd ever had.

As I write this page, my typewriter is falling apart before my very eyes. For weeks it has been shaking, and now and then something, a bolt or small piece, would fall onto the table. But I've just ignored it. I haven't the money to repair it. Help!

July 31, 1983

I am grieved that I'm keeping up so poorly. Did I mention our forthcoming trip? I have yearned every summer to take my kids to the Aspen Grove Family Camp in Utah, but it's quite expensive. So I wrote and enquired, having learned that they have people there who lecture. They wrote back and invited me to be one of their lecturers, speaking twice a day in return for our stay there. We get food and a nice cabin to stay in. And I can sell books there too.

Katy and I had a private walk to the park tonight. The other kids are with Gerald in the city. He wanted to take them to a kind of meditation fair. I enjoy getting the kids alone. In a gang they can be entirely too much.

August 22, 1983

In Utah I did a very bold thing, a spontaneous thing actually. I left a copy of "Letters from a Motherless House" with Hap Green at Bookcraft, who has published so many of my books. I perceived that he had something of a liberal streak in him, so I told him a little about the manuscript. He was quite interested and agreed to read it.

One horrendous thing happened at the Family Camp. A really, really terrible thing.

I wrote of it in a three-page letter to President Gordon B. Hinckley, with whom I had had several positive communications. I told him of my attending a talk at the Aspen Grove Family Camp given by a popular speaker in the First Quorum of the Seventy, Hartman Rector, Jr. I wrote:

> I have never heard a talk in which the voice of the Lord as I know it was so conspicuously absent. This talk was given in an outdoor setting on a lovely summer evening at the Aspen Grove Family Camp, where I had been invited to be a participant. My four children were with me.
>
> The voice that I heard was a voice of bigotry, of self-righteousness, of condescension and patronization. The general thrust of the talk was how special we Mormons really are. An unkind humor permeated the talk from beginning to end. He joked about Catholics whom the Lord obviously loves because we converted 50,000 of them last year, and about people in India who have great suntans and who worship their cows.
>
> "And now let's talk about San Francisco and the homosexuals. Brothers and sisters, I want you to know that homosexuality is nothing more than an addiction, like an addiction to drugs or to cigarettes, and you simply get over it. But it's tougher. And do you to know why it's tougher? Because Satan himself is one of them, and he wants these men!"
>
> At this I heard someone clomping down the steps from the benches above. Yes, my fifteen-year-old daughter who had been sitting toward the top with other young people. She was sobbing, tears running down her cheeks. Her fists were clenched and she was shaking with anger as she sat down beside me.

"Let's leave," I said to her.

"No," she said as she glared at the speaker. "I'm going to sit right here."

I kept my arms around my daughter. More laughter, more jokes. The speaker smiled. My daughter cried. During the closing prayer she got up and ran and I followed her. We talked long into the night. I held her close and told her that this man was not representative of the church leaders that I know and love.

President Hinckley, there is false economy in worrying about the billions of waiting spirits and forgetting about the young people of the Church who are anxious to hear a voice that is consistent with the voice of the Lord. And when the voices in the Church are not—they do not hesitate to go elsewhere.

Thank you for listening. Thank you for your enormous efforts in dealing with difficult things. I send my best wishes and appreciation.

Carol Lynn Pearson

After leaving the Family Camp, I called Brother Hanks and asked if I could see him briefly to ask his opinion on something and also to give him the manuscript we had talked about. He was very gracious, and told me to come right over. Jan came with me and we went up to his home, a lovely place overlooking the city.

We just chatted a bit and then I told him the whole story about the awful experience at Aspen Grove. When I concluded he sadly shook his head and said some things I'm choosing not to write here. Brother Hanks agreed with my intention to write to President Hinckley.

Next day Jan and I went out to lunch with Leonard Arrington. Odd thing. Leonard suggested that I should move back to Utah—because he is looking for a wife. I laughed. (His dear wife Grace passed away last year, and honestly he has been seriously out courting.)

Still catching up on the Utah trip. I had gone to Bookcraft to pick up some more copies of *A Widening View*, but they had run out of the first printing of five thousand in just three months. So they called and arranged for me to get some from the nearest Deseret Book store. I did.

A clerk followed me out and said she needed to hug me and tell me I had prevented her from committing suicide. She said she was just on the brink when she opened one of my books and read the poem, "Time for the Gulls." She decided she would just have faith and hang on.

That short poem refers to the famous story of the seagulls saving the early Mormon pioneers in Utah from starvation when a cricket infestation was devouring their crops. Actually that little verse is one that I too have read over and over in times of trial.

Dallin Oaks (now serving on the Utah Supreme Court) called me on Saturday. He wanted to know where to get a copy of my poem about the woman and the violin. This is "The Steward," and I told him it is in *The Growing Season.* He told me he needed it the next morning to use teaching his priesthood class. "There are men who really need this message," he said.

September 13, 1983

Catching up again. A couple of weeks after sending my letter to President Hinckley, there was a letter in my mailbox from Church Headquarters.

> Dear Sister Pearson:
>
> I read your letter of August 17th with dismay. I very much regret the experience which you and your daughter had. I hope that you and your daughter will accept my apology on behalf of the Church and the speaker for any injuries done. Please be assured of my earnest desire for your happiness and that of your daughter within the framework of the Church and the gospel.
>
> Sincerely,
> Gordon B. Hinckley
>
> P.S. Thank you for the book which you sent me, "The Growing Season." Its contents are beautiful.

Last night I read to the kids a newspaper account of the Druze Muslim community and the Christians now involved in a war in the Middle East. And the big news of the day is the shooting down of the Korean jet over Russian territory last week—a terrible thing—269 people killed.

I want to record one thing I said in church Sunday before last. The lesson was on the millennium. I raised my hand, stood up and said that we must be careful how we present these things to our children, recalling how Emily had come home a few years ago in tears from having been told that before the millennium great destruction was coming—and she might be spared if she was doing everything right, but her friends who did not have the gospel were going to go up in smoke. "I don't know what was actually said, but that's what Emily came away with. That is, of course, a terrible way to get one to feel any kind of a fondness for Christ."

Later. I am amazed! I am astonished! I just hung up from talking with Hap Green, the new manager of Bookcraft. He is *very* excited about "Letters from a Motherless House." He has about three chapters left to read, but he described it as very profound, making a statement that *must* be made. He said it's not often he reads something that is absolutely new to him, but there are things in here that he's never even thought about. "Profound" was a word he kept using. He likened it to Thomas Paine's writings before the revolution.

I could not believe my ears! I asked him who else had to approve a manuscript. He said, "No one." He is the one who makes the decisions. He said he knew it would be disturbing to some people, but that it's a very important statement and has to be made. I told him, as I said before, that this could be the very thing that would give the Church the only good public relations material it's had on "the woman question" since maybe ever. To have something of such good sense come out of Utah, from a Mormon publisher, would generate such good will for the Church that it would be remarkable.

I am amazed. Amazed.

September 27, 1983

Leonard Arrington called from Salt Lake to tell me happy birthday and we talked for a while. I told him about Hap Greene's response to "Letters from a Motherless House." He was astonished, said that would indeed be a first for the Church if Bookcraft published the book.

And about the annual "Women's Meeting." When I was in Utah last I spent a little time with Elaine Cannon, General President of the Young Women organization. She told me her hopes for the forthcoming Women's Meeting, that she wanted something of comparable dignity to a priesthood meeting, that what she was constantly working for was for women to be taken seriously.

Well. Barbara Smith (General Relief Society President) and Dwan Young (General Primary President) gave nice, pat little talks—read every word. What a setback for speaking when the Church got that device in the Tabernacle that allows the speaker to both look at the audience and read at the same time. Dreadful! I find myself tuning out the instant I know a talk is being *read*. Elaine Cannon was brave enough to just speak, and she said some very good things.

But the highlight (read: lowlight) of the occasion was Gordon B. Hinckley giving the final and most weighty address. (The women spoke for eight minutes and then Hinckley spoke for twenty. I told Elaine to have him speak at the first and to take no longer than the women.) Anyway, he got up, looked at the Tabernacle filled with expectant faces, and said, "As I contemplated the arrival of this day on which women all over the Church would come together, I said to myself, 'What a big day for the hairdressers!'"

I went into shock. I could hardly believe my ears. There was a laugh, of course. But it was not a good, warm laugh. It was sort of a surprised, insecure laugh. And he said those words without even a twinkle of the eye or a smile on his face. I can take a good joke. I love a good joke. But this particular statement dramatizes so effectively the problem that exists in the Church—women are not taken seriously. Women are trivialized.

And his talk was filled with—some good things, of course—but also the expected patronizations: "I want you good sisters to know that God loves his daughters just as much as he loves his sons." When that statement needs to be made, we are still in trouble. When that statement sounds as strange to our ears as would the statement to the Brethren, "Dear Brethren, I want you to know our Mother loves you as much as she loves her daughters"—then we will have made progress.

At the end of his talk he assured us that any legislation geared to making the two sexes neutral was not good legislation. To even make that statement shows enormous ignorance.

As we got into the car to come home, Robbie McArthur, who was driving, said, "Hey, how about that hairdresser statement?" I was not going to bring it up. But as long as she did I said that I thought it was in pretty poor taste. Three of the four women in the car agreed.

Last week I went into the city and Gerald spent an hour showing me how to use the word processor that he uses at Bechtel. It's really a wonderful machine, and I am very anxious to get one. As soon as I get rich.

I had a good talk with Steve Covey at church on Sunday. He and his wife Sandra were visiting. During Sunday School we whispered for a few minutes and then I said, "Brother Covey, you already know everything being said in this class. Come out and talk to me for a bit." So he followed me out and we sat in the foyer and talked for half an hour. I told him that since his specialty was human relationships (he and I had talked years ago and we did a few projects together), I wanted him to be aware of what I had experienced since last I saw him. He had asked about Gerald, didn't know we were divorced. I told him the whole story—and how the Church's perspective on homosexuality is tremendously shallow. He nodded his head in agreement, saying that we really don't understand. He was most impressed that Gerald and I are still good friends; he said that's highly unusual. Someone very close to him is going through a divorce after ten years of agony, and she and her husband are bitter enemies. He told me I should write something about divorcing and remaining friends. That both Gerald and I should.

Emily is truly wonderful. Last night at supper on my birthday eve, she had everybody go around the table and say how they love me and why. At her turn she went on and on about how she got all her wit from me and how I help her do this and that, and how I help a lot of other people. Aaron said he's glad that most of the time I'm not a brat. Johnny said he's grateful I conceived him. Katy said she loved me but she couldn't say why.

October 5, 1983

I'm going to Utah tomorrow morning. Several important meetings on projects.

Importantly, I have a meeting with Hap Green of Bookcraft on "Letters from a Motherless House." He is still very interested. He told me he had run into Marion D. Hanks and said to him, "I believe we have a mutual friend."

"Who's that?" asked Brother Hanks.

"Carol Lynn Pearson."

Hanks then said, "I hope you are giving her as much exposure as you possibly can. Get her out there to the whole world."

"I couldn't agree more," Hap said.

He then asked Brother Hanks if he had read the manuscript I had left for him. He had not, but said it was on the top of a stack of things to do. Hap said, "Well, I don't want to say too much until you've read it, but let me just say that I am very impressed."

My meeting with Hap Green at Bookcraft was marvelous! We were together about two hours. He had finished reading "Letters from a Motherless House" and told me all he needed was to get a response from Duff Hanks about it. He would then go through the manuscript and pencil those places that he felt might well be softened a little. He said there would not be major changes, that it would not be good to water it down. "Right now it's a blockbuster," he said.

As Hap and I were meeting, Paul Dunn (General Authority) happened in. He greeted me warmly and said that he hopes I'm continuing to produce, that there aren't many like me. He said I have a voice the women of the Church need to hear and I need to keep it out there.

Our conversation included the bad health of President Kimball. Brother Dunn said, "I suggested once that all of us retire at a certain age, and that met with great resistance from some of the Brethren. One stood right up and said, 'I was called for life!'"

That evening I had an experience that was not so thrilling. I was brought to Utah by the Department of Health for an event on sex education for families. They were featuring one of the educational films I had written for BYU Motion Pictures, "River of Fire." After the film was shown, I spoke briefly, giving the history of how and why the film came to be, and something of my beliefs on the benefits of a "counter revolution" to the "sexual revolution" which sees sex as something unrelated to romantic love. I suggested that the idea of restraint can be seen as a valid way to achieve the kind of love relationship most of us yearn for.

I was not prepared for the hostility of some of the crowd. I had a barrage of comments about my approach being terribly unrealistic, that you can't ask kids not to have sex, that all you can do is to prepare them to be safe by using birth control.

Three of my cousins were there and told me I handled myself beautifully, but I was really surprised by the turn of events. I am not used to being so totally shot down.

Saturday afternoon I went to Algie Ballif's house where we met with the core group of the Alice Louise Reynolds Club, the old guard of Utah feminists. Helen Stark, Algie, her sister Thelma Weight, Anna Tylor and various others were there, about twenty in all. This was a private reading of "Letters from a Motherless House." I knew they would be thrilled to hear it, as they have spent so much of their lives waiting and doing what they could to aid the cause. And they loved it. They were tremendously moved. Helen Stark said, "This is the prophetic voice." I was glad we had this occasion. Many of them are not long for this world.

November 4, 1983

Hap sent to me an article out of the *Church News* on the "Coverup" of early Jewish goddess worship—a report of an archeological symposium at BYU. Raphael Patai was there, a scholar whom I quote in my Motherless House book. The material, of course, I already knew. But I was stunned to see that the *Church News* would so off-handedly report it. They really don't know the implications. But how fortuitous that they should publish it now. It gives a stronger plank for my forthcoming book to stand on.

Not a dream, but something else I want to report on. Every few months or so I am startled out of sleep with the awful, sinking feeling that I am temporary. It dawns on me in a stark realization that one day I am going to die—that one day I will wake up no more. There is nothing comforting about the sensation—it is cold and dark. I feel cheated and violated. The sensation passes before long but it is profoundly unpleasant.

Why are we temporary?—at least our present manifestations? I like being who I am. I like my body. I like my children. I like my friends. I like my work. Why is all this temporary? The giant mystery. And I cannot grasp it.

Thinking about my motion picture script on the life of Joseph Smith, which will never be used. And the concept of obedience to authority, which is so intriguing to me. Joseph's life is saved by Alexander Doniphan, who said no to his superior officer who commanded Joseph's execution. Later William Law says no to Joseph, who is his "superior officer" and begins a train of events that takes Joseph's life. Fascinating, this "obedience to authority" business. I so admire those who choose conscience over authority.

December 11, 1983

A report on my trip to Utah. The most significant thing first. I think I made some good strides toward the publication of the Motherless House book.

On Tuesday evening I telephoned Marion D. Hanks and told him I was coming to Utah the next day and I thought it might be very profitable if we could visit on the manuscript. He said yes, he could do that. He said he would be free Wednesday afternoon and I could come to the temple and see him there. He is now temple president.

Him: Do you have a temple recommend?

Me: No, I do not.

Him: Then I'll have to meet you at the door and bring you in.

He said he had not finished reading the manuscript but that he would make an effort to do so by Wednesday. He told me he has been sick—had vertigo and was for two weeks flat on his back and nauseated, unable even to move. Harsh.

I telephoned Hap and told him I had the appointment and asked if he might like to come. He said yes, he would and changed some appointments so he could be there.

Just before one-thirty I was in front of the temple, where I waited for Hap. Brother Hanks met us and ushered us into his office. We sat around a table and chit chatted for a minute. Then he looked over at Hap and said, "What are we going to do with this firebrand revolutionary?"

We all smiled and I said nothing.

"I read it all," he said, "last night and this morning." He paused and looked at me. "It's a big bite," he said.

"I know," I replied.

"Well, it must be said," he went on. "And it will be said. And to a large measure it's true."

We were together for a full hour. And at no time did he try to dissuade us from publishing it. There were a couple of main concerns he had. One was that I give good documentation as to places and names, etc. I told him I was planning a bibliographic essay at the end and that I could document every historical assertion.

His major question was that it seems to call into question our accepted method of revelation and the process by which we receive our scriptures. I agreed that it did. He didn't say therefore my premise and evidence are wrong. But rather he said it raises this question and what do we make of it? So who has been speaking to us from heaven all this time? And why, if all this is true, have we gotten ourselves out on such a long limb? How did all this happen?

He suggested—and I felt good about this—that I find a place to underline the integrity and sincerity of those who in our history and present have been "receiving the messages."

Hap said that unlike some writers I am very good to work with and have been amenable to making some changes if they would not destroy the potency of the book.

"It certainly is potent," Brother Hanks said.

"What I really want to ask you," went on Hap, "is how will such a book be received by the Brethren?"

"Well," said Brother Hanks, "I can think of a few that will find it very disturbing. The vice-president of the Church, Brother Hinckley, will not, but I can think of some who will. However, I can think of many who will find it refreshing and delightful and informative."

He further said that one of my poet friends had come to him and told him how horrified her daughter was when she went through the temple, vowed never to go back, because it verified a woman's place in the Church that she could not accept. He went on to say that he doesn't understand that. I assured him that I understood it.

As we left I said to Brother Hanks that he must look for a place in the temple ceremony where the Mother in Heaven can be added.

I don't recall his words exactly, but he indicated that the thought certainly seemed reasonable.

December 21, 1983

Last week we had a scare. Gerald had been breaking his health at work, trying desperately to make a success of this new job. And he became ill. His doctor diagnosed pneumonia. And then began to suspect AIDS and took some tests. Gerald soon felt better. And the tests did not find anything. So he is feeling encouraged.

January 1, 1984

Catching up here. Gerald came out early in the day of Christmas Eve, and we all went to the movie "Yentl" with Barbra Streisand. I loved it, a very important statement about the need of women to participate in the life of the spirit.

We had a pleasant Christmas Eve. I read to everyone "The Other Wise Man" by Henry Van Dyke. It's a wonderful story (I had read it for my lesson in Relief Society), and Gerald and the kids really enjoyed it.

Gerald wanted to lead everybody in a peace meditation. The children and I meditate together from time to time. So this Christmas Eve Gerald led us, visualizing our light and energy going out of ourselves and joining together and moving to heal and bring peace to the world. Gerald incorporated Christ in the meditation and our being grateful for him. It was all quite lovely. Then we watched the "Sing it Yourself Messiah" on television, a wonderful event where five thousand lay singers gathered in San Francisco to sing with a professional orchestra, led by a professional conductor. Then we sent the kids to bed and filled the stockings and brought out the guitars I had bought. Each child received one.

Gerald especially loved the "Sing it Yourself Messiah" and said to me, "Blossom, next year, let's be there to sing it in person."

18

GERALD IS FLYING NOW

January 1, 1984

Gerald is not well. New and various tests showed that it is a form of AIDS. Gerald tells me there is a good treatment just developed, 95% effective, using the bone marrow of a near relative. The children know only that he is not well. We have been meditating on him and praying for him. I am hoping for the best.

January 16, 1984

This is a sad day. I got a letter from Hap today telling me that Bookcraft cannot publish "Letters from a Motherless House." George Bickerstaff, senior editor, had talked with the owners of the company, and the consensus was that the potential dangers with the book make it impossible for them to do it.

I was so hopeful. I thought perhaps a miracle was in the offing. But it is not to be. They voice hope that I will just shelve the project.

Shelve the project? How could I sleep in peace or die in peace if I did? Today is the first national holiday honoring Martin Luther King Jr. I honor all those who sacrificed for a cause. And tonight I watched on television a docudrama on the eight women who picketed for over 300 days against a bank's discrimination against women. The closing theme song of the docudrama on King asked the viewers to "keep the dream alive" I must keep my own dream alive. Not to is death.

January 17, 1984

This morning I telephoned Doyle Mortimer, publisher at Randall Books in Utah. I had left him a copy of the manuscript and we had only discussed it briefly before he finished reading it. He acknowledged today that it is fascinating stuff but says even if he wanted to he "wouldn't have the guts to publish it" right now. He said the gender of God has never troubled him because he's a man. And probably the closest we can come to finding answers to the question is to study the words of the prophets and study the temple ceremony. "If the Father wanted us to know more about the subject of Heavenly Mother, he could easily tell us. But it will have to come through the prophets." I hung up the phone, shaking my head and saying to myself, we don't even speak the same language.

February 29, 1984

I've been shopping around for computers specifically for word processing capabilities. But it's been such a hassle and so complicated and so much money that I don't have—and I've become really discouraged. Supposedly I could improve my output considerably with one. But my typewriter is looking better and better to me. And I like having the hard pages in front of me. I love the pages. For the moment I'm putting the idea away.

March 5, 1984

Another addition to the history of my Motherless House manuscript. I was filing my materials when the phone rang. It was Diane Orton, who, with her brother, owns Bookcraft. I had told Hap that I would be interested in having Diane read it.

"I loved it!" was her first statement to me. "But my women's intuition tells me that I don't feel we should do it right now. I'm afraid it will make trouble for you."

I told her that I had been preparing myself for years for whatever trouble there might be.

She had let her sister read it, who is more of a feminist than she is, and the sister loved it, said she thought Diane ought to buck everything at Bookcraft and get it published. In fact, the sister let her husband read it, not sure of how he would react. He loved it!

She went on to say that if I do publish it myself and I got into trouble she would do everything she could to see that it did not affect my standing at Bookcraft. I told her I had people offering to loan me money for the purpose of publishing it and she said she might be able to help in that way, but it would have to be a very private thing.

We talked for a long time, close to an hour. Her final words were, "I just thought it was marvelous."

March 12, 1984

I had a wonderful adventure on Saturday night. A couple of months ago I saw a notice in the paper about a forthcoming poet's Dinner and Competition. Just for fun I entered three poems. It was a dinner at Spengers Fish Grotto in Berkeley. There must have been four hundred people there. Anyway I won TWO MAJOR PRIZES. There were a number of categories. "Your Voice" won first place in the short free verse category. And "Activist" won third place in the long free verse category. I was wishing I could read my poems; I read them so much better than the man who read them. Nonetheless, it was quite thrilling. This was an out-in-the-real-world gathering of poets from all over the Bay area. And I won two major prizes!

Here's my first-prize poem:

Your Voice

I would take your voice
And fill a tub with it
And soak in it for hours.

The vowels and consonants
And little laughs
Would articulate around me,
A sound sauna,
Caressing and deep.

And then I would
Take your voice
And roll it out
Like a blanket
And lie down in it
And let it hum me to sleep.

March 30, 1984

Gerald called last night and confirmed it. After all the blood tests the doctor told him that everything is wrong with his blood that could possibly be wrong. He does have AIDS and it is progressing. He's been working with all these alternative methods of healing and will continue to. And do whatever else the doctor recommends.

I can hardly bear this. Gerald is a beautiful person. I don't want to lose him. I don't want him to lose what could be good years of learning and growing. I don't want the children to lose him. And how could Emily bear it? She is closer to him than to anyone in the world.

Gerald is not giving up and I must not either. He is aware of cases of AIDS that have gone into "remission." Medically it is still a great puzzle. In the paper today is an account of the decision of the S.F. public health commissioner to close the gay bath-houses. Of course. Casual, uncommitted sex has always astonished and repelled me. And to pursue it in the face of death is something I cannot even begin to grasp.

The children and I will continue to pray for his good health. And I will do everything I can to help him. Perhaps there is hope.

Constantly I am brought up against it. Life. What is it all about? Is there really some final sense to all of this? Really a larger reality than mortality? I have written faith-promoting poems, and they make sense. But I have never had an experience that reveals to me personally a surety of life after death. I have longed for such. Where is life as it ought to be—sure and comfortable and simple? Everything in my life is churning. Where will it all end? Only with my own death. And there will be days of happiness in between. And days of sorrow. And I will do the best I can. And how I hope, hope, hope there is Somebody in charge of all of this.

And even now, I can hear Gerald say, "Well, of course, Blossom. You know that. *You're* in charge of it. We're *all* in charge of it. And we're learning what we have to and moving on to something better." And now as I write those words the tears come for the first time. Dear Gerald. Dear good, beautiful Gerald. I don't want him to go.

April 1, 1984

Gerald's will to live is very strong. But he does have some things getting in his way. He is dealing with some hard stuff the Church left in him, very self-negating stuff. He remembers vividly the horror that would pass through him each time in the temple when he would raise his hand to the square and promise that if he did not keep the promises he made in the temple he would "allow his life to be taken."

And he remembers how he and others have been told that they would be better off with a millstone hung around their necks and to be cast into the sea than to be guilty of being homosexual. (Many a Mormon suicide, I know, has come from being told that.) I am surprised that Gerald is having such strong feelings regarding the Church right now; I thought he had put that away. But I guess none of us ever puts it away really; we are always enlivened by the wonderful stuff and tormented by the cruel stuff, the unenlightened stuff.

I am doing everything I can to help Gerald and to bless him. Last night on the phone he told me that I constantly amaze him, that I am a "magnificent being."

April 3, 1984

Last night Gerald was here. One reason was to bring a painting of Trevor's that he wants me to take to Utah next week: Trevor is going to arrange to sell it. Gerald will need the money. He has not been able to work and I'm sure his money will run out soon.

The other reason was to tell the children about his illness. They have known, of course, that he is ill. We have consistently prayed for his health and often I have led them in meditations to visualize a restoration of his health.

We came up to my bedroom. Gerald sat on the grey couch, Emily beside him. I sat on my bed with my arm around Aaron, and Johnny lay on the bed at my feet. Gerald had already talked with Katy, who was now in bed, and told her only that he was quite sick and was going in the hospital for some tests. He told the children simply and clearly what was going on—that he has AIDS. They are all acquainted with the word and know what it means. He also told them that he didn't feel it was going to be fatal, that he knows men who have survived and that he is determined to do the same. Emily began to cry and embraced her father. I felt Aaron's tears running down my hand. I could not see John's face, but his first words were full of tears. There was a long silence before anyone spoke.

I told them that of all people who have AIDS, Gerald has more to live for than any, and that we were all going to help him. I told the children of the book, *Anatomy of an Illness*, in which Normal Cousins tells of healing himself through laughter therapy. I told them they were to collect all the jokes and funny stories they could and pass them on to Gerald.

This is when Johnny spoke, voice quavering, to tell us that in the book Gerald had brought out with him, *Baby Divine*, she had made herself well by laughing.

A little bit of comic relief. These children are so amazing. They feel things very deeply; they are not shallow in any way. And yet they had enough resilience to lift the mood, to make Gerald laugh several times. They are very courageous and strong people.

April 4, 1984

And in other news. Yesterday the Reorganized LDS Church, a denomination that also sprang from the "Restoration," announced it was giving the priesthood to women. I called Elouise Bell on the phone tonight and she told me that it was on the news yesterday. It was not on KSL, the Church-owned radio station, but it was on all the other channels. And it was buried in the Church's *Deseret News* on a back page. According to the story a revelation was received. And they said that with all the changes that have come about in the world there is no reason to withhold the priesthood from women. This step may not benefit Mormon women; it may even be a detriment, as the Brethren will *not* want to follow the lead of the "fallen" church.

April 10, 1984

A word on General Conference. I attended two sessions on Sunday, up at our chapel, shown on a large screen. Some quite remarkable things were done. Women spoke at General Conference for the first time. Six women! Such a good move. They were chosen from the outgoing and incoming Relief Society and Young Women presidencies.

And two new apostles were appointed who have not spent all their lives working their way up in the hierarchy. New blood is being infused into the top echelons. Russell Nelson, famous surgeon, and Dallin Oaks, past President of BYU. This is really an encouraging sign. Oaks is someone I have long respected. His appointment surprises me. His dismissal as President of BYU was very poorly done (the press says he read about it in the paper), and there had been a lot of talk about run-ins he'd had with Ezra Taft Benson.

April 19, 1984

Monday Emily and I went in to visit Gerald. He looked better than I thought he would. His color was good and he seemed in good spirits. In fact his doctor had come in earlier with some good news—Gerald's T-cells were up, the measurement for white cells in his blood. That was very encouraging. Yesterday I went in again and spent a couple of hours with him. The fact is that no one, after being diagnosed with AIDS, has lived past two years. But they are learning things all the time, and maybe there will be a breakthrough. Or maybe Gerald can be a miracle case.

April 25, 1984

Gerald is now out of the hospital. Yesterday in the headlines was the news that the virus that causes AIDS has been isolated. This will lead to an eventual way to prevent it. Next month the doctors will begin treating Gerald with a thing called "interlocken," to build an artificial immune system.

April 27, 1984

Yesterday in the newspaper there was a small headline on page 22 of the *S.F. Chronicle* that says, "The Church Says It's OK to Call God 'Mother.'" It's out of London and says, "God is not a male deity and can be addressed as 'our Mother,' according to a report yesterday by the Church of Scotland." It goes on to say that it is in response to women feeling alienated and distanced by an exclusively male description of God.

Last week I got a letter from an old high school friend, whom I asked to look at the manuscript of my Motherless House book from his point of view as an expert in comparative religions. When I began reading the letter I knew I didn't have the strength at the time to read it fully just then, dealing with all that I have right now. I skimmed it and my heart and my stomach sank.

He reminded me of what a responsibility I have to my readers who love me and who I have influenced so greatly. He said the book felt like it was written by someone who in fact hates men, wants to develop a whole new mythology. I have judged God and found God wanting. I couldn't read any more. I will read it sometime in the future. I am so vulnerable right now. I cannot bear to disappoint people, cannot bear to be judged harshly.

Most people who have read it have been enthusiastically supportive. Are they just being nice? No. But what am I to do? Can I afford financially and emotionally to lose my whole base of influence? Is it possible that things as they are, are as they ought to be? No. I cannot believe that. But I have to let it rest for a little. I can't handle everything at once.

April 29, 1984

Yesterday I took the kids into San Francisco to see Marcel Marceau perform his one-man mime show. It was quite wonderful. My favorite of his sketches was "The Maskmaker," in which the happy mask gets stuck on his face and his body goes through agony trying to get it off.

Afterward we went to Gerald's apartment where he cooked us a wonderful dinner. Gerald is still terribly weak. His hand was shaking as he stirred the soup. But he wanted to do that.

May 4, 1984

I will be driving along alone in my car and suddenly I will realize that I'm crying. Often I don't have the reservoir of patience and of good humor that is needed to be a good mother. So much saddens me. The threat to Gerald's life is a huge sorrow. I am baffled at my failure to get a publisher for "Letters from a Motherless House," and so confused as to what my next step ought to be. And the fear of nuclear war is more and more in the conversation, and should we or should we not sign the "no first use" pledge.

I have often found myself remembering the statement from Robert Lewis Stevenson that my mother wrote in the letter to her children the Christmas before she died. "When the day dawns, face it with a smile, a whistle, eager to labor—happy if happiness be your portion, and if the day be marked for sorrow, strong to endure."

I have had days when happiness has been my portion. Being strong to endure, I suppose, is all one finally can do on days that are marked for sorrow.

I gave Gerald another hundred dollars yesterday so he could pay his rent. But I can't do much more. I don't have much more.

May 14, 1984

Yesterday was John's fourteenth birthday and Mother's Day. He spent Saturday afternoon and night with Gerald in the city and they prepared a nice dinner for us Sunday afternoon.

Sunday morning I spoke in Stake Conference. I was asked to take ten minutes to speak on a Mother's Day theme, and I was happy to accept. I began my talk with a statement from a recent interview with one of the new apostles, Russell Nelson, saying that, "Next to motherhood, there is no more satisfying calling than that of a physician." I then suggested that we often give lip service to statements that there is no greater calling than that of motherhood, but that most of us don't believe it.

How would we react if we overheard a young college student consulting with his advisor who asked what his goals for the future were and he replied, "Well, I wish, of course, that I could make the wonderful contribution of motherhood, but since that is deprived me, perhaps I will become a physician."

The congregation laughed, and I went on, "We laugh because the idea is absurd. We don't really believe what we claim to believe. On the other hand, how unquestioningly we accept statements we've heard over and over from young women, such as, "I don't think I have what it takes to be a doctor or anything. I guess I'll just be a mother."

I went on to point out how our society gives only lip service to the importance of motherhood, and therefore we live in a world in which too often *things* are more important than *people*, in which economic and technological advancement is more important than human advancement, in which sending a man to the moon is more important than creating the kind of human beings that could live in peace and love and sanity on this planet.

I quoted anthropologist Ashley Montague as saying that men must understand that it is the work of the woman that is the most important work in the world, "for it is in the home that human beings are formed and human beings create the world according to the kingdom that is within them."

I said I know that finally the female contribution and the male contribution are of equal value and should be in equal balance. But what we have least of we should value more. And right now we value more what we have the most of—male-oriented things.

I suggested that we try on this Mother's Day to change our consciousness a bit, that we look at the mothers in our homes and those who do the work of mothering and nurturing elsewhere as people involved in the most significant of all work. And also that we bring into our consciousness a stronger concept of our Eternal Mother. I concluded:

"How our respect for motherhood might escalate if we could hold more closely in our minds and hearts and in the flow of our lives that Being who is our Heavenly Mother. We know that our eternal source is male and female, as is our mortal source. May we determine today to cultivate a better reverence for motherhood—both mortal and divine. For this I pray in Jesus' name, amen."

My talk was very well received. Many people told me how important it was and how they enjoyed it.

May 21, 1984

Catching up here. Yesterday I spent all day in San Francisco with Gerald. I accompanied him to his appointment at the clinic. I wanted to meet his doctor and ask some questions.

One whole floor of one of the buildings has been converted to an AIDS clinic. I was told that this morning the waiting room had been just packed. There were about eight there when we were waiting. Two had come in on canes. Several had the lesions on their faces that denote the cancer, Kaposi's Sarcoma. This is a tragedy of monumental proportions. Each of these boys has people who love him. Each of them wants to live. And they are dying rapidly. Since the epidemic began, the number infected has doubled every six months.

We saw his doctor. A young doctor, Dr. Abrams, is in charge of the whole AIDS program at the hospital. They had trouble finding a doctor who was willing to take it on as his sole responsibility. He said that Gerald's lungs appear to be in very good condition. But something showed up in the bone marrow, a form of tuberculosis. The hope in Interlocken was not well founded. That was bad news.

Gerald was depressed after that visit. We talked for the first time of the very real possibility of his imminent death. He came out Friday evening and spent the night and Saturday here. Emily was gone to a movie. Aaron went to a party. John was at the Fathers and Sons outing without his father but with the good men in the ward. After we put Katy to bed, Gerald and I had a pleasant evening. I asked if he would like me to read some of my poems to him. He said he would like that very much. He asked if I would hold him. So we lay on the couch holding each other while I read for perhaps an hour. He was so grateful.

Then we talked. Gerald wants to be cremated. He is going to send for a quart of wild flower seeds that he saw advertised. And he wants to have his ashes mixed with the wild flower seeds and divided into packets that will be sent to a list of his friends. We talked about the children, how hard it will be on them. Especially on Emily. He said he's been planning to work with Emily on a meditation and make her promise to do it daily—an exercise on loving and letting go.

All this is so unreal. It washes over me many, many times a day and chills me.

Gerald's parents came out for two days. It was hard, but good.

June 1, 1984

Before I left for Utah, I telephoned the Simonton Clinic in Ft. Worth, Texas. They've long done impressive work with cancer patients, treating them from a psychological point of view. I spoke with a therapist there who has treated 13 AIDS patients and was encouraged at the results. He said they are all well and he felt they could stay well as long as they maintain the changes in their lives that are necessary. I had talked with Gerald about it and he wanted to try it. Knowing time was of the essence I told the clinic to reserve two days this weekend.

I called Republic Airlines on which I have earned a free ticket and gave it to Gerald. I also gave him the $630 fee for the therapist and $250 to cover hotel and food. A funny thing happened as I called the hotel. The girl taking the information asked for my name, and when I gave it she said, "This wouldn't happen to be the writer, would it?" I laughed out loud and told her yes, and then I asked her if she couldn't help us get a room less expensive than the $85 she first quoted. She said yes, how about $40. You see, once in a while it pays to be famous.

Gerald was, of course, enormously grateful for this. He had been planning to have a garage sale to raise money for this trip. After going to the grocery store last night, I am now left with just over $300 to my name. And I have seven weeks before royalties come in. One way or another I'll be able to make it. I always do. No matter what comes of it, I have got to feel that I did everything I possibly could do, which I have done. And will continue to.

July 17, 1984

Gerald is in the front room preparing to leave this life. And I am doing what I can to make him comfortable.

I will back up and fill in what I can. Gerald's time in Texas had not proven fruitful. I had planned a vacation for the children and me to go to Utah and then to L.A. to be with my sister Marie for a few days. My brother Donald wanted to take the boys and me on a river trip for which he was a boatman and the boys really wanted to do it. Gerald's health had maintained about the same for a while. I was hesitant to leave, but he wanted us to go and the kids really needed it. He said it would make him happy to know they were having a good time. He had people set up to help and I did too.

I called Gerald every other day while we were gone. He had developed great pain in his feet and it was hard to walk. He spoke more slowly and without the usual inflections. Once when I called him he said he had spent the previous night screaming. I told him I would come home but he told me not to. The next day he told me things were a lot better. Since our friend Lynn Ann and his friend from high school, Judy Young, were going to be spending time with him, I decided to go ahead with plans to take the kids to Marie's for a few days.

At Marie's I spoke to him daily. He was losing ground. His speech was very slow. He asked if he could stay here and not have to go back to the city. I told him of course.

We came home a day earlier than planned. When I walked in the door I knew there was no hope. Dear Gerald. He sat on the black couch in his blue robe—so expectant and happy to see us—thin, transparent almost, the body of an old man. And we had been gone just ten days. There was a strange, frail demeanor that I'd never seen before. We all kissed and hugged him. I sat down by him on the couch and put my arm around his shoulders and had the kids recount a little of our adventures. He could not participate much, but he tried. I put them to bed, then talked to him again.

I heard the front door open and close and knew that Emily had gone out. I went out on the front porch and she was sitting crying on the step. "He's already dead," she said. "He's already dead."

The next few days are a blur. I sent Emily, John and Katy to my friend Margy Potter Andersen's to stay the week so I could get organized with Gerald. Aaron wanted to stay here, so I let him. I slept on the couch in the family room while Gerald was on the couch in the living room. I made a list of the things we would do each day: medication, humor therapy, soaking his feet, meditation, listening to the tapes made by his therapist.

We did what we could and then he slept. He woke a lot and said things. Once he said impatiently, "Come on, come on." I asked what he meant and he said he was sitting in the audience of "La Cage au Folles" and couldn't wait for it to start. He did this more than once. This was a great sorrow to me; he never got to see the show. He bought himself a ticket, but it was for the night he was in the hospital. Another time he said, "Blossom, I want to be in the country, north of the river."

I got out my guitar and sang lullabies and other songs to Gerald. He enjoyed that. And in the night when he was having a hard time, I got out his Walt Whitman book and read some poems to him. Oh, Gerald and Walt Whitman! Oh, Gerald and the wide, huge heart that wants to embrace all and know all and experience all and dare all. His expansiveness has always frightened me. But I accept now, just accept and love and do not demand to understand.

One night as I lay with him I felt hot vomit on my back. Should I not write the most dreadful, dreadful things here? But that is part of it and it is there. I cleaned us both up. And tried again for sleep.

I felt so helpless. But I remained strong for Gerald. He always saw me pleasant and loving and doing everything I could.

I called the children who were with Margy and had each speak to him and tell him goodbye and that they loved him.

July 19, 1984

It is now the next day. Thursday. Gerald left us. He is flying now, like he always yearned to fly. Gerald was never content with things physical. He always wanted more. And now he has it all.

This morning he could not communicate when I spoke to him. Yesterday morning he spoke his last words. I said to him, "Hi, Gerald." He opened his eyes and said, "Hi, Blossom."

About one o'clock this afternoon I noticed that his breathing was a bit more shallow. And all morning his shoulders and arms had been cold. So I stayed close to him, one hand on his forehead and one on his hand, and talked to him and told him how much we all loved him and that it was okay for him to fly now. Soon his breathing became more irregular and then it just stopped.

I said, "Oh, Gerald, you can fly now. Now you can fly!"

I closed his eyelids. Then I took some nice-smelling oil and put it on his face and shoulders.

And then I went about the business of life. I called the children. I told them Gerald had just left his body and I wanted them to try to experience with him some of the things he was experiencing—moving through the tunnel toward the light, being greeted by the Being of Light that we know as Christ, experiencing freedom and relief.

Aaron was the only one in town, and I asked him if he wanted to come over before they took the body away. I suggested that he might not want to. But he had been here through these bad days. And he said yes, he wanted to come over. So he did. He cried. I hugged him. And then the man from the mortuary service came.

That's all I want to write tonight. I'll try to finish telling the story tomorrow. Gerald is gone. Can I believe it? I have cried this last week again and again. But tonight I am at peace.

Goodnight, Gerald. I love you.

19

THE WAGONS MOVE ON

July 24, 1984

The first Sunday after Gerald was with me, I had intended to go to church and explain everything to the bishop so they knew what was happening. But I had had only a few hours of sleep so I asked my friend Anne Mauss to go in and explain everything. She reported to me that it was all received with great understanding and compassion.

In fact, Anne was told this is not their first experience with the situation. A young man moved into the ward and told those who first contacted him that he was gay and he would not be participating. They checked on him from time to time and learned that he was in a hospital in Berkeley, very ill with AIDS. Men from the Elders Quorum went in to visit him a number of times, and then arranged daily rides to the hospital for his mother who came from Utah to be with him. I had told Gerald that the bishopric was aware of our situation and also what they had been doing for the other young man. He was glad to know of it.

On Monday Nola Merle Christensen, the Relief Society president, showed up at the door with a loaf of bread. She hugged me and asked what they could do for me, for the children, for anyone. I suggested we could use a little help with yard work. The next morning she and her husband Ted and their son Todd showed up with their tools and went to work in the back yard for several hours. They worked a miracle.

Anna Lea Spencer, my visiting teacher, had called me as soon as she learned what was happening, and said, "I'm not calling to ask if you need anything. I'm calling to tell you to put a pad of paper and a pen by your phone because I'm calling every morning at nine to see what needs to be done, and those things will be done." I have always known that one of the best features of the Church is how it can mobilize people to help one another in times of need. I am very grateful.

Gerald had indeed ordered the wildflower seeds to be mixed with his ashes and planted. I asked his friend Jay to take them up "North of the river." There is a spot there they often went for a meditation retreat.

This morning Bill Graham called to tell me that on Thursday the San Francisco Gay Men's Chorus is going to have a gathering in Gerald's remembrance. Gerald was greatly loved and admired by a lot of people there. They honored him especially for co-chairing the national tour of the chorus.

Sunday evening we had a private memorial service here in the home—for just the children and a few friends who had been helping us. I conducted and asked Bob Johnson to give the opening prayer. I had a few things I had brought from Gerald's desk, which I felt represented some of the things about him that were important to me and that I shared with the small group.

There was a card from a friend saying, "Words are not right for you. Light is." Even when there's been so much confusion and pain, that light never went out.

There was an article from the paper about the swami who crossed the Berlin wall in a balloon to show that borders needed to be transcended. Gerald always wanted borders to fall and to show that finally we are all one.

There were some Emily Dickinson poems that he had copied:

"Because I could not stop for Death –
He kindly stopped for me –
The Carriage held but just Ourselves –
And Immortality...."

I also read a Walt Whitman poem, which Gerald had marked and which I had read to him recently: "Did someone ask to see the soul?"

I had invited others to bring along a thought they might have on life or immortality and on Gerald's influence on them. Lovely things were said, including his good humor in the last days when things were so difficult.

I then read a few excerpts from the book *Life After Life,* and led everyone in a meditation/visualization: Seeing Gerald in his best of health. Then seeing that his body could no longer contain his spirit. Laying him down and watching as the breathing became less and less. Seeing the spirit body, a body of light, raise from the physical body, move through a tunnel, move toward a light, toward that Being of Light that we call Christ, who receives him with great warmth and unconditional love, reviews his life and leads him on to a place of greater learning.

I had them pause for a moment to silently tell Gerald anything they might not have said or anything they might want to say again, and then listen for what Gerald might want to say to them. They then waved him on as he moved further into the light.

The final thing was that I took the candle that I had brought back from Gerald's apartment—the one, in fact, that I had given him for Christmas and had kept burning with other candles for the entire service—and I gave everyone a candle which they lit from Gerald's. I asked them to contemplate light for a moment, and to think of their own light and of the time when they would each have their own meeting with the Being of Light. I asked them to make some resolves about their light so that it would burn as brightly as possible.

I then gave the closing prayer, releasing Gerald with all love and asking for blessings on all of us.

We then ate and had a good time. Everyone told me how much they appreciated the evening. One told me I had created a "paradigm shift."

Emily and John told me the evening was very helpful for them. Emily said that at the end when she was saying goodbye to Gerald, he split in two, and one Gerald came and wrapped itself around her heart and the other one moved on into the light. That night and yesterday Em maintained beautifully, so helpful and patient. Today has been more difficult for her. She cried, and I told her that was okay, she doesn't have to be strong all the time.

That is all I can write now.

August 1, 1984

I must write a little, even though my time is so pressed. I am spending all the hours I can this week writing my short Christmas book for Bookcraft. Did I mention that? I think not. On a trip to Utah, I visited with George Bickerstaff and with the new manager, Steve Evans, on another project. Steve mentioned that they did not have a new Christmas offering and that he can always sell a short Christmas paperback.

Right then I thought—there's my house payment. With all the expenses around Gerald's leaving, I had—for only the second time in my life—not had enough money to make the house payment. I had left a check in an envelope with my dear Anne Mauss with an instruction that when I telephoned her she would put it in the mail. So I instantly committed to myself that I would come up with a good Christmas story.

Lying in the back of the truck with Johnny and Aaron on the way to the river trip with Donald, I said a prayer and instructed my mind that before we got to the river I would have a great story with particular elements in it—like a "laugh and cry at the same time" ending. One thing came, and then another, and then another. And within about one hour, the entire story fell into place, a very *good* story with a surprising, heart-warming twist. "A Stranger for Christmas."

Next day I sat under a tree by the river and wrote it all down in outline. When we got back I went into Bookcraft and read it to Steve and George. By the end both of these men were moved to tears and said, "Yes, we want it!" I told them I needed an advance of $1500 today and that I would get the story to them within a few weeks after I got home. Steve wrote the check. I called Anne and told her to mail the envelope.

Monday I started writing and am now on page 21. It's very good. I'll do seven pages a day until it's done.

This afternoon I received a telephone call from Brother Hanks. I had written to him last week, informing him of the death and telling a few of the particulars. He greeted me with: "I have to take off not only my hat but also my shoes when I talk to you. If anybody wants to see a real saint, they don't have to look on the ceiling of the Sistine chapel; they just have to go and look at Carol Lynn Pearson."

I told him that I had just done day by day the thing that needed to be done so that I could sleep well that night.

He said he had read my letter last night and wept and tried to call me at that time. I was glad that he called. It helped.

The strangest thing. I dreamed that Gerald is back but I'm not glad to see him because I know he will have to die. He is taking a shower. There is water all over the floors of the house. I can feel the water squish through my shoes as I walk.

Then at breakfast Emily was telling me she dreamed about Gerald. I said I had too. So we compared dreams. And her mouth fell open as I told her about mine. In hers, Gerald was back and she wasn't glad to see him. She knew he was going to die. And he was in the shower. And there was water all over the floor and she could feel it on her feet.

Is that not amazing? I've never shared a dream connection like that with another person.

August 10, 1984

Before Gerald's death it did not occur to me, but immediately afterwards it did. Perhaps I should write something. Perhaps I should just write out our story as it happened, showing what each of us learned, showing how we were able to find a better way than hatred and hostility.

There is room I believe, for a story such as ours. In fact, a need for it. Everyone has someone in their family or among their friends who is homosexual. We are all in this life together. We need to love and respect and help one another. I mentioned this to my stake president this morning and he was supportive of the idea. Perhaps telling our story is part of what Gerald and I came here to do.

August 27, 1984

And back to my theme of delighting in and distressing over the Church. In Sunday School yesterday, the lesson was from the Book of Mormon on General Moroni forcing the King-men to fight against the Lamanites even though they didn't want to. The discussion led to being loyal to your country and Brother C. (one of the truly best men in our ward) brought up the idea of what do you do when your country is wrong? The teacher said that you still uphold whatever government you are living under, and that if we obey our leaders (church or national) and they are not right we will not be held accountable for any wrong done.

I could not keep my hand down, of course, and said that history has shown us dramatically that we cannot just follow orders. The My Lai massacre in Vietnam—Andersonville in the Civil War—Hitler's henchmen—in all these cases people committed atrocities just because the person above them gave the orders and they felt they must obey. But they will finally be held responsible. The great moments in history have often come from one person saying "no" to authority. We must learn to rely on our conscience.

The teacher said he could accept about fifty percent of what I was saying. "But," he said, "I would certainly be wary of relying on my own conscience. We have to rely on the voice of the Prophet. This church is based on law and order. The priesthood is based on law and order."

Later I raised my hand again and recounted the story of Hübener in Germany, the young Mormon man who saw that his country was doing wrong, felt he must resist, printed pamphlets, all against the advice of his branch president, his "superior church officer," and was ultimately excommunicated from the Church and executed by the Nazis. Later Hübener was reinstated, posthumously of course, in the Church. I concluded by saying, "My vote is *always* with the human conscience."

Brother C. and I talked about this after class finished. He said that only in the case of the Prophet of the Church could he abdicate his responsibility to himself in favor of anyone. "If the Prophet spoke and said 'this is the word of the Lord,' then I would feel bound by that, no matter how I personally felt about it."

I do not feel that way. See how far I have fallen? I do not even have the same concept of prophethood as one is supposed to who belongs to the Church.

Later. My brilliant Emily just now came home from spending the weekend at Margy's, to be with her daughter Kristinea who just spent a week here with us. Em reported to me on the Young Women's lesson in church yesterday. The teacher told them that women are not to have careers, and that if they do go to work and put their children in day care centers they are ruining their lives and going against the plan of God. Also that the Equal Rights Amendment is evil and would result in rape no longer being a crime, legalizing homosexual marriages, etc. She further said that you needn't look to being in love with the person you will marry—that if the two are good, righteous people they will have a complete union with God and that will make for a very successful marriage. The teacher also has a testimony that polygamy is the true order of things and believes it will be brought back into the Church again.

Now—how's all that for something to help in my attempt to make my daughter love this church?

September 27, 1984

Forty-five years old. Is it to be believed? At eight the children and I are meeting in the family room for a party. I intend to read to them excerpts from my diaries that I have written on birthdays in the past. The first was when I was 17. I had not realized my diary was now such a massive thing. I would like the kids to have a glimpse into my life.

Next morning. We read my first five birthdays. Was I ever so young? And next week I want to go through all the rest of the birthdays with the children. They seemed to enjoy it.

This morning I spoke to a literary agency in Boulder, Colorado. I felt that this story could have a national appeal and I knew I was not capable of making it happen. A contact told me Peter Livingston was excellent. He's in Boulder but spends a lot of time in New York. I called his assistant and she sounded responsive to my description of the book about me and Gerald. I'm sending her some samples of my work, and she's sending me information about their agency.

A light-hearted detour here. Last week Emily and I ushered at Doug Henning's magic show in San Francisco. Aaron came too. Aaron and I both got to go up on stage to help the magician—Aaron with an imaginary pack of cards, me with putting the chain around a trunk with Doug's wife handcuffed in it. Then Doug stood on the trunk, was covered for a moment, ducked down and instantly changed places with his wife. I then gave back the key and they opened the box and Doug popped out of the trunk in a new costume. I do love magic. It's nearly as mysterious as life is.

October 9, 1984

Yesterday I got a phone call from Alice Price of the Peter Livingston Agency. She said they were very interested in the book I described. She had discussed it with Peter, who is still traveling, and he too felt it was very timely and right. They want me to write a book proposal, specific to a format they use, devising chapter outlines and probably a sample chapter.

She said she felt the story was terribly important and could be an inspiring piece. I will give it my full time until I have what they want. They will then approach publishers. This agency takes fifteen percent for their work. This may prove a really fortunate connection. In a way it will be hard to write this book. Just in doing the outline yesterday I found myself crying. But I'm used to that. I have a solid center.

October 22, 1984

Today I am completing the first chapter of the book about Gerald. I feel that a straightforward narrative is the best way to go. Yes, it's hard for me to write it. But I also feel a strong sense of peace about it.

Went to a presentation featuring the new biography on Emma Smith, Joseph's wife, written by Linda Newell and Valeen Avery. I had been looking forward to it for a long time. Purchased a copy and have begun reading it. Evidently it does a very thorough job of documenting the polygamy era, giving overwhelming evidence that Joseph lied to Emma and that tremendous subterfuge went on. Linda said that doing all that research on polygamy was very painful. She said in the midst of it she called her co-author Val and asked how she was doing. "I'm just sick," Val said.

Linda teared up a little as she spoke. "I didn't want to learn all that," she said. "I didn't want Joseph to lie to his wife." Evidently Emma lied too—to her children late in life, telling them that their father never had more than one wife.

At the event I also spoke to D., a young man who's written important things on subjects of church history and has become convinced that not all has been truthfully told. His very orthodox wife is threatening divorce. She is convinced that her eternal salvation rests upon her marriage and that her husband's changed beliefs could lead her down to hell. This is so sad. They love each other. They have three children. I told D. that I think the Church's emphasis on the importance of the family dissolves in the face of one member's changing perception of the Church. When that happens, the Church is terribly divisive to families. D. is in a lot of pain.

I can sympathize with that. I remember when I first seriously entertained the idea that not *all* the things the Church told me were true. But along with the fear and the disillusionment and sense of betrayal and anger, I sensed an undeniable thrill—a delight, an ecstasy.

Could it be true?—was it *possible* that things were *not* exactly as I'd been told?—that God was *not* the Great General Authority in the Sky with his multitudinous wives over behind the curtain bearing unending spirit children?—that God had *not* really given all his power and authority to a miniscule percentage of his children and commissioned them under pain of enormous regret to convince everybody else that this was the only way and to join the Church?—that maybe billions of spirits were *not* now pressing against the barbed wire fences of spirit prison waiting for us Latter-day Saints to take a trip through the temple vicariously for them?—that perhaps femaleness was *not* an afterthought and eternally auxiliary?—and on and on and on?

Since I decided there are often better answers to all the big questions than are written out in the Mormon manuals I have indeed been much happier—with myself and with God and with life. And even with the Church.

Speaking of which, in Sunday School class the other day Brother H. was discussing "the chosen people" as per a concept in the Book of Mormon. Brother S. raised his hand and said that the older he grows the more uncomfortable he is with the idea of anybody being "included out." What a nice surprise it was to hear him say that. The person next to him volunteered that he felt the same way, but since we do say we've got the only true church it means everybody else's church is not true, so there you are. Another volunteered that it's just that we have got *all* of the truth and others have just a *part* of the truth. This seems to satisfy most Mormons, I find. We've got it *all* and everyone else has just a *part.* My contribution was that I think God "chooses" different branches of the family for different works.

November 25, 1984

Aaron gave a talk in sacrament meeting today; it was the first talk he had ever given and he did quite well. A year or so ago he told me that he would *never* give a talk in church. But for the last several months he has been president of the Deacon's Quorum and done quite a responsible job. He was assigned to find one of the deacons to give a talk and he decided that he wanted to do it. I was quite amazed. And pleased.

I think one of the best features of the Church is to give young people an opportunity to develop themselves in this way. He was to talk on something about Thanksgiving. I suggested talking on being thankful for our problems as well as our blessings. Gave him examples. J.C. Penney: "I am thankful for my problems; they have made me grow stronger." The Cunningham boy who burned his legs so badly they were supposed to be amputated, but with a great deal of effort he broke world records as a runner. And Jimmy Durante, who turned his "nose problem" into something that made him rich and famous.

Aaron gave a good talk. He did not read it, but told it, for which I was grateful. I was proud of him.

December 23, 1984

Just about ready for Christmas. Don't think I've mentioned—*A Stranger for Christmas* has been out for a couple of months now and is doing very, very well. I have been giving readings from the book for groups and it has gone over really well each time. Anyone I meet that wants one and can't seem to afford it, I give them one. A little girl in Katy's class said her parents had just sent four hundred dollars to assist in the relief effort in Ethiopia (drought/famine) and they didn't have money left for any more Christmas things. So I gave her a book signed to her family with thanks from me and from all the Ethiopians. A little black girl who had wanted one told me her mother didn't have the money for one, so I gave her one. And lots of other people.

I'm getting excellent feedback about the book. Trevor Southey called me and said it made him weep and he wanted to get ten or twenty to give as presents.

Back to the story in "Stranger," I've been thinking about the whole idea and decided that we ought to do it. That is, take in a stranger for Christmas. I prayed about it—that we could find the right person, and talked to the kids about it. They were agreeable. Without Gerald here, this will be a different Christmas anyway, and I felt it would be good for all if we made our focus on something more meaningful than just our own selves. I called my friend at "Battered Woman's Alternatives" and asked if they had such a need. They didn't. I made more calls with no results.

But the right thing just fell into our lap. Gladys—dear Gladys Martineau—passed away yesterday afternoon. She had been failing for quite some time, and I had been stopping to see her on my evening walks. Her son Julius called me last night to tell me she had gone and to ask if I would speak at her funeral. He's been living with her with his two young boys. This morning I asked the kids if we should invite them to spend Christmas Eve and day with us, and they were agreeable. At church I invited him. He started to cry and said that would be wonderful.

And as always I am glad to know that my work is out there helping people. A friend called to tell me that her mother had said, "Next time you talk to Carol Lynn, tell her how her poem 'Unfed' helped me." Her husband was dying and she did not feel she had adequately expressed how much she loved him. When she read "Unfed" it really hit her. She copied it and kept it in her Bible. She would read it several times a day and then go in and tell her husband how much she loved him, even when he was in a coma.

UNFED

We feed one another in rations,
Serve affection measured to
The minimum daily requirement,
The very acceptable least—

While love bursts our larder
Wondering amazed
Why we are afraid to feast.

December 31, 1984

The end of the year. It will not be hard for me to let this year go. It has been a hard one.

The day after Christmas was the funeral for Gladys Martineau. Her seven children were there with all their various needs and expectations. Some are bitterly anti-Mormon. When they planned the funeral in the bishop's office one of the sisters refused to shake the bishop's hand. And they did not want the bishop to speak. They wanted me to speak.

In my talk at Gladys's funeral, I used the symbol of her sewing—all those wonderful embroidered patchwork coats and such. I said that Gladys's life was like that—a beautiful stitching together of a variety of pieces and experiences and qualities that made her the woman that she was, and is.

Her kindness and compassion. She was always giving the beautiful flowers that she grew in her yard. Once she learned that a columnist for the *Contra Costa Times* was ill in the hospital; she had read his column for years and enjoyed it. Not well herself, she fixed a basket of flowers and delivered it to him.

Her toughness. She told me that when a young man consistently ignored her rule about not bringing her daughter home late, she was waiting for him with the garden hose and let him have it.

Her universalism. This was the best moment of my talk. In Gladys' mind there was no place for borders that divide people, religious borders, borders of nationality or economic status. When Gladys was a little girl she was laughed at in Sunday School for praying in Spanish. She went home crying and told her father what had happened. He told her that she must forgive the little girl who had laughed at her, for she didn't know that God was really a Mexican.

"Oh, is he, Daddy?" Gladys had said.

"Of course he is. I've always prayed in Spanish and he's always answered my prayers." So Gladys learned that God was indeed a Mexican. And that God is much more. And of course that God is Mother as well as Father. Gladys loved her church, but was also quick to condemn any elitism or bigotry she saw within her church or any other church or not in a church at all. She was equally at ease with her sisters in the Relief Society and with her sisters in the Eastern Star, her good Masonic friends. Gladys was indeed bigger than all boundaries.

I felt good about my talk. I knew I had many disparate attitudes to please. And I did. The family was thrilled.

And so ends 1984, a very difficult year. May 1985 bring many good things.

20

WRITING THE STORY THAT I LIVED

January 6, 1985

Trying to comprehend the fundamentalist groups that are devoted to practicing polygamy today. The very idea of being the *only true splinter group* within the *only true faction* within the *only true church* absolutely boggles me. Like being the only true closet in the only true room in the only true house—never mind that there are billions of beautiful houses in the neighborhood. The fundamentalists believe that the Mormon temples are now in the hands of Satan and that when Christ returns the temples will be given to the true priesthood—them—and they will physically live in the temples. What kind of a God would think up a plan that "saved" or "exalted" the tiniest fraction of the human family and sent the rest to lower places and even to outer darkness? I stand all amazed.

January 16, 1985

As I am working on the book about Gerald and me, I am going through many of the early diaries. One thing that I am terribly impressed with is that those pages also contain so much material documenting the Woman Question within Mormondom. The whole thing is there—all my experiences and questions and doubts and the stories that I received from other people. I think all that is terribly important and will one day be a valuable journey.

Something nice happened today. Stephen Sondrup, one of the officers of the Association for Mormon Letters, telephoned to tell me that I have been given one of their annual awards. They have various categories, and I am receiving an award for two decades of contribution to Mormon writing in a variety of genres. This is lovely, of course. I have been received so well down at the grass roots level of Mormon readership, and that's the most important place, I think. But it is marvelous to have some recognition, too, from the more critical, scholarly folks. I am very pleased.

January 23, 1985

In the mail yesterday was an overnight express letter from *Woman's Day* magazine. Last week I had sent a letter of inquiry to about six magazines on a possible story about my experiences with Gerald. When I saw the express letter I knew it was not a rejection slip. The letter was from Judy Watts, Associate Articles Editor.

"Thank you so much for sending us your sensitive and very affecting article proposal. My colleagues and I read it with great interest. I would very much like to talk with you about the proposed story. Please call me collect at ...."

And then this morning before eight-thirty, I received a call from *Redbook* magazine. A woman there, Julie Steinstorfer, told me that *Redbook* wanted to buy the article for their "Young Mother's Story" feature. She said they pay $750 for this kind of article. I was up front with her and said I had also heard from *Woman's Day* and needed to study things through. A few minutes later she called back and said that the $750 fee was negotiable.

A few minutes later I called Judy Watts of *Woman's Day*. I told her that *Redbook* had called and what they had offered. She said she was sure *Woman's Day* would offer more. A little while later she called back and said she had talked to the editor-in-chief, who said that they could offer $1,500 for the article. I told her it sounded good and that I would get back to her. Isn't this quite wonderful? *Woman's Day* reaches over 7,000,000 readers; *Redbook* about half that.

January 26, 1985

A quick update on developments. Thursday I received by overnight express from *Redbook* a copy of their magazine and several copies of the "Young Mother's Story" feature. Also a letter from them, saying, "Carol, each month we receive several queries and manuscripts from wives and mothers who have discovered homosexuality among their husbands, children and close friends. However, none seemed to capture the subject with such feeling and detail as you have."

Also Thursday I got in touch with Peter Livingston, the agent that has been interested in representing the book. He is in New York at present and was very excited to see the great interest shown by these two magazines. We both felt he could pursue a book contract better now, but he did not have my materials with him. So I sent by overnight express a package of the letter I had sent to the magazines and a chapter of the book and information about me along with a couple of my books.

Yesterday afternoon Judy Watts of *Redbook* called again and said, "I really hate to bother you—but we wondered if you had given any further thought to our offer." I told her that I had and that my agent was studying it to see how it might best be worked into something in conjunction with the book. Judy said that of course they could print a statement that there is a forthcoming book that tells the story. She said she had spoken again to their editor-in-chief, who said to tell me that they would be willing to give me more space than we had originally talked about—and that they would be willing to talk about the possibility of doing it in two parts in two issues. Oh, my. This is all pretty overwhelming.

February 2, 1985

I am being fought over! How fun is this? *Redbook* called during the week, offering me $1,500 for between 2,000 and 5,000 words. Later *Women's Day* called with their offer of $2,000 for between 4,000 and 5,000 words.

And Wednesday the agent, Peter Livingston, called to tell me that he had heard from Random House, who is very interested in the book. He was told, "It has to be passed by the big boss, and if the boss does not hate it we will be offering a contract." Peter said if I could hold off the magazines for a week or so he might have a deal and the publisher might want to be involved in the decisions about the magazines. Things are happening!

And at a luncheon in Salt Lake for the outgoing and incoming presidencies of the Young Women's and the Relief Society, my ordeal was brought up. (I know Brother Hanks has been singing my praises.) The new Relief Society General President, Barbara Winder, said that it was a very thoughtless thing for me to take Gerald into the home like that—what if the children would have contracted the disease? Elaine Cannon then gave her feeling—that it was the most saintly act she had ever heard of.

Just this minute I opened a letter from Richard Cracroft responding to my letter thanking him for his words at the Association for Mormon Letters event, giving me my award. He had been our bishop back in Provo, and I felt he would appreciate knowing what happened after we moved.

His letter was filled with admiration and appreciation for what I had done. And with an admission that his many years in church leadership has convinced him that homosexuality is a condition that cannot be changed. He told of desperate situations, and of a suicide. Suicides happen over and over and over again. I am more and more driven with the knowledge that I must write this book.

February 5, 1985

I must report a miracle. I believe the project of the book regarding my life with Gerald must be terribly important. I think it is being guided.

Yesterday my agent Peter Livingston called to tell me he had heard again from Random House and that they were prepared to offer a contract on the book. They are going to call me right away to see if we are agreeable about how the story should be presented. Peter will then negotiate on the business. They are offering an advance of $10,000 to be paid in three installments. That is, Peter said, "respectable."

But yesterday afternoon I was plunged into another problem. Gerald's parents are quite hurt by the idea of me writing the story.

I was devastated. I cannot deal with hurting people. If I feel I have offended someone even on the highway, I hurt for hours. So I grieved all last evening and night. And I do understand what Gerald's parents are feeling about making this story public.

By coincidence—or maybe miraculous timing—last night was the showing of a network television movie, "Consenting Adult," about a family who has to deal with discovering their son is homosexual. Marlo Thomas and Martin Sheen were in it. I called the Pearsons to talk to them and also to tell them to be sure and watch the movie. Velma said they were just getting ready to watch it. I told her I would call back in the morning.

The movie was generally very well done. It did not attempt to validate all of the elements of the gay world. But it did stress the need for love and acceptance through all the differences. This morning I got both Ed and Velma on the phone and they were both pleasant. I asked how they felt about the dramatization they had seen last night. Velma spoke first, saying they thought it was well done. "But," she said, "we couldn't really identify with the parents because we never rejected our son."

So I took it from there. I told them that I loved them a lot and that I want us always to feel good about each other. I told them that whether we liked it or not we are pioneers out on a frontier that is terribly important and that we have to help others who are coming behind us. I told them I had gone back and forth about using my name on this writing and that I decided that my Mormon following, more than anybody I could think of, desperately needed to hear what I had to say, to counteract the bigotry and self-righteous judgment that so often exists. They agreed. I said I knew I would be taking risks, but that I was willing to do it. And that I had talked with the children extensively and told them that some insensitive comments might come to them because of it. They felt they would be okay and that this was something their father would want to have happen.

I told Velma and Ed that I could go ahead with the project only if we all felt good about it. I even cried a little, and not for effect. They kept agreeing with everything I was saying. They said that last night they let their neighbor read my letter and the neighbor said that if their friends couldn't stay with them through knowing about this then they weren't their friends in the first place.

Much more was said—we spoke for over half an hour. They are with me in the project. And they told me that they love me. This is so important to me. So important. I could not proceed without this. I prayed hard last night for a miracle. And I am so grateful.

February 7, 1985

Yesterday I received a call from Charlotte Mayerson, editor at Random House in New York. She told me they are very impressed with my forthcoming book and think it could be a fine thing.

She asked me some questions. Such as if I maintain as an active member of the Church. I told her yes, but that I also am a maverick and something of a heretic. She asked how. I told her that I am an uppity woman, that I speak my mind, that I am a feminist—but that still I am in good standing and very well-liked by the members of my congregation.

She asked how my church will respond to the publication of this book. I said that there will be some who will say, "Well, I'm sorry she had to go through all that, but I wish she had just kept it to herself." But that others—and this will be the majority—will say that they are very grateful I was brave enough to come out and talk about that because nobody has perfect lives and we need to be able to benefit from one another's experience.

She asked how my children felt about the publishing of the story, and I told her they knew there might be some who would make rude comments, but that they knew the project was terribly important and that their father would very much want to have it done. I told her also about Gerald's parents being with me on this.

She told me some things to consider that would strengthen the story in certain ways, and then call her on Friday.

February 19, 1985

Over the weekend Katy and I were in Canada. I had been invited to speak at a Relief Society function in Toronto. The women loved my talk. I told some of my good Mormon jokes and they loved them. That evening I spoke at a youth fireside. The stake president was very pleased, said I was wonderful.

Katy had a good time playing in the snow with the kids in the family. And we were taken to dinner at the "Top of Toronto" restaurant at the top of the highest free-standing structure in the world. It turns around for a wonderful view of the city.

And it was cold, ten degrees below zero. I was freezing, even in my fur coat that I bought to go into Russia.

February 28, 1985

In Relief Society Diana Rice gave the lesson on the Godhead. She handed out a list with various qualities written under each of the headings: GOD THE FATHER, GOD THE SON, GOD THE HOLY GHOST. Some little ways into the lesson at what felt like a reasonable time, I raised my hand and said, "Diana, can you just take one minute to tell us something about God the Mother?"

She blanched a little and then asked me if I would like to take a minute and do that. (I felt I could do this to her, as we have talked on the subject at great length and she read my Motherless House manuscript and loved it.)

So I got up and said basically that I felt that probably half of what we call the Heavenly Father is really the Heavenly Mother and that I know our Source embodies both, and that I feel it's important for us to recognize more fully that God encompasses both female and male.

Nobody was offended. Everything was fine.

Then today as I gave the Visiting Teaching lesson to Felicia Van Wagenen in her home, I added that I felt it important to include the Mother in our concept of the Godhead. Her husband was sleeping in the other room and he got up and came in and said, "You sound just like my mother." I happen to know his mother, definitely a feminist, and he brought me up to date on some things.

She is the "Spiritual Living" teacher in her ward Relief Society, and a few weeks ago when she was to give this lesson on the Godhead she told her presidency that she wanted to bring in the Heavenly Mother. "Oh, we can't do that," they said. "We can't talk about her."

"Why not?" Sister Van Wagenen asked.

"Oh, she's too sacred."

"Is she more sacred than the Father?"

Anyway, Sister Van Wagenen is related to Richard Anderson of the religion department at BYU and asked him what he thought. He encouraged her to go ahead and include the Mother in the lesson. So she did. I told him to tell his mother in Utah that I am pleased and proud.

Speaking of which, a week or so ago my own visiting teacher came by, Anna Lea Spencer. She gave the lesson very properly. Then I said something about the Mother.

"Oh, yes," she said. "For years I have addressed my prayers to the Father and the Mother."

I nearly fell over. Then I quizzed her and she told me she has addressed her prayers that way in family prayer too. I asked if any of the children felt strange about that. "If they did, they never said so." Surprise, surprise.

Last week I had another battered woman here; I'm sure I've missed mentioning some of them. This was a good black woman named Shirley who had her two grandchildren with her. Her daughter had been killed by the daughter's estranged husband who stabbed her numerous times right in front of their seven-year-old boy and three-year-old girl. He threatened to kill Shirley next. I had the three of them just overnight. My kids are always very helpful and warm to whoever is here.

When Shirley walked in, her kids were immediately at home. The little girl crawled right up into the bed in the guest room. Shirley was amazed. She said that's the first time since her mother's death that the girl had gone to bed without Shirley being in it with her. And the kids let her leave them with me while she and the Battered Woman's Alternatives woman went on some errands. She said they'd never let her leave before. But they were perfectly content to stay. She was amazed. And she commented several times on how good it felt here. So peaceful and loving.

Yesterday I started my rewrite of the book. I decided I could spin my wheels forever, so I sat down to the typewriter and wrote a new beginning. It was terribly exciting. I am having a good time.

March 12, 1985

In Utah I had a good visit with Mary Bradford. She spoke at the same event I did. She asked about the Mother project and volunteered that her children for years prayed to both the Father and the Mother in their home. They just did it on their own.

Which reminds me to document a horror story that Carol O. told me. Her son just got married and an older friend of his was giving him some advice. "When I got married I said to my wife, 'You've got five years. I'll give you five years, and if by that time you've made yourself into the woman I want you to be, then that's fine. If not, you go.'"

I asked if maybe he was joking. Carol said she asked her son that very question and he said no, he was serious. The son then asked the friend if his wife gave him a similar ultimatum. "Of course not!" he said. "I hold the priesthood."

My dear Larry Roupe picked me up and took me to his place for a short visit. I told him about the book I'm writing about my life with Gerald, and he reacted very strangely. He is afraid that it will hurt me, that it will bring strong repercussions from the Church. He knows so many people who know me and love my work and put me on a pedestal; they don't want to know all of this. He was really quite agitated. Dear Larry. I know how much he loves me. But the book will be written.

April 9, 1985

More about my trip to Utah. I spoke with a group of Mormon (or former Mormon) gay men. I read them the first chapter of the book and they were very excited.

One of the men there was especially bitter. He had been married, had two children, had sung in the Tabernacle Choir, had been a temple worker, had gone through every possible Church-related program to cure his gayness. He said, "I hate the Church—I despise the Church."

Toward the end of the meeting a friend of Trevor Southey's came, a straight man who has been one of the heads of Church Social Services. He was thrilled at the idea of the book. And he drove me to the airport so we could talk a little bit.

When he said something to the effect that the gay problem in the Church was nothing compared to the woman problem, I told him about my "Motherless House" manuscript. He was very excited about that, said that for years he and his wife and children had been praying to "Father and Mother" together.

Coming home I jumped back into writing the new book. Just today I finished chapter four. Still feeling good about the book. Really good. My pain has been lifted. I can write almost cheerfully.

A terrible thing in Utah. There recently was the conviction of a man for the ritual murders of a woman and her baby. The Lafferty brothers, leaders in one of the fundamentalist polygamous cults, received a "revelation" to "blood atone" a dissenting sister-in-law and her child. They did so, cutting their throats. (Blood atonement: the bizarre doctrine that Brigham Young did teach for a period of time in early Utah that some sins can only be atoned for by having one's own blood shed.)

That terrible, true story of the Lafferty brothers was made into a TV series in 2022, "Under the Banner of Heaven," adapted from the 2003 book of the same name. Every now and then a story from the dark history of weird or renegade Mormons makes its way into public consciousness. This is one of the worst.

While I was in Utah I spoke with my friend M. She said she understands Dan Lafferty; she knows how religion can drive someone crazy. When she was eighteen and again when she was twenty she had a nervous breakdown. "It was a religious thing." She heard voices from God and was tearing off her clothes and running toward the sun when she was caught and taken to the mental hospital. She thought she was in the temple; everyone was in white and she was being robed in white. "If somebody's mind is highly impressionable or twisted," she said, "religion can drive them crazy." She has had to be careful all her life.

May 2, 1985

Last week I took John with me to Los Angeles. I had accepted a speaking engagement from the Fullerton Stake there. I decided it was John's turn to come with me and I arranged a wonderful thing for him. He is deeply enamored of film animation and is now taking a class in it. Last year when we saw *The Secret of Nimh,* I saw the name of Don Bluth as producer. I knew Don briefly as we worked at the BYU Motion Picture Studio. I tracked him down and asked if my son and I could come and take a tour of the Studio. He was glad to hear from me and said of course.

The Studio is called "Sullivan Studio" and is a wonderful, wonderful place. When Don came out of a meeting he gave me a big hug, said I'm looking wonderful and that I'm quoted in his ward all the time. He then proceeded to take us on an hour and a half tour of the Studio, introducing us to everyone and showing us all the steps in preparing an animated film. Right now they're making "An American Tail," which he is co-producing with Steven Spielberg, the story of immigrant mice who come to America from Russia. Don is clearly having a wonderful time with his work. We had a great visit and my John was thrilled. I told Don to find something that I could do for him sometime. He said maybe I could write him a story. I said I'd love to. They're probably moving the Studio to Ireland in a few months.

My talk to the women of the stake went really well. "Where Love Is" was their theme. Often at these events the stake presidents are there and tell me they wish the men could have been there.

I believe I have not written since Peter, my agent, told me we've received an offer for a television movie. I am really stunned. This is a very prestigious group out of New York, "Entertainment Partners." They have produced so far: *A Christmas Carol* last year with George C. Scott, *The Body Human* series, and numerous other impressive programs.

May 12, 1985

Just a note from Mother's Day. At church today I did something interesting. Sister P. caught my eye as I was passing the library and I went in to see how she's doing. Obviously not well. She is caught in her pain and just suffers. She has allowed herself to become a doormat, does things for everybody and has no time for anything for herself.

I talked to her and told her as I have many times before that she has got to do something to protect her own being. She said again that there is no time for her to do anything for herself. I told her it was time she got some help and some support.

So I grabbed her and took her into the bishop's office. I sat her down and put an arm around her and said, "Bishop Sutton, on this Mother's Day you see before you a woman who has tried all her life to do what's right, has given and given and given and has got herself into a position where she's been reduced to a zero. She is in great pain and there is nothing coming in for *her*. She supports everyone else in the family and no one supports her. I think it's time that Sister P. gets some help and some encouragement."

My children brought me breakfast in bed for Mother's Day as usual. I had requested Aaron's hashbrowns and fried eggs and orange juice. Yesterday I got a new nightgown from all of them. And all day they have been kissing and hugging me and telling me they love me and thanks for being their mother. I am very lucky—very, very lucky.

I just read the newest *Dialogue*. There are enormous historical problems regarding the Church. There's a lengthy article on post-manifesto polygamy (after the Church leaders officially said they were allowing no further plural marriages). I have long been aware of the duplicity that was practiced by Joseph Smith and the others in the early days of polygamy, but I did not know that other presidents of the Church routinely lied about the practice. Joseph F. Smith even went to Washington and under oath denied that Church authorities had sanctioned any polygamous marriages since the manifesto.

I was really stunned at that. In spite of the fact that I have not for a long time accepted the "only true" position of the Church, I was stunned. I do not buy that the end justifies the means. We all do things that we would not necessarily broadcast, but to lie under oath is something I would never dream of.

A week ago today my editor, Charlotte, called me from Random House to tell me she had read the six chapters I sent. She wants a whole new approach, says it is too much a recounting of daily events. She wants it more selective, more dramatic. I've been studying it through and I believe I know what she means. I had been thinking "pure documentary." I was giving a history. That's not what she wants. I was initially devastated. But I'll have to look on what I have now as raw material and just start over.

I am looking at my writing these days more critically. These diaries are not particularly well written. They are valuable for the information that is in them. But it would be nice if they were also beautifully written. Sometimes when I really set myself to the effort I write well. But I am not a natural genius at writing.

May 28, 1985

I wrote seven good pages today. I think I'm getting closer now to what will really be workable. I'm not being tied quite so much in detail to what actually happened. But I'm staying completely true to the spirit of what happened. I found myself crying several times during the writing today.

And then this afternoon Bob Fuisz came out to see us, one of the producers of "Entertainment Partners," the group that is interested in making the television movie of our story. I told him it was important to me to have the children in on the meeting, so we arranged it for late afternoon.

We had a really wonderful time. I like Bob a lot. A dynamite New Yorker, also concerned and sensitive. What interests him, he said, is that it is a story about the dignity of the human spirit; it has meaning. He's not looking at this as an AIDS story—it is a love story about a whole family. The next step, he said, is to get a terrific screenplay and take it to the networks. Then if they could get a really good name like Joanne Woodward, it could be a media event. He said if this really happens, we have no idea of the kind of impact it could have.

I will continue to see if I have good feelings about it in thinking and prayer. It is an opportunity that does not come more than once in a lifetime. And if it can be it will be.

June 1, 1985

I watched a half-hour program on San Francisco General and the AIDS ward, very well done, showing the tremendous caring the nurses and doctors and staff and volunteers are investing in the men there. It was hard to watch it, of course. One of the people quoted Jerry Falwell as saying that AIDS is "God weeding his garden." How quick we are to judge.

June 3, 1985

I drove with Anne and Armand and Ruth Mauss to the "Bay Colloquium" at San Jose State. One presentation was a paper by excellent scholar Margaret Toscano examining the idea that Joseph Smith initially ordained a few women to the "fullness of the priesthood" and had further plans for women to perform more priestly functions than they later were allowed to do.

After she finished and people were commenting, I stood up and said something like—

"I appreciate all the good information Margaret has given us, but I find myself filled with a lot of conflicting emotions about this. She just said that we need priesthood to provide a framework for the inner spiritual life that we all need. Now, I have quite a nice inner spiritual life going, and I'm not sure I want the Corporation messing around with it. She has pointed out the ways in which priesthood promotions and hierarchy have not served the men very well. I'm not sure I want that to be happening to the women too.

"Right now there is a marvelous equality between the Mormon sisters. True, it's right down at the bottom, but we are essentially equal. I don't know if I want us to get the same kind of competition going that the men seem to have. I know that some women need to be given permission to feel that they are spiritually valid. But I also feel that making us feel there's something we don't have is like selling water to those that live beside the river."

I received a lot of enthusiastic response to my comments. But I was reminded, and I know it's true, that most women will not see themselves as valid until the institution validates them. So I would vote yes if priesthood for women came up. But that would be my second choice. My first choice would be a change in perception that would make us all aware that the power is ours already. Is it ours already? I say that and I think I believe it. Because I see so much power in places where Mormon priesthood has never traveled, I have to believe that God's power can be tapped into in lots of other ways.

Have I ever written on these pages a little fantasy I had once regarding how God might answer if ever interviewed about the priesthood? Maybe He (She/They) would say, "Priesthood? Priesthood. Oh, yes, that's what my dear Mormon children call my wonderful power, isn't it? Yes, I remember now. Do you know what they call it in India? Do you know what the Navajos call it?

Do you remember what they called it in 'Star Wars'? Yes, 'priesthood,' that's what my dear Mormon children call my great power."

High heresy. How dare I even write it down?

June 12, 1985

I wanted to mention some charming letters I received from a second-grade class whose teacher had read to them *A Lasting Peace.* One little person said, "I think the story was super. Your very thoughtful to let us use the book. I like Sol because he never lied. You have very neat handwriting. Love, Phillip Antonopoulos."

Very neat handwriting. I love it.

June 13, 1985

A dilemma was just thrust upon me. Mike Flynn called me from Utah. He has been rehearsing *The Dance* at the request of the Promised Valley Playhouse, a theatre run by the Church in Salt Lake City. The musical is scheduled to go on in two weeks. When Mike was casting the show he cast a black boy as Brad, the seventeen-year-old kid who has just suffered a heartbreak.

When the Promised Valley people found out that a black boy was rehearsing, they said, "No. A black boy cannot be at the dance with a white girl. No." They asked Mike to recast that part. I was really blown away by this. There is no romance going on between Brad and Janet. They are together as friends; she's sort of helping him out. I'm really surprised that it was that big a deal to them. As it stands now I would rather cancel the show than tell the black young man that he cannot be in it. Making that change would be a statement that I will not make. "We pretend that you're okay, but you're really not."

June 14, 1985

Next day. *The Dance* at Promised Valley Playhouse is cancelled.

June 28, 1985

I've been working on the book; that's about all I do. I'm into chapter eight now, and generally I like what I'm doing. Did I mention that my editor Charlotte responded to the first three new chapters that they were "a zillion times better?"

July 17, 1985

Interrupting my work for an important news report. One hour ago I got a phone call from Western Union, I was out picking up Katy, so I had to call them back. The woman said, "Yes, I have a message for you from Bob Fuchs. It reads: 'I have just received a commitment from CBS to develop a story based on your book. I am off to Europe. When I get back we will start the search for a writer. Congratulations. And my best to the children.'"

I could not move for a minute or two. I called John and Katy up to my room and told them about the message and had a prayer with them that everything will go well. Then I called Emily in Chicago; she is there visiting with the Arandas. Aaron is on a fifty-mile hike.

This is scary. But there is such potential for good here that I cannot be a coward.

September 2, 1985

Labor Day. The summer has gone. So absorbed in writing the book that I did almost nothing else. So much to catch up on.

As to my trip to San Diego. I went down to speak to a church event, a ten-stake single women's conference. The highlight of my time there was a visit I had with a woman named Betsy F. She gave a presentation in a workshop called "Recovering from Child Sexual Abuse." We were able to have a private visit. I have only recently been made aware that this problem is one that is serious in the Church.

I'm sure I have not mentioned here the story of a friend of mine who told me her personal story. She grew up in nearby Concord, California. Her father sexually abused all four girls as they were growing up. Only when she moved away and went to BYU did she get counseling and really understood what had happened. She then called her bishop back home and tried to do something about it. That went nowhere.

She later moved back to this area, now has three children, and caught her father abusing a niece. She told him he was either going to jail or going for long-term counseling. He is in counseling now. The explanation that he gives is that they had a number of children right off the bat and his wife was not sexually available to him; her energies all went to the children. He knew it would be terribly wrong to go to a prostitute or anything like that. Somehow he decided it would be best kept in the family and he gave his attentions to the young girls.

I had heard a couple of similar stories before, but thought it must be a rare, rare thing. However, I'm afraid it is not so rare as it ought to be. I received from a good source the story of a BYU student, a young woman, who was in a class in which abstaining from sex before marriage was emphasized. The young woman innocently raised her hand and said, "Except of course, for the 'patriarchal prerogative.'" Shocked, the teacher responded, "Please see me after class."

This horrendous problem continues to be a very significant one in society at large, likely in all religions, and certainly within Mormondom. Again the notion of male "authority" presents itself for careful examination—as does the impulse to first and foremost protect the reputation of the institution and the reputation of the priesthood holders of the institution (a phrase in Mormondom that means "most men.")

Speaking at the San Diego Women's Conference, 1985.

September 9, 1985

What an exciting day! This morning my agent Peter called to tell me that the producer and CBS have found a writer that they want to do the script for my story. He wants to come out and see me next week for four days. This is Robert Anderson, a major Broadway playwright. When Peter told me this I was truly stunned. What marvelous good fortune. He is the author of such plays as *Tea and Sympathy—I Never Sang for my Father—Silent Night, Lonely Night.* I have long been aware of his work, have read or seen the ones just mentioned.

I immediately ran to the library and checked out all of the things of his I could find. (I do mean *ran*; I ran to catch the bus; Emily drives our only car to school now). And this afternoon I read one of the short plays, *You Know I Can't Hear You When the Water's Running.* He writes wonderful dialogue. This is a very big day.

September 20, 1985

Had a wonderful four days with Robert Anderson. He called last week. I was meditating and had the phone off the hook and he couldn't get through. Then when we spoke I apologized for that and we laughed about it. He said his first wife was a Mormon, said she had a lovely voice and I have a lovely voice and do all Mormon women have lovely voices?

He said when the project was first presented to him he was very interested and asked if there was a book. They told him no, there was not a book. (I guess Fuiz remembered I had only a couple of chapters done when he was here.) Bob never works on a story like this for which there is not a book, but he had agreed to come out and meet me and see if he could get enough story. He was delighted when I told him the book was done, was to get rewrites but was done. He asked me to send overnight express a xerox of the manuscript, which I did.

Monday he arrived. Called me about noon. Said, "It's a beautiful, beautiful book. I was in tears all the way on the plane." A limo brought him out here just after one-thirty and we worked all afternoon. Every day that he was here a limo brought him over in the morning and came to get him when he called in the evening. Bob said, "I came here to find out if I wanted to do the project, but reading the book answered that; I definitely want to." He asked me dozens and dozens of questions, trying to get at details from which he can build dramatic scenes. He kept saying, "I can't figure out what Gerald thought he could find with a man that he couldn't have with you."

I cannot possibly even capsulize all our conversations. I will just jot down a few things. He's very concerned about getting the authentic Mormon background in the story. He wanted to see the book I quoted from, which was *The Miracle of Forgiveness* by Spencer W. Kimball. He called it a very "pompous book." I gave him to take with him President McKay's *Gospel Ideals* and the Sunday School manual, *Christ's Ideals for Living.* They represent the best of Mormon thinking, and I really don't want the story to show just the worst, even though I myself have found plenty to criticize in the Church.

I showed him lots of papers, files, Gerald's notebooks, poems, went over with him all of my books (he thought I was terribly prolific) and even got into my diaries.

The first evening we had dinner with the children. I had cooked a turkey. Afterwards I had the children perform and talk and generally get acquainted with him. Aaron played the guitar. Katy did a piano piece. I told Bob that John had given up music for art and reptiles and amphibians. And Emily sang, wonderfully, of course. Afterwards Bob told me my children are "enchanting, just captivating."

Last night, while I went to Katy's back-to-school night, the kids entertained him with our old home movies and with old tape recordings of Gerald.

Bob wanted to see the church. I arranged to get the keys and we went up. He also wanted to see the place where we first lived here, the BART station, and a few other places.

All of my stories would remind Bob of lots of his stories and he told me as much about his life as I told him about mine. His second wife (the first died of cancer) was Teresa Wright, the actress (I saw her in *Morning's at Seven* in New York). Bob has had affairs with innumerable women, but not during his two marriages; he was faithful to his wives.

He had great romances with Audrey Hepburn (she wanted to marry him, but he knew he couldn't give her a child and she wanted one badly), Ingrid Bergman, Deborah Kerr, the list goes on and on. He said, "I am an intellectual person, but also a very sensual person. Actually I've spent a great deal of my life in bed." We talked about casual relationships and my inability to understand anything of the satisfaction Gerald and others seemed to find in them. He came closer to understanding. He said, "I have never made love to a woman without it resulting in a profound appreciation of that person."

If Bob had not accepted this story, they were going to use the man who wrote *Pippin*. Bob has turned down lots and lots of stories; he turned down doing the screenplay for *The Sound of Music* because he didn't really like the story. He turned Bob Redford down when he was asked to do *Ordinary People* (he wanted to but was already committed). Turned down the Jonas Salk story recently. Did the Patricia Neal story five years ago.

Bob left last night very enthusiastic, very full, having had a wonderful time. He'll come back for two weeks in a short while. CBS wants him to have the script in two months; he told them no way, maybe three. Anyway, we were both awash in all the experiences, the possibilities.

September 30, 1985

Thursday Richard Lindsay called me on the phone. He's the head of the Church's Public Relations Office. He wanted to know the story about the Promised Valley Playhouse incident with *The Dance*—the black performer and the cancellation. So I told him everything. I didn't query him too much about his personal view on it, but I got the feeling that he felt perhaps it could have been handled otherwise. We had a good conversation.

Also I had a call from Dr. Lewis Ribner, the psychiatrist I contacted through my new friend Betsy in San Diego. I wrote him asking for information that would give any light on child sexual abuse in a Mormon context. He said that it was true that a really large percent of his own practice in the area of child abuse is with Mormon families. And he said that in the "Parents United" program there that deals with sexual abuse, he's sure that at least twenty-five percent of the cases are Mormons.

Now, I'm sure that not 25% of San Diego's population is Mormon, so what does this mean?—besides the possibility that Mormons are referring other Mormons. He said it's long been an understanding of the professionals in his area that child abuse in general, sexual and otherwise, is high in the Mormon population. I asked him what dynamics he felt contributed to this. The first thing he said was, "Well, your church doesn't listen to the women." He said that time after time he has seen it occur that a woman goes in to the authorities to tell about a situation; then the man lies, and the authorities believe the man and not the woman.

He also said that a contributing factor is that in Mormondom there is such an emphasis on the family, a self-contained little unit, and on the church being a self-sufficient unit, that too many times, because of an unwillingness to involve outside resources that could help, situations have gotten worse and worse.

October 15, 1985

Some horrendous news: Steve Christensen was killed by a bomb in Salt Lake City this morning. This is the man who had purchased and brought to light the "Salamander Letter," that strange document from history that calls into question some things about Joseph Smith's first vision. Another bomb was set for his business partner, who was his partner also in owning the letter, but the bomb killed that man's wife instead. Christensen was a bishop. I heard him speak at the Sunstone Symposium, clearly a fine man. When my children came home from school we prayed for the families involved, and I burst into tears.

October 17, 1985

More and more bizarre. Yesterday came the news that another bomb had exploded, critically injuring Mark Hofmann, the man who had initially acquired the Salamander Letter. Then later came the news that police had found bomb-making equipment in his house. Evidently he had a bomb in his car that he was taking somewhere else and it accidentally went off, injuring him severely. This is insane; I can't even compute all this.

November 3, 1985

I gave up giving updates on the terrible events in Utah. So confusing, and happening so fast. It appears that Hofmann was involved in a scam of some kind, probably forgery or selling non-existent documents, and needed to destroy people who were ready to expose him. One of his goals was to discredit the LDS Church through unearthing documents that called major points of Mormon history into question.

That was indeed the case. Hofmann is now serving a life sentence in the Utah State Prison. To learn more of this wildly strange and sad story of the man who forged hundreds of historical documents and performed two murders, check the internet or see the Netflix three-part documentary series, Murder Among the Mormons, *premiered in 2021.*

I have been getting excellent response to the manuscript from several of Gerald's close gay friends. John Chidester called me after he read it, truly ecstatic. He said he had been reluctant to read it because he didn't know how much I really understood, but he learned that I understand it all. He went on and on about how balanced it is and how he could not criticize a word. He said his only difficulty with it is that it won't be out until next fall and there are so many people right now that need it so badly. He so wants to give a copy to his former wife and to his mother.

He said that when he finished it he had a lightness and a feeling of healing regarding his own life that he's never experienced before. I was thrilled to hear him say all this. So far I'm getting rave reviews from my Mormon friends and rave reviews from my gay friends and that is quite a large distance to cover. Two of my friends that read it said it changed their lives.

November 20, 1985

Let me get down some thoughts that I may not have expressed for a while on these pages. I am feeling better about being a member of the Church than I have felt in quite a long time. My "widening view" has gone up and up and out and now I am beginning to zero back in. I do not for a moment accept the egocentric position of the Church as far as exclusive authority goes. I think we are one branch of God's human family, but as I observe the various branches I see many good reasons why I can feel comfortable in my particular branch. "Grow where you are planted" says a good philosophy. One cannot affiliate with all systems, just as one cannot marry all people. One specializes. And when I throw out all the stuff about the Church that I find harmful or that I don't believe, and look at what's left, there is really a lot that is left.

The way I see it now, I am not in the Church because of the past or because of the future, but only because of the present. The past—church history—is fraught with pitfalls. I could not possibly be in the Church if I had to believe that in every step of the history God's hand is clearly revealed; I don't believe that to be true at all. And as for the future—I don't believe that only Mormons or maybe especially Mormons will be better off in the world to come. I do not stay in the Church because it will get me a better place in heaven.

I find that I can feel good about being a Mormon solely because of the *present*, because in a very real way the Church can serve as an excellent tool for me, helping me do the things that are important for me to do. I can lift and serve other people very effectively in this organization. I take my Visiting Teaching very seriously. Sister L.'s family is in a mess; I have been trying very hard to get her to make an appointment with a family counselor whose name I gave her; and I call her and send her things in the mail that I think are appropriate to her situation. And Sister T. is trying to work out a marriage that may not work. Her husband left for a year and then came back, but it is not going well. She has no cause of her own and I have been helping her find a good place to direct her energies and not just wait around for her marriage to be all right. She has just signed up to be a volunteer for the CAP Child Abuse Prevention program that goes into the schools. I gave her the number for that.

And I do good things with my speaking. And with my Relief Society "Social Relations" lessons. And I appreciate the good concern from others that my children get. Did I mention that the Brethren of the ward painted our house? Remarkable. And that Wally Jones took a day off work so he could drive Aaron to the second day of Scout Camp in order that Aaron could attend both his father's memorial service and the Scout Camp too. It is good to be a part of a community of very good people. I am encouraged that perhaps I can work out a permanent way to remain a Mormon and feel good about it.

Last weekend I spoke in San Luis Obispo. Katy came with me and we had a good time. I knew that Barbara Smith was going there to speak as well. She was released last year after serving for ten years as General President of the Relief Society. We happened to be together on the same plane. So I gave her a hug and sat by her and we visited all the way down. Barbara is a fine woman. She has been experiencing more of life recently and told me about some major challenges in her own family. She has been learning some significant things about how other people live, some of the real problems in the world and in the Church. "I thought every woman was just like me," she said. She told me she learned a lot from those committee meetings in which we informed her of "women's issues." Barbara and I hit it off very well in our conversation, so I pressed her for a few things. I asked how seriously she was taken by the Brethren during her time as Relief Society General President. It depended, she said. Sometimes her requests were taken very seriously, such as when she asked Paul Dunn for things regarding the dedication of the Monument to Women in the Nauvoo Garden.

Barbara had recently been a speaker at President Kimball's funeral. She said this is the first time to her knowledge that a woman had spoken at the funeral of a prophet. She said Sister Kimball had asked for her. Barbara actually heard it on the news before Gordon Hinckley called her.

I talked to her about my ongoing concern over the tremendous lack of balance in valuing things male and female and she agreed. I pointed out to her that in my talks I refer to the Father and the Mother in Heaven, and I asked her if she would feel comfortable doing that. She said that sometimes she quotes President Kimball or someone else in referring to the Heavenly Mother, but since it's not scriptural she has not felt that she could do it herself. But she did say that once she said to Sister Kimball, "There ought to be a Prophet and a Prophetess, and you would be the Prophetess. And a Patriarch and a Matriarch." Sister Kimball agreed.

I felt to tell Barbara about my own experiences and about the book I am writing. She was very interested and very impressed, calling what I did "highly courageous." She said that she has a friend who has eight children and has been left by her husband who is a homosexual. The friend is of course having a terrible time trying to work things out. I told her to give the friend my number and have her call me. She did call me, the next night in fact.

Sunday afternoon I spent with my editor, Charlotte Mayerson, of Random House. She came to San Francisco for something else and stayed over a day so she could see me. We went over the manuscript page by page for the final changes that she's making. A few fairly major things were touched on, which I will be adding a bit to clarify. She wants to see Gerald suffer more rather than just go off happily to his new life. And something on why it was okay that I shouldered all the financial burden and he got to spend his fortune on the Gay Men's Chorus. We had a good visit. Charlotte is very enthusiastic about the book.

Spent yesterday replying to two letters from Bob Anderson. He's got his first draft of the screenplay done and feels he has been "true to the rich story." He said he was asked to do the screenplay for *An Early Frost*, which was on TV last week, in which a family discovers their son is gay and has AIDS at the same time. He said the story didn't interest him and he was glad he waited for mine.

An Early Frost *was the first ever television motion picture to deal with the AIDS crisis. It received a great deal of attention.*

December 3, 1985

Katy said something the other day that just blew me away. We were home alone, lying on my bed, and I said, "Katy, tell me a story." "No," she said, "you tell me one." It is so hard to get Katy to perform in any way, except on the piano. I try and try and she will not sing and she will not dance. Often she just kind of hides away. So on this occasion I said, "All right, Katy, we'll make up a story together. I'll start and you finish my sentences."

I started a story about a horse and Katy added one word or maybe two to all my sentences. She would *not* take the story and run with it. After five minutes or so of laboring, I said, "Oh, Katy, why won't you tell me a story?"

Katy sighed. "Oh, Mom—I am not a story teller—I am a story *tellee*." I nearly fell off the bed laughing.

December 31, 1985

Our Christmas was a happy one. Emily said it was one of the best she's ever had, that she felt happy and content and in the Christmas spirit. On Christmas Eve we watched "A Christmas Carol" on TV with George C. Scott, produced by Bob Fuisz, who is the producer of our story. I gave Emily a copy of Zeferelli's *Romeo and Juliet* movie. And *The Secret of Nimh* to John. And a microphone to Aaron for his music work. Katy wanted a horse but settled for a hamster.

The kids and I were able to do some good things. We decided to "adopt a family" through the county social services. We got a mother and her eighteen-year-old son, who live in nearby Pittsburg. She lost two other sons in one year. We went to Gemco all together and spent about one hundred dollars on food for Christmas, and clothing, a watch, and perfume.

The room mother and I had Katy's class do the same thing. We found a mother and four-year-old girl that were not being taken care of and we had the kids in class bring in money and clothing and toys. One little boy brought in twenty dollars. I had gone the day before and read to the class *A Stranger for Christmas* and introduced them to the needs of the family we had been given. This little boy said, "Can I bring twenty dollars?" "That's a lot of money," I said. "But if you want to, it would be a wonderful thing."

And on Wednesday night all the kids from church went to a warehouse to help prepare Christmas things for needy people. I'm so glad we could do this. I am grateful to be among the healthy, physically and emotionally and spiritually. I am happy.

One last thing of interest. Friday I received a phone call from a reporter at the *Deseret News*, Glen Warchol. He is doing a series for the paper on homosexuality in the Mormon Church and had heard about my work. I was stunned. I did not think this Church-owned newspaper could do such a thing. My initial thought was that I didn't want to talk to anybody in the press until the book came out, but the more I talked to him the more I felt that the time is now to do whatever I can.

I liked Mr. Warchol. He said he is finding that many people in Utah deny that there could possibly be a homosexual problem in the Church. And he's talked to lots of gay people who tell him things like, "The homosexual is the lost sheep in the Church that nobody goes out to find." I told him that I wanted to talk to my agent and to Gerald's parents before I committed myself to an interview. I did. All of them thought it would be fine. So I called back and said I'll do it. It's a big deal and I want to make sure it's done right. This is sooner than I'd thought. But I'm ready. And 1985 is gone. It was not easy. But it was good.

21

FROM "GOOD MORNING AMERICA" TO "OPRAH"

January 13, 1986

A massive amount to catch up on. Just got back from Utah late last night. Glen Worchal from the *Deseret News* came to Jan's and we did the interview there. We spoke for hours. He had read my manuscript by that time. He asked me questions like: "What do you think of the suggestion that AIDS is God's retribution to sinners?" I responded with Luke 13, Christ asking if the men who had the tower fall on them were less righteous than the others. He wanted to begin the story with the way my ward helped. I told I wouldn't be able to tell it without crying. He wanted it anyway. So I did. And I cried.

I told him a few things I hoped he would emphasize in the article. I said, "Recently Mother Theresa came to New York to open a hospice for AIDS patients, calling them 'children of God.' We Mormons shouldn't need to have her tell us that. We already know that. Gerald sang 'I am a child of God' a hundred times. And it was just as true of him the day he died as the day he was born."

Glen is a non-Mormon. He knows the story could be axed before it is in print, but he is very hopeful for it. And his bosses are more and more excited about it and about my participation in it. Their hope is to just do it and let the Brethren read about it in the paper.

In Utah I saw a woman I had met a few years ago when we were both talking about women in the Church. She has been working on the huge study the Church has financed to find out what women of the Church really think. She said the results are now being computerized and are not what the Brethren were hoping to hear. Relief Society comes off looking really bad. And it appears that the authorities are not going to act on any of the information that has been discovered.

I walked outside with her and learned that she has gone through a divorce from her husband who teaches in the same department at BYU that she does. Their different ways of looking at the Church "tore the marriage apart," she said. I put my arms around her and told her that broke my heart, that too often I have seen the Church, which prides itself on what it does for families, become the divisive factor if someone in the family is not in lock step with the others.

January 15, 1986

The famed Herb Caen of the *San Francisco Chronicle* put a little note in his column yesterday: "I can't get it out of my mind—the newsquib about the Mormon Church excommunicating an AIDS sufferer who was seeking spiritual comfort and forgiveness. Anything else you'd care to know about the Mormon version of Christianity?" This story was big news in Utah. Even the *Deseret News* carried it.

Something happened after sacrament meeting that just blew my mind. A sister whom I visit teach, R., spoke to me for a moment. Then she laughed and said, "Oh, I have an AIDS joke for you." Before I could even respond she went on, "Why is AIDS called the miracle disease? Because it takes fruits and turns them into vegetables." I was so shocked I could hardly breathe. "That is not funny," I said. I left the building and went up to my bedroom and cried. Joel, a friend of mine with AIDS, was cooking dinner for me and the children—while R. was telling me that joke *in the foyer of the Mormon chapel.* How far—how very far we have to go.

The last night Joel was here I gave him a foot bath. It is one of the most truly delicious, relaxing, pleasurable experiences one can have. I washed and massaged his feet in warm water for some minutes. Then I dried them and massaged them again with oil. Most of his Kaposi's lesions are on his feet, bruise-like marks under the skin.

January 29, 1986

Yesterday was an incredible, awful day. The spaceship *Challenger* exploded just after it took off from Cape Canaveral in Florida. It had seven astronauts aboard, including the first civilian to go up, a school teacher in New Hampshire. The pictures in the newspaper this morning of the families left behind were unbearable. I don't understand it. Are we all here just at the mercy of happenstance? Is there some final reason for all of this horror? As Emily said when she was just tiny, "Mom, I wish we could see what life really is instead of just how we're in it."

And a bit of recent philosophy from my children. Katy and Aaron were rummaging around for some food on the day before grocery shopping day. "I'm going to have an ice cream cone," said Katy. "Good luck," snorted Aaron. "There's no ice cream." "Then I'll just have the cone," said Katy, happily munching into an empty cone.

So that I could put an accurate statement in the bio I had to prepare for Random House, I called Bookcraft to find out how many of my poetry books had sold to this point. They have sold 46,028 of *The Growing Season,* 18,232 of *a Widening View*, 10,203 of *I Can't Stop Smiling,* and 3,284 of *Beginnings*, after we got the book publishing rights back from Doubleday, who had sold at least 25,000 copies. Before we closed down Trilogy Arts we had sold about 140,000 copies of *Beginnings* and *The Search*. So that totals just under 250,000 on all books of poetry.

R. called and apologized about the AIDS joke, said she had been feeling terrible about it. I forgave her and went out of my way to make her feel better.

There were a number of letters to the editor in the *San Francisco Chronicle* regarding the young Mormon man in Ogden, the AIDS patient. One of the letters was mine:

> "Regarding the story of the AIDS sufferer who was excommunicated by his Mormon bishop in Utah, I would like to point out that the decision was a local one and would not have been handled the same way by every Mormon bishop. I have a friend who is also suffering from AIDS and who moved two times after his diagnosis. He dealt with two Mormon bishops who, upon learning of his condition, were very supportive and gave him healing blessings through an 'administration of the priesthood' and the laying on of hands. I personally applaud the two bishops who chose in this difficult extremity to bless rather than condemn.
>
> —Carol Lynn Pearson, Walnut Creek."

February 6, 1986

I spent money. Two wonderful large bookcases, one for either side of the piano. It's not that I'm excessively rich these days. I finally paid last year's taxes out of Bookcraft's royalties. And I managed to pay my tithing just before the end of the year. I received the last payment from Random House. Now I won't be getting anything more until the *Woman's Day* payment. But I'll manage.

Glen Worchal called yesterday from the *Deseret News*. It looks like the series will run this weekend.

February 14, 1986

The publisher of the *Deseret News* killed the series. I just hung up from talking with Glen Worchal. The series was scheduled to start on Sunday and run Monday and Tuesday. Saturday night came the word that it was killed. Jim Mortimer, the publisher, who had told Glen he was *not* going to take it to the board, took it instead to Thomas Monson who relayed the essence to President Ezra Taft Benson. We don't know whether or not Benson read it. But the decision was "Why do our readers need to know about this?"

Just last November Benson became President/Prophet of the Church. There is a "new style of leadership," as the new Prophet is ultra conservative. Glen said they have been instructed that "the paper is to carry out the goals of the Church. It is to be regarded as an organ of the Church."

He said he and many others on the staff had hopes that the *Deseret News* could become a really fine paper, something like the *Christian Science Monitor.* "But now I know that this place is never going to change. I want to get out of here as soon as possible. That's how many of the good writers here feel."

February 21, 1986

It appears that the "new prophet" has a son who has a lot of power in Utah now, and certainly with his father—Reed Benson, former National Chairman of the John Birch Society. Glen said that recently a series for the paper had been prepared on day care but was killed because the new prophet does not believe women should work outside the home.

Last night I called Emma Lou Thayne, the "token woman" on the *Deseret News* board. I wanted to know if she had been made aware of all this. She said yes, she had been and she's been thinking of me. She's just sick about the whole thing, says she has been "very discouraged for a long time," and that it's gotten worse over the years. That's what is frightening to her. She said it would be a marvelous breakthrough if the *Deseret News* would run my story, but there's nothing to be done.

She's going to talk to Thomas Monson, but she has no delusions that she'll be really listened to. "I feel like I'm just a little barking dog. I go 'yip, yip, yip,' and they pat me on the head and say, 'That's all right.'" She said she's had some success in talking to Hinckley, but now Hinckley does not have the power; Benson does.

We talked a long time. Emma Lou has gone through her own struggles and I feel she and I are in a very similar place. She loves the Church, she loves being a Mormon and working in her ward. This is her home. And she's not about to abandon it. But when these kinds of things happen—and they happen often—she says to herself, "Who needs the Church? Why are we doing this?"

I was glad to talk to her. Emma Lou is a truly great woman; I've admired her unceasingly for years. What are we going to do? What is going to happen to me in the fall when my book comes out?

I will write more on this, but now I am too tired. In fact, I am heart-broken. Maybe, finally, I can't be a Mormon. I want to. I love the Church. But maybe, finally, I really do not belong.

I had written to Bookcraft to tell them about the project before they read about it. They had not responded and I was wondering if they were alarmed. So I called to ask them. George Bickerstaff greeted me warmly and when I asked if they had written me off he laughed and said they would never do that. He added, as he has said many times, that my creativity is highly valued at Bookcraft, and especially my good nature.

"With the position that you have, Carol Lynn, you could have become arrogant and demanding and very hard to work with. But you have done none of that. You have always been a great joy to work with. And Bookcraft will always feel that way about you."

February 25, 1986

An update on the *Deseret News* story. Emma Lou called last night to tell me she had spent forty-five minutes with Thomas Monson and she was very, very discouraged. She approached him from the standpoint of his "come back to church" editorial that was in the *Church News* at Christmastime. And she told him what a wonderful thing it would be for the Church were they able to take the offensive on this and promote this beautiful story. "Carol Lynn has been a model for young women and for others for years. This could do a marvelous service. The book is coming out, a movie is coming out, and what better thing than for the Church to get behind it and help it?"

Brother Monson was unmoved. "These men are very, very unfeeling," she said. Brother Monson said that from the article it appeared that Gerald had never made an effort to get over his homosexuality.

No effort! I told her of the years of anguish Gerald went through, the fasting, the praying, the horrendous decisions that he had to make. "Of course," she said. "I know of the anguish."

President Kimball's stand, Monson said, was that it was a choice and something you could repent of.

"But what if that stand was wrong?" asked Emma Lou. "That stand is not clinically sound."

Monson also did not like Richard Cracroft's statement in the interview that these young men should seek professional help. The Brethren want everyone to stay within the bounds of what the Church offers.

"*The Miracle of Forgiveness,*" Emma Lou said, "has caused a lot of guilt and sorrow and division where there should be none."

"Who has the real power in Salt Lake these days?" I asked.

"Reed Benson," she replied.

As a reprieve from all this I have been practicing the piano. I took lessons for about a year in my early youth and have only played by ear and fiddled around since then. But I got out "Lebensraum" by Listz and have been working on it. Very fun and very satisfying. I even played for my dear professional pianist friend Anne Mauss, and she was amazed. "It was perfect," she said.

March 2, 1986

Emily and I just returned from receiving her Patriarchal Blessing (a once in a lifetime event for Mormon people, generally in their youth.) It was wonderful, really lovely and inspiring and lifting. We went to the home of Alan Johnson in Danville, a sweet, pure, gentle man. I was so hoping and praying that it would be a good experience, and it was. He put his hands on Emily's head and set out many good ideals for her to strive for. It reflected many of the good, wonderful qualities that I know Emily already has. It blessed her to be intelligent, to study, to serve, to be filled with light, to bless others, and to excel in accomplishment. It spoke of her father, that he was given authority to watch over and help her.

After the blessing was over, Emily asked if that reference was to her Heavenly Father. "No," he said, "that was your earthly father. I've never felt impressed to make a statement quite like that before." And the blessing spoke several times of the Mother in Heaven and how She loves Emily and will be close to her. That dissolved me into tears. Afterward I asked him if he mentions the Mother often. "No," he said. "Very rarely do I do that."

It was really a thrilling, lovely thing. In the midst of my discouragement with the Church over other things, I am glad to have a wonderful experience like this. I wish every young person could have such an affirming, inspiring experience.

March 11, 1986

And then some downers to add as well. Yesterday I got a letter from Glen Warchol, the *Deseret News* reporter:

> A siege mentality seems to have taken hold under the new Prophet. They are attempting to shut down all information that doesn't 'advance the goals of the Church,' as the new power structure sees it. Censorship has become rampant at the *Deseret News* and offending passages border on the absurd. Morale is in the basement.
>
> A friend of mine at the Associated Press in SLC has put together a story on the changes made by the E.T. Benson regime. It deals, in part, with the amount of power son Reed wields. The Church is desperate to stop the story. It also gets into some of the problems at the paper, including the dismantling of the AIDS project.
>
> I'm going to get as much of my stuff in the article about your story as soon as possible. I doubt it will hurt your book sales in the fall. This wasn't an easy decision and the fact that it will cost me my job is the least of it.
>
> They can't win all the time.
>
> Sincerely,
> Glen Warchol

Aileen Clyde called me the other day. She and I had worked together on the committee that Barbara Smith had called. She wants me to speak to a group of women at whatever point we can arrange my being in Utah. She said that to her observations "things are worse for women in the Church now than they've been at any time in the history of the Church."

She said the lessons in Relief Society are obviously written by men for what they want women to be, that the meat and the challenging thinking that used to be in the lessons is gone now. They're redesigning the lessons, she said, to essentially make them all spiritual living lessons.

And I got another call a day or so before that from Joan Ritchie, that wonderful woman in New Mexico who entertained Katy and me as we went there for me to speak at her Relief Society overnight conference in Santa Fe. She told me a discouraging story. A week or two after the conference, the stake president called in the Relief Society presidency and the bishop and informed them that there would be no more overnight conferences for the women, that it was not appropriate to take "wives and mothers" out of their homes overnight, that it sends a message to the women that home is a bad place to be. Joan disagreed strongly and told him many great successes of the conference, how the women developed such love for each other, went home stronger, how the divorced young woman for the first time felt accepted and a part of things and has been a different person ever since.

Joan assessed that what really happened was this: the men saw the women come home from the conference vitalized and strengthened and they were frightened. Men don't know how to deal with women who are becoming stronger.

Joan was devastated. She had prayed, had received what she felt was wonderful guidance.

March 20, 1986

Just now Emily and I were talking about some things, some of her friends who are having difficulties. Emily said, "How did you guys do such a good job with us? I want to know so I can do everything just like you did. Except for the colored dishes. And the rules on the TV. And your singing in the grocery store."

I laughed. I make the kids each use one set of dishes, plate, bowl, cup, different colors so we know whose is whose. After we eat they each wash theirs in the sink and put them away. And when a cup or a plate is left in the living room, we always know whose it is.

April 4, 1986

I received a copy of a talk given by my General Authority friend Brother Hanks on March 11 of this year, just last month, at a BYU devotional. Some time ago I sent him a letter telling of Gerald's death and the circumstances surrounding it.

In his talk he said:

> "I have to share with you as I finish today a letter I received from a marvelous human being you would know and will know because her story is going to be published. Years ago I performed the temple wedding of this woman and her husband. He was what we call a homosexual man and tried very hard to suppress that need. He was not successful and the marriage ended but the partners remained friends. I read now from her letter:

> 'Dear Brother Hanks:
>
> I am writing now because I want you to know that last Thursday my former husband passed away a victim of AIDS. He was here in my home where I was taking care of him. Toward the end I read Walt Whitman to him and played Beethoven for him and told him how much we all loved him and I did what I could to make him as comfortable as possible.
>
> Last night the children and I and a few close friends held a private memorial service for him here at my home. It was a wonderful event and we are all able to release him with love. The children will miss him a great deal. I will too. He gave a lot to all of us.
>
> Somewhere there is sense to this. I have been granted a great deal of strength to help me through it, and for that I am grateful.'
>
> Then she compliments her loving bishop and stake president and friends and others who have supported and sustained.
>
> I go to sleep some nights and wake up some mornings thinking, 'I read Walt Whitman to him and played Beethoven for him.' And then I tell the Lord, 'Lord, if today I can approach that kind of Christian quality I will be grateful.'"

I felt tears now as I typed this. Dear, kind Brother Hanks. I am so blessed to have him as a friend.

April 29, 1986

I am typing on a borrowed typewriter from the place that is fixing mine. For a year or so I've been typing without a good left margin. But then the carriage return went out. One day I may go to a computer/word processor, but I'm still reluctant. And I still don't have the money. And I have a sentimental attachment to my old typewriter and a moral objection to high technology.

Speaking of high technology, this morning we have news of a serious nuclear accident in a plant in Russia. It must be very severe in order for them to let the information out. The Scandinavian countries were experiencing ten times their usual radiation and investigated. It's all a mess, just a mess. The world is mad to allow tampering with forces that obviously can destroy us all.

While I'm on the world scene, I will just mention the big Libyan crisis. The Libyans have a long history of terrorism and finally Reagan said: no more. We went in and bombed certain targets to disable their capabilities. Should we have? I felt ashamed of us. I know there's plenty of reasons why something had to be done. But to take the initiative and bomb anybody is a dreadful, dreadful thing to do. Surely there must be some better answers.

I got a note from Barbara Smith, urging me to put the book away for a few years, saying it will put me and my children in a whole different light and might be harmful. She said people will read new things into my writings that they have enjoyed for so long, and she doesn't want that to happen. This should not surprise me. I guess I'm in for a lot of different responses.

Last week Cory Maxwell (now publishing director at Bookcraft and son of General Authority Neal Maxwell) called to ask me if they could see the galleys of my forthcoming book. He said that Deseret Book has a copy of the galleys and that Bookcraft has been getting calls asking about the book. What??? Deseret Book has a copy of the galleys of *Goodbye, I Love You*? I was stunned.

Evidently a bookstore can send for an advance copy to determine if they're going to order it. So the galleys are circulating! Yesterday I got a note in the mail from the wife of someone at Deseret Book. She said her husband had brought the galleys home and she asked if she could read it. He said she could have it for a day, but that there were lots of other people waiting in line for it. Here's her note:

> My heart is so touched by what I have read. I wish I could put into words the feelings I'm experiencing as I think through *Goodbye, I Love You.* My heart aches—yet you didn't seem to lose sight of yourself and that very most important thing—love. I don't understand homosexuality. I'm actually horrified at the thought. But I too believe we have a responsibility to love—no matter what. Thank you for your portrayal of Christlike love. You have touched my heart tenderly and gently and I want to thank you for that.

So there is my first unsolicited response to the book.

Last week Bob Anderson called. His third draft of the screenplay is now with the top network bosses at CBS. Everyone continues to feel very good about it.

May 7, 1986

I spent this morning writing a letter to Richard Lindsay, head of Church Public Communications. I decided to take the initiative and let him know exactly what is going on with my book so that there will not be unnecessary apprehension in Salt Lake.

Since I last wrote, my agent Peter called to tell me he's sold the book in Germany. A top publisher there was in N.Y. for the weekend, read it, wept, and offered 30,000 marks.

Charlotte called from Random House to tell me they've got me on *Good Morning America.* Is this even to be believed?

My trip to Colorado, New Mexico and Pennsylvania for speaking engagements went very well. Must mention one moment. In the Pittsburgh home of Pat Mathews, Stake Relief Society President, there is a wonderful stained-glass window, ten or twelve feet tall, an arch with a nature setting with beautiful features. Sunday morning when I woke up, I came out of my bedroom to see that the sun was just beginning to come through the window. The top quarter was flooded with light. It was stunning. I sat down on the stairs and watched for a half hour or more as slowly, slowly, slowly the light filled the entire window. Each little piece of glass was transformed into something gorgeous. It was a unique meditation, a beautiful experience.

The conference the day before on Saturday was great. They had anticipated five hundred women when they invited me, but the registrations kept coming in, and they actually had 710 women. Saturday evening they presented a "play," a really fine presentation featuring great women of both America and the Church—Dorothea Dix, Susan B. Anthony, Marian Anderson, Anne Sullivan, Helen Keller—and Mary Fielding Smith, Amanda Smith and Zina Young. It was very well done, just the kind of celebration of women that I love to see. Part of it was musical and as the cast was performing the song from *Mary Poppins,* "Sister Suffragettes," calling for "equal rights with men," I turned to Shirleen (counselor in the Stake RS Presidency) and said, "What kind of heresy are you teaching your women back here?"

She giggled and said, "Isn't it wonderful?"

I find that just about everywhere I go, if you scratch a Mormon woman, you find something of a feminist, whether she would ever call herself that or not.

May 16, 1986

Speaking of keeping diaries, what a coincidence happened recently. 1—The Relief Society asked me to give a mini-class on diary keeping for homemaking day. 2—Last week Jan Hilton asked me to cover her seminary class in the Cambodian branch while she's out of town and to speak on diary keeping (she knew nothing of the R.S. request). 3—Last night Brother Anderson came home teaching and gave his message on the importance of keeping diaries (he also knew nothing of the two things mentioned above).

In my two presentations I showed examples of my diaries, traced my history in diary keeping, and gave reasons why I think it's important, primarily to help one lead an "examined life." Truly I do think that all these pages have served me marvelously to face more clearly what I'm doing and why I'm doing it and what I'm really thinking.

May 19, 1986

I received a letter from Richard Lindsay of Church Public Communications on Saturday.

> Dear Sister Pearson:
>
> Thank you for your kindness in writing. Our thoughts and prayers have been with you through this difficult time. Our appreciation also for alerting us to the upcoming book and the television motion picture to follow. We had been aware, independently, from media journals that they were

forthcoming, but your thoughts and comments were particularly helpful in better understanding your motivation and purpose.

Our prayers will continue for you and yours.

Sincerely,
Richard P. Lindsay

He also enclosed a "recent statement on Chastity and Fidelity" that he thought would be of interest to me. There was nothing even remotely new in it. "Unnatural affections, including those toward persons of the same gender, can be overcome. Homosexual relations run counter to God's eternal plan."

June 10, 1986

Last week was our "Peace Child" weekend. A very good experience. John and Katy were both in this musical that has been performed now thousands of times in many different countries, empowering children to be our leaders in world peace.

I had read to one on the committee my peace poem, "To All Women Everywhere," and they asked me to present it at the beginning of the program. So I did, at all four performances.

To All Women Everywhere

Let us sing a lullaby
To the heads of state.

They are our little boys grown up
And they have forgotten the sound
Of their mother's voice
And they need to be
Sat in the corner
Or given a good shaking.
Are they too big for that?

Then let us sing until their fingers
Fall from the fateful button
And they put the guns
And tanks back in the toy box
And remember that their mother
Told them we do not
Hurt one another.

Let us sing until they
Close their eyes
And dream a better dream.

Let us sing them to peace.

As I was talking on the phone to my brother Warren on Saturday night he told me a stunning thing. A couple of weeks ago Arthur Haycock was released as personal secretary to the President of the Church—because of a conflict over the presence of Reed Benson in the administration of the Church. This was printed in the *Salt Lake Tribune*. Haycock is an institution in Salt Lake. He's been there through five different presidents.

Later I was talking to Martha Bradley of *Sunstone*, and I asked her if she knew anything about the Haycock affair. She said that yes, she knew more than she was supposed to know. Evidently Brother Haycock was objecting to the presence of the "Benson boys" constantly at their father's elbow helping him run the Church. Haycock said, "This is not how it's done; this is not how we do things here." And in a group of people Reed Benson humiliated Haycock, really tearing into him. The next day Haycock was let go.

Quite amazing. Evidently the *Deseret News* said he had been appointed a mission president or temple president somewhere. That's what they do when the General Authorities want to get someone out of Salt Lake City. Everyone knows that some years ago Ezra T. Benson himself was sent to Europe to get him out of the way. What a faith-demoting story all this is.

June 21, 1986

My darling Emily is eighteen years old today. What a wonderful day. What a wonderful person.

I woke her up this morning with her friend Ann Hilton playing "Happy Birthday" on her violin outside Emily's bedroom window, then serenading her while Em ate the breakfast in bed I had prepared. She was surprised and thrilled. Then the telephone began to ring. I had arranged for all her best friends to call that morning. Emily wanted to walk in the hills and be alone for the coming of the very moment, 11:14. Just now she and the others are downstairs watching *Romeo and Juliet* which Emily got for Christmas.

I got a letter last week from Brother Hanks. I had sent him an advance copy of *Goodbye, I Love You.* He said that reading the book was "a tremendous experience" for him and that it, like all the experiences he's had with my life or writing was "ennobling and humbling." He did express some concerns that I have shown so many of our failings as Mormons that it casts a negative light on the Church.

The next day I called Charlotte at Random House and asked her if reading my book had changed her perception of Mormondom. She said that it had, a lot. "I was pretty much anti-Mormon, I would say. In the town that I grew up in there was a Mormon family, very self-righteous and smug. And later one of my writers got a divorce and the Church came down hard on him. When I read your book I saw a lot of things about your church that I didn't know and that I was very impressed with. Like the community service. And when your church came through for you at the end I was very surprised. I had really expected them to be quite mean to you. But they were wonderful."

"So reading the book made you feel a little more warmly toward the Church?"

"It made me feel a lot more warmly."

I believe I struck a balance in telling the good things and the difficult things both regarding the Church and regarding the homosexuals. I did what I had to do.

June 30, 1986

A major, major thing to report. Last week Carol Schneider of Random House's publicity department called to tell me that not only has Deseret Book ordered *one thousand copies* of the book, but "they have requested that I come for an autograph party in their Salt Lake store during what they call General Conference in October." I was stunned. And so thrilled I could hardly sleep. This is more than I had hoped in my wildest dreams.

And what does it mean? Surely the galleys must have been read by a number of people, certainly some of their superiors who are General Authorities. Anyway, I congratulate them for being brave. And they will not be sorry.

Yesterday Carrie, assistant in the publicity department, called to read me the schedule of the tour. It will cover thirteen cities: New York, Boston, Philadelphia, Washington D.C., Cleveland, Detroit, Chicago, St. Louis, Houston, Salt Lake City, San Francisco, Seattle, and Los Angeles.

It will start in New York with the *Good Morning America* appearance on Friday, September fifth. In each city I will have four to six interviews per day. Carrie and I talked for some time about the questions I would like interviewers to ask me. She was very impressed with what I suggested, and she said, "You're going to be fine. I can't think of a question anybody would throw at you that you can't answer."

My enthusiasm is rising. I am very, very excited about the tour and the release of the book.

And Saturday was a remarkable day. I believe I mentioned that I was invited to be the keynote speaker at the annual conference of Affirmation, the independent support organization of Mormon and ex-Mormon homosexuals and lesbians. There were close to two hundred participants in all, a very few of them transexuals. Several things surprised me. Many of these people still hold their Mormon doctrine very, very close. They believe in the Church and its ordinances and its theology and work very hard to make some way for it to fit them.

So many stories I could tell. I met a couple from Orem, parents of a young man who just informed them six weeks ago that he is homosexual. They came with him so they could learn more and be of better help to their son. "There is so much pain in this room," the mother said. "Such pain. These men are hurting so badly. I don't want them to hurt like this. There is one thing I know. My son Mike did not *decide* to be a homosexual. He *discovered* that he was a homosexual."

In every session I heard a man cry and saw many with tears in their eyes.

I spoke in the afternoon. As I was introduced and went to the microphone, there was extended, *very* extended applause.

I spoke for about an hour. I told my story, told about the book, and then I told them some of the things I hoped for. From the heterosexual community I hope for better understanding, for healed relationships, for fewer inappropriately encouraged marriages, for fewer gay suicides.

And I told them that what I hoped to see from the homosexual community was responsible behavior, giving heterosexuals less opportunity to judge them harshly. I spoke of my feelings toward promiscuity, that it is emotionally and spiritually debilitating as well as clearly now physically disastrous. I quoted Joseph Wood Krutch: "If sex has come less often to be a sin, it has also come less often to be a supreme privilege." I feel it should be a supreme privilege. I quoted Margaret Anderson: "In real love you want the other person's good; in romantic love you want the other person." I quoted my own poem about joining eros, erotic love, with agape, Christlike love:

Double Wedding

Let's have a double wedding,
You and me
And Eros and Agape.

Let us post interchangeable notes
On bedroom wall and refrigerator:
"Love thy lover" and "love thy neighbor."

Let us kiss shoulders and eyelids
And the cut fingers of small children.

Let us serve one another
Apple blossoms in vases
And quartered fruit on trays.

Let us write poems
And wills to each other.

Let us have nights as friendly lovers
And days as loving friends.

And let the four of us,
You and me
And Eros and Agape

Stand in line together
At the grocery store
And at a golden anniversary.

I told them that I hoped gay people would come to see their sexuality as part of their larger life rather than as the overriding fact of their existence. I said that as women have in the last centuries repudiated the concept that "biology is destiny," so gay people must repudiate the notion that "sexuality is destiny." There are still many choices that can be made.

I told them I hoped they would respond with love even to those who are not treating them with love. I quoted Edwin Markham:

> They drew a circle that shut me out,
> Heretic, rebel, a thing to flout.
> But wit and I had the will to win:
> We drew a circle that took them in.

And I closed with a prayer that each of us can do the best we can to exemplify the love that Christ came to teach.

When I finished, they gave me a very long and emotional standing ovation. We then had a question-and-answer period. The final question was from a young man who said, "As soon as you're through talking, can I come up and give you a hug?"

"Of course," I said. And he did.

At lunch I deliberately sat at a table by a transexual woman. She had blonde hair, a rather attractive face, long red nails on her large hands, and she had a kind of sad, humble, naïve purity about her. She had been converted to the Church in the army, had subsequently married a woman, but all her life had felt that *she* was really a woman, sort of felt that in her marriage she was in a lesbian relationship. "It's not so much the sex I'm interested in," she said, "it's the love." Her brown eyes were very sad, very hungry.

July 7, 1986

A little update out of Church headquarters. A very knowledgeable friend called me on Saturday and told me among other things that her sources tell her that Reed Benson has been put in as official secretary to his father, President Benson, the position from which Haycock was released.

Her sources further tell her that President Benson *twice* presented the name of his son Reed to the Quorum of the Twelve as the man who was to fill the vacancy in their ranks—and both times the Quorum rejected him.

This could still be in the realm of gossip—*but* Armand Mauss (noted sociologist and my friend) told his daughter-in-law Annie (my close friend and

Visiting Teaching companion) that this story is correct. Armand is well connected with what's going on in Salt Lake.

What? The only true Prophet makes a very important pronouncement to his twelve apostles, who reject that pronouncement!

Yesterday I wrote a letter to Dallin Oaks, now a member of the Quorum of the Twelve:

Dear Elder Oaks,

As I was sitting in Relief Society today following along in the manual during a good lesson on integrity, I noticed that in the full three pages of examples and quotations, not one was by or about a woman; all thirteen were by and about men. Two of the men were non-Mormon, Moliere and Gandhi, and the rest were LDS leaders or men in the scriptures.

I began to feel again, as I often do, that femaleness is invisible—that, after all, women seem not to count for much. Surely it would not be difficult to find a few historical or scriptural or LDS examples of women of integrity. To put out a lesson in 1986 given to women by a woman, pointing to thirteen men and not one woman, should make us all ashamed.

I found myself raising my hand (I often raise my hand, and the members of my ward understand me and love me for it), and standing up to observe that integrity is not only a masculine characteristic, but surely a feminine one too, that I could not think of the word without remembering Joan of Arc, and that we could well remember Mother Eve in her commitment to obey the higher law above the lower law.

At any rate, I found myself wondering, "Am I the only person who is noticing this, or who even cares?"

And I remembered that some years ago I wrote you a letter at BYU calling your attention to a brochure that went out totally devoid of any suggestion that women were a participating force at the university, after you had earnestly pled with the faculty and staff to take their women colleagues more seriously. You thanked me graciously and in fact reprimanded the responsible office. I know that you were sincere then in wanting to include women more fully in the life of the university, and I assume you would be equally so today in wanting women to feel in all appropriate ways included in the life of the Church.

I can't tell you how many of my good women friends have chosen inactivity in the Church because of this. I am not going to do that, but I am going to continue to raise my hand rather frequently and possibly write a letter from time to time, which I think is what a woman of integrity is supposed to do.

I hope you have an active mental file and better yet a physical file of things pertaining to the position of women in the Church. Knowing your mother as I did, I'm sure that this is something she too would urge you to consider.

I'm grateful, Elder Oaks, to have you in the important position that you occupy. The women in the Church are the best you're going to find in the entire world. Wallace Stegner, in assessing the strength and dedication of the Mormon pioneers, complimented them highly and then said, "Especially their women; their women were incredible." I love Mormon women. They deserve the very best. And often they do not get it.

All best wishes to you personally and in your important assignment. I am well and happy, as are my children. I have many things to be grateful for.

Very Sincerely,
Carol Lynn Pearson

22

"FOR SUCH A TIME AS THIS"

July 23, 1986

When I got back from Utah, there was a letter here from Dallin Oaks. He thanked me for my good letter and said that he agreed with the points I had made, that we do need "best efforts" and "patience" as we work toward improved performance in that area. He also said he was aware of some of the difficulties I have lately gone through and wished me well. I thought it was a good letter and was glad to get it.

Last night Robert Anderson called me from New York to tell me that CBS has turned down the movie project. He was very disappointed. It seems a new "boss" was put in and brought with him his own projects and got rid of some that were already developed. That happens a lot. Bob says he doesn't regret doing the script of my story. "It's been a wonderful, enriching, inspiring experience," he said.

I am disappointed too, of course. But I have not been thinking about the movie a lot or putting a great deal of hope on it. The book is going so well that I feel very satisfied.

July 30, 1986

Yesterday morning a woman from *People* magazine called me. She wants to fly out next week to interview me and take pictures. This was cleared through Random House, of course. They consider it a real "coup," said it is very hard to interest *People.*

And Charlotte told me everyone who reads the book is very excited about it. She said they might even get a second printing underway before the first printing is out. First printing is thirty thousand.

August 6, 1986

The book is here in front of me. *Goodbye, I Love You* arrived this morning by overnight mail from Random House. I am extremely pleased with it. The cover is a gold-yellow background with the title in large dark blue letters. The subtitle reads, "The true story of a wife, her homosexual husband and a love honored for time and all eternity." And then my name. To the left and under that is a lovely red rose and a dead rose with their stems touching. It is very effective. Trevor Southey, my dear artist friend, and I brainstormed on something for the cover, and that is what we came up with. It really does look great. And, of course, the title was inspired by the last words that our daughter Emily spoke to her father over the telephone. "Goodbye. Goodbye, I love you."

And yesterday was a big day. I spent all afternoon with Kristin McMurran, the reporter from *People*. She was wonderful, a young woman, very open and unspoiled and very moved and thrilled by the story. We talked for a long while, her just asking me questions and me responding. *People*, she told me, has twenty-three million readers. What an amazing thing, to get to address twenty-three million people!

August 17, 1986

I am feeling the stress. I have spent weeks doing nothing but making lists and doing things and crossing them off. All the logistics of getting ready for three trips—the time with the family at the beach house, then the trip to Utah, then the trip to New York City—have been absolutely staggering. Everything—the correspondence, phone calls, checking on this and that, buying the Plymouth Voyager and insurance, refinancing the house, taking calls from people who need to talk—I am going crazy. This afternoon I locked myself in my bedroom and cried for a while. I haven't cried for a long time. But I needed to. I'm at least functional now; I can go on.

August 31, 1986

I have finished the Utah part of the tour. And it all went wonderfully well. I am thrilled.

Wednesday morning I taped something for all three television channels for the evening news and also taped a thirty-minute talk show for KSL, "Talkabout." I was able to say what I wanted to say. The next night I was on "Prime Time Access" on KSL, and they taped twice as long as they had intended. Some of Bruce Lindsay's questions threw me a little, but I was told I handled all the questions wonderfully. Channel Two kept pushing me to take the General Authorities to task and I kept avoiding that; they made an editorial comment that the book shows the Mormon leadership not to be sensitive to the homosexual condition.

From the outset people were grabbing me to talk and calling me on the phone in my room and leaving messages. I knew that would happen. That's why I wrote the book. I knew there were all those people waiting for a little help:

"Last night because of the things you said on the news, I was able to talk to my husband and tell him that our son is gay."

"My father read the book and cried a while and said to me, 'I want you to thank that woman for writing this, thank her for me.'"

Similar statements came time and time again.

The mother of a gay man told me she's going to set up a family support group for Utah families who have a homosexual member. She got a P.O. box that day and I subsequently announced the information at all of my interviews and in my talk.

I was sent numerous flower arrangements from Random House, friends, people I don't know. When I checked out I had the hotel send the flowers to Primary Children's Medical Center.

Friday evening was my talk at the Sunstone Symposium. I had, of course, been looking forward to it with enormous anticipation. There was a large crowd; they opened the doors connecting three ballrooms. I'm sure at least fifteen hundred people were there.

I had a firm outline, but did not read my talk (I do not believe in reading talks). The response was better than anything I could have hoped for. I received a standing ovation. There was a good, good spirit in the hall. I succeeded in what I wanted to do, which was to cultivate understanding and avoid divisiveness. After I finished I entertained questions and the good spirit continued. A lot of gratitude was expressed and a lot of reaching out was done. My dear brother Donald gave a beautiful closing prayer. The whole thing could not have been more thrilling.

My friend and visiting teaching companion Anne Mauss was there and told me that Jerry Cahill, Church spokesman, was at my talk. Armand Mauss had lunched with someone at the Church offices who had been told that Cahill was appointed to see to it that I had the "broadest possible latitude" to do what I wanted to do, as they felt there would be a lot of good come from this in the long run.

All day Sunday I spent with a reporter, Dennis Leabow, who was flown in from the *Los Angeles Times Magazine*. A photographer came also and we had a very good day. I spent the evening with Sharon Swenson, a reporter from *Utah Holiday.*

The *Los Angeles Times* reporter wanted to get some pictures of me at Temple Square, so we went over there. As we looked sort of professional, we were stopped and asked if the pictures were for publication, being told then that we had to have clearance. We waited a while and finally the young man came back saying he had talked to Jerry Cahill, Church spokesman, who said it was fine, and for me to take all the pictures I want.

Monday I had a very good interview with *This People Magazine* (LDS Church-oriented publication). The reporter kept telling me how incredible I was. Also two more radio interviews, including the University of Utah station.

Must back up. Saturday morning I was on KTLK radio, a talk show, call in. I was interviewed for about half an hour, and then we took calls. The first one to call in was a crazy lady, who assured us that if we had the right kinds of laws that would let us execute a few of those homos the others would never do it again. A few calls later I heard Gerald's father's voice on the line. He challenged the first caller, saying, "If you saw a bunch of those homos lined up and you saw one of your loved ones among them, would you say, 'Pull the trigger'?" Then he identified himself and he and I talked a minute. It was, of course a very emotional thing. My kids were listening to this at their Uncle Donald's house and were amazed.

I sold nearly four hundred books at my table at the Sunstone Symposium. So now I have enough money to pay the end of this month's bills. And for that I am very grateful.

Charlotte called me in Utah. She said that Random House is thrilled to see what's happening. Waldenbooks had called me earlier, telling me that they had sold out their thirty-five copies in three hours and were trying to get more as fast as possible. Charlotte said that all the instant action in Utah has put the book on what's called the "Ingram Best Seller List." She said Random House has now gone into their second printing.

I received two very moving calls from two different gay men, now married to women and really wanting to stay in their marriages. They both said that my book had given them hope and encouragement to stick to their decisions and to be successful and be understood. Both consider my book to be a "marvelous breakthrough" in their lives. This makes me very happy. This is why I wrote the book.

September 13, 1986

I am in Chicago, and taking the first opportunity I have to catch up on all my adventures. The tour is going extremely well. My first morning in New York I was on *Good Morning America.* I felt good about the interview.

Charlotte, my Random House editor, called on the phone and said that I made things sound so easy, that I need to emphasize more of the tragedy and the conflict and make people want to read the book. As she was speaking to me, however, the publicity head, Carol Schneider, came into her office and was appalled that Charlotte was saying that to me and started crying right in front of her, as she had while watching the show.

I was taken directly after to Cable News Network's "Take Two" for a live seven-minute segment. Then I had lunch with Charlotte and Peter, who happened to be in New York at that time. They were very excited and thrilled at what is happening with the book. It's now in its third printing, of 10,000.

Later I went to Penn Station and took the train to Philadelphia, just over an hour's ride. As I was about to leave the train a young woman came up to me and said, "Are you the woman I saw on TV this morning who wrote the

On tour to promote *Goodbye, I Love You*.

book?" She said it sounded very interesting and she intends to get it. That was the first, and then it happened a number of times.

In Philadelphia I had some very good interviews. A woman caller asked how the children were handling the idea that maybe their father had not gone to heaven. I said that I was quite content, as were my children, that Gerald was in good hands, that he was continuing to grow and to learn. And this, I said, is not in conflict with the Mormon construct of eternal life. We believe strongly that every person on this earth is given every opportunity to fulfill their potential. Mormons call this "eternal progression," I said.

The woman responded, clearly moved, "That's beautiful."

Monday I spent in Boston, the first show being "The Lovell Dyett Show." He is a large, tender black man, very interested in talking about the Church. He wanted me to describe being a Mormon and what kind of Mormon I am. I said I am a faithful, participating member who raises her hand whenever something is said that I think needs a second opinion.

"Not in the Mormon Church," he said. "You don't raise your hand in the Mormon Church!"

"Sure you do," I replied. "You raise your hand *kindly,* but you raise your hand. I've got plenty of good Mormon friends who want to talk about important issues, and who do."

That evening in Boston I had a wonderful time with the *Exponent II* women. They had set up an evening for me at a room at Brandeis University. A man that purchased two books told me he was from Church Social Services and that he had seen my half-hour KSL interview and thought it was wonderful. I asked if he had been in Utah then. He said no, that Social Services in Salt Lake had sent the interview out to be used to help train the workers in dealing with this problem.

As he told me that I began to cry right in front of him. I was so thrilled, so pleased to know that already what's happening is far beyond what I expected.

Tuesday I was in Washington D.C. Good interviews. Spent the afternoon with old high school friends who happen to be living there now. It was great, talking over all the adventures and sorrows that have beset us all. Good, good, meaningful time. I had to be spirited away to get to the airport.

That night when I walked into my hotel room in Cleveland the phone was ringing. A man's voice said he was calling from Paris, France. I asked if he was joking and he assured me he was not. It was six a.m. there and he and his wife, who were members of the Church, were calling me together. They had moved there from Utah and he is president of a company in Paris. He said he and his wife both read the book and were profoundly moved. They have a situation they've been dealing with for years, not exactly like mine, but similar, and they have for seven years looked for a person that they felt they could talk to. They did not feel that bishops and stake presidents would be able quite to understand what is happening to them. They both independently, after reading the book, decided that I was the person who could understand and who could help them. They wanted to fly in and spend a few hours with me, and as soon as possible.

I was stunned. I assured them I did not feel to be the fountain of any wisdom that could not be otherwise obtained. He said they were not expecting that, but they were very, very anxious to talk with me. I told them this weekend in Chicago would be the first opportunity. He said fine, they would fly in and meet me in Chicago. So—tomorrow morning I am seeing them. Is this not amazing?

The most memorable thing in Cleveland was the *Merle Pollis Show.* I had been warned about him by a couple of people, saying he sometimes was pretty tough and tried to "get" people. So I was prepared. When we first met he said, "I don't know what to think about you. I don't know if I love you or hate you or am angry at you or what." I gave him a hug and told him he had no reason to hate me.

He said, "I must tell you that I have a huge prejudice against the Mormon Church and a huge prejudice against homosexuals." So we took it from there.

He said he reads twenty books a month and that it had been years since he read something that stirred him up and involved him and moved him like my book did. And he said over the air that he wanted everybody to go out today and buy this book, going on and on about how important it is. And he said over the air that whatever negative feelings he had about me had dissipated. As I left the building he gave me a kiss.

Spent an early evening casual get-together with some Mormons at the home of Neal and Becky Chandler. An old friend from BYU, a gay roommate of Gerald's, K. had traveled to be with me. He was so thrilled to have the book out, had called me on the phone to tell me it had prompted such a wonderful conversation between him and his former wife, R. She had told him to tell me she's been waiting twenty years for this book. And their conversation helped them a lot to come to some understanding about how to deal with the children having to realize that their father is gay.

As we talked about the Church and what remarkable progress it is to have this book available, he reminded me of something he may have told me before but I had forgotten. Prior to their marriage he and R. had counseled with Apostle Spencer W. Kimball, the go-to authority for all sexual problems. He was very kind and encouraging, but he said to R. something she has had to live with all her life. "If you are sufficiently feminine," he told her, "you can save this man." She did not save him. What a burden to have to carry!

At the first event in Detroit, at the TV Studio where we were to do "Kelly and Company," I had a message to call Lenore Romney, the wife of the former governor of Michigan, George Romney. I called her and she said she had tried to get tickets to come to the Studio but they were all taken. She said she wanted me to know how proud of me she was. She had seen me on "Good Morning America" and I looked so beautiful and handled everything so well about the Church. She said she knew this was a subject we all needed to know more about; even she needed to know more.

October 7, 1986

So, so good to be home! I feel dreadful that I have not kept up with this diary, but there was absolutely no way to do it. So I must take the time to go way, way back.

Regarding the couple that came to Chicago from Paris to see me. Their main problem was one instance of infidelity on his part. He had suffered a great deal of guilt over it and she had been devastated and it had been a great wall between them for years. They had talked about it but had never been able to get rid of the wall. Something in my book, they said, gave them both a vision of love and forgiveness that they had never known before. I just listened to them talk, threw in a little philosophy from time to time and read a few poems. They especially loved this one:

The Forgiving

Forgive? Will I forgive, you cry.
But what is the gift, the favor?
You would lift me
From my poor place
To stand beside the Savior.
You would have me see
With his eyes, smile
And with him reach out
To salve a sorrowing heart—
For one small moment
To share in Christ's great art.

Will I forgive, you cry.
Oh, may I—
May I?

They were thrilled with our visit and had decided that as long as they were in the country they would go to Salt Lake and visit with a General Authority and clear things up once and for all. They had made an appointment with Elder Faust, one of the Twelve, and they were also going to tell him that my book is the greatest thing that's happened to the Church in years and years and years.

In Los Angeles, I addressed the Miller-Eccles study group in Pasadena. It was in a large backyard and there must have been 150 people there. Good crowd, intelligent questions. One comment in particular I remember. A man asked, sincerely and not challengingly, if the final answer to the problem of homosexuality wasn't just a healing blessing of the priesthood to relieve one of the problem. I asked, also sincerely, if he knew of any instances in which this had occurred. No, he said. I said that I did not either. A woman then rose and commented that maybe what we should be doing, rather than looking for the priesthood to heal them, is to call on the healing powers of the Lord to heal us of our attitudes and our prejudices. I thought that was quite a remarkable thing to hear.

I did a number of interviews in Los Angeles, TV and radio. One that I especially recall was the taping of "Hour Magazine," one of the most important ones. I was exhausted. But I had to brighten up and get my adrenaline going. The host was Gary Collins and he started out with something of a joke on the title, which made me uncomfortable. So, not feeling good about where he might be going, I just took over the interview. I felt very good about what I said and the way it all went. When it was over the audience asked a few questions and then I was taken off. Suzanne Wickham, the West Coast Random House person, said it went extremely well. "Nobody takes over an interview from Collins, but you did it," she said.

On the 20th of September I flew home for a couple of days. It was wonderful to be home. Wonderful. The children seem to have managed very well in my absence. Both Jan Tyler and Lynn Ann Somppi, my dear and responsible friends, had taken good care. I had called the kids almost daily and they seemed to be happy and moving along.

I continually asked them if they had received any comments at school or anywhere that made them feel uncomfortable, and they said no, they had not. And now that I'm home I asked them again. Nothing negative has been said by anyone. Everyone who has called here at the house had only good things to say. And they've been receiving a lot of support in the ward.

While I was gone Emily said to me one evening on the phone, "Mom, I find that I'm missing Dad less. I sort of feel like he's out there now, alive and doing his good work and helping all these people to understand, and so I just miss him less." I was really happy to hear that. And they all seem to be very proud of me for what I'm doing. I continue to tell them some of the good stories that come back to me, and they are happy about them. "You're so rad, Mom," Emily said. "So rad. I'm so proud of you."

Elouise Bell called from Provo. She has heard nothing but positive response to the book, which surprises her because she felt there might be various reactions. In fact, she told me that on a page of the *BYU Universe* there was a list of books recommended by professors, books every student ought to read. *Goodbye, I Love You,* was recommended by George Pace. This amazed us both, as he is a very conservative religion teacher, one we knew as very anti-feminist. I was so pleased to see him recommend this book.

Merla, Gerald's sister, called from Idaho. She was very excited and said that everyone up there is just thrilled with the book. Merla said, "This is the best thing that's happened to the Pearson family in years."

When I got back there was a note to call Dr. Abrams, the doctor who had cared for Gerald. I had intended to send him a book but had not done it yet. He told me that strangely he had just happened upon the book. At an airport he went into the gift shop to find a paperback book, but somehow found himself browsing in the hardback section, picked up my book, was caught by the word "homosexual" and opened it to see Gerald's name. He then flipped though the book and saw *his own name*. Of course he bought the book, read it, cried a number of times. He told me it is a "major contribution to understanding." I am sending him two books today.

So many mothers of gay sons have called. Night before last one called me from L.A. Her son is gay and she said how helpful the book is, and how she feels the Church has to address this more realistically. Last night her son called me, just ecstatic, saying, "I can't believe the change in my mother since she read your book. She's called me twice today as I've been reading it, saying, 'How far are you now?' and is so anxious to talk with me about things. It is a huge, huge change, and I'm so *grateful* to you."

The fact that the stories seem all to be about gay men and boys is pertinent here. It took some time before society (and certainly the Church) acknowledged the experiences of lesbians.

I had to make another trip to Utah for what will always be remembered as my Deseret Bookstore Day. At the autograph party at their store in Orem, an unending stream of people came through, gay men, parents, former wives, just people. I was driven there by Debbie, head of general books at the downtown store. She and I had a very good visit. Her enthusiasm for what's happening is huge.

Later, when we got to the downtown bookstore in Salt Lake City, there was a line of at least twenty people waiting for me. And for about three hours there was not a letup. Such a stream of grateful people—a woman whose son died of AIDS, more gay married men, former wives, and people who didn't let on but I knew they were in pain. Truly it was an astonishing day. The Deseret Book people told me they checked their computer and found that *Goodbye, I Love You* has broken every sales record they've ever had for the sale of one book in one month.

October 16, 1986

Before I continue to catch up, I will just write about yesterday while it is still fresh on my mind. I was on the *Oprah Winfrey Show* yesterday. Last week the Oprah person, Diane Hudson, called me and said they were very interested and wanted to talk about having me on right away, said the only day they could do was Wednesday. Carrie at Random House had to pull me off something in Minneapolis in order to make it happen.

So Tuesday afternoon I flew out to Chicago. Took a cab to my hotel, the Ritz Carlton, a great place. Had time to relax and take a bath and get a pretty good sleep. Was expected at the show at 8:15 a.m.

The show was really overbooked, too many participants. Oprah came into the green room to meet us all. She's a very warm, nice person and I liked her a lot. I gave her a hug from Emily and later got her to sign an autograph to Emily.

I was given quite a bit of time to briefly tell my story, then answered a few questions. My shining moment came when I took on a caller who told how his wife brought other women home and sometimes he joined in the orgies and it was "a fantasy come true."

I felt a rush of fury and said, "You know, there are a lot of 'nightmares' also coming true for a lot of people who are reaping the bitter fruits of a sexual revolution gone far too far. The emotional devastation as well as the physical ailments seen today are certainly evidence of that. It's time for a certain amount of sacrifice, of commitment to one other person, of putting someone else's needs before our own." The audience applauded loudly when I finished. That was their only spontaneous applause.

As I report on all this now, these many years later, it almost seems like a dream, or like some fine plot that was orchestrated by powers beyond my own. I know that this whole adventure that I lived out and shared was a turning point for a huge number of people in the way they viewed themselves, viewed a dear but frightening family member, or viewed our religions and actually our whole social order.

While Gerald and I never, ever spoke of the possibility that I would write our story, more than once he said, "Blossom, you know that you were put on earth for a purpose greater than to write nice little poems. And you know that you and I made an agreement before we came to this world that the two of us had a large work to do. I am so sorry it's so painful for you, but we agreed to do it."

Of all the letters that have come to me—and there are about eighty by now, there has been only one from someone who took me to task for writing the book. A Mormon woman felt I was "adding fodder to today's immorality." How could I say something like, "Oh, Gerald, you can fly now?" Don't I know he gave up the right to fly when he broke his temple covenants?

I will never be able to number the positive stories. Just a moment ago I received a call from Helen Schlie, a Mormon woman who has a bookstore in Mesa, Arizona. She wanted to pass on to me that she has received such positive response to my book. I asked about negative response and she said she has not had *one* negative comment. In fact, she said, a man called her in the middle of the night in tears to tell her how much the book meant to him.

And this one is deeply moving to me. A young woman who grew up in one of the most outstanding families in our ward here in Walnut Creek, called me from Provo. She and her fiancé had read the book out loud to one another and she had cried all the way through. She said, "When we finished I had to sit still for an hour just feeling the experience. The genius of the work is making people feel all that and feel it so deeply."

23

MY LITTLE UNAUTHORIZED FREELANCE MINISTRY TO THE OUTCASTS

October 20, 1986

A woman called to tell me an interesting thing that happened in her Relief Society. The teacher went into a tirade against homosexuals. This woman got up and left, cried in the foyer, and then went home. In a little while the bishop appeared with his wife at the door.

"I've come to apologize for the Relief Society teacher," he said. "I saw you crying and before I was able to get to you, you were gone. I asked a sister what had happened. I then read the teaching manual and there was nothing on homosexuals in the lesson. What the teacher did was uncalled for. And I personally apologize for the pain this brought you."

That teacher was released from her calling the following month.

Last week a man flew in from Utah to talk to me—married, gay, father of four, very distressed about what to do. He had come to hate himself. Three years ago he met a man and fell in love, the first time he had ever been in love, and the first time in years he did not feel suicidal; he saw some good in himself, he felt some of the darkness lift.

I had no firm answers for this man. I tried to help him look into the future knowing he will have to make a choice that will mean a huge sacrifice either way—and try to make whichever sacrifice will bring him to a better place of peace.

Incidentally, this man is very rich, works in computers, and wants to give me a computer and laser printer and word processing outfit. He said it would thrill him to do that. He is so grateful for my book. And he also wants to fund other things that might help in developing a better understanding of homosexual people. I told him if it would thrill him to set me up with a computer that I would certainly allow him to do that. He assured me it would thrill him enormously.

This man's name was Bruce Bastian, a name that meant nothing to me then. I did not know that he was co-founder of the software program WordPerfect and that he would go on to become a prominent philanthropist doing remarkable things in the world as well as an ongoing blessing to me and my family. I emailed him just now, asking if I could tell the story using his name and he said, "Of course you may use my name. I would be honored and flattered. I love you, my dear!"

And I must tell the story of Brad, who lives in San Francisco and who was a convert to the Church. I sat by him at the Affirmation dinner, and as we were talking he said, "You know what makes me want to give up?"

"What?" I asked.

"Knowing that in the next world I want to be where people like you are, where Jesus and God are, and knowing I can never be there. It just makes me want to give up."

"Brad!" I said, "How can you say that?"

"Well, it's true. I'm gay."

I tried my best to convince him he was wrong, but what is my word compared to the word of Spencer W. Kimball?

As the evening ended, Brad hugged me and said, "Oh, I wish I had a friend like you."

I replied, "Brad, I would love to be your friend."

He came over and went to church with me a week ago. He hadn't been to a Mormon Church in eight years. But he told me he wanted to come with me. He cried as he told me how much he loves the Church. For a year in Provo he went to his bishop every Sunday for a priesthood blessing to help him be asexual until the next Sunday. When he saw that no change was taking place in him, he said to himself, "If I'm destined for the lowest place after I die, I'd just as well go now." And he determined to end his life.

He was in a position where he could collect medication, so he gathered large amounts of pills. One evening he drove up to the Provo temple. He figured there would be kind and helpful spirits in that area and when he passed over there would be someone willing to help him. So he took the pills. He sat there on the grounds of the temple and felt the waves of blackness coming toward him. He lost consciousness.

He must have walked away after he was unconscious as the next morning he was found in a field, spread-eagle on the ground. It was so cold that his metabolism had slowed and the work of the pills was not complete. A BYU faculty member found him on his way to work and got him to the hospital. Brad was in a coma for two weeks.

He decided God wanted him to stay alive. He moved to San Francisco and again talked to the bishop and stake president, who were very kind to him. They refused to excommunicate him, even though he said they should. "It wouldn't do the Church any good to excommunicate you and it wouldn't do you any good," they said. But Brad dropped out of activity, knowing there was no place for him in the Church.

He loves the Church. As he and I sat together during sacrament meeting, and I took the little piece of bread and the sip of water and he did not, Brad was in tears. Afterwards, he said to me, "The Mormon people are the luckiest people in the entire world. They don't even begin to realize what they have. I go to the Mormon Church every day in my heart. And I go to the temple every day in my heart."

What can I say to Brad? Only that the Church is wrong on all of this, that when his time comes he will be welcomed into a heaven where God and Jesus are. And where I will be too.

I thought that perhaps I could type Brad's story without tears. I was wrong. Incidentally, Brad's full story is one that I tell in my book, No More Goodbyes: Circling the Wagons Around our Gay Loved Ones.

The next weekend, last Saturday, he came to my house because he wanted to do some yard work here. He and John worked together and made the front of the house look wonderful. Then Brad and I went for a walk around the reservoir.

H.D. called from Seattle. He has been a bishop twice and said that on one occasion one-third of the men in his "singles ward," both active in the Church and inactive, were gay. He held a support meeting for them in his home once a week. He sent six homosexual men off to the temple to "live happily ever after" with their wives. Later he learned that five of the six had been excommunicated.

Got a call from a woman in North Carolina, who was so moved and grateful for the book. Her husband left her a couple of years ago. He was threatened, she said, by her competence as a woman. Often he would raise his right hand to the square and command her to do what he wanted her to do. Again, I bow my head and say shame, shame, shame on our patriarchy. I seem to be reaching a much wider group of people than those involved with the homosexual issue. I seem to have now my little unauthorized, freelance ministry to the outcasts, those who have really been hurt. I just cheer them and lift them and tell them they're not alone and that they are loved by God and can move on and make a good life.

A woman called who just needed someone to talk to. Her missionary son had just come home after serving fifteen months in Wisconsin. She was devastated. He claimed there was no room in the mission field for the gospel of Jesus Christ, it was all so regimented, so statistically oriented, so really inhuman, he had no time just to be kind to people. He didn't fit. So he got on a plane and came home.

I told her that if he really was not making a difference out there that maybe coming back was an act of courage on his part. But I wanted her to convey to him from me that if he chose, he could go back on his own terms and refuse to be a part of whatever he saw that was not happening the way it should happen. "If we allow them to drive us out," I said, "we let them win. We can stay and kindly make waves and insist that our point of view be recognized."

She called me a couple of days later to tell me that her son had gone back to the mission field. They had talked for eight hours. He had been impressed with the things I had said, and some things she was saying. He thought about the people he had been teaching who were preparing for baptism. Anyway, he decided to go back. She was thrilled and very grateful to me for helping her.

Incidentally, she is going to send me a copy of the newsletter that the mission sends out. They have three lists that they put the missionaries' names on, depending on the success that they have in number of baptisms and other statistics—each list suggesting one of the levels of glory in heaven. Those at the top are listed under "Celestial Kingdom." Those who achieve less are listed under "Terrestrial Kingdom." Those who achieve even less are listed under "Telestial Kingdom." As often as I hear stories like this, I am amazed. What head, heart, spirit could come up with something like that?

This same woman told me she has another son in the Italian mission. He was seeing some of the nonsense start to happen and finally decided, "To hell with statistics. I'm just going to love the people."

Another moment of comic relief from my children. On the last week of school Katy finally wore some darling clothes that Emily had been begging her to wear. "Oh, Katy," Emily said. "You look so cute!"

"Yes," said Katy. "It's Nerd Day."

October 23, 1986

I got a call from Frank McEntire, wanting a copy of *Goodbye, I Love You.* He works in the Church offices, so I asked him if he had heard any scuttlebutt about the book there. "Nothing negative," he said. "The people I talk to love the book. Bill Evans, head of Special Affairs, said he loved it and the book was a great service to the Church."

From curiosity, I just looked up Bill Evans on Wikipedia and read: "2012—LDS public affairs leader Bill Evans met with several high-profile LGBT activists in Salt Lake City at the Alta Club, including the national Human Rights Campaign director, Dustin Lance Black, Bruce Bastian, the Utah Pride Center director, and the director of Mormons Building Bridges."

Yesterday afternoon I got a call from Senator Orrin Hatch, Republican from Utah. I had met him a long time ago in Provo. He said, "I loved your book. It is a wonderful contribution to the Church and to everyone else."

He went on to tell me that as he has worked with homosexual people in his government work and earlier as a bishop, he found that he could not condemn them. "I know what the Bible says and all that, but there's something else going on here. These people did not choose to be homosexual."

I asked him if he interacts with the Brethren in Salt Lake, and if he would put in a good word for the book. I said that I hadn't heard from them, but I assumed there must be some concern there. He said he certainly will put in a good word, that he could see how some of the Brethren might be troubled about it, but "that's just too bad." He ended with, "Let me know if there is ever anything I can do for you."

Later in this account you will read of something that Senator Hatch tried very hard to do for me.

Last night James Drake, the musician I've spoken of who is head of the Organ Department at Utah State University, told me again how thrilled he is with the book. "It's the best thing that could ever be done for gay people in the Church," he said. A lot of his organ students are gay and he sees the torment they are going through in regard to the Church.

He remembered being told that a group of gay men had gone in to meet with Brother Hinckley, asking for recognition in the Church. He asked them to leave his office.

An actor friend of his had gone to Boyd Packer for counseling before he went on his mission. Without looking up from his desk, Elder Packer told him, "You'd be better off dead."

A married gay man he knows went to President Kimball for help and was told, "When you get out of the shower, don't look at yourself in the mirror while drying."

As he was an organist, I asked about the two female organists that I was told are now official organists on Temple Square, along with the three men. He said it's not as good as it looks, that the three men get paid $30,000 a year or more, Cundick, Longhurst, and Christiansen—and that the two women get paid nothing, play only when the men are not available or for special occasions like Women's Meetings. This is a disappointment to me.

He also told me he had heard that the Brethren had asked me not to write my book. So I guess that totally baseless rumor is going strong.

Sunday I spoke at the sacrament meeting of the Walnut Creek First Ward, which meets in the same chapel that we do. Bishop Hurd had addressed the congregation some weeks ago and spent ten minutes telling everyone how wonderful my book was and that they must read it. And his counselor who called me about speaking couldn't say enough about the book. I gave a good talk, geared to everyone who is hurting, everyone who had something delivered into their life that they didn't ask for. Used some of the poems. Everyone seemed to love it.

October 30, 1986

Yesterday afternoon I spoke to one of the editors of the *Ensign,* Giles Florence, who wanted to talk to me about an assignment he's been given. Under the direction of their new advisor, newly-appointed Apostle Joseph Wirthlin, he's been instructed to come up with some articles on homosexuality. I told him I thought it could be a great step forward, unless he was instructed also to just bolster the party line that it's simply a sin and if you do A B C, you'll be okay. He said he never would have taken the assignment on those terms.

He also said that the thing that struck him most about my book was how I went into the Woman Question. He feels that's something that definitely needs to be looked at. We're going to keep in touch.

November 3, 1986

Yesterday was a good Sunday. I invited the children to direct our monthly fast as a fast of thanksgiving for the fact that our book has gone so remarkably well. And I stood up in testimony meeting and said how grateful I was for that, and especially thanked the ward for being such a good part of the story, and that I was thrilled to be able to hold them up to the world as an example of how people ought to deal with crises and help one another. I told them of all the "outcasts" I've been hearing from, the people in our Mormon community who don't quite fit the picture we like to paint. And I reminded us all that the Church is not a club for those who are perfect, but a clinic for those who are flawed, who are struggling to improve, which means all of us.

November 17, 1986

I can't keep up to date on the many calls I'm continuing to receive. Just an hour ago I got a call from L., a young man in Newport Beach. He's gay—from a very prominent Mormon family—served a mission—has been suicidal. His father told him, "You're dead to me; we won't have a relationship in the next world as you are lost for eternity." His mother said, "Homosexuality is an abomination in God's sight and in my sight."

"All I want is to be seen as a human being with dignity." He started to cry. We talked for quite a while. I asked him to drive up and have Thanksgiving here with us. He said he would think about it.

November 30, 1986

The young man I mentioned a couple of weeks ago, whom I invited to drive up for Thanksgiving, did come. And it was very good for him. And for us. My children were, of course, very warm to him, and playful. His father was a bishop and saw some of the literature on the subject, saying that these individuals were to be referred for shock therapy. He was sure if he mentioned his feelings, he would be sent to the shocks, so he talked to no one. He adapted. Every time he had any sexual feelings, his body turned them into a seizure.

His parents sent him to doctor after doctor. His physical state was so precarious that one doctor thought he might just stop breathing. Consequently, his parents had to check on him several times in the night to see if he was still breathing. In college he was suspended for failing all his classes. He became absolutely non-functional.

When he first told his parents that he had had his name removed from the records of the Church and why, they disinherited him. They told him they were putting in their will a stipulation that everything goes only to those children who, at the time of the parents' deaths, held a current temple recommend.

Two weeks ago his sister in Orem called and cancelled her invitation to have him come for Christmas. She said, "We don't know yet how homosexuality develops, and I just can't risk my boys being around one."

A strange and wonderful thing happened his last night here. I had taken L. with me to pick up Katy from the horses. I was fixing supper at the bar and he was across from me, drawing in his sketch pad for his art class. He was drawing my face from the photo on the back of *Goodbye, I Love You.* He continued to tell me about his feelings, that it was hard to be around living, lively things, to just be and allow himself to live. A part of him tells him he cannot live, is not worthy to live, must die. "It was hard to get that close to the horses," he said. "Horses are alive, they just are allowed to be. I'm envious of horses. People have more respect for the sexuality of horses than they do for my sexuality."

Sobs stopped his words and he dropped his head onto his drawing pad. I walked over behind him and put my arms around him. I sat on the stool beside him and held him for a few minutes. When he raised his head from the drawing pad, I glanced at the picture. There was one tear at the corner of his drawing of my eye. One of L.'s tears was coming out of *my eye*! We were both amazed.

I asked him if I could have that picture and he said yes. This morning as I went into the kitchen (he left very early) I found the picture on the counter, with this message written under the face. "There is only a smudge of a tear left there. Maybe with more love, tears can be wiped from the eyes of others also. How can I ever repay your love? God bless you all. Love, L."

And today Bruce Bastian flew in with my computer! As promised, he flew in with seven boxes of things: an IBM computer, color monitor, laser printer, disk drive, lots of software. After he set it all up, he spent a while instructing me, but I am still so unclear on almost everything. What an incredible gift! And what a dear, good person.

The day before Christmas Eve a lovely thing happened. Kendall Bean (concert pianist and composer) and his wife Karen came over with their friend Sharee Fitzgerald. Kendall played a song he had written and Sharee sang it. He wrote the song with Queen Esther in mind, but wants to dedicate it to me. It's a thrilling song. "For such a time as this I was brought forth . . . ." I was extremely honored.

December 30, 1986

Another new turn in my life. This afternoon Emily left for Utah for a semester at BYU. I am not yet facing the reality of her being gone. I have cried only twice in her presence, once just before she left as we had a special prayer together. This takes its place with other of the realities of life, and life moving so quickly, that I cannot grasp. Last night I lay on the couch holding Emily, with the fire in the fireplace and the Christmas tree lights on. And we talked about some of the things we have to look forward to. Emily is so beautiful, so thrillingly charming and lovely and interesting and interested and gifted and capable. And so loving. I am truly in awe of her. How did I come to have such a wonder in my life? Emily has pulled me and blessed me and confounded me and intimidated me and delighted me for eighteen and a half years. Oh, Emily, Emily, thanks for being.

24

"TO BE REJECTED BY SOMETHING SO WONDERFUL AS THE MORMON CHURCH IS ALMOST MORE THAN A PERSON CAN BEAR"

January 22, 1987

So I have converted to my computer. It's wonderful for writing and printing letters! I can write them quite quickly, and they are printed instantly and quietly. This, obviously, is my first page of computer diary.

I am ashamed that I have not written until this far into January. But my life is still not my own. Here are just a few of the highlights.

On Emily's first day at BYU, in her Book of Mormon class, the teacher, with a Polish accent, said, "Pearson? Pearson? Are you related to our favorite prophetess?" Emily laughed and admitted that she is. She said she's handling her notoriety well.

I had to go to Utah for some speaking engagements. Em and I did some shopping at the Deseret Industries just for old times' sake. We had a ball and got some cool stuff.

The next morning we got up to watch ourselves on the CBS Sunday Morning News with Charles Kuralt. The leading segment was our story, "Double Dose of Tragedy." I thought it was well done. It certainly made clear the pain of those who have both AIDS and the condemnation of the Church at the same time.

They had shot lots of footage when they were with us in California. The program showed the whole family at prayer, a statement from Emily about remembering her father, two statements from me, one in which I got emotional. They also showed the family in Idaho I had referred them to. The father made a very strong statement: "Unfortunately we have here a doctrine that is rooted in homophobia and superstition from the past, which is very hard to get over." I have been very careful not to say anything that strong, but I'm glad he said it.

The program also had a statement from an interview they did with Dallin Oaks: "Love the sinner and condemn the sin." And an injunction that the repentant sinner must forsake his sins and move on. He said that marriage is not considered "spiritual therapy" for the homosexual condition. Brother Oaks looked uncomfortable as he spoke.

And after two years I had another flying dream! I have been yearning for one. In this dream I wanted to show others how, so I was allowed to levitate off the floor and fly around in the room. It was really a wonderful feeling.

Last night I found a slip of paper John had brought home from Sunday School, a quote from Apostle Marion G. Romney: "I remember years ago when I was a bishop I had President Heber J. Grant talk to our ward. After the meeting I drove him home. Standing by me, he put his arm over my shoulder and said: 'My boy, you always keep your eye on the President of the Church, and if he ever tells you to do anything, and it is wrong, and you do it, the Lord will bless you for it.' Then with a twinkle in his eye, he said, 'But you don't need to worry. The Lord will never let his mouthpiece lead the people astray.'"

I found myself instantly troubled at this and kept the boys after our usual chapter reading to talk about it. I told them it was my hope that they would grow up to be good members of the Church, but also that they would be thinking members of the Church. I said I thought the statement on that paper deserved questioning. I told them some of the stories from history when ordinary people did terrible things and then blamed it on their superiors, saying, "He told me to. I had to do what he said—he's my leader." They already knew, of course, of the horrors of Hitler and his henchmen.

I told the boys they could never shift responsibility for their actions to anybody else—not to the president of the Church or to anyone, even their mother.

I continue to get very good response to *Goodbye, I Love You.* Yesterday I spoke at the BYU Management Society in San Francisco. I asked before I began how many had read the book, and about two-thirds raised their hands. That's quite remarkable. They were very responsive to my talk. A couple of questions showed some ignorance and a simplistic faith in the prophet: "We know that God has told the Prophet homosexuality is wrong; we just haven't tried hard enough to find out how to cure it."

February 5, 1987

I have spent a huge amount of time on this computer, answering the many letters that I have received. Each gets at least a note back. I'm current now, and that feels good.

The article in *People* magazine finally came out last week. It was a good article. Peter, my agent, said he had been receiving some more calls with interest for the movie rights. And Random House has been receiving more requests for interviews. Yesterday I was on the phone with three different radio stations, one in Milwaukee, one in Phoenix and one in Denver. The Phoenix station kept me on for two hours. There were lots of calls. A number of Mormons who had all my books called in and had good things to say. Some sad calls too. One young man told of a friend of his who had been kicked out of the house by his parents and then learned that he had AIDS. He had, just the night before, hung himself.

Someone from *This People* (unofficial Mormon magazine) called me yesterday on another matter. I asked if the interview they did with me was ever going to appear. She said probably not, that the editor had become a little anxious and didn't want to take any chances. She said some were concerned that I am now an advocate for homosexuality, seeing that I have become the hero of the Mormon gays.

Had another long conversation with a gay Mormon man, R. He planned his death on the anniversary of Hemingway's suicide, drove up to Idaho for that purpose, but a spiritual experience stopped him from doing it. He had read my book five times and was extremely grateful to me. He spoke of himself as a pioneer. I read to him my poem, "Pioneers." He cried. He had been through lots of kinds of therapy, especially aversion therapy, not the shock kind, but the kind that makes you vomit.

I am so, so weary of hearing the same story of pain. We have got to do better.

February 7, 1987

Wanted to mention meeting Jess Groesbeck at the Sunstone Symposium. He is a psychiatrist who now works in Salt Lake. He was very anxious to talk with me and couldn't say enough about my book. He felt that my appearance at the Sunstone Symposium last August was absolutely historic. He said, "I thought, as I watched you there, that you accomplished for homosexuals what Alex Haley did for the blacks in his *Roots*. Never again will they be non-people."

In the mail today I got a note from Peter Herford, the CBS producer for the program they shot at our home. He said:

> Response to our story has been heartwarming and troublesome at the same time. Mormon civilians—just members—have responded positively, in some cases painfully. But Church officials are on the war path. It is sad. Rather than recognize the problem the Church has in dealing with the homosexual community, the Church has—in its official arm—become defensive in the extreme. I hope they get beyond their official anger and deal with the real problems. Thanks again for your help and support.

February 18, 1987

Trying to get caught up so I can go to London in good conscience for the book tour for the British release of *Goodbye, I Love You*. Just now I had an interview with someone from the *Daily Express* in London. He flew up from L.A. with a photographer. Good interview. They're coming back at three to get a photograph with the children.

Yesterday in the *Church News* there was a major article, "Apostle Reaffirms Church's Position on Homosexuality." It contained statements from Dallin Oaks that were missing from the CBS interview. The thrust of the thing was that there is a single standard and that everyone, no matter what their inclinations, is bound by the law of chastity: no sexual intercourse outside of marriage, and of course marriage means the union of a man and a woman. Asked about the terrible guilt homosexuals feel, he replied that anyone disobeying the commandments ought to feel guilty, to feel alienated from God.

The thing, I believe, that is not being dealt with here is that the homosexual orientation is an authentic thing, that there are people in our population who are not qualified for marriage as we know it, who—through no choice of their own—have unalterable feelings that go in a different direction. And what are they to do? Nobody answers that question adequately. What are they to do?

March 10, 1987

Just got back from London yesterday after a very, very long and exhausting trip. And now I have only one hour to get a good report in here.

I stayed in Durrant's Hotel on George Street, a pleasant, small place. Had trouble sleeping through the night as I kept thinking it was time to get up. Sunday I had all to myself. I slept in, ate, walked over to Hyde Park to listen to the speakers. Monday I started the interviews. I was received warmly everywhere. First I did *TV AM,* their major morning show. I was told I'd have five minutes, but they kept me on for nineteen. Then later another TV thing, a taping of their show patterned after Donahue.

I had received a letter from Wendell Ashton, LDS Church mission president in London, inviting me to dinner. He used to be editor of the *Deseret News* and then head of Church Public Communications. Our connection had been a good one. His wife Belva is a fine woman whom I had talked to on several occasions about our mutual concerns regarding women in the Church. I called and had a good talk with them and then Belva called me back and invited me to stay with them in their flat for my second week. I gratefully accepted. So on Saturday I took a cab over there.

They were wonderful to me, gave me the key and told me to come and go as I wished. The first night they took me out to dinner for a great meal at the famed "Serpentine" in Hyde Park. They had both read my book and were very impressed. Wendell said he understood that some of the gays were using it as their *Ensign* (official Church magazine). Belva said she cried after she finished the book and thought it was just wonderful. In Salt Lake the hairdresser she went to is gay and is one of her favorite people.

The next morning I got up at five with them and went to a "sunrise service" for the missionaries at St. Albans. The sun did not rise, but the morning was lovely and misty. It was Fast Sunday, and their intent was to rededicate themselves and call on the Lord to help them achieve their goal of 150 baptisms in the mission during the month of March. Wendell told me they usually get just under a hundred, but he knows they could get 150. I had such mixed feelings as I saw those young men (and two women), those dear, sweet, sincere young people. I felt again the tremendous clash inside me about the Church. I'm all for going out and trying to lift people's lives, and I think in many ways the Church does that. So I'm with them. But not without feeling the reservations I have about much the Church is and does.

I had an interesting thought there at the sunrise service. At the Ashtons, I'd been staying in the "General Authorities Suite." It had a large bedroom, large bed, sitting room, private bathroom. The first night I was there I remember washing my hands at the sink and thinking, "Maybe we need to remember that just as important as Joseph Smith seeing God in the sacred grove is Joseph Smith seeing God in other people, such as in the man who had no boots and so Joseph took off his boots and gave them to him." I played with that idea that night and found it quite intriguing. Few of us will see God in a sacred grove, but all of us can and should see God in other people.

So there at the sunrise service the idea was made even more concrete. They passed out a paper with song lyrics printed on it. "Oh, how lovely was the morning," the song about Joseph's first vision, and on the other side of the paper, "As I have loved you, love one another," a favorite of mine. The same idea I had been playing with. The other side of the vision is love.

And then another addition to the thought came as I watched my favorite of all the plays I saw there, *Les Misérables.* When Jean Valjean is being taken into heaven at the end, he says, "When you love another person, you have seen the face of God." I know that is profoundly true.

Just this minute my phone rang. Louise Degn from KSL asked me to be on their *Prime Time Access* when I'm in Utah next week. She thought the viewers would be interested in the response that I've had to my book, and also she said I might want to reply to the rumor that I've been excommunicated. One person had called and asked her about that. I don't think it's a widespread thing, but I believe there are *lots* of stories out there. I'll be happy to be asked about any of them.

I asked Louise what news is there in Utah and she mentioned that two weeks ago President Benson had given an address on women at BYU, which also went out as a satellite offering across the Church. She said it was just terrible, a speech right out of the fifties, instructing women not to enter the workforce, not to get careers. "Women, come home, come home from your typewriters, from your nursing stations, from the factory, from the café—come back to your homes."

And back to my time with the Ashtons. I must write down some of the things Belva and I talked about. I won't write down everything, as certain things should remain private. But my commitment to history showing the fuller picture is very important to me, and so I'm going to write down some things.

Belva was on the General Board of the Relief Society for a long time, and saw the whole thing deteriorate as Correlation came in and put the Relief Society down further and further on the charts. It was happening at the end of Belle Spafford's reign as president, and when Barbara Smith took over she found she had little power. The budget was taken out of the hands of the Relief Society, they could not call their own counselors (Barbara Smith had one of her requests for counselor rejected and a perfect stranger put in her place), could not have control over their own lessons, could not make their own plans for going out into the various stakes for visits, lost the *Relief Society Magazine*, etc. She remembered Belle Spafford saying about the change as it affected the Relief Society, "They closed us down."

Seeing how crippled they were as leaders, Belva and Alice Smith offered to write a letter that Barbara could sign, a letter to the Brethren telling them how they viewed all that had happened and asking for some concessions. Barbara agreed and sent the letter over to their advisors, the General Authorities who supervised them. Barbara was called in by one of the lowest on the ladder (whose name she would not give me) and he "tore her apart." He told her never, never to do anything like that again, never to question the decisions of the Brethren. Barbara went back to her office and locked the door and sobbed and sobbed. She didn't go home. Her husband called that evening and she didn't answer the phone. Finally he went to her office and found her just devastated.

Belva was very sad and bitter about all this. "Intelligent Mormon women hurt inside," she said, "but they conform for the greater cause." (Belva sees the greatest cause as the Church; I personally see a cause greater than that, truth in general.)

Belva spoke of going out to dinner once with several General Authorities and their wives. She joined in the conversation twice, and then noticed that no other woman was saying anything. So she shut up. "All evening long only the men spoke, only the men. The women said nothing. Afterwards I said to Wendell, 'Spare me that again; I never want to go through that again.'"

I really enjoyed talking to Belva; she is a very good, devoted, perceptive person.

March 25, 1987

Back to President Benson's strong statement against "working women," calling for all the women (especially mothers) to "leave your typewriters, leave your nursing stations; come home." My friend Elouise Bell, still a professor at BYU, told me huge numbers of people were up in arms about it. She told me that the day after the talk, five nurses resigned at Utah Valley Hospital.

A woman at the Ogden conference told me she was in the temple and overheard a woman say, "What did you think of President Benson's talk? I can't decide if he was speaking as a right-wing politician or as a prophet." Another woman joined in, very vehemently saying, "If you have any shred of testimony, you would know he always speaks as a prophet!"

I understand the Church Office Building was deluged with phone calls from irate women. Lynn Ann told me her sister, a single mother in Orem, said she'd be happy to quit her job and send all her bills to the Church.

And, of course, I still get so many messages from gay men and their families. A woman in Southern California called. Her son is dying of AIDS. "I didn't realize you could hurt so much," she said. "My son has his sense of humor, his contagious laugh, but sometimes he gets very low. I went to a talk last week at our 'Know Your Religion' series. The speaker said we're seeing God's scourge of the last days, AIDS. I just began to shake. The bishop is thinking about excommunicating my son. I told him if he does he'll have to excommunicate me too."

April 6, 1987

Today I had a phone call from David Sundwall of the Health Resources and Services Administration in Washington, D.C. He has read *Goodbye, I Love You,* and invited me to come back there to make a presentation to a group of people in a national program of AIDS treatment. I told him I'd be thrilled to come. This is the kind of thing I'd hoped would happen. I will be taking Emily and making an adventure out of it.

Another telephone call. And another. The minute I hear a young man's voice: "Sister Pearson? You don't know me, but . . ." I know him. I know him. I know his whole history, mostly his whole heart, and I know his whole pain as well. Today M. and I talked for an hour. He grew up in the Church, worked with his bishop, but continues to feel as he has always felt. He had promised himself that if he ever had another homosexual encounter, he would kill himself. Last month he did, and he tried to commit suicide. He was referred to me by the therapist he's been working with, a Mormon woman who called me some time ago in desperation to know what to do with these young men.

"I had a dream after I was disfellowshipped," he told me. "I dreamed that Christ appeared to me, and he touched me and it was wonderful. I thought that after that I was going to be changed. But I wasn't changed. And I was so disappointed, so angry. I thought, if Christ healed the lepers and raised the dead, why couldn't he do something for me?"

Might it be because there's really nothing there that requires healing?

Last night I met with Jan Cameron, who founded the LDS gay support group HELP, and Dave Willis of LDS Church Social Services. They're working with Victor Brown Jr. and John Carmack (both General Authorities) on a pilot program to give some support to families of gay people. They told me that part of it is a support group for gay men led by Bishop Roberts, whose ward I spoke in the other night. Willis is disillusioned with the way the Church has handled all this, knows there is a huge need and wants to do something so that families don't have to make a choice between the Church and their children.

They feel good about Brother Carmack's attitude and help to them. They don't feel good about Victor Brown Jr. "He acts very overbearing," they said, "doesn't really want to be involved." Willis of Church Social Services said Brown's approach is very simplistic and misleading.

I asked if Victor Brown had read my book. Jan said yes he has and that he felt I had "lost it."

"She doesn't understand gospel principles," he said. And he was troubled about something I said about the Mother God.

April 18, 1987

Must report on my interview with the woman from the *U.S. News and World Report,* Murial Dobbin. She came out on Thursday with a photographer and we had a very good interview. Her quest is to find out what the Church is doing and can do in regard to the pressing social issues of the day. The status of women is high on her list.

She said, "It is such an anachronism to have an organization that keeps women as second-class citizens." A few years ago she had an interview with apostle Boyd Packer, who assured her that Mormon women are very, very important and very happy. And Barbara Smith assured her the same. "Barbara kept patting my hand and showing me all the beautiful handiwork in the glass cases. I remained unconvinced."

She had read my book and was very impressed with it. We talked a lot about the response I've had, and I showed her a few of the letters from the general Mormon readership. My main point to her was that I believe the Mormon Church (here I speak mainly of the People Church) is quite ready and quite capable of meeting some of the difficult problems. I am very heartened by the response I've had to my book. And I told her that I feel better about being Mormon now than I have in some years. And that I believe this Church belongs to me too, not just to somebody in Salt Lake City. I have a huge ancestral, emotional, spiritual, financial investment in this Church, and I consider it my right and my obligation to do everything I can to help the Church be everything good that it can be.

She questioned whether the leadership is responsive to the questions and criticism of the members. I told her about my writing to apostle Dallin Oaks last year to criticize a Relief Society lesson that quoted 13 men and not one woman. I told her he had written back saying he agreed with what I said and that we needed to do better in this and also needed patience while we did it.

May 19, 1987

First a report on current things. I could hardly sit through sacrament meeting on Mother's Day; all the talks were themed to "The Restoration of the Aaronic Priesthood." It makes it only slightly less obscene to realize that the theme for the whole month was the priesthood; it was not a deliberate slap in the face. Just thoughtless. Particularly because women, of course, cannot be ordained to the priesthood.

Between sacrament meeting and Sunday School I grabbed Ted Christensen (former bishop and very good thinking man) and said, "Am I the only one here to whom it seems very strange that we should be talking about the priesthood on Mother's Day? Here we have the one day in the year on which we can legitimately extoll the powers of womanhood and what do we do? Talk about the priesthood."

He said, "You're right. It does seem a bit strange." As we continued to talk I said I didn't know if I would say anything to the bishopric, being already pegged as the resident dissident. "Why don't you talk to the bishop?" I asked. "Tell him that if we have a whole year of Sundays devoted to things male, we can certainly have one week devoted to womanhood."

"I think I will," he said.

Yesterday evening Ted called me and said he had talked to the bishop and they had agreed to have the month of August have the theme of womanhood, and he was asked to give the major talk. Ted wants me to share with him some of my thinking on the subject.

I had not mentioned this to the children; I don't air my complaints about the Church with them. But after Ted called I told them the story because I want them to realize you can *do* something about the things that trouble you. I asked them if they had noticed the fact that at sacrament meeting on Mother's Day we talked about the priesthood. John said, "Mom, you realize I never notice *anything* about sacrament meeting." Aaron had not noticed. Katy said, "I noticed, Mom. I noticed it was Mother's Day and we were talking about the priesthood and I wondered why." Good for Katy.

Speaking of Katy, I must write down a wonderful thing she said. Well, two really. She and I had a major conversation about honesty after Katy said a thing that was not true. When we finished, Katy said, "Mom, you know what I think honesty is?"

"What?" I asked.

"I think honesty is like soap, like soap that covers you all over and makes you all clean."

"That's wonderful, Katy," I said. "You use such interesting images. I think when you grow up you could do some really good writing."

"Maybe I could," she said. "You know, sometimes, sometimes I have this—this squirt of similes."

Isn't that great? A squirt of similes!

I did a wonderful thing Monday night. I look Lynn Ann to a poetry reading on the Berkeley campus. Yevtushenko, the Soviet poet, read from his poems and it was *wonderful.* He came on stage with a big red jacket over his shoulders, which he then threw off and proceeded to speak in quite good English. He is a very large man, very dramatic, with a deep, expressive voice. He read some poems in English, and some in Russian, after which his translator read them in English. It was truly thrilling.

One of his poems was about loving America, and loving Russia. It ended, "There are oceans of malice between us. There is the Atlantic Ocean between us. But we will swim toward one another." I so love that image. Katy got excited about it too, when I gave my report to the kids.

The next night I gave them Yevtushenko's history at dinner and then read one of the poems from the book I bought. "I want to be everyone and everywhere." They found the whole thing quite interesting, including Aaron. And John was inspired to get out an album of *Rush* that he loves and have me read aloud some lyrics that also talk about getting rid of borders.

I am so glad that I went to see this poet. It was thrilling, really memorable. I had a sense of watching a prophet at work.

Speaking of the words of a prophet—a bit more about President Benson calling the women to "come home" from their employment. I was talking with Robbie MacArthur, who said that her daughter-in-law told her she knows quite a few young married women in Utah who are quitting their jobs and having the family go on welfare.

Also, I had been invited some months ago to do a mini-class in Relief Society on "Turning your hobby into a career." But last week Kathleen, the woman who had invited me, told me I was being bumped. Our Relief Society president was very concerned about Brother Benson's statement and did not want to do anything contrary to it. Kathleen and I laughed about it; she is a nurse and has always worked part-time. She's not going to quit her job and does not like the additional guilt. I've talked to a number of women around here who feel the same way.

I am now going to eat some lunch and then will write about the trip. My frequent lunch these days is a carrot and cabbage salad with nuts and raisins and a little mayonnaise and nonflavored yogurt; it is wonderfully healthy and good.

May 26, 1987

So to the trip. Washington D.C. But first St. Louis. It was good, though a mixed bag. I flew to St. Louis first, as the *Sally Jesse Raphael Show* decided they had to have me on their show about women caring for declining husbands. It was a very good program. Her theme was that in this day of throwaway relationships when someone does not meet your expectations, what is it like to stay with someone "for better or for worse" when the "worse" really does come.

I was brought in for the last segment. There have been only two interviews on which I found myself showing emotion: the CBS interview and this one. There was something about the way Sally said, "You crawled into bed with Gerald when he was dying. Why?" Emotion washed over me and I experienced the whole thing again.

I flew from St. Louis to Washington to meet Emily and a couple of my high school friends, Aniene and Mary. We drove around to see the sights and had a wonderful time: the Lincoln monument, the wall on which were inscribed the names of the Vietnam casualties, the Jefferson monument, and a wonderful statue of Einstein. We stayed in a hotel that night and enjoyed it very much, ordering room service and being luxurious.

The next day was the meeting. I felt it went very well. I liked David Sundwall, head of the Health Resources and Services Administration, the man who had invited me. He gave a presentation, then I spoke for about thirty-five minutes. Then they asked questions of us, including Emily. They seemed to be very impressed at our presentation.

Right in the middle of my talk the Surgeon General appointed by President Reagan, Dr. Koop, walked into the room with his assistant, carrying their copies of *Goodbye, I Love You* for me to sign. They stood at the door as I finished my talk, then Dr. Koop said a few things to the group. Afterwards I was given to understand that they might be asking me to do something in the future. I will do what I can, of course.

Em and I also went to New York to see my editor at Random House, Charlotte. She was very taken with Emily, and we had a good conversation about the new book that, at her suggestion, I am working on. Might not have written much about it here. Charlotte said it would be a shame not to have a second book lined up, and she wanted something both fun and meaningful about being a single parent. So that's what I've been doing in the midst of everything else. Charlotte wants to make sure it shows the hard stuff along with the sweetness and light. Some of the chapters she's read look too "tied up with a blue ribbon." My successes need to be more "hard won." I make it all look too easy.

We also went to the top of the World Trade Center. And we took the boat around the island. I was very ready to come home, very ready.

Yesterday Brad Adams came to visit with me and give me a few lessons on the computer. This is the man who tried to take his life up at the Provo temple. He's such a dear, good person. And he's suffering quite a lot of conflict and negative feelings. He recently learned that he is virus positive. As we were talking about some of his stresses and his needs, he asked if I would give him a blessing. "I don't care if you don't have the priesthood," he said. "I'd like you to give me a blessing. Sometimes when I'm really, really low, I give myself a blessing. I place my hands on my own head and give myself a blessing."

At that moment my heart broke. That Brad or anyone would have to give his own self a blessing! I thought about it and told him I would be glad to, if he would do the same for me. So after supper we came up here to my room and said a prayer and then gave each other blessings.

I did not feel uncomfortable; I felt fine about it. I did not, of course, use the word "priesthood." I placed my hands on his head and gave him a blessing of every good and encouraging and warm and loving thing that came to me. He appreciated it a lot. And then for a few minutes I continued to stand behind him with my arms around his neck.

"The Mormons have got to stop being so rejecting," he said. Then he broke into sobs and couldn't speak for a while. "To be rejected by something so wonderful as the Mormon Church is nearly more than a person can bear." Again my heart broke for Brad. And for all the others out there who are outcasts. How can we do this to them?

Then Brad gave me a nice blessing, and I appreciated it. He said that he saw me singing heavenly songs and blessed me with the peace and the stillness that comes with a beautiful garden. Brad is constantly thrilled at the work my book is doing. And he sees me as a "maypole" around which many, many people will dance.

As I write here of the yearnings of so many gay people that I have come to care for, I am realizing that in calling them "homosexuals," and making the "sexual" part the criterion on which we judge them, meaning "acting on it," we are missing a major mark. We tell them they should not "fall in love" with each other, which is not possible.

Romantic love, I believe because I know, is truly one of the most awesome and mysterious experiences available to humans. To issue a ban on those feelings, to call them evil, is cruel indeed.

The thoughts above were prompted by this paragraph:

I'm keeping very busy, of course, but still I have time to feel. I started to write a poem, "So much love and nowhere to put it." It is hugely frustrating. I suffocate in my own perfume. I am out giving love to so many people, while I yearn so to be able to give love to just one. I am receiving love from thousands of people, needing to receive love from *one*. Even the universe does not take the place of *the one*.

Being in love colors everything, sweetens everything, energizes everything. To my experience nothing compares to being in love. Not religion. Not service. Not being loved by thousands of people because I have changed their lives. The ecstasy, of course, moves into a more practical stage. Still, nothing comes close to being loved by and loving one person. As I wrote years ago:

Seeing you seeing me
Took my breath away.

I never knew there were
Grand Canyons in me
And Mona Lisas
And Sistine Chapels
And the Alps—

Until that look,
That amazed, amazing look
Crossed your tourist face
And I became the newest
Wonder of the world.

It is hard to know, to *know* that "sweet mystery of life" and then to live without it. And we are asking our dear gay people to live a whole lifetime without it.

May 31, 1987

This morning I had a run-in with our gospel doctrine teacher. Jim M. who I am pretty good friends with, got going on this "true authority" thing. He said that although ministers of other faiths might be perfectly sincere, still in the eyes of God the Father they are still, as we read in John 10:8, "thieves and robbers."

I didn't even raise my hand. I said, "Oh, Jim, come on. You can't mean that."

He tried to defend himself, and other people jumped in and said that we can't make such an assumption.

I further volunteered, "Yesterday as I read an article about Mother Teresa to my children, my son Aaron asked, 'Mom, do the Mormons believe that Mother Teresa is going to hell?'" I replied that not exactly hell, but some feel she won't be in the "highest heaven." I said that all Mormons I know admire her enormously.

"Of course," said Jim. "She does good work. But she doesn't understand the teachings of Christ. And if at some point she doesn't accept the gospel she will end up in the kingdom of the 'good and honorable of the earth' but not in celestial glory."

"But Jim," I said. "It would take Mother Teresa about five minutes to go through the ordinances the Mormons say she needs to have done. And it would take the rest of us about a hundred years to get to where she is in our spiritual development. Mother Teresa doesn't understand the gospel? Jim! She's been out there *living* the gospel for more than 50 years!"

Just now John walked into my room and said, "Katy, did you give Juliet a bath?"

"Yes," said Katy.

"She doesn't *need* a bath. And if you ever do it again, would you please wash off the bar of soap?"

I burst into a laugh. "John," I said, "is there cat hair on the soap?"

"Yes," he said. "It's disgusting."

I laughed and said, "Well, better the cat hair is on the bar of soap than on Katy's tongue."

June 8, 1987

A report on my most recent trip. I flew to Atlanta, as months ago I had been invited to speak at the national convention of Gay and Lesbian Parents, and to receive their annual "Media Award," which in the past had gone to Phil Donahue and to Abigail Van Buren. The award itself was one thousand dollars. They also gave me a beautiful crystal blown glass dogwood sculpture. Had a very good time with them.

I was the speaker at the banquet. The other major award they gave was to a drag queen, "Charlie Brown," who had raised $80,000 for people with AIDS.

I started my talk by saying, "I have never before shared the platform with a drag queen, and I can't wait to tell my bishop." They loved it. I gave a good talk, telling my story, emphasizing the relationship of Gerald and the kids, and urging them all to be the best parents and the best former spouses and the best people that they can be. Everybody gave me "rave reviews."

July 7, 1987

And now about the puppy. I've mentioned, I'm sure, Katy's single-mindedness in her desire for a puppy. "Puppy" has appeared on my grocery lists. "Get Katy a Puppy" has appeared on my lists of things to do. I have found Katy in tears.

Another dog around here is absolutely the last thing I need. I guess the final straw was a few weeks ago when Emily was pushing the other children to see if they were hiding any strong feelings about what we've all been through in the last three years. The boys seem to have generally taken it in stride. But as she pumped Katy a little, Katy said, "Well, about once a day I sit down and cry because of the things I can't have, like my daddy and a puppy."

Katy, being the number 4 child, has always had the tail end of everything. So I caved. I can't give her her daddy, but I can give her a puppy. So—I did.

Katy is ecstatic. It was love at first sight. Puppy love, of course. The puppy is a Keeshond. Her full name is Bridget Baby Brown Eyes, but she is generally known as Bridget.

Yesterday we drove to a waterslide in Pleasanton and took the puppy with us. I was so in admiration, as I often am, as I looked at my four children, so full of life and interest and enjoying each other so much.

One more little thought about my Katy. She has moved downstairs and has cleaned out all the excess stuff in her room. She was throwing away a little bottle of perfume I had given her. I said, "Katy, save this. You'll want it in a couple of years."

She replied innocently, "Will it smell better in a couple of years?"

August 14, 1987

In Utah at a wedding reception I spoke with Phyllis Van Wagenen, Lola Redford's mother. Phyllis moves in the uppity Mormon women's circles in Utah, and I asked her if she had any news for me. She said she had been told by her friend Shirley Paxman, who is close to the family of Gordon B. Hinckley, that word has been given to the *Ensign, Church News*, etc. to quit quoting or referring to Church President Benson's recent talk on women, and to lay off the issues he addressed: having very large families, no careers for women, etc. She also said the Brethren are doing their best to keep him out of state as much as possible.

I have a note here that I made to myself in my day-planner at church. Hymn number 296. "Our Father, by whose name all fatherhood is known, Who does in love proclaim each family thine own...."

And where, I ask, is the Mother, by whose name all motherhood is known?

September 2, 1987

More about the *Sunstone Symposium* in Utah. Phyllis Tribble gave a good address on finding feminist themes in the Bible if one scratches below the surface.

The first session was on the changing nature of the family, somewhat of a response to President Benson's controversial address, and many got up to make statements. I got up and said, "Wouldn't it be wonderful, as we observe the 'changing nature of the family,' if we saw a change that affected our eternal family, so that we no longer had to live spiritually in a one-Parent home, but could finally be the children of two Parents? And wouldn't it be wonderful if the Prophet, rather than instructing all the mothers to 'come home,' would invite the Heavenly Mother to come home?" This was greeted with much applause.

A woman was there making a TV documentary on women in the Mormon Church. She had noticed me that first night and asked if I would be

Katy, Aaron, Carol Lynn, Emily, and John.

interviewed (she didn't know who I was). I agreed and made what I felt to be a good, faithful positive statement about how Mormons continue to be good pioneers and that we can meet the women's issue and other issues intelligently. And that we have a wonderful, though undeveloped, plank in our platform that tells us God is both Father and Mother. Developing that would be a good boost toward valuing equally maleness and femaleness. I quoted writer Virginia Woolf: "Men and women are different; what needs to be made equal is the value placed on those differences." And I noted that nowhere is this done, not internationally, not nationally, not in the Mormon Church or any other church I know anything about.

Another difficult story about the fruits of President Benson's talk. Yesterday B.C., a member of my ward, brought over some paint he bought for me; my friends from Affirmation have volunteered to paint the inside of my house. B. and I talked for quite a while. His son just got married a year or so ago. He's supposedly in college, but not doing well and so dropped out. The wife, now pregnant, because they had been encouraged not to wait to start their family, had a job in preparation for the coming of the baby. They have no financial security; B. and his wife have been helping them. In response to President Benson's talk, the wife quit her job so she could do the right thing and stay home. So she stays home all day and watches television until far into the night. And the husband scrambles.

September 17, 1987

Yesterday afternoon my phone rang.

Me: Hello?

Her: Hello. Is this Carol Lynn Pearson?

Me: Yes.

Her: This is Ann Landers.

(Two weeks ago Ann printed my "To an Adopted" for the second time without my name on it. The first time, a few years ago, I and several friends wrote to correct her. When it happened recently. I wrote my agent, Peter, and he sent a letter to her.)

Me: Well, Ann! How are you?

Her: I'm humiliated is how I am. I have here in my hands a letter from your attorney. I can't believe how all this happened. I am so sorry. And I hope you can forgive me.

Me: Of course! It's worth it to get a phone call from you.

Her: A number of people wrote and told me your name should be on that poem. You must have an awful lot of fans out there.

Me: Well, there are a lot of people who read my poetry.

Her: I should think so. It's beautiful, just beautiful. And I have a statement coming out in a column giving you credit for that poem.

Me: I would like to send you the book that it's in.

Her: Please! I would love that. And I'm sure there will be others in there that I will want to use, and when I do I'll do it right and give you full credit.

Me: And that other book that I know my agent mentioned...

Her: Oh, yes, I have that right here in front of me. *Goodbye, I Love You.* Senator Orrin Hatch sent it to me and I read it, a beautiful story. I'm looking at your picture on the back of your book. You're a beautiful, beautiful woman. And now that I know your name, I will never forget it again. It will be emblazoned on my mind for the rest of my life.

I told her again how thrilled I was to talk to her and that I appreciate tremendously the work that she does. I often read her columns to my children and we talk about how we would respond to the problem and then read how Ann responds. We had a fine conversation. For history, here is the poem she had printed in her column, "Author Unknown":

To an Adopted

I did not plant you, true.
But when the season is done—
When the alternate prayers
For sun and for rain are counted—
When the pain of weeding

And the pride of watching
Are through—

Then I will hold you high,
A shining sheaf above
The thousand sheaves grown wild.

Not my planting,
But by heaven my harvest—
My own child.

On Sunday I had the kids watch with me the movie of *The Shoes of the Fisherman,* from the novel by Morris West. It was one of Gerald's favorite books. A fictional story about a Pope who assists in averting international disaster. The current Pope is here in San Francisco today and I wanted the kids to have some background on all that. Such a good story.

Another brand-new thought has held my mind for several days now. On the airplane I read the book *We* by Robert A. Johnson, a Jungian psychologist. The book investigates the need for the feminine in our world that has so entirely sold out to patriarchal values. And as I read this paragraph, page 19—"It is the feminine qualities that bring meaning into life: relatedness to other human beings, the ability to soften power with love, awareness of our inner feelings and values, respect for our earthly environment, a delight in earth's beauty, and the introspective quest for inner wisdom"—I was suddenly struck with the paradox that in spite of the fact that the Mormon Church is maybe among the last bastions of patriarchy, many of the *works* of the Church are the works of what Johnson calls "femininity"!

One of the things the Church does best is to insure relatedness to other human beings. And in spite of frequent unrighteous dominion, there is the explicit attempt to soften power with love, as the description of use of the priesthood makes clear. To some extent we're encouraged to be aware of our inner feelings and seek for personal revelation. We are told to "clean up our ditch banks and plant gardens and not to go deer hunting just for sport," and to remember that the earth has a soul and to care for her as well. Introspection? Well, prayer and meditation are high on the list.

There is too much that seems to ask us to listen for the outward orders and too little asking us to listen to the inward orders, but there is the potential there.

So. I have been thinking about this a lot and it interests me. I don't know what it means. My mind just got to it. But it interests me.

Monday night Katy and I took our first tap dancing class through Civic Arts. It was fun and Katy had a good time. Which is a breakthrough; she has not been a dancer or anything like unto it.

And now something absolutely delightful: Tuesday night I gave Katy a wishbone to wish on with me. She took it and thought a minute and said, "Mom, I can't think of anything to wish for." Isn't that marvelous? Katy and her puppy are very happy.

October 5, 1987

Another trip to report on. My main purpose in going to Utah was to speak at the AMCAP Conference (Association of Mormon Counselors and Psychologists). They had invited me many months ago.

It was really a thrilling, remarkable experience. There were more than three hundred people there, the biggest crowd they've ever drawn. I was told by someone who talked to one of the officers that several of the Brethren were not very happy about my selection as their keynote speaker.

I spoke at the first session. Mostly I told them about the experiences I've had in this last year, about the people I've been hearing from, the people in great pain who are out there waiting for them to come to their assistance. I used the good story of Brigham Young dismissing General Conference and sending out the wagons with supplies to rescue the people on the plains, the handcart companies that met an early winter in Wyoming. I told them that they had to be the rescuers now, to load up their wagons with all of their professional skills and all of their compassion and understanding and love. I had many, many of them tell me how much my book has meant to them and how they appreciated my talk. Some said they were certain my work was the reason the Brethren, like it or not, are addressing this subject.

Must mention the Church's "Women's Meeting" that was held last week, televised out to all the chapels. All three women in the Relief Society Presidency spoke. And apostle Russell Nelson. All of them spoke as if they were speaking to a group of small Primary children. One of the counselors said that we have lesbian women and homosexual men in the Church and they are under the same obligation as the rest to be chaste. Her talk was on understanding people, but she never even approached trying to understand and include these outcast men and women. Jan Cameron, who founded the support group "HELP," said she was so angry with the talk that she just cried.

I was unhappy with Brother Nelson's talk. He had a condescending demeanor that he never would have used in speaking to a group of men. And he said the most amazing thing: "Sisters, we know you have problems. We know your kitchens are too small. We know there are financial problems." And that concluded his list. Kitchens too small! The problems of Mormon women make a too small kitchen the absolute least of things! It was truly discouraging. And I was interested to see that the chapel was only about a fourth full. A couple of years ago, when Gordon B. Hinckley made his infamous comment

Kent Burnett, organizer of the AIDS Names Project, holding Gerald's name on a block for the AIDS Memorial Quilt, 1987. Thousands of blocks featured the name of someone who died in the pandemic.

about the "hairdressers," the crowd was overflowing into the recreation hall. I guess women are getting the message that there's not much there for them. A number of good individual statements were made, but I felt that as a whole it was a real low.

October 25, 1987

A long time since I wrote. Mostly just work. Work, work, work is all I do. I am not necessarily proud of that. My tray sometimes is empty, but I continue to give. I push myself daily, and the only recreation I take is a walk to the park or up into the hills so that I will be healthier and live longer and be able to work more. I do enjoy my walks, however, and I look at the trees and the sky and the clouds with wonder and am amazed that I can move without being plugged into anything, that I am alive.

A week ago I was the keynote speaker at a women's conference at St. Mary's College in nearby Moraga. It was sponsored by Battered Women's Alternatives and AAUW (American Association of University Women). I spoke on love as the approach that women must use if we are to bring femininity to temper our male society. Used a lot of my poems. The response was tremendous; in fact they gave me a standing ovation.

A couple of weeks ago I got a letter from apostle Gordon B. Hinckley. I had sent him a very good article on how the Catholic Church is dealing with AIDS and suggesting we could have a similar approach. His letter was a

The AIDS Memorial Quilt on display in Washington, DC.

thank you note, and at the end he said, "I appreciate the good you have done and are doing."

December 3, 1987

Spoke to Bookcraft Publishers today; the secretary told me they've had a large response to Ann Landers giving out my name to the poem she had quoted. She has answered more than thirty calls from people inquiring how they can get *Beginnings* (now out of print), very emotional people who say they've exhausted the bookstores and the libraries. One woman begged her to read her the poem over the phone and when she finished the woman was in tears.

December 5, 1987

I sent this letter off today:

Dear President Hinckley,

You will not be receiving regular complaints from me, but I love the Church too much not to voice an objection to the picture in the *Church News* that I received yesterday.

I was stunned to see the portrayal of the hand of God as a nice white hand, and the hand of Satan as one of darker color. I had so hoped we were beyond that. A friend of mine who is of minority background found this to be very painful; he said that it and many other things make him feel like a "marginal" member and one definitely of lesser value.

Do not take the time to respond to this letter. But am hoping you will take a minute to see what policies are in place that will move us toward a more sensitive portrayal of our brothers and sisters of darker color.

I send you very best wishes and appreciation.

Very sincerely,
Carol Lynn Pearson

December 18, 1987

Received today a welcome letter:

Dear Sister Pearson:

Thank you for your letter of December 5th. I am taking the liberty of passing this on to those who are responsible for the publication of the *Church News*. Certainly nothing should be done which might create the impression that we regard those with skin of a different color as being inferior. It is the teaching and doctrine of the Church that all of us are children of the same Eternal Father.

Every good wish to you for a very happy holiday season.

Sincerely,
Gordon B. Hinckley

And I must record a magical, wonderful dream:

Mikhail and Raisa Gorbachev are in my home where we are having a wonderful conference about how to achieve world peace. As the meeting ends, I give them two of my books. Later Mrs. Gorbachev calls me from Moscow to tell me how much she has enjoyed the books. We have a good conversation and I say to her, "Oh, Raisa, do you realize the position you are in to do such a lot of good? You could host a conference of all the first ladies of all the countries and discuss women's issues and how women can help obtain world peace." I am so moved as I say this to her that I begin to cry.

I woke up and went right to my keyboard and wrote Raisa a letter, telling her about the dream. I will find an address and send it to Moscow with the two books that I gave her in the dream. This was truly a thrilling experience, leaving me with such a great feeling.

That's a good place to end this year's writing. Here's to world peace. And to the solving of all our major problems.

25

MY FAMOUS LETTER TO THE BISHOP

January 10, 1988

Last night I attended a historic occasion. For the first time in Mormon history, I believe, an event was held in a chapel specifically for homosexual people. It was a dinner held in the San Francisco chapel for three groups: Bishop Roberts' Saturday morning group of gay men who come each week just to talk, San Francisco's Affirmation group, and HELP, the parent support group.

It was really quite remarkable. I knew a lot of the people who were there, of course, and I was inundated with their ongoing appreciation and received more and more stories of how *Goodbye, I Love You* has been extremely helpful to families.

I sat by Bishop Roberts and we talked during dinner. He has been receiving a massive education in dealing with these people. His stake president is very supportive, but some who don't understand are pretty alarmed that he is seemingly so soft on homosexuals. A couple of people reported him to the General Authorities, saying he is gay and his counselors are gay. And the other day he received a call from another bishop who tore into him for "accepting the homosexual lifestyle," and said Bishop Roberts shouldn't even be in the Church.

He is really a wonderful man, has a countenance of purity and kindness and real honesty. After dinner he spoke for a few minutes, and expressed some of his hopes for continued dialogue and better understanding. "Are we going to beat up another generation of children who are gay in the Church or are we going to lift some of their guilt? Some of the greatest men I know in the Church are gay; they are the best disciples of Christ you could ask for. I'm not a very good administrator; the stake president tears his hair out over that. But I think I'm a good minister, and that's what I want to do, minister as Christ would minister."

We spoke after the meeting was over, and he said that the answer was to pray that the Prophet will receive a revelation about how to handle this. "The current prophet, President Benson?" I asked.

"He might be just the one," the bishop said. "He's a farm man, knows some of the more earthy aspects of life."

January 31, 1988

Reba Keele of BYU told me about a major study that was done about women's attitudes about the Church, which has been generally suppressed. Evidently the higher educated a Mormon man is, the more likely he is to be active in the Church; the higher educated a woman is, the less likely she is to be active.

I was put in touch with a family in San Diego, and speaking to the father I learned that there is a group there, solely a Mormon group, and *so many* have the same story—an active LDS father, bishop even, who has molested them. Some stories run that the father gets a slap on the wrist and no further action, goes on being even a bishop after he has sexually abused his daughter or daughters. He agrees with me that this is another huge problem in the Church, says he thinks the Brethren know it is major, but don't know what to do about it.

Something especially sad. My dear old BYU theatre friend Tom Macaulay has AIDS. I knew he was "getting over pneumonia," which often means AIDS. I called him. It's true. He sounded in good cheer, but we both know what is coming. Very sad here. I love Tom so much.

Have to record here something funny and true that Katy said. We were watching a comedy routine on TV and something came up about "birth control devices." I was a bit uncomfortable. I said to Katy, "Katy, what's the very best birth control?"

"Withdrawal," she said.

"What?" I was quite startled. "And what is withdrawal?"

"It's like when you just move back and don't even get involved in the first place."

A couple of days ago David Sharpton called from Salt Lake, one of the men I've spoken to concerning their work with the Church. David is a gay man who has AIDS and has been a useful resource to many. When he called, he was very sick and feeling terrible about some interference in his hopes for the Church's new Department of Homosexual Concerns. He's afraid it's just the old "cure" program in a new dress. Alan Gundry, who was the Church's liaison between the Department of Homosexual Concerns and Affirmation, has been told now he can't speak to groups. He was going to meet with Affirmation in Salt Lake, but can't now. Evidently the newsletter of Affirmation published a report that David gave at the L.A. meeting, and that got the attention of some of the Brethren. I knew things could not go smoothly on this. Evidently Brother Gundry and Victor Brown, who is the new head of Church Social Services, do not view homosexuality in the same way. Gundry knows that going celibate is not the same as going straight. Brown thinks there is a cure for the homosexual.

I'm meeting with Gundry in two weeks; we'll have to see how all that goes.

February 13, 1988

Got a call from James Drake, an organ professor in Utah, who had before called and said how he loved my book. He told me of a young man in England, a gay man who found himself at the end of his rope, then miraculously found my book in a bookstore and found it to be hugely helpful. He was, in fact, taking the missionary discussions and discussed his homosexuality with president Wendall Ashton. He reported Ashton as being very understanding, saying, "That's the way the Lord created you, just as he created me heterosexual." Ashton said he had done some studying into Church history and was convinced that Evan Stephens, who wrote so many of the hymns in our hymn book, was gay.

February 28, 1988

I spoke to a good crowd in Logan, six hundred or more, much larger than usual. Talked to a lot of appreciative people afterwards. Alice Smith was there and came to lunch with us. On the way there I quizzed her a little about the stories Belva Ashton had told me of their dealings as the Relief Society Presidency with the General Authorities when they were trying to salvage a little autonomy for the Relief Society after Correlation destroyed such a lot. She told me essentially what Belva had told me. And it was a sad thing for Alice to remember.

I took Katy to Welfare Square, where we took a tour around the bishop's storehouse and saw the movie about the welfare program of the Church. Very impressive. Then I had an hour with Alan Gundry, the head of the new Department of Homosexual Concerns in the Church. He is a very good and kind person, who realizes we do not have the answers. He said, "Ten years ago I would have said all these guys can be changed, but I know now that's not true." His goal for the department is to help everyone love one another and to realize that we're all brothers and sisters. He's just going to be collecting data right now, listening to people's stories.

March 9, 1988

Dear Bishop Sutton,

Being a person who feels free from time to time to voice a criticism, I feel I should also from time to time voice an appreciation.

I would like you to know that I very much appreciated that in your confirmation of your daughter on Sunday you referred to her Heavenly Mother and her Heavenly Parents. It may be difficult for a man to understand how excluded a woman can feel in a system that uses only masculine terminology. We are in profound need of acknowledging God as Mother as well as Father.

I hope that your Sara and all the young people in our ward will continue to hear frequent acknowledgement of their Mother.

Thanks for your ongoing good work.

Sincerely,
Carol Lynn Pearson

March 13, 1988

A lovely Sunday morning as I look out my window here. This is really a gorgeous place to live, and I am very grateful. Our church meetings are now one to four, so we have the mornings free.

Speaking of church. I had another run-in with our gospel doctrine teacher. I am quite fond of Brother M. in an odd way. He is very sincere and welcoming of Katy when I have her stay with them, as she is very good friends with his daughter. But he is such an arch conservative. In his Book of Mormon class he was talking about the Church being led astray by the teachings of men, and remarked that one way he observes this is in the number of women who work outside the home, in opposition to the Prophet's counsel. In the last ward he lived in, in Orinda, in his priesthood quorum, *all* of the men had wives who worked, and when they had a lesson on the subject, they didn't take it seriously. He began his statement by saying there would probably be some who would want to challenge him on what he was about to say and ask to meet him in the parking lot.

So when he finished, I raised my hand and said, "Well, Jim, I'll be glad to meet you in the parking lot, on behalf of all the good women in this ward who work, either because they have to or want to."

March 20, 1988

In the last two years I have received in person, by phone or letter, hundreds of stories from people anxious to be heard. A recent one wakes me up in the night. And somehow I have to see that it is preserved.

M., a woman from a nearby community, called me a week ago today, having just finished reading *Goodbye, I Love You*. As she cried and began her story, I knew she really needed to talk to someone, so I invited her to come over and we could talk in person. So on Friday afternoon she did and we walked down to the park.

I have never been with anybody suffering with more raw pain. If I'd known how fragile she was I might not have taken her outside. She cried as we walked, and then we sat down at a table at the park and she cried more. In all the people I have been with, I don't remember actually crying myself as I talked to them, but I did with M. I put my arms around her and cried with her.

I kept wishing I were taking notes as she spoke. She put everything so well, so poignantly, and the story is so horrendously dramatic.

She and E. were married for eighteen years, and she was very happy. She was very much in love with him. He was the only man she'd ever loved, ever made love with. Three years ago he became ill with what they thought was the flu. Finally, on a visit to the hospital, she learned from her husband that he had been diagnosed with AIDS. He told her that on one occasion, when he was coming out of a concert in San Francisco alone, he had been attacked by three homosexual men, who all raped him, and that's how he must have contracted it. Just the story of the rape nearly killed her, she loved him so, to think he had gone through that. She felt raped herself. And then to know he had AIDS from it. Her world crashed. She went home from the hospital that night and wrote his funeral service, selecting the scripture, "Rejoice in the wife of thy youth and be ravished with her love." She had always loved that image, always loved the word "ravished," felt sometimes that she felt more passion for her husband than he did for her.

They had two children. A boy, fourteen, took one look through the door at his father in the hospital on a breathing machine and ran the full length of the hospital and fell unconscious at the feet of his aunt.

A week later E. died. M. stayed with him all the time, brought each of his brothers in to say goodbye. She told him she loved him and would never marry again and they would be together forever. A look of pain crossed his face like she had never seen. Even after they told her he was gone, she told him again that she loved him, and "a tear fell out of the dead man's eye."

No mortuary would take him. They put him in a body bag. When they found a place that would take him, it had to be a closed casket; they wouldn't prepare him, shave him, etc. No one in the family was told it was AIDS. Everyone was told it was leukemia. After the children were in bed, M. would sit on the kitchen floor and scream her pain.

Two years after the death, she found a medical clinic number in her husband's things, and wondered why he had gone there, as their health provider was Kaiser. She called and asked if he had been there for an emergency. She was told he had a very thick file there. She called her sister, who flew in and together they went to the clinic and demanded to see the file. "Multiple Partners," the file said. He had been in often, treated for gonorrhea, syphilis, herpes, hepatitis. The nurse didn't want them to take the file, but they told her she could give it to them now or after a lawyer demanded it. M. took the file to her doctor at Kaiser, who spent an hour with her, deeply distressed for her, said that her husband clearly had many relationships with men.

Again she was destroyed. Now all her memories were violated. She had been betrayed. And she couldn't talk to him. She went home and screamed at her husband, "God damn you! I will never be buried by your side!" She said to me, "That's all I had left, the only way I could hurt him, to not be buried by his side. My name is on the tombstone, but I screamed at him that I would never be buried there."

She can't tell her children. Again she sits on the floor after they are in bed and weeps and screams. The betrayal and helplessness is overwhelming. And she doesn't sleep. She keeps books by her bed for the three a.m. reading, the four a.m. reading, the five a.m. reading. Over and over she recites a particular Emily Dickinson poem.

I am the first person she's been able to talk to who knows what she's been through. She's been to counselor after counselor, but none of them understands at all.

I made her promise that on Monday she would call her doctor at Kaiser and get some medical help for her depression and her sleeplessness. I told her to call me after she's talked with her doctor.

I tried to encourage her to find a way to divide her feelings about her husband, to take the part of him that was the terrible, betraying part that caused her so much pain, and put it in a box and hand it over to God and say, "You deal with this; I can't." And to keep the other things, the good things, and allow them still to be. I told her, and I know this is true, that the dark part of him, strange and baffling and destructive though it was, did not erase the fact that he did love her, did do all the good things she knew he did.

She said, "His co-workers told me how much he loved me. They said his face would light up when speaking of me. How can this be?" I told her that, strange though it was, it could be. He did love her, as Gerald loved me. I was often told that Gerald lit up when speaking of me, that others knew he loved me dearly, as did I. I am able to keep that part of it, to turn over to God the other part that will always baffle me. I have come to peace concerning it. M. has no peace.

I have been praying for her constantly since Friday. I'm encouraging her to participate with the wives' support group that has been organized.

Oh, what is the sense to all the pain in this world? M. is an unusually intelligent, beautiful, tender woman. How can this be? I rationalize my own difficult situation in that it brought the opportunity for me to use it to help a huge number of other people. But what is M. to be doing with this? Why must her anguish be so great? As I held her, she rocked back and forth with the pain and cried and cried.

Dave Willis, of LDS Church Social services called me to bring me up to date on the events of "the Church and the homosexual." He was very discouraged. Evidently the dinner that was held in the San Francisco chapel alarmed some of the Brethren in Salt Lake. They withdrew Church sponsorship from the parents' support group. When John Carmack (the supportive General Authority) left, it was the end of anybody's enthusiasm officially. Victor Brown, Jr., who has been over the local pilot program of HELP (Homosexual

Education for Latter-day Saint Parents), didn't want it to be anyway. Brother Willis has been chastised for his involvements in this outreach to gays, told he was wrong and told to stay away from it. Bishop Roberts was instructed to disband his Saturday morning Group. But he has reassembled them in a family home evening group. All this is indeed discouraging.

May 2, 1988

On Tuesday the 26th, I received a phone call from the office of the assistant to the Surgeon General asking if I would be willing to serve on an advisory board to the AIDS Task Force in Washington. They are organizing an eleven-member advisory board, comprised of nine medical people and three lay people, of which I would be one. David Sundwall has recommended me. I told her yes, I would be pleased to be on the board. She said the responsibility would be that I would have to travel to Washington twice a year. I will receive further information.

I'm glad to be able to do this. Maybe I can help out a little and it would be most interesting. And, of course, it is a significant honor.

Did I mention I'm going through the Old Testament stories with the kids to make sure they know them? I have been remiss about this for years. For one thing I have some very ambivalent feeling toward Bible stories; many of them I cannot even begin to see as the "word of God." But I do want my children to know them. A couple of weeks ago I quizzed John, "Now, what does the rainbow signify?"

"The rainbow signifies," he said, "God's promise that he would never again destroy the world by flood. *Next time He'll get us by fire!*"

No wonder John is currently an atheist.

Coincidentally, the very next day there was the most remarkable rainbow in the sky that I have ever seen. Ever! For the first time in my life I saw a *full,* complete rainbow, both sides and even a little of the top. It was stunning.

The following consists of excerpts from a five-page letter I wrote to my bishop. I was indeed an involved and committed member of my ward! The full letter is in my archives and also in the complete diary.

May 9, 1988

My letter to Bishop Sutton, a copy sent to both of his counselors, Wally Jones and Rand King, our stake president, William Parmley, and two General Authorities, Gordon B. Hinckley and Dallin H. Oaks:

Dear Bishop Sutton and Counselors,

Knowing, as I do, that the three of you are good and caring men, I believe that you have concern for the feelings of the members of the ward. Consequently I feel comfortable in sharing some feelings with you.

One of the roles that life has assigned me is that of defender of women, which role I am happy to take. I have for more than thirty years been a careful observer and documenter of the various ways in which our society and our church demean women and consistently value things male over things female, despite rhetoric to the contrary.

Of all the things I have observed, none has been more remarkable than what happened in our ward yesterday on Mother's Day. I love our ward. When people ask me why I don't move back to Utah, a major part of my response is that I love my ward in California. I have wonderful memories and great appreciation for this ward and for this ward's current bishopric. But the memory of yesterday will remain with me as an enormous sorrow. I will start at the beginning.

Precisely one year ago, as I was sitting in Sacrament Meeting on Mother's Day, it suddenly dawned on me that all of the talks, *all* of the talks, were in commemoration of the priesthood. I thought to myself, "This is not happening. They would not do this to us. Here we have one day—*one* day out of the year on which it is legitimate to focus on women, on the powers of the female, possibly on the eternal and theological implications of motherhood, and instead we devote that day to honoring the *priesthood?"* The printed program assured us that the "theme of the month" was priesthood restoration, but that was thin justification. By the time the meeting was over, I was fairly shaking. I wished that the talks would have been on food storage; we could have forgiven it as an oversight. But to have talks on the male priesthood on Mother's Day carries the unavoidable feeling of insult, rather like spending Martin Luther King Day talking about how blessed we are to have been born white. After the closing prayer, carnations were handed out to the mothers. I had to wonder what the flower meant.

I was not the only woman in the ward who noticed. Both of my visiting teachers, without my bringing it up, said, "How did you like the way they snubbed us on Mother's Day?" But women are good and forgiving and supportive and take what they're given and make the best of it. However, I did convey to the bishopric through a respected third party that I felt a real mistake had been made.

On the Sunday before Mother's Day of this year, one of the women in the ward said to me, "What do you think we're going to have on Mother's Day next week? Do you think they'll give us the same treatment?" I assured her I was certain they would not.

So yesterday. Both major speakers addressed themselves fully to the restoration of the priesthood. I was embarrassed for Brother Curtis, who made a difficult attempt at the beginning of his talk to acknowledge that it was Mother's Day and tried somehow to tie that in with the subject he'd been asked to speak on. "Isn't it wonderful that motherhood and priesthood work so well together?" I sat in disbelief. After the closing prayer the women were asked to stand so we could receive a pink carnation.

I may be the only one in the ward who is writing you a letter, but be assured I am not the only one who is feeling precisely what I have expressed.

Directly after Sacrament Meeting, a member of the Relief Society Presidency grabbed me and asked if I could please take ten minutes at the end of the lesson and give some thoughts to the mothers, as they had noticed that nobody had prepared anything really to commemorate the day, and they were also grabbing some Primary children to come in and sing. I told her that of course I would.

I know that the bishopric is not the enemy. Consciousness is the enemy. Each member of the bishopric is a good man, whose hard work and kindness have been appreciated by me and my family. The problem here is not just the simple one of a failure to plan ahead with a little sensitivity. And the result is not just somebody's hurt feelings. What happened yesterday is symbolic of something so vital and profound that it demands our very best attention. Why is our collective consciousness on what we do to our women so low? How can we, year after year, decade after decade, allow one half of the human family to be placed in a secondary position and consider it appropriate?

Today in the newspaper I read, under the heading "Why Women Can Wear Pants but Men Can't Wear Skirts," something I have known for a long time: "This double standard exists because men have higher status than women in our society. It is acceptable to take on the trappings of those who have higher status than we do. But if men dress like women, it's not acceptable. We aspire to upward mobility, not downward mobility."

And we wonder why many women are opting against motherhood in favor of traditionally male pursuits? Or why many women who do devote themselves primarily to traditionally female pursuits do so with the vague feeling that, much as they love it, they're viewed as holding second prize? The Church should be actively engaged in promoting the status of women, the respect given women, not in continually diminishing it.

On page 92 of the current *Ensign*, Elder Hinckley is quoted as saying, "Woman is God's supreme creation. Strong and able women today fill responsible posts in industry, government, education, and the professions. The whole world looks with respect to the Prime Minister of Britain, a woman of demonstrated ability and great capacity in carrying forward a program designed to strengthen her nation and its people. We were all impressed with Golda Meir serving as Prime Minister of Israel. It is wonderful to witness this great renaissance. I think it will continue to grow for the blessing of people everywhere."

There is indeed a "great renaissance" going on in the world, in which women are being acknowledged and empowered, and it is and will be a blessing to everyone.

And is there such a renaissance going on in the Church? Many of my close women friends have left the Church, despairing that such a renaissance is possible. I have chosen to stay in the Church, determined to be a force in assisting that renaissance to happen.

And slowly it is, I think. Slowly more and more people are asking questions: Where are the women in our history? Why did all the prayers in the Bible go up for a boy child instead of a girl child? Why are women in the scriptures so invisible or so clearly second class when they are visible? Why do we emphasize the eternal family, but not find it strange to worship God as a Single Parent? Why are we given the impression, through scripture and story, that everything really important on this earth has been done by a male God and His male children? Why does the historical suppression of the knowledge of God as Mother look like "a conspiracy" (to quote a fine review of a BYU symposium as reported in the *Church News*)?

Why are Mormon women who go to work to send a son on a mission or perhaps to send a child to college or to ensure music lessons for their children made to feel guilty when they deserve all the support they can get? Why are Mormon women so subject to depression? Why did the husband of a friend of mine say, when she asked him what he would do if he had been the one born a woman, "I guess I'd just make the best of a bad deal"? Why do so many Mormon women go through the temple once and refuse to go back again or go back with great reservations? Why did I notice last year in a Relief Society lesson given to women by a woman, that thirteen examples and statements were from men and not one was from a woman? Why did it take Sonia Johnson to point out that women were not allowed to pray in sacrament meeting? Why can a non-member male serve as Sunday School president, but a faithful woman member cannot? (A woman can rule Great Britain or Israel, but not the Sunday School?) Why did the General Presidency of the Relief Society and the entire General Board have the distinct feeling when the organizational changes were made a few years ago via Correlation, that they were being asked to step further to the back of the bus? Why has a recent Church-sponsored survey shown that the more educated a man is the more likely he is to stay in the Church, and the more educated a woman is the more likely she is to leave?

The questions that are being asked go on and on. It may be possible to dismiss this letter because, as we know, Sister Pearson has this thing about women. Dear Brethren, this thing about women is one of the most profoundly important issues that exist today, affecting the family, the nation, the world, and surely the Church at the very center. Maleness and femaleness, on every level, are out of balance, and the resultant ills are frightening. To say more would require a book, not a letter.

My goal is to raise awareness. My wish is that each of you would look at every program, every policy, every talk, every lesson and ask if it promotes or undercuts the self-esteem, the general status of women. I know that you love your wife and that you want the best for your daughters and that you feel concern for the well-being of all the women in the ward. The women in this ward are marvelous people. I love them. They deserve the very best.

The renaissance of women that Elder Hinckley spoke of is a reality and is not going to be reversed. With or without the Church it is, with all its confusion and possibility for excess and error, going to move forward and sort itself out and bless the world. I sincerely hope that we can all be a part of it.

As to the immediate incident that prompted this letter. The obvious justice would be to take next Sunday, which is the official day to commemorate the restoration of the priesthood and devote it to a belated celebration of womanhood and motherhood—not a "program" with little ditties about how perfect mothers are, which sometimes makes us feel worse going out the door than we did coming in—but powerful, dignified discourses on womanhood and motherhood in history, in our lives today and in our eternal tomorrow. If you could do something so magnificent as that, how proud of you I would be! That, of course, is too much to ask, so I humbly ask for your ongoing awareness and small or large moves in a good direction.

I thank you for reading this letter. I thank you for being the good men that I know you to be. If I have made you uncomfortable, I do not apologize. Discomfort, even pain, as all women know, is the only way a birth takes place. We are in the process of giving birth to a new and better vision of women, and we must go through our labor.

I am including here a copy of a poem I wrote last night. You will find the analogy extreme. It is extreme only in degree; the two examples come from the same consciousness.

Again, I offer you my appreciation and pledge you my support. I want to continue to give service in the ward and in the Church in whatever way I may be useful.

I send this letter with my very best wishes and hopes for increased understanding.

Very sincerely,
Carol Lynn Pearson

Civilized

My society is more civilized than
The Chinese.
In China
Where they can have only one child,
Sometimes when the five-year-olds
Show up at school,
Black bangs trimmed
Above wide black eyes,
Seven faces are little boy faces
And one face is that of a little girl.

And silent at the bottom of the river
Move thousands of tiny female bones.
And the Mother of the Universe moans.

My society is more civilized than
The Chinese.
We know that girls are as good as boys,
And so there are as many women as men
To sit in a chapel on Mother's Day
To celebrate the priesthood
Because the priesthood given to men
Is the theme of the month,
Of the year,
Of the century.

And the women stare at their laps
Where a pink carnation lies.
And the Mother of the Universe cries.

May 15, 1988

An update on my adventure with the bishopric. I knew the letters would be delivered on Thursday, and I found myself anxious during the day. I do not like any kind of unpleasantness or to cause unpleasantness for anyone else.

At ten that night the phone rang.

"Hello?"

"Sister Pearson? This is Bishop Sutton."

"Oh. How are you, Bishop?"

"Fine. Thanks. I received your letter today and I'm calling to thank you for it. I don't think there's anybody in the Church who could have said the things you said so eloquently or as effectively. My consciousness has been heightened and I do appreciate it."

We talked for quite some time. I told him that I very much appreciated his call, that I have a high regard for him. He said that there are a lot of people that he really doesn't care what they think of him, but there are some people whose opinions he values a lot because he respects their judgment. And he wanted me to know that I'm one of those people.

He said that they are now planning to give the month of October to the theme of womanhood and motherhood, and he would be pleased to have me help them plan such a thing and possibly be one of the presenters. I told him I would be happy to help in any way.

I found it interesting that later on Chris, the bishop's wife, was especially warm to me. (Did I mention that they live just up the court, a ninety-second walk away?) She said the bishop had let her read the letter, which he doesn't often do.

"One could explain in several ways what happened last Sunday," she said, "but the fact remains that it did happen. And all those things you said are true and they do need to be looked at and somebody has to say them."

I told her I was very impressed with her husband, that the bishop is a very good man.

I also wrote letters to the stake president and to Elders Hinckley and Oaks, telling them of my very satisfactory conversation with my bishop, who, I said, is a very fine and honest and intelligent man. And I offered to send them something from time to time for their files on "Women."

And now on to lighter things. John's birthday was on Friday. I served him breakfast in bed and we sang to him. As he came in from school I had playing on the stereo as loudly as I could his favorite "Pink Floyd" album, which I hate. I had balloons on the door and the wall, his kindergarten picture, cut-out of his hand in kindergarten, a book he wrote in kindergarten. And I blew bubbles on him as he came in.

I had written a poem the day before, which I read to him.

John Leaves Home

Surely you're not going without me?
Surely you're not taking your stereo
And leaving your mother?
Surely, John, a policeman will find you
And bring you home.
We're not finished!

I read to you *The Little Red Hen*
And talked about industry.
I read to you *Animal Farm*
And talked about equality.

But I have not read to you yet
Les Misérables
Or the complete works of Shakespeare,
And if I don't
Who will?

I have discussed with you at the dinner table
My hundreds of news clippings
On American-Russian relations
Acts of heroism and horror
The birth of a panda
And Ann Landers' columns on
Drug abuse, sending thank you notes,
And teenage pregnancy.
But next month and the next
Newspapers will come out
And if I don't
Scour them for things
You need to know about
Who will?

Ah, you are laughing.

Oh, John, take me with you.
Tuck a little mother in your head
And every now and then let her speak.

Take me with you.
You need to cease being a child
But I need always to be a mother
And if you won't let me
Who will?

26

SISTER PEARSON'S EXTRAORDINARY SACRAMENT MEETING TALK

May 22, 1988

Such a lot to catch up on. I have been thinking continuously about the new book I want to write about the Divine Mother, not sure what form it will take. Sad that I could make nothing happen with *The Motherless House,* but I'm not through yet. Have a story in mind. But I'm not a novelist. I'm far better on idea than on execution, far better on thought than on style. Sometimes I find myself raging, as Salieri raged in envy about Mozart, that my thoughts are better than my talents. I am just now reading *The Women's Room* by Marilyn French. She has a wonderful voice, a wonderful style. How does one get there?

Last week I read and finished *The Chalice and the Blade* by Riane Eisler. What an experience! Most of the historical information was not new to me. But some of her synthesizing did give me brand new thoughts. I love her terms "Partnership Society" and "Dominator Society." That diffuses such a lot of the threat, I think, when one addresses changing the system. Men often can only see the present or its opposite, which would be when women rule, without considering there is another option. "Partnership" is a wonderful word. And to show that this other option worked and worked well for hundreds of years before war was even invented is a marvelous contribution.

I read the book mostly during jury duty. Had to go back several days. Two attorneys quizzed us to see if we were suitable jurors. The attorney for the prosecution said to me, "Mrs. Pearson, you tell us you are a writer. Most writers think they are smarter than other people. I wonder if you might let your very active imagination take over in this case and come up with your own story rather than what actually happened."

I replied, "It may be that I would see a possible scenario here and a possible scenario there, but I'm a smart person, and I would be able to bring it back to reality and judge on the evidence presented." However, I was one that the attorney for the prosecution dismissed. The good thing was that all that waiting gave me a chance to read *The Chalice and the Blade.*

On Thursday I got letters from both Elder Hinckley and Elder Oaks. Very formal, as I had expected.

Brother Hinckley said:

> Thank you for your recent letter and the attached letter to Bishop David Sutton.
>
> I appreciate the sensitivity that you show. I would encourage you to continue to work with your local priesthood leaders.
>
> I appreciate your efforts. May the Lord bless you always.
>
> Sincerely yours,
>
> Gordon B. Hinckley

And Brother Oaks said:

> Thank you for your recent letter sharing a copy of the communication you sent to your bishopric. I have read this with care and concern, and will keep it, as you suggest.
>
> Thanks also for what you said about my talk at conference.
>
> I hope you and your children are getting along well.
>
> Sincerely, your brother,
>
> Dallin H. Oaks

Last week Katy and I went to Back to Camp night. One little story to illustrate a point. I was sitting by Sister K. on the floor, leaning up against the wall as we all sang from the program, "Where is Heaven" by Janice Kapp Perry. "I wish I could remember the days before my birth, and if I knew the Father before I came to earth …"

I turned to Sister K. and said, "Wouldn't it be wonderful if these girls could sing, "the Father and the Mother?" She looked at me with a little surprise and said, "It doesn't bother me a bit."

It bothers me. More than a bit. And I think it bothers the harmony of all civilization.

Thursday was the AIDS benefit at the Civic Arts Theatre, a gala affair and performance by the various musical theatre groups in the county to raise money for the AIDS task force here. They had asked me to give a staged reading of twelve minutes of material from *Goodbye, I Love You.* Of course, I told them I would love to.

It was quite a remarkable evening. And being a person who usually underplays things, I must be honest and say that they were truly stunned with me.

A woman sang beautifully a song from *Mame,* Alma Sayer, and when I walked up to speak to her after the program was over, she looked at me and said, "Son of a bitch—you are such an incredible actress!"

And Lareen Fender, Emily's former ballet teacher, spoke to me, crying, and said it was one of the most remarkable experiences she's ever had, to see me up there performing like that. "Your presence on that stage was electric. Every person in the audience was in the palm of your hand."

John Hetzler, my friend Marsha's husband, who also performed, told me they should choose a play especially for me and let me act again.

"What play would you choose?" I asked.

"Eleanor of Aquitaine," he said.

"Do you think I could do Eleanor?"

"Do it? You could do it in your sleep. You could *phone* it in! But don't."

It was a wonderful evening. They raised five thousand for the cause. I sold books and gave the profit to the AIDS task force.

How I do miss the stage.

I had asked for a dream on whether or not my new story could be a play and I dreamed that yes, it could be. I've been giving some thought to this. The Tonys made me think more of it. One day I may be in a play again.

June 12, 1988

Last Wednesday Joanne of Battered Women's Alternatives called to see if I could take in a woman and her two children for one night. I said yes. In a couple of hours she brought over Pat and her eight-year-old son and two-year-old daughter. Pat's husband had tried to kill her that morning. She clearly had no resources, financial, educational or cultural. She watched wrestling on television and preferred it to anything else I offered her.

And an interesting story I must record. Pat came away without a hairbrush or pajamas. I found a hairbrush that was not in use and gave it to her to keep. And I told her I would loan her a pair of pajamas for the night.

I had two pair of pajamas that I love. Seldom do I buy anything nice for myself, but some months ago I found some lovely silky pajamas, and I bought two pair, one blue and one scarlet. I have worn them alternately. So I put on the scarlet ones and took the blue ones down to her.

The next morning after she packed, the pajamas were lying on the chair in the front room. I looked at them and I said to myself, "I ought to give her those pajamas."

"But," I replied, "I don't want to give her those pajamas. I love those pajamas. And at the shelter they'll give her some things."

"You must give her those pajamas."

"She would not appreciate them like I do. They look really nice on me."

"You must give her those pajamas."

"If I had some old pajamas that I didn't want anymore … "

"Wait a minute. A couple of days ago you wrote a poem called 'I Was Naked and Ye Clothed Me Not' and now Christ comes to your door with her tangled hair and her two difficult children and you say, 'If I had some old pajamas that I didn't want anymore?' Is that what you would do if Christ himself came to your door in need, you would look for some old rags that you didn't want anymore?"

"Of course not."

"Give her the pajamas."

I picked up the pajamas and handed them to her. "Here, I want you to have these. You can take them with you."

"Oh, thank you. They were very comfortable."

I miss my blue pajamas. I really do. And I am ashamed that it was such a struggle for me. But now I am using it for comfort. Christ and I can be twins, He/she in my blue pajamas and me in the scarlet ones.

The other day Anne Mauss called to tell me something her daughter Jennifer had just said. Mike had taken Jennifer to an opera in the city, *Noah and the Flood.*

Jennifer was talking about "the bad character." And, as Anne quizzed her, Jennifer said, "You know, the one that said in a big voice, 'I will send down the rain and I will destroy you' and all that stuff."

So Anne had to tell her daughter that was God Himself she was talking about.

"Oops, sorry," Jennifer said.

And there you have it. Another show of how we do our children a disservice and let them believe everything they hear about God. We have painted God in such a way that he is "the bad character," and often he is. In the Doctrine and Covenants he often is.

I seem to write Very Long Letters. I can't imagine how I found the time. Seeing in front of me now another five-page letter, this one to my General Authority friend, Elder Marion D. Hanks. I wanted to share with him the adventures I'd had regarding the publication of Goodbye, I Love You. *Much of that is shared in this diary account, so I will select just a few excerpts.*

June 5, 1988

> Very dear Brother Hanks, …
>
> Missionaries get to report on their experiences, and, while nobody in Salt Lake has asked what I have learned, I have learned quite a bit, and I would like for it to be in someone's files, just for the record. And I believe you would be sincerely interested in knowing how my adventure turned out.
>
> I have been thrilled at what has happened. I feel that my book has accomplished more than I even hoped for. I knew that there were risks involved, but I also felt that the positives would far outweigh the negatives. And that has been the case.

I have received over five hundred letters to date, two of which questioned my judgment in writing the book. All of the others have been from people who wanted to thank me or share their own difficult stories or give me support or ask support for themselves, or for their son, or for their husband.

These letters have come from all over the world, and most have come from members of the Church. The largest group (I have them in categories in my filing cabinet) are filed under "LDS, General," meaning the writer is not gay and has no gay son or husband or related problem, but just wanted to thank me for giving them a better handle on something that has been so terribly difficult to understand. All this has been very faith-promoting for me. From what I have seen, we as a people are anxious to do better than we've done on this very difficult subject.

I have seen parents and children communicating for the first time in years, discovering that they don't have to let doctrine or policy come before the love they feel for one another. I have seen young homosexual men feel that maybe, just maybe, there is some other explanation for their condition than their own wickedness and some better option than suicide. I have seen wives and former wives of homosexual men be able for the first time to talk about their situation and know they are not alone and that it wasn't their fault. I have seen married homosexual men count the cost and recommit to their wives in a choice that is more painful than most of us can even imagine, and other men who may divorce have some better way to explain themselves to those they love. I have seen support groups organized for families of homosexual people, and I hear from them of little miracles.

I know that one of your concerns was how the world at large would perceive the Church through my book. All the letters that I have received indicate a much more positive than negative response. Typical of these is a letter from a woman in Massachusetts. "Knowing relatively little about the Mormon Church, I got an impression of it through your writing as a warm and loving group." A number of people have asked me if just anybody can attend the Mormon Church, and I have found myself recommending it to many who have contacted me.

You will be interested, I know, to learn that my children have received only positive response to the public telling of our story. This I consider a miracle, as I was certain there would have to be some unpleasant encounters. However, there have not been. Every one of them reports that anyone who has brought it up, at school or church or wherever, has done so only in a positive way. I am unendingly grateful for this.

I have also talked on the telephone to hundreds of people. I was advised to get an unlisted number, but I didn't think it fair to do that, so instead I had a second line put in and I have had the very rewarding experience of talking to a lot of people who really needed to talk to someone. I have heard lots of stories, not just related to homosexuality. I have been hearing from outcasts of all kinds. Well, I suppose you do too; this is nothing new to you. But I am continually impressed with the amount of pain that is out there. And I continually have to question how well we are doing in addressing that pain.

No one that I have talked to, no parent, no wife, no brother or sister, has said, "Aren't we glad we have the Church to help us deal with this problem?" Instead, very large numbers have said something to the effect of, "How I wish the Church could be part of the help on this instead of part of the problem."

Take, for example, the wife who called me from Southern California. "My husband is in such anguish that every now and then it nearly brings him to suicide. He wants to be cured and free from his homosexual feelings, like they promised him he would be if he married and was spiritual enough and prayed and fasted enough and watched his thoughts and read the scriptures. But it never happens. And he knows he's not being righteous enough, or it *would* happen. I know his feelings are never going to change. Why can't they just help him to accept that so he can stop feeling that he's a terrible, wicked person?"

Here I told of my friend Brad going up to the Provo temple and taking a deadly dose of pills because he thought kind angels would be at that place to help him over. And his intense devotion to a church that he knew despised him. I also told of some of the steps forward I had seen in Church-related agencies and their being short-lived because of pressure from the top. Those too are described in previous pages of this document.

All in all, I feel tremendously encouraged that we as a people are capable of moving a few steps onto an extremely difficult and distasteful frontier and making progress. I speak of the people down here at the bottom of church hierarchy. To this point the answers we have received from the top have been woefully inadequate and often counterproductive. (I heard a professional in the field describe the Church's response to all of this as "A marvelous shirk and a blunder.") The pain that is out there deserves our best attention.

You may find it interesting that I feel more comfortable being a Mormon just now than I have felt in quite a few years. I feel somehow that I have done something important and rather painful for the Church, which needed badly to be done, and I have not only been allowed to do it, but have been appreciated for doing it. At least that is what I have received from mail and telephone and from the good people in my own ward and stake. I have no way of knowing what are the sentiments of the higher leadership. I continue to teach my Social Relations lessons in Relief Society. Women tell me they love the lessons and that they leave feeling better than when they came.

I have times of sadness, but I have a lot to be grateful for. Thank you for reading this letter. I just wanted to report to someone, and I continue to think of you with fondness and appreciation.

This letter does not need a reply. Just put it in your files. You have too many people needing you.

I send very best wishes and love.

Very sincerely,
Carol Lynn Pearson

July 10, 1988

A major catching up again. We've been back from Utah for a week now. The day after we arrived in Provo I dropped the boys off at BYU for Youth Conference. Aaron, now 16, had an experience there that I must record and that still makes me angry.

It was his first workshop on the first day. V.C., whom I do not know, gave it and it became for Aaron exactly what Hartman Rector's talk at Aspen Grove was for Emily. V. started in on homosexuality, saying it was the evilest of all the evils and that Satan had figured out how to destroy the family. Aaron was very upset. He got up and left.

He waited until noon when all her workshops were done and then went back in and talked to her. I have encouraged my children to speak up when they feel it is right, but especially Aaron has not yet learned the kind of tact that lets him do it kindly. Anyway, he let her know that she was "the most bigoted and ignorant woman" he had ever met.

"Would you like to talk about it?" she asked, smiling and inviting him to sit down. He told her she didn't know what she was talking about regarding homosexuals. She continued to smile and said, "This is the Church's position. These men can change and that is expected of them." Aaron argued that they cannot change, that they're just that way. He began to cry in front of her and she continued to smile and quote the Church's position. He said, "Wipe that smile off your face and listen to me!" By the end of the conversation she knew who he was and he asked if she had read my book. No, she hadn't. He told her that maybe she should. And he left.

I felt bad about this. You would think that the woman would have enough compassion that when speaking to the child of a man who was a homosexual, a man whom the child loved, she would make some kind of gesture of understanding or at least say, "Well, there are a lot of things we don't quite have figured out." But she just smiled and quoted the Church's position. Her smile was what Aaron was most furious with. And I can see it now. I don't know the woman. But I know Mormons who have that self-satisfied smile that never goes away.

Aaron and I talked about this encounter. I told him that every once in a while he was going to meet someone like that who would make him very upset, and that he had to accept it as something that was just part of life. I encouraged him to learn how to deal with people smoothly and not rashly. I have had years and years of training in how to take the dissenting point of view. Aaron is just a kid. But I'm glad he spoke up.

Before I forget. I got a letter from the Society for the Blind in New Zealand. They want to make *Goodbye, I Love You* available in braille. That is good. I sent it on to Peter, my agent.

My old friend Byron Fisher told me a marvelous story about my old English teacher at B.Y. High, Anna B. Hart, a dear, sweet, sensitive soul. Byron is good friends with her son John, from whom he got this story. After Mrs. Hart retired, she visited John in the San Francisco area. One of the things she had always wanted to do was to walk across the Golden Gate Bridge. So her son arranged it and dropped her off to walk.

As she was midway across the bridge, she was so moved by the sight and the experience that she stopped and opened her purse and took out a notebook to write a poem on the occasion. She was immediately arrested by Bridge Security, who told her that she could not commit suicide there. They figured she was writing a suicide note and was going to jump. It took John some hours to get her released, to assure them that she was only planning to write a poem. That, of course, is not funny. However, it is hilarious.

The day after we got back was the Fourth of July. Senator Orrin Hatch called me on the phone from Provo after the big parade there. Charlotte had sent him from Random House an advance copy of my new book for comment and he said he loved it and would write a fine statement and send it to her. This is the book I've been working on for a year now, *One on the Seesaw: The Ups and Downs of a Single-Parent Family.* I was very happy to have him call me. He expressed again great admiration for all that I'm doing and asked about the kids. He told me some of the things he's doing in Congress, said the AIDS bill was mostly written by him.

July 23, 1988

At church on Sunday Kathleen M. told me an interesting story. She and I have had a running commentary on "working women." She is my visiting teacher, and has for some years worked as a nurse. She said that at the hospital where she works there is a new technician, a young woman who had been working at the LDS Hospital in Salt Lake and who told her this story. Not long ago, President Benson was in the hospital for a cataract operation, and she was among those who accompanied him down to the car.

After she helped him into the car, this conversation ensued:

Him: Young woman, are you married?

Her: Yes, I am. My husband is a student.

Him: I hope the time will come soon when you will be able to have a family and stay home to raise the children.

Her: Well, to be honest, President Benson, I was uncomfortable with your talk on the subject of women working. I am a convert to the Church. I have always been taught to be independent and productive, and I love my work, and I believe that after I have children I will find some way to continue in my profession.

President Benson did not reply. He just smiled at her as they drove off.

Last week I got a letter from Brother Hanks in response to the one I had sent a few weeks ago.

"Dear and Beloved and Respected Friend,

Your letter greeted me after a brief time of absence and played the part of a warm circle of light in a cold and dreary world. I appreciate your letter and appreciate you."

He said he had heard very few critics of me or my book.

And he said I need never shield him from the blessing of my friendship. Which, in fact, he found himself doing with Jeff Holland for whom he has high hopes of contribution to the Church. What a sad indictment of our Mormon system that such a lovely man as Brother Hanks would have to withdraw from a man so as not to taint him in the sight of others.

I sometimes have received a feeling of sadness from Brother Hanks. A statement like "a warm circle of light in a cold and dreary world" troubles me. Does he not have the personal happiness he deserves? I suppose the situation is his being a very sensitive man in a system that is sometimes abrasive and abusive and anti-spiritual. In other letters he has also given me a glimpse of sadness.

July 26, 1988

I wrote back to Brother Hanks. Here are just a few sections:

> You indicated you might like to share my letter, but would keep it confidential. There is no need for that. Use it in any way you might like. I find that being 'out of the closet' with my frequently unorthodox observations is the only way I can maintain in the Church.
>
> Speaking of which, I am enclosing here a copy of a letter I sent in May to my bishopric. Peruse it as you have time and put it in your file on 'Women.' My bishop, who is a good man, called me the night he received it and thanked me for it.

> And, speaking of 'cold and dreary,' I really don't think life is intended to be as cold and dreary as sometimes the Church seems anxious to make it. I hope you have a good group of kindred spirits among all the 'Stepford Wives' or 'Stepford Brethren' that the system seems magically to produce among so many who are called to high office.
>
> I have recalled a statement made by Rabbi Harold Kushner (*When Bad Things Happen to Good People).* An ancient Rabbinical saying is: "God will hold us responsible for all the wonderful things on earth that we refused to enjoy. Would that be a great theme for a conference talk?

I concluded the letter with best wishes and love.

July 31, 1988

What a fun day I had yesterday. I wrote two country western lyrics, a good poem, went to lunch with friends and played cards until late with Katy.

My country western: "No teacher never taught me how to put you in the past tense ..." And "Your love is like lightning—it never strikes twice in the same place ..." Too bad nothing will ever come of these.

Last Sunday. Talks in sacrament meeting just about sent me out the door. Theme of the month is obedience. New, young, enthusiastic, frighteningly orthodox couple spoke. Her prime example was the Israelites having been commanded to go and wipe out a city of Amalekites, kill every living thing, men, women, children, infants, camels, donkeys, oxen, sheep. And the Israelites did kill *most* of them, but spared some of them. And they were severely chastised by God for their disobedience. I could hardly sit there. *This story is part of the ongoing pattern of the triumph of patriarchy in its violent march over the gentler, goddess-worshipping cultures.* I felt ill.

And then her husband gave his talk on the fourteen points of following the prophet that Brother Benson gave a couple of years before his reign as Prophet began, which act was seen by those close to the situation as his paving the way for himself to have a stronger position when he arrived there. "The Prophet is the only man on earth who speaks for the Lord in everything," the man said. "His word is more important than the scriptures. He doesn't even have to have earthly knowledge on the subject he's speaking about. And the Prophet will never lead the people astray."

Hey, even the twelve apostles today do not take every word that comes from the Prophet as the word of the Lord. Sometimes they vote no. I believe the information I have received from several very good sources that the apostles turned down President Benson's two requests to have his son Reed put in as a new apostle.

I looked around the chapel to see how much damage I thought was being done. It didn't appear that anyone else was listening.

Yesterday Katy came home from a week at Girls Camp. This was her first time and she really enjoyed it. They slept in their bags out under the stars and washed their hair in the lake. And everyone behaved, and a good time was had by all. This is one of the very positive things about the Church. It's wonderful to have a group of people that you can send your children off with and feel perfectly comfortable with the care and the leadership and the atmosphere. Katy and I sat together in my big, black leather recliner here in my room and rocked and talked for a long time. She is about as tall as I am, but still very thin, so we fit. And it was lovely to hold her. We do that often. I love her ideas.

And John is getting ready to leave for the California Institute of the Arts. An emotional time for me. I have tried to bite my tongue and just let him be, disorganized though he is. After a blowup last week, I wrote a poem, "Don't Push," which has a wonderful first line, "The minute the doctor said 'push' I did, and I've got to stop now because you're eighteen." Writing that helped me. I've gotten better. (Sort of.)

Cal Arts is very expensive, as are most colleges these days. But I decided that giving this to John would be worth even taking out a second mortgage on the house. (I am still not in the "wealthy" category.) A great blessing came. A couple of months ago I was talking to my friend Bruce Bastian on the phone and as he inquired about each of the kids I told him of John's acceptance at Cal Arts and of my going into high gear to pull it off financially. "Could you use some scholarship money?" he asked. Such a blessing. Such a good, good man.

Last night, Sunday, I had Nola Myrl and Ted Christensen come over for dinner and to talk to John about his bicycle trip. Did I mention that John is insistent that he is going to bicycle to school, riding from our house down the coast to Valencia in Southern California? And the Christensens had, years ago, taken their seven children on a bicycling trip from their home in Walnut Creek all the way to Salt Lake City. They brought a video they had made from pictures of the adventure, and they gave John some advice and encouragement. They are such wonderful people.

And so this is why I stay in this strange institution we call the Mormon Church. Because Nola Myrl and Ted are such wonderful people. And hundreds of others I could name. Not that they're the *only true wonderful people.* But they're *my* wonderful people, and I'm not going to turn my church over to Boyd K. Packer and the like. There's a lot of work to be done, and I'm going to do my share of it.

August 19, 1988

Yesterday John left home. I have been holding my heart. My little John, sweet boy, frustrating, dear, charming, delightful person. Gone.

We both set our alarms for five-thirty. I had prayer with him. Made him a waffle and bacon and orange juice and egg drink and watched him eat. Then

I made him take a jacket he didn't want to take, took a few pictures of him setting out, sent Katy to bring down Aaron, and we three waved him off as he pedaled up the court.

John left his bedroom light on, as he often did, and I turned it off. He left a pair of pants on the floor of the bathroom as he often did, and I picked them up. I cleaned up his breakfast dishes. I almost cry writing this. I am a mother.

Oh, my dear John. I hold my heart and let you go.

As we continue this journey of sharing information from my diaries, you will receive fewer stories about my children. They are moving into adulthood and, while I felt I could share their lives when they were children because they were mine, I feel that increasingly their lives belong to them and their stories belong to them.

August 23, 1988

Yesterday Katy came in to tell me she'd started her period. As she had been applying a certain necessary care to her dog Bridget, she said with a giggle, "Mom, I'm in heat! I just started." I got out my *Encyclopedia of Women's Myths and Secrets* and we read pages about how menstruation has been viewed over the centuries. I then took her out to eat. After which I wrote a poem about it. Which I really like. "In Celebration of the First Menstruation."

IN CELEBRATION OF THE
FIRST MENSTRUATION

Katy,
Who has of late been putting
Pads and panties
On her Keeshond dog
Bridget Baby Brown Eyes,
Loped long-legged and twelve and sweet
Into my room today and giggled,
"Mom, Mom, I'm in heat!
I just started!"

I pulled her down
Into the big chair that we
Used to not quite fill
And made sure she understood
That a menstruating woman
Is of the devil
That she must not
Look at the sun, sit in water

Speak to a man
For she is unclean
Or enter a church
For she would defile it.

And I stroked her
Innocent freckled skin
And bright braided hair
And told her to keep in mind
That she is, as St. Jerome said,
Formed of foul slime.

Katy laughed. "Right, Mom!"

And I told her all that was from
A bad period
Men's period
When male was god and jealous
And said what was what

A period that luckily menopaused.

But that there was an earlier time
When woman's secret was sacred
When the Great Goddess
Gave the blood of life
And all worshipped joyously
At her royal fountain
When girls "bore the flower"
A flower that flows a future fruit
Making her a marvel
A time that is due again.

Then I gave Katy five and said,
"Hey, woman, let's go celebrate!"
And we went right out under the sun
And Katy spoke right up to the man
And ordered a BLT and we ate.

We clicked our cups to flowering
And Katy giggled and blushed and bounced
And blessed the restaurant
With her presence.

Aaron was the only one home last night, so I read it to him and he grunted.

Back to John for a moment. A couple of weeks before he was to leave, Bob and Joyce Anderson came home teaching (Bob is our former bishop). He had called and asked if he could give John a blessing. I said certainly, that I was going to ask if he would do that.

A note here. It is true that I have significant questions about the "exclusivity" of LDS priesthood authority. But I do not have questions about a good LDS man having access to divine power in this particular way. And just the power of love and concern and kindness, which Brother Anderson holds abundantly, is something that I would be glad to have John blessed with.

As he stood up to give the blessing, Brother Anderson asked Aaron if he would like to join him, and then he asked me if I would like to join them. So we all put our hands on John's head and Brother Anderson spoke the blessing, a very lovely, encouraging blessing of protection and wisdom, etc. I was not going to ask to be included in this, though I know it is even written in priesthood lesson manuals that a woman may be invited. But I was glad that Brother Anderson thought of it on his own.

It is important that we understand the history of women healing in our church. In my 1973 book, Daughters of Light, *I tell numerous documented stories of women in the early Church giving healing blessings, with the brethren or acting independently. Complaint came to Joseph Smith that women had administered to the sick "by the prayer of faith, the laying on of hands, or the anointing with oil." After considering the matter, Joseph replied, "Who are better qualified to administer than our faithful and zealous sisters, whose hearts are full of faith, tenderness, sympathy, and compassion? No one." In the same chapter, I quote President Joseph Fielding Smith in the February 1907 edition of the* Improvement Era *saying: "If [a wife] is requested to lay hands on the sick with [her husband], or with any other officer holding the Melchizedek priesthood, she may do so with perfect propriety. It is no uncommon thing for a man and wife unitedly to administer to their children, and the husband being mouth, he may properly say out of courtesy, 'By authority of the holy priesthood in us vested.'"*

September 12, 1988

Yesterday in church I was asked to read a poem of mine, "The Lesson," that was reprinted in the Church's *Young Women's Manual.* The teacher gave the girls a lesson about God. "He … He … He … He … who begat His daughters," she taught. Amazing. I gave a few thoughts as I read the poem and at least made mention of our Heavenly Father and Mother. Oh, it is so deep, so very deep. Can we ever root it out and plant new seeds for a better harvest?

September 25, 1988

Bishop Sutton called me on Thursday to take me up on my offer to help him plan October's sacrament meeting talks, which are to be on the theme of womanhood. I talked to a few women in the ward to get their ideas on what might be said or what makes them feel uncomfortable in the Church. Jan Hilton didn't like to be segregated with "this" is for men and "this" is for women. Birdene Keddington said she didn't like in the temple to feel beneath a man all the time; and where are the women in the Book of Mormon? Another said the church structure is fine, but the attitude of many of the men is awful, they just can't deal with a capable woman. Another said she feels guilty and overwhelmed too much.

Anyway, I went in at 5:30 with Anne Mauss to give the bishop some ideas. I outlined the kind of talk I would give if I were asked to do it, a philosophical talk on how this mortal world in its fallen state has obscured the ultimate equality of maleness and femaleness; how the Old Testament tells this clearly, that women were property; that Christ brought a revolutionary view of women, treating them as equal to men in ways that challenged social norms; that this did not last, as in the dark ages there was serious debate in church councils as to whether or not women had souls; that with the Restoration came a good new thrust toward equality, that we have backward and then forward motions, and must continue to move forward. That today, as always and in all cultures, as Margaret Mead found, basketweaving, if done by men is highly regarded, and basketweaving if done by women is low in status. Etc. Etc. Etc.

The bishop said, as I concluded, "Can you recreate that talk on the 30th of October?"

"Yes, I can," I said, "But I need forty minutes; I need the entire time."

"Fine," he said.

Anne was blown away. Again.

October 10, 1988

At General Conference, Brother Hanks used a statement I had written to him in a letter and suggested that it would be a great theme for a conference talk: "God will hold men responsible for all the wonderful things on this earth they refused to enjoy." So great!

Did I mention I'm having hot flashes? And I only just turned 49. Katy stole my periods. She started right in the middle of my last one and I haven't had one since and I don't think I will have. Instead I'm having hot flashes and I hate them.

October 17, 1988

Katy was at the home of her friend J.'s family and was asked to give the blessing on the food and said, "Dear Heavenly Father and Mother."

Afterwards the father, Jim, our gospel doctrine teacher, said, "Katy, I noticed you said the prayer to both Heavenly Father and Heavenly Mother."

And he took out the Bible and showed her that the correct order of prayer is just to address the Father.

I asked her if he made her feel uncomfortable. "No," she said, "but I think maybe I made him feel uncomfortable."

Something lovely happened today. I got a letter from a woman in Provo who used to work with my Daddy at the County Welfare Department. She came up to me last week as I was in Utah and told me who she was. I asked her what she remembered of Daddy and she said a lot. I asked her if she would be willing to write me a letter telling me about him.

This afternoon I opened her letter and found a story titled, "He Cared." In the second paragraph I read, "Lelland Wright...."

What a great and wonderful thing. I sat there and cried as I read it. She told a story of a woman that Daddy had helped while he was a case worker with the welfare department there. Others had treated her with great disdain, but Daddy stepped in and gave her authentic help and respect and helped her change her whole life and even graduate from BYU and become a successful professional. I was thrilled.

I read the letter to Aaron and Katy before supper and they both were impressed with it. I will send copies to the siblings and other relatives. So lovely!

I've been working hard on my talk for Sacrament Meeting. So far the talks about "Woman" this month (yes, "Woman" has been the theme of the month) have not been very progressive. To be told that women are wonderful and special and that men and women have great but separate gifts, does not do it for me. And the two youth talks. One a sentimental story of a girl who does not appreciate her mother and the mother goes out to buy the girl some new nylons for a dance and she has an accident and never comes back, and then the girl appreciates her. And another talk telling us that we should show gratitude to our mothers and thank them after a nice dinner and wash our own socks.

Well, maybe that's better than nothing. Or maybe it isn't. I don't know.

November 1, 1988

Yesterday, Sunday, was really a monumental occasion, definitely historic. I gave my talk in Sacrament Meeting. And I made a tape, so this talk is now in my archives.

I worked hard on the talk; it was the top priority item for weeks despite all my traveling. I didn't want to just read it, but I did follow my text pretty closely, as I wanted to be sure to say things just right and not wing it, for winging it on this sensitive ground might be dangerous. I don't know that I could quite say stage fright, possibly that, but also a tremendous excitement carried me all morning.

A youth speaker went far too long. And I could tell I was going to either have to cut a lot or go way over. I chose to go way over. After the women and young women in the ward sang "Sisters in Zion," I was on. I had asked the chorus to go back down after their number, as I wanted them to be able to see me and me them.

So I walked to the podium and began. It was not easy. The room was charged with interesting energy. I could feel in my pores that I was working harder than I ever had to give this speech well. I felt that I was swimming upstream the whole way. And I knew there was no going back. So I pushed on, as if I were in a blizzard, to mix my metaphors. I was sweating, and it was not a hot flash. But I was also enjoying it and I knew I was doing the right thing.

I finished and sat back down. The closing song was sung and prayer said.

Anne Mauss was the first to reach me. She had made her own tape recording and was sitting up close. She had tears in her eyes as she hugged me and thanked me. She then stepped to the bishop and said, "Thank you for letting her do this, and thank you for not turning on the red light." She was surprised to have the bishop smile and give her a little hug.

The next person to reach me was a man in the ward I do not know, who told me he saw my son taping it and said he had to have a copy for his wife, who is inactive in the Church because of these issues.

One of the major (we feared) chauvinists in the ward, David B. said, "This is the first time I have heard you speak and you spoke by the spirit. The spirit was very strong. I need to have a copy of the talk to send to a woman in the east I'm trying to interest in the Church, a feminist woman. I think this would help her. I really liked the way you put it at the end, that it is not a battle of women against men, but of all of us against a limited consciousness." A number of other men spoke to me appreciatively.

Before I left the stand Bishop Sutton shook my hand and thanked me. His face was flushed and his eyes looked like he had had a near-accident. But he was smiling.

Many of the women were ecstatic. Birdene Keddington, our chorister, said, "This is the best thing that has ever happened to this ward. And the best thing I can imagine happening to any ward."

November 28, 1988

Further reporting on my talk. I have played the tape for a number of people and all have been thrilled with it. Mike Mauss, Anne's husband, said he had listened to the tape three times and he has appreciated it more each time. His father Armand Mauss, prominent sociologist, said it was "magnificent."

Two rather unusual things happened at church yesterday. They may have been just flukes, but both stood out in bold relief, as I notice every detail on this subject. And, of course, my talk was given just four weeks ago.

It is the usual pattern, when a couple give the prayers, that the woman opens and the man closes. I know that order is a requirement with the talks.

To my surprise, Jim M. gave the opening prayer and his wife gave the closing prayer. Wally Jones was conducting, and in talking about the possibility of choosing emergency preparedness items for Christmas gifts, he said, "We have often been sent information on this subject from the Sisters and the Brethren in Salt Lake." I could not believe my ears. We *always* hear "Brethren and Sisters."

And in reading *BYU Today* I found a very good talk by Jeffrey Holland and noticed "your daughters and your sons," which is not the way we say it, and also "sisterhood and brotherhood." That was not accidental. Tiny things. But a good sign.

27

MRS. POTATO AND THE MORMON WOMEN'S FORUM

December 6, 1988

I had a thought as I was climbing out of the shower the other morning. I remain humbly unsure of precisely what or who "God" is. There is something wonderful and meaningful that we call God, I do believe. And I've been comfortable with the Mormon anthropomorphic deity if it includes the Mother. Of course, whatever is, *is*, and I'm not about to try to dictate. My thought was remembering that when Gerald told the kids about Santa Claus, he was always careful never to say, "There is no Santa Claus," but always to let the secret be, "*We're* Santa Claus!" Now, I am holding the possibility that perhaps the truth is—not that there is no God—but that in some amazing way, *we're* God, little pieces of God. I know that's tremendous heresy from a Mormon point of view. But I think we need to take more responsibility for blessing the world and creating good things and not just praying that God will take care of it all for us. A thought.

Had a number of people come to meet me recently. Just last week, two men from Canada traveling through, gay, both have AIDS. And a woman from Walnut Creek, so moved by the book that she couldn't stop talking about it, brought me flowers. And a man from South Africa who had been in the "staged reading" they did there of *Goodbye, I Love You*. I went on walks with all of them. I consistently tell people my only talking time is my walking time and if they want to visit with me, we'll walk together. They are happy to.

I missed an evening session of Stake Conference, but Anne gave me a report and said an unusual thing happened. Toward the end Stake Patriarch Alan Johnson was called on extemporaneously to speak. He came up very emotionally, she said, saying he wanted to bear testimony that our Father in Heaven loves us and that we can receive that love. And also that our Mother in Heaven loves us and we can receive Her love as well. For the rest of his talk he spoke of "them," consistently referring to God as our Father and Mother. Anne was very impressed. (This is the good man who gave Emily her patriarchal blessing and spoke of her Mother in Heaven.)

Tonight I'm going to tape the final two hours of Joseph Campbell being interviewed by Bill Moyers on PBS. "The Power of Myth." It's wonderful. Sunday night Aaron watched some with me and even he was interested. Campbell is marvelous. I read quite a bit of him when I wrote "Letters from a Motherless House."

An amazing moment. He was speaking of how a society's structures indicate the values that inform that society. At one point the cathedral was the highest building anywhere. Then the castle was the highest building. "A perfect example of this is in Salt Lake City," he said, as the camera focused on the temple spires. "First the temple was the highest building. Then the state capitol became the highest building. And now—(and of course we see the looming giant at 50 East North Temple)—the tallest building is the Church's office building, where the business is run. That is the story of Western civilization."

I invited Rozan and Brad Gautier to dinner on Sunday night. Brad is Aaron's new priest's quorum advisor. We had a wonderful time, had Aaron play guitar. Then I read them the "Walk in the Pink Moccasins." Brad had come up to me after my Sacrament Meeting talk and asked for that part. After, he said, he could just shake his head and say, "How did all that happen? Men would never sit still for that."

Rozan said, "What can we do to change things?"

I told her, as I always tell people, to raise their hands, write their letters, talk, read; told her about *The Chalice and the Blade.*

I feel very good these days about my mission. I am doing things. I am getting braver and braver and doing important things.

And now I'm tired and going to get ready for bed.

January 10, 1989

So pressed. *So* much I need to do and so little time to do it. But I am way behind on this diary and must catch up. Important things to record.

Another monumental step. Last Wednesday the 4th I spoke at the Mormon Women's Forum in Salt Lake City. This is a feminist organization established last year, dedicated to discussion of gender issues and working toward equity of women and men within Mormonism. They invited me to speak and I gladly accepted.

As soon as I arrived I telephoned Kelli Frame, a cofounder of the Forum with Karen Case. Kelli was the woman who had invited me. She was very upset. "A terrible thing has happened," she said. "Channel Four interviewed us and distorted it to make it look like we're a bunch of militant women demanding the priesthood. Karen and I are just devastated."

I turned on the ten o'clock news at my brother Donald's house. "Group of Mormon women picking up where Sonia Johnson left off ... (picture of Karen with baby) this woman aspires to the Mormon priesthood." Showed

Gordon B. Hinckley and read statement that only God gives priesthood, and women ought to focus on their privileges instead of what they don't have.

The next morning Kelli and Karen picked me up and took me to TALK radio, where I was interviewed by talk-radio host Jim Dabakis. The show went well. Call-ins. Nothing difficult. I get a lot of appreciation on those kinds of shows.

During the day I called the Church's Public Communications Office and spoke with Don Lefevre, telling him that these women are no more radical than the hundreds that meet annually at the Sunstone Symposium. I told him I was going to be speaking at the Forum and if they would like to send a representative from their office I would be glad to have them do that.

What I am personally calling for is, I believe, much more radical than that women should be ordained to the priesthood. I'm calling for a complete paradigm shift, to see things in a totally different way, to rethink history together, to rethink who we are, to put femaleness and maleness side by side in partnership.

After dinner we went to the University of Utah where my talk was to be in the Fine Arts Auditorium. Jan Tyler had arranged for an audiotape and a videotape. Two television cameras were there. And various reporters and photographers. I was, however, not as nervous as I had been at the sacrament meeting talk in my ward. Still, I knew this was a momentous occasion.

The talk was very well received. There were about 350 people there. I got much more emotional at the end than I had anticipated. And I talked for an hour and a half. I didn't know it would be that long. But the audience was riveted. At the end they gave me a very long and enthusiastic ovation. After I went back to my seat they were still clapping and I stood up again.

A lot of my friends and relatives were there. My cousin Helen's daughter Cindy (soon to be Dr. Bateman) told me it was the single most important and best talk she had ever heard in her entire life. Gloria Firmage told me the talk was wonderful. She said she saw there the woman who works for the Church's Public Communications Department on women's concerns, that she was having lunch with her the next day and intended to underline for her everything that I said. Gloria works as a specialist for the Relief Society, and answers phones a lot, speaking to women who call in with their concerns. There are a *lot* of questions. "Every woman I know," said Gloria, "has these issues, either repressive or explosive."

Just this morning, Marie Cornwall called me from BYU. She was at my talk and said it was wonderful. She works on a committee for the Church that has to do with women's issues and wanted to know if I am going to make the talk available. She and her colleague who were there want to show it to some of the leaders in Salt Lake, especially, she said, the Church's women's presidencies. And, she thought, some of the Brethren too.

Marie Cornwall and I talked quite a bit about the surrounding issues. She said the problem, of course, is not just what the Church is currently doing to women, but to spiritually growing people of any kind.

When I said that since the ERA we don't have anything to "come up against," to talk about and raise issues about, she replied that the Church itself is serving that function now with its increasing authoritarianism and bureaucracy. That's what is facilitating our critical thinking. Also, she said that at a recent history meeting of some kind, right in front of Boyd K. Packer, LDS historian Jill Derr prayed to our Heavenly Parents.

What a really exciting adventure this all is. What took us centuries to get into will take us centuries to get out of, but there are certain pivotal moments. And today, for the Mormons, is one of them.

Lighter things: 1—some of my high school friends were at the talk, and it was so great to see them. 2—a woman at the talk introduced herself as Robert Anderson's niece (my NY Broadway playwright friend Robert Anderson); he had told her about our great visit and especially commented on how pure he perceived me to be. He said, "Carol Lynn is so pure it frightened me." 3—my brother Donald loves his two little girls. He is a great father.

I went to lunch with Aileen Clyde and Francine Bennion, with whom I served on that committee for General Relief Society President Barbara Smith. After I moved to California, they continued to work for Barbara as specialists on developing a seminar on depression that would go out to all the women in the Church. Barbara was thrilled with it. Showed it to a Church committee of men and women, who said, "Why is this just for women? Men need it too. Can you do it for both?"

"Of course," said Barbara. They spent another year revising it. Then they presented it to the Quorum of the Twelve. Instantly it was killed. "Why talk about depression?" the Brethren said. Barbara Smith "went into grief." And Francine and Aileen were devastated, have never recovered.

I feel I wrote about this long ago, but that it is still a major sorrow for the leaders requires that I mention it again.

Back home, I got a call from Phyllis Nibley. I had sent the sacrament meeting talk tape to her and Hugh for an evaluation. She said they both felt I "stated the case very well."

I went into tithing settlement on the 18th and the bishop kept me for half an hour anyway. "I want to give you some feedback I've received on your talk, Sister Pearson." He went on to say that numerous people, men and women, had contacted him to say how much they appreciated it. Just that day a woman told him that my talk made her feel better about being a woman than any talk she had ever heard. He said the major negative response was from the Relief Society Presidency. They had reported to him that "It just didn't sound like what we're receiving out of Salt Lake." To which the bishop smiled and said to me, "Of course, maybe that's why you felt to say some of the things you did."

And in the larger world big things are going on. Last month the Soviets had a terrible earthquake, devastated large areas and killed over 50,000 people. I sent a hundred-dollar check to the Red Cross for them. A pittance, but if everyone did something, needs would be taken care of. And we are about to inaugurate a new president: George Bush, not always a kindred spirit.

Christmas Eve afternoon Rob Epstein and Jeffrey Friedman came here to see the family regarding the TV movie they're producing on the Names Project, the quilt honoring those who died of AIDS. These two men have already won an Academy Award, "Best Documentary," for their 1984 film, *The Times of Harvey Milk*. They were very taken with the children, and I'm sure they'll use us somewhere. I got a thank you note from them saying that "the love here was palpable."

January 18, 1989

Got back from New York this morning at 2:30. Pretty much a wasted trip. The *Geraldo* talk show people had contacted me some time ago as they were doing a show about women married to homosexuals. I truly did not want to go, but finally agreed to. The show was embarrassing. Geraldo just poked around in sleaze for a full hour. But I didn't fall for it. The rest of the panel had not had the experience I've had of dealing with inappropriate questions and they fell into his trap. He saved me for the end and ran out of time so I only got to have a minute or so. My statement was very good and the audience applauded. But it all was very much not worth my time.

January 29, 1989

A lovely morning as I look out my window. I am grateful for mornings; have not always been. I have a good life, a lot of happiness and satisfaction, and a lot of important work to do.

I am reconceiving my "Motherless House" project. I was up walking in the hills two days ago and it sort of fell into a different shape. And I think it will work. In "Letters from a Motherless House," the fine little manuscript that was never published, the basic story was me, myself, writing letters to God the Mother, telling Her the terrible, historical things that have been going on in the family without Her and asking Her to please come home.

But what if I used the same powerful historical information not to tell their stories, but *let them tell their own stories!* I can already hear their voices—a Paleolithic woman, an Egyptian woman, a Greek woman, a Gnostic woman and so many others, each speaking their own lives from the pages of the book. I really like this idea.

Bit of ward news. I've been released from my Relief Society job as Social

Relations teacher, which I've had for eight years and really enjoyed, and am now "inservice leader" in the Primary, helping the teachers learn how to teach.

Did I mention getting a call from Somebody Skousen who attended my Mormon Women's Forum talk in Salt Lake? One interesting thing he said: his uncle Cleon Skousen had read and loved *Goodbye, I Love You* and was passing it around to all the family. That book seems to have cut across so many boundaries, from the liberal to the ultra-conservative. And of course I am so grateful.

I caught Katy bathing *the neighbor's dog* in our bathtub the other day.

Last week Sarah Shummer called me from Sunstone East, asking me to speak at their symposium. She had heard that my Mormon Women's Forum talk was wonderful. I told her if I could have two plane tickets I would come. I'd love to take Katy and visit Washington D.C.

I decided to let Aaron and his rock band practice in our carport. I insisted that he write some letters to the neighbors telling about his band practicing there (he put down two layers of carpet to help muffle the sound), and I had him add to the letters: "Remember this is keeping five teenage boys off the streets and away from the drug dealers." So now I've got the band here. There could be worse things. And Aaron is very determined with his music. I feed the boys waffles and they eat whatever else they can find. There is one who smokes and I am after him to stop. He quit for three days, but went back "because it's addictive, you know." I get so damn mad at the tobacco companies for what they're doing to young people especially, and so mad at the young people for falling for it.

February 2, 1989

When I wrote my last entry about being released from my Relief Society calling I underplayed it. I think now it is highly likely that the bishop received a call from one of the Brethren in Salt Lake asking him to curtail my power in the ward. It came to me on Sunday when Birdene asked me in a whisper in the hall, "Did you resign from your job in Relief Society?"

"No," I said. "They fired me." As I said those words I knew they were true. I need to meet with Bishop Sutton to get clear on this.

Tuesday night was unbelievable. I, willing person that I am, went to the stake preparation meeting for Inservice Leaders, went with Rozan, who is my friend and also the Primary president.

The woman teaching the class I attended on how to help teachers of children be better teachers was a very good woman; I will say nothing against her. What I am railing against—*railing against*—is the mentality that created that hour. She had spent, I'm sure, at least twenty hours preparing. She had filled the room with homey little things to make a décor that would inspire us. She gave us handouts up the yin-yang, all cute and gimmicky, such as a little lunch bag labeled, "Primary Is My Bag," out of which we could make an invitation to give to all the Primary teachers in the ward to lure them to monthly preparation meetings. I also got a bear sticker, a heart clip, a heart cookie in a plastic bag, a pencil with sheep all over it (a reminder to feed the sheep) and a little stuffed sheep that this woman had made for each of us. Also a little bag of candy.

And she gave us some tips on how to make our presentations interesting. Such as skits. She told of a very effective skit she and three other women had put on for their preparation meeting. They each were a different kind of potato. One was Mrs. Instant Potato, who did everything right away, and she wore a box with "Instant Potato" written on it. Another in her own box was another kind. And another. Our teacher had been "Mrs. Baked Potato," as she let everything cook for a long time so it would be just right. Her costume was a brown skirt, topped by a yellow blouse for the butter, you know, and a white scarf for the sour cream.

I felt like I was having an out of body experience. I saw the whole world with all the pain going on and the women who desperately need help, need to hear what I have to say to and about women, and because my saying it is so dangerous, I had been taken from my excellent teaching position and been recycled to become Mrs. Potato. I looked around me. Untold numbers of women hours going into gimmicks. I had to look down and put my hand over my eyes. I don't remember ever wanting not to be somewhere like I wanted not to be there.

Out in the hall, I paced like a caged animal. When Rozan and I were alone in her car, I let go. I couldn't speak. I began to sob. I told her about the presentation. "With a dozen unanswered letters on my desk from women whose children are dying of AIDS or are contemplating suicide, with all the phone calls I get from women who desperately need to hear the things I am being asked not to say—*I DO NOT HAVE TIME TO BE MRS. POTATO!*" She burst into laughter. And then commiserated. She understands. Of course.

I woke up in the middle of the night and thought and cried. Yes, I must speak with the bishop.

And on the subject of women. Monday Emma Lou Thayne called me from Salt Lake and we talked for nearly an hour and a half. We are kindred spirits and perceptive of all the same things about the Church. She has spoken out on issues as the only woman on the board of the *Deseret News*, owned by the Church. (Such as recently when they interviewed forty prominent people for their New Year's resolutions, and there was not one woman represented.)

She told me of some tiny things the Brethren were contemplating doing in terms of giving women "better ground." Why do I have such mixed feelings about this? Why do I feel the Brethren are being dragged kicking and screaming into some slightly more enlightened view of women?

Emma Lou told me of a young woman close to her who went on a mission to France and had a terrible experience, so much pressure to get the statistics looking good. After she came home, the girl had some of her friends from the mission field over. Seven of the nine of them were in therapy.

Another friend told me about S., her relative who went on a mission to Japan and felt the same "statistics pressure." On one occasion a Japanese woman was ready for baptism, then backed out just before the event. The mission president sent the woman and his wife into another room so the wife could persuade her. S. went in as interpreter. The mission president's wife said, "Now, the Lord has been very good to you and he wants you to join the Church and he will be very disappointed in you if you don't."

S. listened and prepared to translate, but found she could not say those words, so she said in Japanese, "The Lord loves you very much and he doesn't want you to join this church unless you feel good about it."

The woman did not join.

February 5, 1989

Well, I was premature about my conclusion regarding the bishop. He assured me that he has heard from no one in Salt Lake about me. It was, in fact, the ward Relief Society Presidency who suggested I be moved. He had already told me that they were alarmed that my sacrament meeting talk did not sound like what they were receiving from the Brethren in Salt Lake. And perhaps, they said, "It was time for a different point of view."

I assured the bishop I had not been delivering heresies in my lessons. I had, however, generally concluded the lesson with something like "that we may be better daughters of our Father and Mother in Heaven." I asked him if that sounded frightening, and he said, "Not to me."

He said, though, that many people in the ward do not want to hear anything about the Heavenly Mother. He said he had heard from some who said he was not doing his job as bishop to let Sister Pearson say those things over the pulpit.

And he told me a very interesting story. I think I mentioned here that last Stake Conference, on the Saturday evening session, Patriarch Johnson gave a very moving talk equally devoted to the Father and Mother in Heaven. Bishop Sutton told me that at a subsequent bishops' meeting, the Patriarch's own bishop, Kay Anderson, brought it up and said he was concerned about it and that he didn't think it was appropriate. The bishops talked about it and when asked his opinion, Bishop Sutton said (and he smiled as he told me), "Actually that's quite a commonly taught doctrine in my ward."

The bishop's job, and he emphasized this, is to keep the ward big enough for all who want to be there, for the liberals, of which we have some, and the conservatives, of which we also have some. I told him he is doing a lovely job and that I very much appreciate it.

So does any of this make any difference? I am out on the front lines, constantly working in the trenches to make the world safe for the feminine, and does it make any difference? I know I have already made some difference. But so slowly. Things go so slowly.

Friday night I read love poems at the ward Valentine Dinner Dance. Everyone loved it. I know—because I can feel it in the room when I read—there is something quite remarkable that happens. No one moves. They are mesmerized.

I worked all week on the new "Motherless House" book. I'm slowly getting back into all the historical research and focusing on how I'm going to do it. And I've just got to go on faith, for my finances are precarious. But I cannot put it away again. I cannot.

Spoke again to B. who had told me terrible things about her and her sisters being sexually abused by their father. Only in adulthood did they check it out with each other and all the memories were the same. B. observed that when woman gets a gut feeling that something is wrong regarding a priesthood holder, the leaders tell her that is "Satan," and she must overcome it and obey.

"They withhold their love if we don't do what they say. We get conditional love from our men and from the Church. If we're good, and do what they say, we'll be loved." When B. and her sisters all wrote letters to their father's stake president and all went up to Idaho to testify in a church court, bringing evidence, he finally was excommunicated. He had been on a mission with his wife and had molested a girl there.

This morning, Sunday, Katy is sick, has been throwing up. But that is not the only reason I am not going to the multi-regional meeting in the Oakland Coliseum, at which Thomas Monson and two other General Authorities are speaking. I can't bring myself to go. It hurts too much. If I can just stay in my little ward here and read love poems at Valentine's dinners and minister to anyone who needs me and be given a place anyway even though I am a liberal and something of a heretic, I can manage. I can be happy being a Mormon. But when I remember Salt Lake City, when I try to fit into the Institutional Church, I collapse inside.

This morning while making waffles for Katy and her friend Corissa who came over, I put on Crawford Gates' "Favorite Mormon Hymns." As very often happens, I found myself crying.

"As the Dew from Heaven Distilling … " The sound thrusts me back into my sweet adolescence at BYU when the Church was still simple and simply true and President McKay told us wonderful things to do and to be, and we did and we were, and we were God's chosen people and grateful to be so, and we were going to bless the world and everything was going to be all right for all of us. The nostalgia overpowers me. Even now, writing of it fills my eyes again.

February 12, 1989

I am so excited about my new version of the "Motherless House"! This week I wrote several very good stories in the voices of Biblical women. The maiden watching the gang rape of the Levite's concubine who had been offered by her father to the mob. The ten-year-old Midianite girl who sees her mother and father and brothers slain by Moses' invaders. And yesterday I wrote the woman who stood up to Jeremiah. These are very good, I think. And powerful. And dangerous. And it must be done. I read them to Anne Mauss and to Lynn Ann and they both were amazed. Anne said, as I know, that I am ripping apart everything by the seams. I am doing major blasphemy. This is true. To look at the horrors done by the patriarchs in the Bible from another point or view, especially a *female* point of view, is something my people have never done before. And I love it.

Last week Kelli Frame called, one of the leaders of the Mormon Women's Forum. They've been getting lots of response to their work, the great majority of it positive, women saying they thought they were the only ones who felt that way. Some of the women who call say things like, "I keep thinking I'm going to have to leave the Church." And some were worried about the fact that on the morning of the resurrection, their husbands were going to have to call them from their graves by the power of their priesthood and so they had to be obedient.

Did I mention Lynn Ann's telling me of her uncle in Montana, who keeps his wife in line by threatening that if he's not pleased with her, come the morning of the resurrection, *he won't call her!*

February 13, 1989

Today Bookcraft rejected my new book of poems, the one I'm calling *Women I Have Known and Been*. Not having heard from them, I called Cory Maxwell, now head of publishing (and son of General Authority Neal Maxwell), on the phone. He said they're quite uncomfortable with the manuscript. "It's not as religiously oriented as the other poems. There seems to be an adversarial tone, a divisive spirit." I asked him which ones in particular seemed objectionable, and he said, "Well, first of all, 'In Celebration of the First Menstruation.' We could never publish anything with that title. Also, 'Obedient Girl" and 'Mastectomy.'"

Here are two of the objectional poems in a volume intended to support women:

Obedient Girl

Everybody was proud of this little girl.
She loved to please and obey.
She got good grades
And she baked good cakes

And she cleaned her room each day.
(And she came home pregnant at seventeen).
She loved to please and obey.

Support Group

You can fall here.
We are a quilt set to catch you
A quilt of women's hands
Threaded by pain made useful.

With generations of comfort-making
Behind us, we offer this gift
Warm as grandma's feather bed
Sweet as the Heavenly Mother's
Lullaby song.

You can fall here.
Women's hands are strong.

Cory also volunteered that my activities of this last year require that they be careful in what they publish of mine. I asked if I was on the black list in general and he said no, but that future things would depend not only on the project itself but on any extenuating circumstances at the time.

To which I replied, "So for example, if in a Christmas book I don't talk about women's issues or give another talk at the Mormon Women's Forum, my manuscript would be favorably received?"

"Something like that," he said.

So there you have it. Bookcraft has become more conservative over the years, and especially now with the son of a General Authority in charge. What can I do? I must do the things I feel I must do. Even my livelihood can't be the first consideration. One of these days I'm going to die. I will not starve to death. Friends will share their wheat with me. And my children will manage one way or another. This is not easy for me. I hate to disappoint people. I'm not used to that. But I've got to get used to it. I feel I'm going in the direction I must go, and I must trust the universe and God and the Goddess to take care of me.

Got a haircut today. That lifts me a little. Read my Jeremiah piece to Anne who was again blown away. It is heavy stuff. I mean, very, very heavy stuff. And she suggested something I've been thinking about myself. She said, "These pieces can't just be on the page. Do you know what happens when you speak them aloud? Incredible! It has to be a play! You have to perform these women!"

Indeed, that is what I have been considering of late. A one-woman play. Scary. Amazing.

Well. Major storms are a-brewing in Salt Lake City over the women. Kelli Frame called me on Saturday to tell me that her stake president is planning to hold a court on her. Her bishop, Richard Van Orden, has been very good to her all along, very supportive of what she's been doing, and refused to hold a court when the stake president suggested it. So the stake president, Klopfer, wants to do it himself, a high council court (women seldom get high council courts, just bishop's courts).

Her bishop had been instructed to ask her some questions:

"Do you advocate open disobedience to Church policies? Such as insisting on standing in the circle when babies are blessed when such permission has been denied?"

She said, "No."

"If there were no unrighteous dominion, would you be able to accept the patriarchal order?"

She said, "No, there has to be something beyond both patriarchy and matriarchy."

"What should we be doing about God the Mother? Do you pray to her?"

"We should be acknowledging her," she said. "And yes, I do pray to her along with the Father. And I feel good about that."

"Is there virtue in being obedient to God's servants even if you disagree with what they're saying?"

"No," she said. And the bishop agreed with her that he would reply no to that too.

This morning Kelli called me again to say that Karen Case's bishop, Mike Williams, called her in last night and told her he was not holding a court on her and he is not calling this a disfellowship; *but* she is not able from here on to go to the temple, take the sacrament, pray in meetings, hold a calling, speak in meetings, even substitute playing the piano in meetings.

Kelli called back an hour or so later to tell me UPI was anxious to get the story. They know somehow that something is happening in Centerville, where Karen Case lives, and they want to give it full coverage. Kelli and Karen and the other members of the Forum board, as well as authors Linda Newell and Linda Sillitoe, and Lynn Whitesides are meeting at four this afternoon in Salt Lake. They're asking the press not to do anything until after Wednesday when they learn what is in the offing for Kelli.

A part of me would love to see this exploding all over the major media to underline that what these women are saying *is actually true!* Can you believe this even: The women are saying we do not have a major voice in this church, and the Church replies, "What? You take that back or we'll throw you out."

Karen's bishop outlined five things she needs to do to repent, but her baby was screaming as he spoke on the phone so she only remembered one of them.

She has to state publicly that she does *not* believe that the scriptures are written from a patriarchal bias.

What? Anyone who would claim the scriptures are not written from a patriarchal bias is a candidate for a mental institution.

And coincidentally in the news these days is the Ayatollah of Iran who has sentenced to death the British writer Salman Rushdie, whose new novel, *Satanic Verses,* blasphemes Islam. A reward of more than three million dollars has been offered any Muslim who kills Rushdie. And a million to a non-Muslim person who might get to Rushdie first. It is now a major international event.

And here we have our own little version being played out in Mormondom. Kill them if they challenge our authority. Kill them. I am ashamed.

At the insistence of my friend Elouise Bell, I called Eleanor Knowles, vice-president of Deseret Book and asked if she thought they might be interested in my new book of poems, *Women I Have Known and Been.* She said very possibly, that they have done a few more progressive things than Bookcraft has done, like a couple of books on divorce. I have spent some time going over the poems, deleting a few lines that might be unnecessary red flags and writing a couple of very safe, inspiring poems. It's ready now to send.

Learned something that outraged me. Huldah the prophetess is not now included in the new LDS Bible Dictionary, though she is in the Cambridge Bible Dictionary on which ours is based and called a prophetess there. And Deborah is included in the LDS Bible Dictionary, but no longer labeled a "prophetess," which she was in a prior edition of this same dictionary.

Bit by bit Church leaders have gone about limiting the power and status of women. Systematically stripping away the little power woman has grudgingly been granted. They have a lot to answer for.

Lynn Ann's sister lost her baby. Even before birth they observed there was no heartbeat. Lynn Ann said her sister's ward had been terrific through it all and that the bishop came to be with her for the last several hours of labor. In fact, Lynn Ann, who hates the Church, said, "This is one of the times in my life when I've had to say, maybe the Mormon Church is okay."

Such a crazy quilt we are of magnificence and shame.

February 23, 1989

Good news from Salt Lake. Kelli called me Tuesday night and told me that her bishop had received a call from Thomas Fyans, General Authority. He asked the bishop if he was taking any action against Kelli Frame.

The bishop said, "No, I am not."

And Brother Fyans said, "Good. See that you don't."

And he was not happy at all to learn that Karen Case's bishop has already taken action against her. Now it is to be hoped that they will give the word strongly to Kelli's stake president and to Karen's bishop. It may be that this protection is motivated primarily to avoid some of the worst publicity they could get in a decade, but I will hope that also there are some of the Authorities who have concern for justice and truth and women.

Went to a meeting Monday night as invited by a woman in Judy Young's ward, Ervina Bertolina. Her "Women's Studies" class assigned each student to form a group and talk about issues. As expected, she invited Mormon women to talk about Mormon women's issues. Nothing much was said that I have not been covering in these pages. All were anxious for better days to come. All over the Church little groups of women are getting together. Or suffering in silence and getting ready to explode.

February 28, 1989

One thing I forgot to mention about the last poetry reading I did from the new book of poems about the experiences of women. We talked about one of the poems that mentions Heavenly Mother. One of the women (whom I did not know) said, "Well, what we do know is that there are many more Heavenly Mothers over there than Heavenly Fathers."

I said, "Well, no, I don't agree with that."

She said, "Well, either you believe in polygamy or you don't."

"Well, I don't!" I said emphatically. She looked a little taken aback.

Is this not amazing? I mean, that one can have such a definite knowledge of what's going on over there, and in such an absurd way.

One more little horror story. Anne told me of a woman she knew in Pullman, Washington a few years ago who had five boys. There was another woman who had five girls, and of that woman she said to Anne, "She's got to get herself worthy of being able to raise a priesthood holder before Heavenly Father will trust her with a boy. Clearly she's not ready for this."

And another story. A friend of Christy's said that her little six-year-old boy came home from church recently and said to her, "I'm made in the image of Heavenly Father, and you're not made in the image of anybody."

Well, yet another one. In my position as Primary Inservice Leader, I sat in on Anne's lesson in Primary. It was to the ten-year-olds, and was on the reformers. It gave fine stories of Wycliffe, Luther, Hus, even Anne Hutchinson, and how the church banned them for disagreeing with its doctrine. (Hus was even burned at the stake for challenging Catholicism.) Everything in the lesson was leading up to the only possible conclusion that conscience must reign supreme over authority.

But no. Correlation took a left turn onto a convoluted journey to get to the point that "Now that the gospel has been restored we can safely follow the prophet and have no reason to disagree." *What?*

Anne had called me on the phone earlier to rant about it.

The latest out of Salt Lake is that Karen Case's bishop was not back-tracking about his five points of repentance, and when Karen said she could not follow them, he said he would have to see about a court. She told him it was her understanding that other bishops had been given the instruction to "let the women be and do nothing to them." Her bishop showed her a certificate he has, indicating that *he* has been made a judge over her. Worse and worse.

And now to the good stuff. I wrote three great pieces last week for my one-woman play: the Christian woman at Ephesus, the witch waiting for the burning, and that great lady Elizabeth Cady Stanton. How I do love them all!

March 9, 1989

A very funny thing happened today. Here in Utah I had breakfast with Ladd M. and his parents and a few other people who were here for a wedding. We were telling a few jokes, and Mr. M., who is a vice president at BYU, told me *my joke* that I had made up all by myself. Probably Elouise Bell had passed it around on campus. Hearing my joke told to me was hilarious!

"The Mafia goes through Salt Lake City and kidnaps the wife of Ezra Taft Benson, President of the Mormon Church.

"Son Reed runs to his father's office and says, 'Oh, Father, Father, the most terrible thing has happened: Mother's been gotten by the mob!'

"'She's *what?*' says President Benson in alarm. 'Oh, thank heavens. For a minute there I thought you said your mother had *gotten a job!*'"

The next day Thursday I had lunch with Eleanor Knowles of Deseret Book. We spent quite a long time together and I felt very good about it. She said there were a few poems that would have to be taken out of *Women I Have Known and Been*, but that the response she was getting from her editors that had read it was extremely favorable. She showed me all around the operation and introduced me to various people. The head of marketing is a woman, who told me she absolutely loved the new book.

There are eight poems they would have to take out, Eleanor said. One is "In Celebration of the First Menstruation." She really liked it though, and is considering slipping it back in after the advisory board sees the manuscript. "The Sins of the Fathers" should stay (the narrative poem about the woman forgiving her father for early childhood sexual abuse). Five out of the six women on her board said they had had very strong negative feelings against their own fathers. None had experienced incest, but all five told of some real emotional or physical abuse from their father.

So the manuscript will have to pass their advisory board that meets on the tenth of next month. I don't know who's on it, several General Authorities, I'm sure. I asked Eleanor if she expected there would be any problem about the book or about me personally and she said no, she didn't think so. And she had asked their manager Ron Millet and he didn't think so either. I do so hope this happens.

While I was in Eleanor's office, I called over to the Church Office Building to see if I could drop in on Elder Hanks. His secretary said he had meetings and people waiting for him, but she knew he would be very upset if she didn't let me in, so she told me to come over just before three-thirty. I also called Elder Fyans' office. He wasn't in, but I left a message with his secretary to thank him for his intervention on behalf of the women of the Mormon Women's Forum.

Brother Hanks and I had a good visit. He spent about forty-five minutes with me. I told him about the situation of the women who had started the Forum. He agreed it was not a good thing to call them on the carpet. But he didn't seem to understand why they felt strongly about addressing these issues. "Nobody thinks men are superior to women these days."

I asked if he felt encouraged about some of the things he's been trying to do in the Church and he said yes. He asked if I had a bishop who was good to me, and I told him yes, I'd had very good bishops. He said he had hoped I wouldn't get a bishop who would try to silence me. He said there are only a few authorities who are worried about what the women are doing, some who think the woman thing will get bigger than the black thing ever was and want to stomp on them.

He gave me a hug as I left. I am grateful for Elder Hanks.

Downstairs I ran into Russell Nelson, of the Twelve. I shook his hand and introduced myself, saying I didn't think we had met. "Oh, yes, we have," he said. "I heard you lecture once at BYU." Embarrassing.

Jan Tyler told me that her friend Frank McIntyre, who works at the Church Offices, told her that recently the Quorum of the Twelve had been given an "Executive Briefing" on the results of an important study that the Church had hired done about the attitudes of women in the ranks. Their reaction was one of disbelief that there was so much discontent, so they had the complete data brought to them. Jan didn't know any more than that.

Cousin Cindy Bateman told me a bad story. She's doing research on Mormon women doctors, trying to find them for an association she wants to create and for some writing she's doing. She told me of finally getting in to see one of the counselors in the Relief Society Presidency, Sister Evans, who had her arms folded across her chest and had Cindy sit feet away.

She was very suspect of Cindy and didn't speak to her as you would think one interested woman would speak to another. Finally Cindy said one of the reasons she would like to find these women is that she understands many of them are inactive in the Church.

"And do you know why they're inactive?" asked Sister Evans. "They're inactive because they've disobeyed the word of the prophet and left their homes for careers."

Cindy could not believe what she was hearing. It really shook her. She is not a radical feminist like I am (No, I am not radical; I am very balanced). She tries to make everything work. And this really hurt her.

Channel Two people found me at the book signing and made me come with them up to the State Capitol where the Names Quilt is on display. They interviewed me there for a few minutes, asking such things as how would Brigham Young feel about having these panels in memory of men who died of AIDS hanging there near to his statue. I said I thought he would approve.

And I told the story of his stopping conference to send out rescue parties to the people on the plains who were caught in an early Wyoming winter, saying as I have said before, that AIDS sufferers are some of today's people on the plains. And reminding them too that King Benjamin in the Book of Mormon said not to ask whether one is worthy to be helped before you help them.

Called Marie Cornwall to tell her I'm making the tapes of my Mormon Women's Forum talk available. She was glad to know, as the director of BYU's Women's Research Institute, and ordered a video and two audiotapes. She has also been a researcher for the Church's Correlation Department, where she studied causes/patterns of Mormons leaving church activity.

She told me of an experience she had with Hugh Pinnock, General Authority, in which they were meeting on the subject of the singles in the Church, and Marie and her committee made a presentation they had worked long and hard on. Elder Pinnock, at the end of the presentation, said, "I know what the singles need. They need to be taught the gospel and they need to repent."

Marie responded that she didn't think they needed to repent any more than other members of the Church, and she was quite strong in her response to him. Someone else interrupted and calmed things down, she said. How maddening.

These are very interesting days. I am going to predict that the next few years will be tumultuous ones concerning women in the Mormon Church. And then I think some breakthroughs will be made.

28

THE CURTAIN RISES ON GOD THE MOTHER

August 23, 1989

On Monday the 7th I read my new play to a small group of people from the ward. I wanted to let the word out gently via some friendly people, so I invited my home teachers, Bob and Joyce Anderson, Birdene Keddington, Diana McClun and Greta Holcolm. Again, it was a major hit. When I was through, Birdene beamed breathlessly, "Carol Lynn!"

Diana said, "It's brilliant!"

Brother Anderson (my former bishop) loved it, and his wife Joyce said, "This might upset some people, but it has to be said."

The next morning Brother Anderson called to give me more comments. No criticisms except that he wanted a few things strengthened even more. "Can't you make Rachel a little stronger? She was a very powerful woman." He didn't have any problem with Emma Smith, said I didn't downgrade Joseph and I upgraded Emma.

I went to Girls Camp for three days. Katy spent the week and loved it. Really marvelous program, devoted leaders, great activities. I spoke on Sunday night at the fireside on diary keeping. Tuesday I spoke to the younger girls on self-development.

Lonnie Wells, who is now Relief Society President in her ward, told me she has encouraged the sisters to change the pronouns when they sing the hymns, so that they sing of "sisters" and not "brothers" and "she" instead of "he." Most of them don't, she said, but she does, and she sings loud and clear. I asked if she would do that in sacrament meeting, and she said she usually does. I often do that myself, but rather surreptitiously.

As I sat eating at camp with a group of the women, it was brought up that the girls' programs in the Church are never as well funded as the boys', nor are they allowed to do as interesting things. Some strong feelings were expressed about this.

And I found myself pointing out that it's more than odd that we have come to refer to the men in the ward as "The Priesthood," and even here at Girls Camp. They're not "the men" or "the brethren." They're "The Priesthood."

A woman cleaning up the kitchen in the chapel may have a can of garbage too heavy to lift, so she of course, has to leave it for "The Priesthood" to take care of.

We're grateful to "The Priesthood" for putting away the chairs after the ward dinner (as if it's being done by some remarkable, invisible force).

"The Priesthood" there at Girls Camp put on a fun skit in which they came out wearing rabbit ears and danced around the stage.

And after the skit, the girls sang, to the tune of "Bye, Bye Birdie,"—"We love you, Priesthood, oh, yes, we do. We love you, Priesthood, and we'll be true. When you're not near us, we're blue. Oh, Priesthood, we love you!"

I'm not making this up. Truly bizarre.

My dear friend Anne reported to me a conversation with her sociologist father-in-law, Armand Mauss, in which he told of some Sunstone people going to speak to some General Authorities, trying to generate goodwill toward the magazine. Apostle Boyd K. Packer told them that if they continue to push, they would place themselves in great spiritual jeopardy.

"There is a core of truth," he told them. "And you're either moving into it or out of it, and when you get so far out of it there's just no coming back."

Kelli Frame called to talk about the Mormon Women's Forum bringing my play to Salt Lake. We'll probably do that in January.

September 10, 1989

I see that yesterday was my wedding anniversary. Twenty-three years ago Gerald and I were married. I've never had a "visitation" from him, but I do believe he is thrilled to see the work that I've been doing.

And yesterday I had a wonderful day shopping for some of the things I'll need for my play. Lynn Ann and I went to several antique stores in Berkeley and Oakland.

I knew what I needed; I've had it clear in my mind for some time: a trunk from which to take out various props and costume pieces as each character appears. A small carpet. A stool of some kind. And I found my trunk! A pine chest really, very attractive—large, plain wood with hinges and a curved top. I love it. $285. A cane and eyeglasses for Elizabeth Cady Stanton. A fan to spray gold for the Greek woman. A silver jeweled belt and neck piece for the Egyptian priestess. A beaded neck piece for the American Indian woman. A long, black chain for the front and back of the witch. I already have a fine wooden bowl for the Ephesian woman to use as she kneads her bread. And Rozan came up with the great idea of my using play dough to do the actual kneading.

All this went on my credit card. Right now I don't see enough money coming in to last me through the end of the year. But that is often the case. Something will come up. It always has.

I have only six weeks before my first performance at the Women's Conference at Saint Mary's College. So excited I can hardly sleep.

September 19, 1989

Working hard on the play. Most characters are clear and ready to go. Rewrote Emma around my mother's shawl—the stunning, embroidered and fringed shawl she bought at the World's Fair in Chicago in 1933. It's been safe in my drawer of treasures, but I believe Emeline Sirrine Wright would be thrilled to have her shawl used in this search for the Mother. I begin Emma's scene by holding the shawl up to the audience and saying "You will not find another shawl like this is in all the city of Nauvoo. Joseph gave it to me. It is beautiful, isn't it?"

Later, after she speaks of Joseph's other wives, she says fiercely, "But no other woman in Nauvoo has a shawl like this!"

Found a wonderful catalogue of unusual musical instruments. Ordered six. Will use them for short bits between some of the women.

The other day Katy and I were lying on my bed and I said, "Oh, Katy, I'm almost fifty! And you're just fourteen. I don't want to grow old and die."

Very seriously Katy said, "Don't worry, Mom. We're eternal."

"How do you know that, Katy? Just because you've been told that all your life?"

"No. I just know. I've always known that."

"Have you had any experiences to tell you that?"

"No. I just know."

October 1, 1989

My play is moving right along. Yesterday Rozan and I went shopping for an area rug and found one that I really like. It's a wonderful, deep red with flowers on it. Found it at Macy's, a $900 rug marked down to $270. It will give a nice, inviting, strong, warm, feminine atmosphere. And for my birthday Aaron spent a few hours in the garage and built for me a lectern that fits over my step-stool for Elizabeth Cady Stanton's speech, which then turns into a small table for Rebecca, the Jewish woman in Hitler's Germany, to put her candles on in honor of the arrival of the Holy Shekhinah, Shabbat Queen, the feminine part of God.

While I was in Utah I gave two "readings" of the play. My cousin Helen Bateman in Provo hosted one and we had about sixty people. Many of these were more mainstream types than "feminist" types, so it was a good test. And it passed with high marks.

I managed to get Ruth Funk there (former General President of the Church's Young Women's organization). I could tell she was with me all the way, and at the end she told me, "This is magnificent!"

Ida Smith, who used to head BYU women's programs, told me that the next day she would talk to the person in charge of BYU's annual Women's Conference and push to have them invite me to perform my play there. I'm glad she will do this, but I know they won't be allowed to invite me.

Max Golightly, my very dear high school drama teacher, came and was truly excited. I had specifically invited Helen Stark, one of the grand old ladies of Mormon feminism, who has done so much for the cause. I remember her coming by and giving me the first little pamphlet that exploded me into serious historical research—about Ann Lee and the Shakers, expressing the radical idea of God as both Father and Mother. She was, of course, thrilled with the play.

The conference at Weber State went very well. Did some TV publicity for them. Did an hour on KSL talk radio. Made it a point to be asked about my current project so I could break the news to Utah.

Drove up to Ogden with Carolyn Tanner Irish, the Episcopalian minister I have mentioned. We had a great visit. She told me her journey of losing faith in the LDS Church's exclusive position of authority, joining the Bahais, healing with the Quakers, going to the seminary and being ordained. She now sits on her father's board with a couple of General Authorities, says she gets along well with them, enjoys them a lot, but of one she said, "I liked him much better before he became an apostle and developed an artifice." I told her about my play and she was very excited at the idea.

I was put in touch with Darlene Hutchinson, who came to my hotel and we had a good visit. Darlene is the woman in the Church's Office of Special Affairs and Public Communications. She advises the Brethren on a variety of "women's matters." I liked her. She said the Brethren asked her to go through the Bishop's Handbook and look at it for sexist language. She made a number of recommendations, all of which they incorporated. I asked her to tell me the things she has observed since she's been there that she would count as steps forward for women. Here they are:

In the handbook she read that a woman who had been raped was to be asked if she did anything to provoke it. Darlene struck that right away and no one objected.

Women or men married to inactive or nonmember spouses are now on the same footing about going to the temple with the approval of the other. (It used to be that the wife had to get the husband's approval, but not vice versa.)

More auxiliary leaders sit on the stand at Conference, etc., are invited into top council meetings, and some now talk at General Conference.

Recently a policy allows a woman to be sealed to more than one man, *if all parties are dead*. (The assumption is: in the next life she will choose which man to spend eternity with; polygamy still reigns.)

No longer does a man have to give permission for cancellation of a sealing requested by his former wife.

Divorced men must answer at temple recommend interviews if they are current on their child support payments.

Darlene had received so many inquiries from women about not being able to stand in the circle for the blessing of a baby even though a non-member husband (clearly without the priesthood) was allowed to participate. She didn't want to even bring up the subject, but she wrote it up anyway, and her fears were realized: the Brethren made the determination that from now on only Melchizedek priesthood holders will be able to stand in the circle. I don't like that decision; it deprives some fathers of a good opportunity. And, of course, confirms that the Brethren would rather take away that right from a non-member husband than give that right to a wife who is a member. "No Women Allowed."

I told Darlene that some of the additional things I thought ought to be done are:

Phase out polygamy altogether, let it go the way of the Adam-God doctrine. She agreed whole-heartedly. I asked her if the Brethren could be persuaded to stop letting men be sealed to more than one woman in the temple. She was hesitant to say much, but did give me to understand that it had been seriously discussed.

I told her that we need to take out of the closet the teaching on the Heavenly Mother and make it useful in our lives and in our worship. She responded well to that.

I told her we need to stop calling the men "The Priesthood." She had not thought of that but agreed with what I said.

I told her the whole curriculum ought to be carefully studied to see how it sounds from a female point of view. She agreed with all I said on the subject.

She expressed her feelings that the Brethren are talking about women's issues and want to make the women happy. I'm sure that's true on one level. How much they try to put themselves in a female mind and really see, is questionable.

Darlene said she really enjoyed my talk at the Mormon Women's Forum in January, that I said things in a very balanced way.

I may be in touch with her from time to time. I told her all about my play and gave her a minute from the Christian woman at Ephesus. She was fascinated.

Had lunch in Salt Lake with Ruth Funk, former President of the Young Women's organization. She is now head of the State Board of Education, and told me that right in the middle of our conversation she realized that she is now trying so hard to do in education what she tried so hard to do in the Church, to empower individuals, but now she is *able* to do that because her power is so much greater there.

I think Ruth was a woman who took more risks on behalf of women in the Church than many others in the hierarchy. She agrees with me that the female presidencies have been getting less and less outspoken. She looks forward to when the Church will be run with the "Teach correct principles and let them govern themselves" philosophy.

Had a short, good visit with my dear Elouise Bell on BYU campus. I dragged Eugene England and Doug Thayer into her office and read to them my Christian Ephesus woman. They seemed to really love what I'm up to.

Waiting for Elouise, I visited with Eugene quite a while. He is studying violence in the scriptures and the symbolic violence in the temple and how it affects our lives. I could tell all this is very hard for him. Two years ago, after he published an article about (against) polygamy in *Dialogue*, he was prohibited from teaching religion. He was very hurt at the way it happened. Dean Matthews had his secretary call Eugene's secretary with a message that he was no longer to teach religion classes.

Now the news after my return home.

Went up to Rozan's this afternoon and watched one session of General Conference. Jayne Malan, First Counselor in the Young Women's Presidency, was the best of all the speakers. Her talk was wonderful, very genuine, showed connected emotion (which so many of the Brethren never, ever show). Elder Maxwell warned against "murmuring," said that we are better off not to find fault, but to trust our leaders because they are being led by Christ.

I don't "murmur." I speak as articulately and loudly as possible. I even hire a theatre. One does not "murmur" on the stage.

It occurred to me while watching General Conference that religion is sort of like education. The really important stuff happens at the bottom, in the classroom. And the higher up you get into the administration (even though you need it to keep things together) the further away you are from where the good stuff is going on. I just want to stay down here at the bottom where wonderful things happen between people.

Had an interesting conversation with my dear artist friend Trevor Southey, a gay man who was pretty much forced out of the Church years ago. He's told me often that there are many things about the Church that he misses deeply, but he cannot accept the "only true church" concept. I told him there are plenty of us that manage to find different ways to look at that.

I said, "Sometimes I see God as functioning like a marvelous, burning burst of fire and intelligence that is constantly sending off sparks all over the earth and all over time, and those who are able reach out and catch a spark and do what they can with that spark. Someone catches a spark and writes it into a book. Someone catches a spark and makes it into a painting or a major invention. Someone catches a spark and founds a church or reforms another.

Bernadette of Lourdes caught a spark and the patterns of her brain translated it into the Virgin Mary. Many others caught sparks and 'saw' them as angels.

"Joseph Smith caught a spark, a very bright one, and the patterns of his brain were nineteenth century, patriarchal patterns and so translated them into what made sense to him, the Father and the Son. I don't think he made this up. I think that is what he received, what he could understand. Which does not mean that is all there is or that other people's experiences with divine sparks were less valid. And Joseph's spark has quite remarkably not diminished, but in many ways gained momentum."

As I said all that to Trevor, he said, "Carol Lynn, that makes the most sense of anything anyone has ever told me about religion!"

October 8, 1989

A good and productive week. Most of my props and costume pieces are assembled. Friday morning I performed the play here at my home for Richard James, a major director/actor in the area, and Kerri Shawn Denison, the best actress I've seen locally.

They were both really stunned. "Awesome" and "Fabulous," they said. They were overwhelmed at the power of the piece and at my own ability to bring each of the separate women to life. They gave me a few minor directorial suggestions, which I appreciated. Like: leaving the costume pieces and props of each woman out of the truck on the stage when their scene is over, so that at the end, I am literally surrounded by the sisters. Love it! I will have Aaron build a coat tree on which I will hang some things.

My musical instruments came: a fine drum for the Indian woman, a wonderful clay ocarina on a leather strap for the Paleolithic woman (such a great, ancient tone), a Greek lyre, a gong for the Egyptian priestess, and a tambourine to introduce Rachel. These touches of sound will add a lot.

I'm still unclear on the title. "Song of the Sisters?" No.

I have sent out a couple of hundred letters to people inviting them personally. I do believe we will come close to filling up the four nights I've rented for "Stage Two," the smaller Civic Arts Theatre.

October 15 1989

It is Sunday. On Friday at St. Mary's College, I perform the play on stage for the first time. I'm staying well, but am feeling a great deal of tension in my body.

Last Friday there was a good article in Maggie Crum's theatre column in the *Contra Costa Times*: "Woman Writes, Stars in Play about 'Mother God.'" So the word is out. No going back.

And a small, good thing in my ward. Last Sunday, after Bishop Sutton presented to Randy Rice the "Duty to God" award, he called up Courtney King and presented her with a Young Women's award that (I believe) he had created. As he did so, he smiled and said in a little aside, "You see, Sister Pearson is educating us on giving equal recognition to our young women."

Did I mention my new title for the play? "Mother Wove the Morning." I like it a lot and am getting good response from it. I think it is lyrical and affirmative, without being accusatory or self-pitying.

Last Friday something quite wonderful happened here at home. When Katy came home from school I sat down with her and Aaron and explained what had to happen over the weekend and asked Katy to vacuum downstairs and upstairs and to dust. Katy got a bit belligerent and grumbly. Aaron grasped her firmly and kindly and said, "Katy, I'm going to be your father for a while." He took her up to her room and *without losing his temper one time* talked to her for at least twenty minutes. Here is some of what I heard:

"Katy, you've got to understand that Mom is under a lot of pressure right now with her play ... she needs all the help we can give ... do you know how much more Mom does for you than she ever asks you to do for her? ... you're a part of this family, Katy, and we love you a lot, but sometimes you don't take your share of the responsibility ... do you know how much you have to be grateful for? ... do you ever just think about being thankful for everything you have? ... I don't like out loud prayers, family prayers, but just to go over stuff in your own mind ... Katy, I want you every night to kneel down and just go over everything you have to be grateful for ...."

I listened in awe.

October 17, 1989

Disaster today. Shortly after five, as I was cleaning the downstairs bathroom and Katy was sweeping, we felt the floor move. "Is this an earthquake?" Katy said. The house began to shake mightily.

I grabbed Katy and we stood under the doorframe, arms extended, pressing against the wood. It seemed to go on and on, major rolling. Then it stopped. We examined all the rooms. No real damage was done. A few things were knocked over and some pictures were askew.

But that good fortune was not enjoyed by everyone in the area. There was widespread damage. A section of the Bay Bridge collapsed onto a freeway below it, killing hundreds of people. Buildings collapsed in San Francisco and in other cities. Fires are now raging in the Marina and other places. Riots in Oakland. It is a nightmare. We have been watching all night on TV. Aaron and Katy and I said a prayer for all the injured and the workers. I have been praying all night.

Life is so fragile, nature so unreliable. People are so wonderful; they move right in and help and do all they can. I am grateful that we are safe. I wish it were so for everyone.

October 18, 1989

News of yesterday's quake continues. We have not been asked to take people in, but cash contributions are requested. I will send a check to the Red Cross. Telephone lines have been down and I've not been able to get messages out that we're okay. Last night Aaron got through to John down in Southern California. This morning I told Katy to keep calling until she got Emily who is in Chicago with our good friends Mario and Dana Aranda. Our Utah people have been calling here. Kelli Frame called me, said her first thought was that I couldn't die before I did my play. Actually, as Katy and I were holding onto the door frame, I had that same thought.

Aaron drove me over to St. Mary's this morning. We set my stuff up in the theatre and I did a run-through. The stage works great for me. An apron was built, so I get to be very close to the audience. I felt very comfortable there and *very excited.*

I now have the swastika arm band for the shirt my Nazi woman is mending. And the two heavy parchment pieces for the Gnostic woman's letters. Prepared a lighting design instruction for the St. Mary's theatre man.

I am *so grateful* I get to do this work. It is so thrilling! A woman approached me at the cleaners and said, "Are you Carol Pearson? I'm coming on Friday. It will be *wonderful!*"

October 19, 1989

Thursday. Just a quick note while I'm waiting for the iron to get hot so I can press my costume. Nearly there!

I rehearsed again at St. Mary's. Picked up my 5,000 flyers from my friend Wes Carlson and took them to the Civic Arts Box Office, where they will be distributed at currently running shows.

I walked up in the hills this evening for exercise and to clear my mind.

I've been forgetting to mention something. When I was at Katy's Girls Camp this summer, giving a talk on diary keeping, I took with me the book in which Elouise Bell used excerpts from my very early diaries, *Will I Ever Forget This Day?*

> July 31, 1961. This evening I began a most significant experience. I am reading *Women of Mormondom* by Tullidge.... I skimmed over a few comments, and then lighted upon this paragraph on p.177: "Presently woman herself shall sing of her divine origin. A high-priestess of the faith shall interpret the themes of herself and of her Father-and-Mother God!"
>
> Whether or not I bear the potential of being a "high priestess" able to sing the themes of womanhood and my 'Father-and-Mother God' to ears other than my own—at least I shall sing them to myself.

I had forgotten that. But when I read it in my diary this summer out under the trees at camp, I remembered it fully. I could see my bedroom again and feel the powerful emotions that I felt. I can remember weeping as I read that passage. I can remember kneeling down and praying with a full and yearning heart that I could participate in that adventure. Tullidge's book was very melodramatic. My youthful devotion seems melodramatic now. But it was so genuine. And it has never left me. That girl was twenty-one years old. Nearly thirty years have passed. And that tremendous need has always been with me.

Tomorrow morning I launch the major work of my life:

MOTHER WOVE THE MORNING

a one-woman play
written and performed by

Carol Lynn Pearson

October 20, 1989

I did it.

And I am very pleased. Tired, absolutely drained, but very happy.

It went extremely well. Aaron and I left the house just after seven this morning and drove to Saint Mary's College. Set up the stage: the rug, the trunk, the two stools, the rack that Aaron built for me. The set looked great.

Judy and Anne came to help me get ready. Judy ran the tape of music I wanted playing before and after and during intermission. Anne did my hair. I put on my wonderful white costume and went backstage to wait.

About a hundred and fifty women came in, all associated with Battered Women's Alternatives. Rollie Mullen greeted them. Lights went down. Stage lights came up. I went on.

Is there a better word than wonderful? *Full of wonder* it was. I have not performed on a stage for twenty-six years. Twenty-six years! And I love it so. I have improved considerably since my college days; life has done that to me, blessed me with joys and with anguish nearly too hard to bear.

And they loved it. I could tell the audience was with me all the way. I could sense what they were feeling, and it was powerful. They laughed in all the places I'd hoped and even some new ones. I became emotional in my expected places, especially telling of the rape of the Levite's concubine. Afterwards many told me there was magic in the hall. At the conclusion they all stood and applauded enthusiastically.

I went over to the luncheon and talked to some of the women. One told me, "I looked around and said: Why isn't my husband here? Why isn't my nineteen-year-old son here? *Everyone* should be here!"

Kathy DeHaven, our vocal teacher, was there with her friend, a therapist, both enormously excited. I asked the therapist if the therapist character in my play worked and she said certainly, that even at intermission she had turned to Kathy and said, "We are watching a family reconstruction. The whole world is longing for its Mother, and women are expecting to find that in men and they can't find it there. You reconstructed the family right there before our eyes!"

I will go now to bed. How incredibly lucky and blessed I am to get to do this wonderful thing. I am so deeply grateful.

October 22, 1989

In looking through the *Church News,* I read the account of the recent General Women's Meeting. President Hinckley: "As I have said from this pulpit before, I am satisfied that God our Eternal Father does not love His daughters less than He loves His sons."

The very fact that someone would make such a statement indicates that a Major Problem exists. Has he ever said to the men, "I am satisfied that God our Eternal Father does not love His sons less than He loves His daughters?" Or, to really push this thought: "I am satisfied that God our Eternal Mother does not love Her sons less than She loves Her daughters."

October 23, 1989

Preparing to open for my one performance at Onstage Theatre in Pleasant Hill, then four performances at Stage Two in Walnut Creek next week. The first occasion of people actually buying a ticket.

Brother Anderson, my former bishop and now home teacher, gave me a blessing tonight. I had suggested it last month when they came, and he said he would be happy to. I also said I would like his wife Joyce and my children to participate. So tonight Aaron and Katy stood with Joyce and Bob Anderson with their hands on my head to give me a blessing. Brother Anderson blessed me to be successful in this very important work, to show to those who will listen the other side of God, and to show the history, both positive and negative of women in this world. He said that the message of this play is important in the same way that the coming down of the Berlin wall is important.

Ran through my lines as I walked to the park. People must wonder to see me mumbling to myself as they go by and perhaps hear, ". . . It is said that if you look into my eyes an enchantment will bring you evil … you may suddenly develop leprosy … your cow may die …."

October 29, 1989

So tired. The play went very well. The theatre seats about 135 and very few seats were empty. Producer/performer makes for a heavy load. Got more flyers. Checked my props, pressed my costume. Got Helen Means, who owns the theatre, to put black flats over the back wall. Worked at six-thirty with a lighting man. Dressed and did makeup downstairs. So exciting. *To sit there and hear the audience come in—so exciting!* I could tell the audience was half Mormon anyway; Mormons talk more than most when they get together.

Stood at stage left, breathing, praying, sipping water, waiting. Blackout. Lights up. I walk on.

I greeted the audience, then said, as I had at St. Mary's "During the earthquake, I hung on to the door frame and I said, 'Oh, please, dear God, don't let me die before I can perform my play *one time!*'" A good laugh at both venues. And here I added, "Yesterday my daughter Katy and I were driving past this theatre on our way to the mall, and Katy saw the sign out front and said, 'Oh, look, my Mom's playing at a theatre near me!'" The audience enjoyed that a lot.

I made one error, but did a great recovery. Brought in the Nazi woman before Mrs. Stanton instead of after her, and had to figure out how to smoothly proceed. No one knew. Actually it's amazing I haven't made more mistakes. The possibility of error in a two-hour production that demands total focus and mastery of any number of physical and verbal and emotional details is awesome. And I think I'm doing remarkably.

The audience applauded enthusiastically, and stood as they did. It was quite thrilling.

So many people that I knew came—and so many that I did not know. Nobody around here has ever seen me act—they think I'm just a writer—and so they are taken quite by surprise. Several people said the bishop was smiling as he left and speaking warmly.

The next day Rozan and I went for a walk in my hills. As we were going up, we passed a woman who said, "Oh, I was on the front row last night. It was so wonderful!" What fun, fun, fun!

October 30, 1989

Yesterday at church a lot of people who had seen my play spoke to me. Ruth Troxel had told the missionaries about it and they wanted to see it but didn't have the money. I told her they could come for free. And she said this play could be a great missionary tool. Surprised smile here. A missionary tool!

Receiving notes from people who saw the play. I can't think how one person deserves to do this amazing work and deserves to receive such honor for it.

November 11, 1989

The world is going through such remarkable things these days. Yesterday the Berlin Wall was opened and hundreds of thousands of East Berliners streamed through to the West, some to stay, some to visit and go back. They were jubilant; TV coverage has shown this amazing thing as it happened. And this morning as I read the newspaper over breakfast I could not help crying. What a wonderful, wonderful thing. The Berlin Wall opening! —and the Mother returning!

On Thursday I went to the *Contra Costa Times* to be interviewed by our theatre critic, Maggie Crum. Had another five thousand flyers printed. Leaving them everywhere. Friends have been helping me.

Last Sunday I went to Sacramento. I had been invited by the Mormon television program there, "Moments of Reflection," to do an interview. Then the Church's Public Relations man there, David Polei, called and asked if I would do a fireside at the same time. I said yes. The fireside was put together in just two weeks, but there was a huge crowd there. Packed, clear through the seats that were put up in the recreation hall and even on the stage. Brother Polei said there must have been fifteen hundred people there.

I gave my good talk on love, using some of the poems. I was "whisked away before the closing prayer" because I had to get over to the TV station.

At the Studio I did scenes from four of the women, then talked with the interviewer, a nice young Mormon man. I was very positive and thrilled and presented it all in such a way that nobody could argue with it. He kept saying, "Excellent … wonderful." And at the end they rolled up the credits: "This program is brought to you by the Church of Jesus Christ of Latter-day Saints."

Miracles are happening.

I had such an interesting experience this afternoon. Called animator Don Bluth's organization to see if Don might have a position for a dear friend who has been out of work for some months.

"Is this *Carol Lynn Pearson???* I have been thinking about you. You have made my day!" He was beyond thrilled.

Don is just releasing his newest animated film, *All Dogs Go to Heaven*.

"Listen," he said to me, "What we need around here are good scriptwriters. Now let's talk. We've got to do something together. At least ten times I've said to my secretary, would you find Carol Lynn Pearson for me? We need her."

To which I told him the whole world has been able to find me, and if his secretary can't he needs a new secretary.

"I like the way you think and I like the way you write, and I want us to work together."

"All right, let's do it."

"You will?"

"Sure."

Well, you'd have to come to Ireland because we're moving there, but then you could come home to write it."

"Okay."

"Okay? You really will??"

"I will."

I told him about my play and suggested that there were some themes in the longing for the absent Goddess that could be pertinent to a story he might develop. He said he would love to see the play.

What fun. I've never had more enthusiasm from someone about working with me.

November 20, 1989

Madly gearing up to perform at Stage Two here in Walnut Creek. On Thursday Dr. Hansen (head of BYU's drama department when I was there), called me from Utah. I had sent him a tape of me reading three of the scenes. "I am amazed at the development of your voice," he said. "Your voice is very, very strong."

November 24, 1989

I opened tonight at Stage Two and it went wonderfully well. I was very much connected to the play and to the audience. All seats (over 150) were full and they turned away people at the door.

In my introduction I said, "And speaking of Thanksgiving, do you know how grateful I am to all of you for coming tonight?" They responded with a sustained applause; that surprised me, and warmed me.

I felt only good things from the audience. They applauded well at intermission, and again when I came back for the second act. And there was a very strong ovation at the end.

I am DOING IT!

I am making people think. L.B. came with a group and said to me, "It makes me see that maybe women shouldn't be so submissive."

I AM DOING IT!

L.C. said, "It makes us see how absurd some of the ideas about women were a long time ago, so we have to know that some of our ideas right now are just as absurd."

I AM DOING IT!

November 29, 1989

Saturday night went just as well. Full house. Again people turned away at the door. Rain. And I had another wonderful time performing.

I had a dress rehearsal on Thursday to which I invited people. Betty Stevenson, my black friend in Oakland who is a convert to the Church, came with eight or ten people. She was thrilled beyond words. Just a minute ago I called her and told her to send more for tonight if she wants. She told me she has been thinking of the play constantly, that it gave her so much, and that she is no longer ashamed of wanting to love her Mother in Heaven. And she loved my black Shaker woman, said she was wonderful.

Katy's friend Rebecca, a Jewish girl who had seen the play, came over yesterday and I asked her how the play made her feel. "Oh, it gave me such a good, warm feeling. It made me feel proud to be a woman."

This is amazing, and is, of course, professionally the highlight of my life! It is really a religious experience.

Monday afternoon Charlie Jarrett, the reviewer from the *Rossmoor News* called me and said, "I never do this, but I wanted to call you and read the review that I'm putting in the newspaper." He then proceeded to read me a stunning review (which will be in my files). Then he identified himself as a former Mormon. He dropped out, having been in a bishopric, for reasons that included what the Church does to women. And his wife too said, "This is a male chauvinist organization. What am I doing here?" Still, he continues to love the Church and is absolutely amazed and thrilled to see what I'm doing. "It feels like a brand-new day!"

I'm getting rave reviews from the Mormons, the Catholics, the Jews, the atheists and the ex-Mormons. What a profoundly important time.

And yet, not all is well in Zion. I had a good telephone interview last night with two young women from the *Student Review*, the alternate newspaper at BYU. They were not allowed to have a woman come and speak on rape crisis as it might offend their conservative financial donors. What? And Kelli told me that in Batina Lindsay's stake the stake president is asking the women in their temple recommend interviews, "Do you support Batina Lindsay?" Batina had given a talk at Sunstone that had a fair amount of strong stuff about women as healers. Dangerous indeed.

And I am so busy being part of the answer to this whole thing! I cannot say how thrilling it is.

December 4, 1989

We keep adding performances. Three more in the middle of this month.

On Wednesday night our stake president, Gary Anderson, and his wife Lynn were there. I had specifically invited them. Just now I got a note in the mail from Lynn, saying how touched she and her husband were and how they welcomed my reminder of our spiritual Mother. ". . . We rejoice in your wonderful success and hope the crowds keep building so that your efforts can raise the awareness of many of our brothers and sisters. We certainly plan to tell our friends about it!"

I called Darlene Hutchinson in the Church Public Communications Office today and told her all about the success and asked for a list of the General Authorities and of the women's leadership. I am going to send a letter to each one and offer tickets for my Utah run.

Maggie Crum, the reviewer for our local paper, the *Contra Costa Times,* gave the play a very good review and then put it in the section of "Prime Picks" for weekend entertainment. A bit from her review:

I always marvel at the man or woman who has the courage to take over

The characters of my one-woman play, *Mother Wove the Morning*, 1990.

Genevieve

Running Cloud

Phoebe

Emma

Elizabeth Cady Stanton

Hilda

Rebecca

Marie

a theatre and put on a one-person performance whose success is utterly dependent on the abilities of that lone individual who gets virtually no support from a set, costumes, music and special effects.

What Carol Lynn Pearson has done is even more remarkable. She not only wrote *Mother Wove the Morning*, she also directed and produced it. And, as the sole performer in a drama spanning 22,000 years, she depicts 16 women in their ongoing quest for a mother creator as well as a father creator. Now that I've seen this enthralling piece, I have the feeling she'll continue to do her play for years to come with ever-increasing success.

A handsome woman with shining eyes and a mop of curly white hair, Pearson brings intensity and vitality to her performance. In addition to having excellent dramatic presence, she forges a bond with her audience and seems to speak to each person individually. The women she portrays have become Pearson's friends, and more than once, as she considered their plights, tears glistened in her large eyes.

Just now I called Maggie to thank her for her review and she told me again how much she enjoyed it, and that her husband who almost never enjoys anything she takes him to, was very enthusiastic about it.

This morning I had a long-distance interview with Doug Wright, my cousin, at KSL in Salt Lake, and then this afternoon with Jim Dabakis at KTALK. Jim asked me if this play couldn't get me into trouble in Utah and I laughed out loud, emphasized how well it is being received here by Mormons and everyone else.

December 9, 1989

Just falling into bed. But I must document these remarkable things while they are happening. I just got back from Berkeley, where I was a smash hit with the Catholics at Newman Hall. More than four hundred very astute Catholics gave me a standing ovation. Such a responsive audience. Laughed in all the right places. Laughed at the first mention of the name "Tertullian" (early Christian leader guarding against heresy) caught all the good little nuances I was playing with.

I used a good joke for the first time to introduce the play. I adapted it from some other joke I heard. My first words to the audience:

Well, the Pope dies and goes to heaven, and St. Peter greets him, saying, "Before you come in we have this little test you have to pass—you have to spell the word *God*." Of course, he does and goes in.

Then Billy Graham dies and goes to heaven and St. Peter greets him, saying, "Before you come in we have this little test you have to pass—you have to spell the word *God*." Of course, he does and goes in.

> Then Barbara Harris, the first female Episcopal bishop—(and at the mention of her name, here came a wild ovation and shouting)—dies and goes to heaven, and St. Peter greets her, saying, "Before you come in we have this little test you have to pass." And she says, "Oh, no, not another test! That's all I've done down there is pass this test and that test—and you know the tests are always harder for the women than they are for the men." And St. Peter says, "Don't be silly, my dear. Spell *Melchizedek*."

Roar of laughter and clapping. I'm going to keep it. A great way to invite people in.

December 12, 1989

We have now added three more nights after Christmas.

On Friday the theatre will give me a check for $2500 as partial payment. What a wonderful thing to make money at what I love the most. Still have lots of bills to pay. And I have yet to pay my tithing for the year. Which I will do. I am certainly willing to pay my tithing if only out of gratitude for the opportunity of having a voice to the Mormons. Very willing.

December 17, 1989

Since I last wrote I've essentially done only my play. Thursday night was totally sold out and they turned people away at the door. Friday and Saturday had only a few empty seats. Mara Keller came; she is an associate of Riane Eisler, well-known author of *The Chalice and the Blade.* Mara was very excited about the play and said she would encourage Riane to see it and to invite me to present it at a conference.

I'm feeling a little tender tonight. A little sad. Maybe it's something post-partum.

December 31, 1989

The end of a year. The end of a decade. In twelve minutes it will be 1990.

The major event of the year, of course, was the birth of *Mother Wove the Morning.* Fifteen performances so far, all received with such enthusiasm and gratitude. There are so many to whom this work is just as important as it is to me.

Today the *Salt Lake Tribune* article about the play came out in Utah. The *Deseret News* article was supposed to come out too, but it did not. Could someone have instructed the Church-owned *Deseret News* not to publicize this play? Strange things do happen in Salt Lake City.

It is midnight. I hear fireworks outside. Happy new year! 1990!

29

PIONEERING THE FEMINIST FRONTIERS OF UTAH AND IRELAND

January 1, 1990

All day has been spent in getting ready to fly to Utah tomorrow. Aaron helped me pack my trunk. We're rolling the stand up in the rug. The lyre is going in my suitcase.

January 9, 1990

The first chance I've had to write since coming to Utah. On Wednesday and Thursday I did some good media appearances. KSL (the Church-owned station) went overboard to do things. I was on their morning news, their noon news and another spot, and they were good to me. I was introduced by Shelly Osterloh in this way: "One of Utah's treasures comes back to the state—Carol Lynn Pearson." I performed the Shaker deaconess scene in my interview with Bruce Lindsay.

The *Salt Lake Tribune* did a good article with a picture; *Ogden Standard Examiner* the same. Ivan Lincoln of the *Deseret News* wrote a good article and had two pictures set to run on the Sunday before I opened. But the story did not appear on that day. We learned that the publisher, Jim Mortimer, had pulled the story, saying, "Hmmm. I don't feel good at all about this. I'm not going to run anything until I check with Elder Faust."

I subsequently called Emma Lou Thayne, who is on their board, and she called Tom Monson, one of the Twelve Apostles. On Tuesday a very short article ran on the entertainment page, an article that amazingly gave no indication of what the play was about. Just this morning I called Ivan Lincoln to get his take on it. He was hugely embarrassed and said, "Here we pretend to be a newspaper and we're just an extension of the *Ensign*." As I already knew, a lot of employees of the *Deseret News* are very discontent, and many keep their eyes open for other jobs. Ivan said someone called and cancelled their subscription over my story not appearing.

This is such a lot of nonsense. This is the same thing they did with *Goodbye,*

I Love You, but they only made themselves look foolish. And neither the *Deseret News* nor the Brethren are going to make or break *Mother Wove the Morning.*

The women of the Mormon Women's Forum have been working their heads off. I am playing in the Salt Lake Arts Center, a 165-seat theatre.

Friday was opening night. We were sold out and quite a few people were turned away. My sister-in-law Susie came with one extra ticket and asked a little crowd if anyone wanted one ticket. She had people grabbing for it.

So my signal came and I opened the door and began my descent down the aisle, saying, "Well, it seems the Pope dies and goes to heaven … " but I didn't even get that far before I was interrupted by enthusiastic applause. What a thrill.

I was then in place on the stage, started the joke over again, thanked them for laughing because some of the women they'll be seeing are suffering severe stage fright.

What a wonderful audience. They were so ready to respond from the very outset, especially to laugh. The play couldn't have gone better. The audience was deeply grateful, gave me a standing ovation. Jan brought down a huge bouquet of roses that Kelli had bought. It was, of course, a dream come true. So many came up afterwards to speak to me. One woman said she was giving me a twenty-one-gun salute.

A friend of Jan's called a couple of times to say that her life has been forever changed by my play. She said every cell of her body was electrified. She has been pulling in people off the street and telling them they must go to this play.

So many people I didn't know were very grateful to me. A woman from Southern Utah hugged me tearfully and said she would like to tell me sometime about how her husband tried to have her excommunicated for healing her son. I told her to write to me; I want all these stories in my files.

Margaret and Paul Toscano, major excellent scholars, were there and were off the chart with excitement. He went on and on about how courageous I was and how everything worked together so beautifully, the writing and the acting and the props and the musical instruments.

Eugene England was there and told me it was wonderful. He's arranging to have me come to BYU to play for his 100 students in his Mormon literature class and others.

January 15, 1990

The play has been going very well. Wednesday and Thursday nearly sold out. Friday and Saturday completely filled with some turned away.

On Wednesday I was sick. I'd been feeling a little uneasy in my stomach for a day or two, but then after eating on Wednesday evening I felt really strange. Just before going onstage I went into the bathroom and threw up. But I went on. Even though sick, I gave all I could and it must have been sufficient, for a woman told me it was the most moving experience of her life.

I continue to get wonderful response from the audiences, standing ovations and huge, huge appreciation. So many, many people telling me such truly remarkable things. A friend of Jan's left a message on her machine that her friend a midwife had been to the play and said she had had many spiritual experiences in her life, and this was one of the greatest.

These few responses I'm writing now do not really do justice to what I am receiving every night. I am getting the most pure appreciation I have ever received in my life. Older women will hug me with tears in their eyes and say they have waited forty or fifty years for something like this to happen. One man said to me, "Take care of yourself. When someone does anything as important as this, there will be those who will try to stop them."

Should mention that on several nights a strange man stood out front stopping people and telling them this pagan goddess worship is the work of the devil.

The Mormon Women's Forum women have been working very, very hard on all this. I took four of them out to brunch on Sunday to talk about an extension, as we were nearly sold out for the entire run.

Speaking of the Mormon Women's Forum women, most of them have stopped going to church. They feel they are under great suspicion and should not waste their energies in supporting the Church. Batina Lindsay and her husband Jim have been very active in the Forum and also active in their ward. Their bishop called in their two teenage daughters separately and warned them about what their parents were doing, said they might have to choose between following their parents and following the Church. The girls were very distressed, and Batina and Jim were outraged.

February 4, 1990

Lots of catching up to do. Extended the play twice. I could not possibly have asked for a better reception. At one performance two BYU coeds left during the Nazi scene. Outside they said, "This is weird. What does the Church think about this? This is just too weird." But none of that compares to the predictable standing ovation and the tears of gratitude.

I am thrilled at the response, but not really surprised. If something like this play had happened when I was living in Utah—or in California—I would have dropped everything and attended again and again and sent all my friends. When I remember the delight I felt in finding *one little crumb* about the feminine in the deity, a little hint in an ancient manuscript—and to know what a rich feast I am now providing in my play—I am thrilled.

Not one General Authority or member of the women's leadership responded to my personal letter and offer of complimentary tickets to the play. I understand. I love Mormondom down at the bottom. I do not love Corporate Mormondom.

With Lex de Azevedo and his mother, Alice King, one of the popular King Sisters, 1989.

I might, however, succeed in getting my friend Elder Hanks there. I called the first week and learned he was out sick with vertigo. I called again on Friday and his secretary said he was between meetings and likely could not talk. I told her to tell him it was not urgent and I would call back. She told him, and he got right on the line and said, "I *insist* on talking to you." We had a good twenty-minute conversation. I told him the play was going wonderfully well and I urged him to come. He said he would very much like to and would check on dates with his wife.

He also said he felt encouraged about some of the things he sees happening in the Church, things he has worked on for a long time, such as the policy that now, churchwide, all missionaries will give a half day a week to Christian service instead of proselytizing. He worked hard for that concept when he was mission president in China and ran into a lot of resistance from church headquarters. He said he will be retired after next year, and I think he is looking forward to that.

He said that before my play got here, he heard someone in one of the council meetings say something negative about it or me. He rose to my defense, as he always does, and the person said, "Oh, I don't doubt Sister Pearson's compassionate heart. I just question some of the stuff she's peddling."

Strangely enough, that night after the performance, some of the women went for ice cream and we ran into Elder Hanks and his wife and two daughters and sons-in-law. His wife Maxine came up and hugged me first and said she had been thinking about me. Then he gave me a hug too. I met the daughters and husbands and they all said they had been talking about the play and were eager to see it.

I've performed three times now in Orem. First on the 20th at UVCC, the community college. They sold out and people kept coming and coming until we had over four hundred there. It was not as vocal an audience as some in Salt Lake, but it was a very warm audience.

On Sunday I called Anne Mauss and asked what was new in the ward. She said the only new thing was the budget. The Church announced that there would be no contributions asked of members for the ward budget, that all that would be taken care of through general church funds, a policy that would equalize all the wards. I can understand that. *But* the result will be a cutting out of all frills, all fun activities that the kids have enjoyed. Our ward budget, coming from headquarters, will now give $56 for the Young Women for the entire year, and $75 for the Young Men. Don't know how that was figured. Anne said that Dix Newell, one of our high councilmen, husband of Sarah, a good and enlightened woman, said in great heat that this finally shows once and for all the "patent, indefensible inequities that exist in the way the Church views the young women and the young men." The young men have the Scouting program, which has no financial limits on it. And, of course, there is no corresponding program for the girls. The girls are stuck with the $56 per year.

Other responses to the play. Ida Smith (director of the Women's Research Institute at BYU), called and told me she loved it. Georgia Faux (BYU professor) called, said it was the most wonderful thing she'd ever seen. Carma DeJong Anderson (artist, writer, producer, activist) called and told me her daughter had seen it last night, and the first time I said the word "Goddess" on stage she began to cry and then just wept. My dear friend the great Mary Bradford embraced me in tears and said, "You did it! You did it!"

On Tuesday the 23rd I gave a performance at BYU. Eugene England had come opening night and then called Harold Oaks, now chairman of the Drama Department, to see if they could have a performance for some classes that wanted to require their students to see it. Harold called me and we arranged to have it in the Experimental Theatre at 6 pm. They paid me $500 for this. I understand that after someone brought in the review and they realized this was "challenging material," Harold Oaks wondered if he had been tricked, but then said they should take a risk and just do it. They had only 250 seats and filled them all, with people sitting in the aisles.

It felt like a conservative audience, but a warm audience. And they gave me a strong ovation. Afterwards there was a lengthy discussion period with lots of positive comments made by both men and women. My dear high school drama teacher Max Golightly was there and loved it, said I had done it so well that no one could possibly be offended. Elouise Bell was there with a lot of her students.

Richard Cracroft, English Professor and my bishop during the ERA business, was there with his wife, Janice. He called me a few nights later and we had a long talk. He was very impressed with the play, but said it left him unsettled. *What do we do now with all of this???*

On the 24th my friend Lex de Azevedo came with family and friends. As he left he hugged me and said, "It was wonderful. It was absolutely a ten. I have no reservations about this." Writer Clifton Jolly came with them and said to me, "You are a witch! You became each one of those women right in front of us. It was incredible!"

Last Sunday evening I attended a meeting of the Mormon Women's Forum committee. Each woman has her own pains and needs and wishes. And they are all *so good.* Before the meeting began Andrea Emmett was telling of some bureaucratic decision of her bishop that hurt her in terms of the way she produces the ward's printed program. She's very tender and even began to cry as she said, "I'm not going to let him or anybody drive me out of the Church. This is *my* church too!" She said she had heard of some bishops and stake presidents that are telling people not to go to *Mother Wove the Morning.* Even if that is true, I am thrilled that there is so little evident negative response.

And I am making money. Tickets are selling for ten dollars, five for students. After expenses I will give the Mormon Women's Forum twenty percent. I have already received one check for over eleven thousand, which allowed me to pay January's bills and put seven thousand in my savings account and pay off the rest of my credit card debt. I am truly, truly grateful. To make good money this way is almost too good to be true.

There. I think I am caught up. In conclusion, I am having a wonderful time. I miss being home. Dreadfully. But I am finally doing the thing that has been driving me for decades. And it is going marvelously. I am very, very grateful.

February 23, 1990

Don Bluth called me on the phone from Ireland today. I said, "Is this *the* Don Bluth?"

"Yes. Is this *the* Carol Lynn Pearson?"

He is coming to the States next month and will come to Utah to see my play and visit with me about story ideas. Don is branch president over there and is overwhelmed with all the pain people have had or are going through now.

February 25, 1990

Home for a week. So glad. Katy and I went to Stake Conference today. The theme was service and it was quite good. One interesting phrase I had not heard before, from one of the stake presidency, was about our moving on the road to "godhood and goddesshood."

More catching up to do. Must report that I did succeed in getting my friend

Marion D. Hanks to the play, along with his family. I saved seats on the front row for them. After Emma, I heard Brother Hanks clapping very loudly even after everyone else had stopped, and the same after Mrs. Stanton. This audience, as many do, gave me a standing ovation, and the Hanks family joined that. Afterwards in the lobby, Maxine hugged me and said they had no idea I was such a wonderful actress. Then Brother Hanks (he has told me to call him Duff, but I can't do that) hugged me and said, "This was more than fine, this was marvelous, and I am proud of you. We'll be in touch."

I gave 26 performances in Utah all together. A few memorable occasions:

A young woman on the front row began to cry as I gave the introduction. I went to her and picked up her hand and held it for a minute as I continued, then kissed her cheek and played the first few minutes with her tears on my lips.

The last week a bright young man in front beamed throughout, then met me in the lobby and hugged me and said this was his second time there and he handed me an envelope. When I opened it I read in lovely calligraphy:

If you listen

You can hear
Sixteen women
Singing

Through her,

And
Sixty billion
Humming along.

Is that not wonderful? It made me laugh and cry. When I saw on the back of the note his name and number, I called and thanked him and asked if he could produce a number of them for me to give to the volunteers who have been working on the play. He said he was so moved by the play when he first saw it that he went out to a special place he goes to at Saltair and prayed that he could find something to give me to thank me for the wonderful gift I had given. Then he went home and wrote this poem. How magnificent. Paul Whiting.

March 16, 1990

Here I am again in Utah.

More bad news about the Church and women. Major journalist Linda Ellerby wrote in her national column "What I learned in Utah," after speaking at a conference here on "Women in the Workplace." President Hinckley also spoke at that conference, laying the blame of society's ills at the feet of women who have gone into the workforce.

An important member of the Mormon Women's Forum, L., who lives in Southern California, has been asked not to make comments in Relief Society and was told that she may not teach classes anymore.

Another friend bemoaned to me how the new Gospel Doctrine Lesson Manual now quotes only General Authorities on the scriptures.

I met a new and interesting Mormon woman, Helen Hinckley Jones, noted writer and cousin to Gordon B. Hinckley. I asked her to tell me something she'd seen happening in the last couple of decades in the Church that was very positive and then something she had seen that was negative. She couldn't come up with a positive, but she told me a negative. She was released as gospel doctrine teacher in her Pasadena ward after seventeen years because the leaders were instructed that the class had to be taught by a Melchizedek priesthood holder. She was not even informed properly; the new teacher just asked her for the manual.

And my sister Marie had a faith-demoting story for me as well. An employee in her department, K., is a Mormon, and recently was telling Marie how concerned she was about the behavior of her son. This is a second marriage and the son has put himself above everybody else, even the step-father, and puts down the girls especially. Marie asked when this started. K. said, "Can't you guess? Just after he was made a deacon. He says, 'I'm the only one in this house that holds the priesthood.'"

I get so sick of this. There are so many excellent things to say about the Mormon Church. But definitely not when you look at the valuing of the genders.

My friend Maureen Ursenbach Beecher, historian/writer, told me on the phone she was so thrilled to observe as she saw the play that I have personally gone through the journey of "The Hero Within"—orphan, martyr, wanderer, etc. and have now become a magician. She was thrilled.

More on Don Bluth here. He flew in from Ireland on Wednesday intending to see my play before going on to Los Angeles. His plane was stuck for four hours in Houston, so he missed my play. Next morning we met for a few hours and talked about scripts for his animation production company. Right now he's preparing "The Troll in Central Park," which is not ready yet. We brainstormed some things that might strengthen the story and he felt good about my ideas. He definitely wants me to write a script for him and to come over to Ireland so we can work on it together.

He said as he left for the plane that he might fly back from L.A. in a day or two to see my play. I didn't think he would, but he did. On Saturday he flew in with his business partner, John Pomeroy, and John's wife Cammy.

My play that night went very well. Good, alive, appreciative audience. After everybody else had gone, the three of them remained. Don embraced me and said, "Can you take another, 'You were wonderful'?"

With renowned animator, Don Bluth, in Ireland, 1990.

"Sure," I said.

John had had a headache all day, and I did my acupressure trick, which got rid of it, and for which he was very grateful. We then went out to eat and had a wonderful time. They were very, very taken with the subject matter of the play and we talked about it considerably.

As I've been reviewing and typing all of this, I keep shaking my head and saying to myself, how did that woman that I was have the guts to do all that? She risked so much. It could have been a tremendous, embarrassing flop. How did her conviction never waver? I remember a quote I heard in college by Emerson that "whatever is true for you is true for other people as well." I really believed that. And it turned out to be correct. Before retiring that play, I performed it more than 300 times.

And so we come to the end of volume one of my diaries. Thanks for walking with me. To be continued. . . .

Love from your friend,
Carol Lynn

Coming in 2026, volume two of the four-part series of *The Diaries of Carol Lynn Pearson.* The book opens with this entry:

April 7, 1990

I just got off the phone from a wonderful conversation with my old friend, Aileen Clyde, who (and is the millennium here, or what?) has just been called as second counselor in the General Relief Society Presidency. Elaine Jack is the president. Chieko Okazaki, a brilliant Asian American woman, is the first counselor.

Aileen was stunned at the call. The day before general conference began she got a call from Apostle Russell Nelson's secretary asking if she and her husband could be in his office that afternoon at 2:30. They went up and he greeted them. Brother Nelson then went into a conversation with her husband about what *Clydes* he was related to, the construction business, and their mutual time in the Navy. They were talking and laughing and getting very much at ease, and Aileen was completely uncomfortable.

They then went into First Presidency counselor Thomas Monson's office, where the very same thing happened. The men went on and on about their mutual experiences, totally ignoring Aileen (later her husband, Hal, said he was embarrassed for what was going on, but didn't know what to do about it just then). After they had had their "good old boys" conversation about the Navy, etc., Elder Monson turned to Aileen and said that she was being called to be second counselor in the Relief Society Presidency, and would she accept? She said yes, she would, and asked if she could meet Sister Jack. (She didn't even know her).

She was ushered through a door into a board room and Sister Jack met her there and with tears in her eyes said, "Yes, you are the woman I've been thinking of."

Aileen and I talked long about the devastating problems that women face in this culture of ours....

But the point of light at the end of the tunnel grows brighter. Such a woman as Aileen Clyde is now in an official position, though the Brethren don't know what they've got and she is well aware that they don't know what they've got. And she is not going to back down. She will be true to herself whatever comes. Though she will have to negotiate and compromise, she will not give up her integrity. She said that too many young women in Utah feel that the women's movement is over and that "we" lost and "they" won, and now all that is in front of them is to find a husband. I can sleep easier knowing that Aileen is there at Church headquarters.

INDEX

Numbers in italics indicate images.

D

O

P

Q

R

Y

Z

ABOUT THE AUTHOR

Carol Lynn Pearson describes herself as a troublemaker and a problem solver. A fourth-generation Latter-day Saint who grew up in Utah and now lives in California, she loves the church that molded her into a spirited feminist and activist, courageous enough to challenge harmful concepts, even those of her own religious community. Her first collection of poems, *Beginnings*, sold more than 150,000 copies, followed by numerous books, lyrics, and stage plays. Her 1986 bestseller, *Goodbye, I Love You*, tells of her marriage to a gay man, Gerald Pearson, their eventual divorce, and her caring for him in her home as he died from AIDS. The profound impact of this story marked a turning point in the national perception of the gay community.